Birding Utah

D. E. McIvor

FALCON®

HELENA, MONTANA

A FALCON GUIDE ®

Falcon® Publishing is continually expanding its list of recreational guidebooks. All books include detailed descriptions, accurate maps, and all the information necessary for enjoyable trips. You can order extra copies of this book and get information and prices for other Falcon guidebooks by writing Falcon, P.O. Box 1718, Helena, MT 59624 or calling toll-free 1-800-582-2665. Also, please ask for a free copy of our current catalog. Visit our website at http:\\www.falconguide.com.

Cover photo: Western Tanager
Back cover photo: Marbled Godwit
Both by Donald Jones.

All black-and-white photos by author.

Library of Congress Cataloging-in-Publication Data

McIvor, D. E. (Donald E.), 1964-
    Birding Utah / by D. E. McIvor.
        p. cm.
    Includes bibliographical references and index.
    ISBN 1-56044-615-3 (pbk.)
    1. Bird watching—Utah—Guidebooks. 2. Birding sites—Utah—Guidebooks.
    3. Utah—Guidebooks. I. Title.
    QL684.U8M35 1998
    598' .07'234792—dc21   97-52145
                                                          CIP

CAUTION

Outdoor recreational activities are by their very nature potentially hazardous. All participants in such activities must assume the responsibility for their own actions and safety. The information contained in this guidebook cannot replace sound judgment and good decision-making skills, which help reduce risk exposure, nor does the scope of this book allow for disclosure of all the potential hazards and risks involved in such activities.

Learn as much as possible about the outdoor recreational activities in which you participate, prepare for the unexpected, and be cautious. The reward will be a safer and more enjoyable experience.

 Text pages printed on recycled paper.

To my parents, who showed me a world full of wonders.

And for Hobbes, who would have advocated birding by taste.

Contents

Wasatch-Uinta Mountains Region

4. STATUS AND DISTRIBUTION CHART

5. UTAH BIRD SPECIALITIES

Acknowledgments

First and foremost, I would like to thank Blair Larsen for her patience and support throughout this project, which frequently took me on the road and away from my duties at home.

The Department of Fisheries and Wildlife, Utah State University, generously provided me with an office and a laptop computer through much of this work, giving me both a base of operations and a means for avoiding transcribing pages of handwritten notes. I relied heavily on the gap analysis of Utah prepared by the Geography and Fisheries and Wildlife Departments at Utah State University, particularly for the compilation of Chapter 5; Doug Wight was instrumental in making this information accessible to me.

I would also like to thank my reviewers, Steve Hedges and Tim Vitale, who graciously agreed to wade through the manuscript, emerging with helpful comments.

A book of this sort is never the product of a hermit scribbling away madly beneath the dim light of a candle in some remote cabin. To the contrary, a book like this only comes together with the generous support of numerous people who share unselfishly their knowledge, experience, and in some cases raw data with the one person who gets to put his name on the book jacket. Thanks to the following individuals who shared their knowledge—the book would be much less without your generosity: Keith Archibald, Heather and Stanley Chinowsky, Keith Clapier, Rebekah Creshkoff, Matt DeVries, Bryan Dixon, Eric Finkelstein, Val Grant, Carlton Guillette, Steve Hedges, Mary Honeycutt, Jeanie Linn, Kevin Loughlin, Tom Lyon, Wayne Martinson, Chad Meunier, John Spence, Priscilla Summers, Pat Terletsky, Cathi Tomsen, Alan Versaw, Tim Vitale, Merrill Webb, Carol Wells, Linda Whitham, and Terry Tempest Williams.

Finally, I would like to single out three individuals whose contributions went above and beyond the call: Steve Hoffman, Director of HawkWatch International; Frank Howe, former Partners in Flight Coordinator for Utah; and Dr. Peter Paton, who generously shared his raw data from his seasons of doctoral work on the shores of the Great Salt Lake.

I would also like to thank my editors at Falcon Publishing; Eric Keszler stewarded the project through its early stages, and Ric Bourie guided me cleanly through the final manuscript preparation and submission process.

Map Legend

Interstate		City or Town	Salt Lake / Salt Lake *or*	
US Highway		Campground		
State or County Road		One-Way Road		
Forest Service/ County Road		Picnic Area		
Interstate Highway		Pass		
Paved Road		Cabin or Building		
Gravel		Gravel Pit/Quarry/ Borrow Pit		
Unimproved Road		Elevation	5,281 ft.	
Railroad Tracks		Hill		
Birding Site	**17**	Mountain	5,281 ft.	
Parking Area	Ⓟ	Overlook/ Point of Interest		
Intermittent Creek/ Spring		Observation Platform or Blind		
Lake, River/Creek/ Canal, Dam, Waterfall		Information/Visitor Center or Ranger Station		
Mud Flat		State Boundary	UTAH	
Bridge/Overpass		Park/Refuge/Forest Boundary		
Marsh or Wetland			N	
Cliffs	Top edge	Map Orientation		
Trailhead	Ⓣ			
Trail		Scale	0 0.5 1 Miles	
Suggested Route				
Gate				

Utah Birding Regions

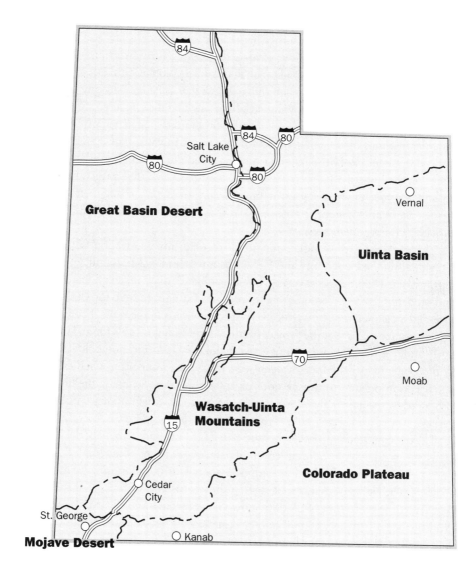

Preface

We all amass a private collection of epiphanies, and many of mine are connected with birds: the Merlin that swooped out of thickening clouds over Stewart Pass in the Wellsville Mountains, its bullet-shaped body rocketing a few feet above my head before it disappeared below a ridge; the Sage Grouse strutting on their lek that reminded me more of a singles bar than a bird courting ritual (lest we forget that we are animals, too); the Flammulated Owl that called outside my tent in the Deep Creek Range; the Black-chinned Hummingbird that hovered in front of a spider's web and plucked the spider from its orb, and then perched just above my shoulder with an air of self-satisfaction; a day on the Wasatch Plateau when I glanced up from my bird data sheet to see a young mountain lion playing like a kitten on the bole of a fallen aspen; the Red-tailed Hawk that parachuted to the ground not 4 feet away as I sat watching Peregrine Falcons testing their wings on a rising thermal. My hope for this book is that it will assist you in building your own collection of memories.

The genesis for this book came about through my association with several individuals in the Geography and Earth Resources and Fisheries and Wildlife departments at Utah State University. Using satellite-derived imagery, faculty, staff, and students from these departments produced a gap analysis of Utah, which included a detailed range map for every species of bird in the state. These and the other resource maps that the project produced are valuable tools for all land managers and planners. Thumb through any major bird identification guide and look at the range maps; the lack of detail can leave you wondering whether certain species occur outside your back door or 100 miles away. Scanning the bird maps produced by the gap analysis project, I saw at once how helpful they would be for birders, novice and expert alike. Fifty of these maps compose Chapter 5.

I also recognized the need for a state-based birding guide. Many of the publications produced in Utah were either out of date, out of print, or incomplete. Utah is an excellent birding destination with 406 species of birds occurring within the borders. The sights of millions of staging shorebirds and waterfowl at the Great Salt Lake, the migration of 20,000 Snow Geese through the Clear Lake Wildlife Management Area, and 18,000 nesting American White Pelicans are all compelling reasons to pick up your binoculars and spend a day here.

Because I wanted to provide readers with a well-researched book, I have relied heavily on the expertise of birders across the state, who generously consented to share their knowledge. The fact that I could gather the information found in these pages is due to the cooperation of those other birders; I owe them a debt of gratitude.

My desire to make this resource more accessible comes with the fear that my efforts will lead to the ruin of something wonderful. It is possible to love a thing to death; we need look no further than Yosemite Valley, the Great Smoky Mountains, or Old Faithful. When I asked other birders for help and advice, I posed two questions: Where would you send people to bird watch? and Where would you prefer people not go to bird watch? I gave careful consideration to both answers. I believe birders on the whole are a conscientious lot, and so I place my faith in you to uphold our reputation and to do whatever you can to protect this resource.

I hope you will find this guide to be a worthy traveling companion. I tried to evoke my ideal of a sidekick in the pages of this book—an amiable comrade who will share essential knowledge while letting me find the path to my own discoveries. May your journeys teem with interesting diversions and abound with feathered companions.

Don McIvor
Smithfield, Utah
September 1997

Though still rare, the Peregrine Falcon is regaining a foothold in Utah. The bird shown above is a captive.

Introduction

The fate of Utah's birds has always rested, for better or worse, with the human inhabitants who have come and gone over many years. It's hard to know exactly what the Native Americans—the Ute and the Paiute, the Fremont and Anasazi, and preceding cultures—thought of the birds around them. Archaeologists have determined that some bird species found their way into the diets of these desert dwellers. Remains of larger birds, including Pied-billed Grebe, Snow Goose, Mallard, Snowy Egret, Golden Eagle, Turkey Vulture, Great Horned Owl, and Sage and Sharp-tailed Grouses, show up in refuse piles near settlements and in debris deposited in cave shelters. We know, too, that turkeys were a regular part of the diet of Native Americans, and that the Indians kept turkeys as domesticated fowl, particularly in the southeastern corner of the state. Turkeys also are depicted among the eclectic fauna drawn on pictographs and pecked into panels of petroglyphs. It's also probable that at least some native peoples held more than a utilitarian view of birds. For example, a Mountain Bluebird was found interred with the body of a cliff dweller in southern Utah. Perhaps it held some religious significance, but it seems more likely that the value of this azure-blue bird of the uplands was simply aesthetic.

The written record of birds in Utah begins with the Dominguez-Escalante expedition of 1776. Like most expeditions that would enter Utah in the next 75 years, the Dominguez-Escalante party was not staffed with ornithologists or naturalists, and their mention of birds was, at best, cursory. Fur trappers and traders were next to enter this largely uncharted terrain. The United States was a growing country; few people in this age of exploration looked beyond the potential economic value of any resource. *Can a bird feed me? Are there enough of its kind to feed the settlers who may come after me?* It is not surprising that journals from those early explorers highlighted the conspicuous and the tasty, to the neglect of the small and hard to catch.

No one who encountered the Great Salt Lake and its tributaries could fail to remark on that area's abundance of birds. In the mid-1800s John C. Frémont visited the mouths of the Bear and Weber rivers, enjoyed a dinner of sea gulls shot by Kit Carson, and in a subsequent journal entry noted:

> The water fowl made this morning a noise like thunder. A pelican was killed as he passed by, and many geese and ducks flew over the camp. . . . The whole morass was animated with multitudes of water fowl. . . . rising for the space of a mile around about at the sound of a gun, with a noise like distant thunder. Several of the people waded out into the marshes, and we had tonight a delicious supper of ducks, geese, and plover.

Mormon pioneers confronted with surviving in the Great Basin Desert were equally preoccupied with the economic value—or harm—derived from birds. Shortly after settlement, organized hunting parties set out to drive all "vermin" from the land, including magpies, ravens, eagles, hawks, and owls. Such persecution and hunting for sustenance took their toll. The clearing of land, grazing, development, and water projects altered habitat, initiating a steady decline in many bird populations and undoubtably a shift in species composition. The Grasshopper Sparrow and the Sharp-tailed Grouse, two birds dependent on desert steppe habitat, were once abundant but have declined dramatically, probably due to grazing disturbance and habitat loss. The Sandhill Crane, once extirpated from Utah by hunting and habitat loss, has made an encouraging comeback since the early 1970s. These are but a few examples.

Despite the rising of the conservation movement in the late 19th and early 20th centuries, state-sanctioned destruction of some birds continued well into the 1930s, as the State Fish and Game Department issued ammunition to hunters to kill hawks, pelicans, and other fish-eating birds.

SENSITIVE BIRD SPECIES OF UTAH[1]

STATUS	SPECIES
Extinct Species	Passenger Pigeon, *Ectopistes migatorius*
State-listed Endangered Species	American Peregrine Falcon, *Falco peregrinus anatum*[2] Southwestern Willow Flycather, *Empidonax traillii extimus*[2]
State-listed Threatened Species	Bald Eagle, *Haliaeetus leucocephalus*[3] Ferruginous Hawk, *Buteo regalis* Yellow-billed Cuckoo, *Coccyzus americanus* Mexican Spotten Owl, *Strix occidentalis lucida*[3]
Species of Special Concern (Due to declining populations)	Northern Goshawk, *Accipiter gentilis* Swainson's Hawk, *Buteo swainsoni* Caspian Tern, *Sterna caspia* Black Tern, *Chlidonias niger* Burrowing Owl, *Speotyto cunicularia* Short-eared Owl, *Asio flammeus* Common Yellowthroat, *Geothlypis trichas* Yellow-breasted Chat, *Icteria virens*
(Due to limited distribution)	American White Pelican, *Pelecanus erythrorhynchos* California Condor, *Gymnogyps californianus* Osprey, *Pandion haliaetus* Sharp-tailed Grouse, *Tympanuchus phasianellus columbianus* Williamson's Sapsucker, *Sphyrapicus thyroideus* Three-toed Woodpecker, *Picoides tridactylus*
(Due to declining populations and limited distribution)	Sage Grouse, *Centrocercus urophasianus* Mountain Plover, *Charadrius montanus*[4] Long-billed Curlew, *Numenius americanus* Black Swift, *Cypseloides niger* Lewis's Woodpecker, *Melanerpes lewis* Crissal Thrasher, *Toxostoma crissale* Bell's Vireo, *Vireo bellii* Grasshopper Sparrow, *Ammodramus savannarum*

[1]Modified from Utah Division of Wildlife Resources, Utah Sensitive Species List, March 1997.
[2]Federally listed Endangered Species.
[3]Federally listed as Threatened.
[4]Candidate for Federal listing.

While the blatant destruction of birds has dwindled, more subtle impacts continue in the present day. Habitat loss is the greatest factor, particularly along the Wasatch Front, where urbanization proceeds steadily. The loss of wetlands is another major concern. In general, though, this is a positive time in the history of birds and people in Utah. More people than ever recognize that birds rely on our benevolence and stewardship. Organizations such as the National Audubon Society, HawkWatch International, and The Nature Conservancy are active across the state.

Utah is gaining a reputation as a birder's destination. With a diversity of avifauna totalling 406 species, found in habitats ranging from alpine tundra to desert canyons, lifetime memories are almost guaranteed. Utah boasts five national parks, more than any other state in the lower 48. Throw in eight national monuments or recreation areas, along with 48 state parks, and suddenly you face more birding options than one vacation could ever handle. In the right park at the right time, you are likely to find Bald Eagles, Peregrine and Prairie Falcons, Chukars, Blue Grouse, Spotted Owls, Gray and Willow Flycatchers, Eastern, Western, and Mountain Bluebirds, Townsend's Solitaires, Swainson's and Hermit Thrushes, Western Tanagers, MacGillivray's and Virginia's Warblers, Lazuli Buntings, Green-tailed and Spotted Towhees, and Cassin's Finches, to name but a few.

Birders at the annual open house at Bear River Migratory Bird Refuge focus on a bird.

One of the keys to Utah's bird diversity is its proximity to two major flyways. Utah lies on the eastern edge of the Pacific Flyway, where numerous species of shorebirds and waterfowl pass through during spring, summer, and fall migration. Often these species turn up in the most improbable places, such as tiny desert oases surrounded by expanses of saltbush and sage—a world removed from the wet Pacific shoreline or windswept tundra where they nest or overwinter.

The second flyway is a hawk migration route along the Wasatch Mountain Range, one of eight raptor migration corridors identified in the West since the 1970s. Numerous destinations in the state provide "center court seating" for viewing this phenomenon.

No other place in the world can match Utah's combination of desert canyons and timbered high country, its gamut of species from Mojave Desert endemics to inhabitants of the Hudsonian arctic zone. And you can explore all of this from a vehicle on a country road or take a weeks-long backpack trip into wilderness.

HOW TO USE THIS GUIDE

This book won't be much help in distinguishing one bird species from another; there already are plenty of good field identification guides on the market. What this guide *is* intended to do is lead you to birding opportunities—112 of them— throughout Utah. It's also a resource to guide you to state and federal land management agencies, and to conservation and birding organizations. To reach the sites in this book, you'll want to travel with a state highway map close at hand. Once on the scene, you'll probably need that field identification guide as well.

The 112 sites offered here are certainly not the only birding sites in Utah, nor on any given day will they necessarily be the best. Caveats aside, during the right time of year and the right time of day, all of the sites described in this guide should provide you with a good experience. If in your travels you pass what looks like an intriguing birding spot that isn't in this guide, by all means take the time to stop and scout the location. And if you discover a new hot spot, please share it with the rest of us!

The sites that follow offer a wide range of experiences for all levels of birders. Some are leisurely strolls through urban parks, ideal if you have limited time or transportation. Others require some advanced planning, at least one night away from home, and perhaps a four-wheel-drive vehicle or canoe. These latter sites are offered for those who would like to plan an extended trip. But a major expedition is certainly not required; most of the good birding in the state can be had from a road or a short walk along a readily accessible trail.

Chapter 1 offers the basics in planning a trip, whether you're out for an afternoon or a week. I've spent many days in the field and so far managed to return from every one of them, but my experiences have led to some consideration for what can make a day afield more comfortable and rewarding. I pass on some of these lessons in this chapter.

Chapter 2 is about gaining a sense of place—an appreciation for the landscape and how it shapes the lives of birds. The chapter will introduce you to the climate and topography of the state, as well as the major habitat types and the species you can expect to encounter in each.

Chapter 3 is the core of the book. It contains descriptions of 112 places in Utah to go birding, grouped into five ecoregions. With a few exceptions, these accounts were written on the assumption that you will be birding in warmer months, when summer residents are present. However, I did include noteworthy species that may be seen during winter or migration only.

Each site account is formatted to provide at-a-glance information. The name of the site appears at the top of the description, followed by these headings:

Habitat: This section indicates the habitat types found at each birding site. To gain the full benefit of this information you should read the section of Chapter 2 that describes major habitat types. Armed with this information, you'll quickly know what sorts of birds to look for. The habitat information will also clue you in about the climate at each site.

Specialty birds: This section appears in the form of a list and identifies any specialty birds occurring at the site. The list is drawn from Chapter 5, which highlights 50

Birding on the Antelope Island Causeway.

species that many birders come to Utah to see. Keep in mind that some of these "specialties" are rare, occur only during migration, and can be tough to identify. You're never guaranteed a sighting. But at the right time of year, a diligent birder will have a good chance.

Other key birds: This list is fairly subjective and contains the species which exemplify each site, along with others of interest that you might expect to see. Absent from this list are the most common species like Starling, House Sparrow, or Rock Dove, which are at best ubiquitous and at worst outright pests.

Best times to bird: This advice takes into account both seasonal and diurnal time. Don't be discouraged if you can't make it during the "best" time; birding at other periods of the day or season can still yield rewards and surprises.

The birding: This section contains tips specific to enhancing your birding: where to hike or drive and where to look for a particular species or activity.

Directions: This section provides enough travel information to assure you'll arrive at the destination. Again, like the site map, this information should be used in conjunction with a state highway map and, optionally, with locally available maps of even greater detail.

General information: Additional tips and tidbits are in this section. There may be mention of other nearby activities for companions who aren't interested in birding, as well as cautions regarding seasonally poor roads, tips on avoiding crowds, or suggestions for other birding spots worth a quick check.

Each description concludes with some "**Additional Information**" to help you plan your outing. The map grid coordinates are from the Utah highway maps. This is the standard map available at any Chamber of Commerce as issued by the Utah Department of Transportation. The elevation of the site, hazards you might encounter, the location of the nearest amenities, the nearest developed campground—public or private—and an agency or organization to contact for additional site-specific information are included here also. Some sites are city parks or cemeteries or, in one or two cases, land owned by commercial industries; in these instances I generally suggest you contact the Utah Travel Council, which will provide regional travel information but not information specific to that birding destination.

The maps that accompany each site description include trails or suggested birding routes and major landmarks. These maps should be used in conjunction with a Utah state highway map, the *Utah Atlas & Gazetteer* (published by DeLorme Mapping, P.O. Box 298, Freeport, Maine 04032) and with maps issued by the USDA Forest Service, National Park Service, Bureau of Land Management, state park, or U.S. Geological Survey.

Chapter 4 provides a checklist of Utah's birds with a guide to seasonal occurrence, notes on habitat type and ecoregion for each species, and an indication of the relative abundance of each species in the state.

Chapter 5 provides greater details for finding 50 of Utah's more sought-after "specialty birds." This list too is subjective, but based on discussions with other birders and ABA members, these 50 birds seem to be among the most desired for life-listers or anyone seeking the more unusual birds in the state. Each description is accompanied by a range map, a description of the species's habitat association, your estimated chance for a sighting, and the better places to look for that species.

Birding Utah concludes with several appendices to guide you through reporting rare bird sightings and finding birding organizations and land management agencies in the state. A glossary of ecological terms is provided along with a list of published resources I found useful in compiling this book and that you may wish to use for expanding your knowledge of birds.

1. Planning a Utah Birding Trip

WHEN TO GO BIRDING

Few birders would deny that spring and early summer are the most rewarding times to watch birds. This is the height of breeding season for all but a few species; activity is at its peak, with birds resplendent in fresh plumage, male birds singing in prominent view in defense of their territories, and the number of resident species at its zenith. This is the time of year you can expect to find those conspicuous and colorful songbirds—warblers, orioles, hummingbirds— as well as other birds such as flycatchers, house and marsh wrens, and the migrant species of sparrows. But birding only during this period would mean overlooking some of the more interesting events in the annual cycle of avian life.

Both spring and fall migration offer the opportunity to find certain bird species in extraordinary numbers. On the Great Salt Lake, Northern Pintail, American Avocet, Wilson's Phalarope, and Eared Grebe form single-species flocks of 100,000 to more than 1,000,000 individuals. Even if you already have these species on your life list, seeing these magnificent flocks amidst this rich ecosystem is an unforgettable sight. Spring and fall also provide the opportunity to find migrant species, often in habitats or plant communities in which they do not normally appear.

The American Avocet forages in shallow water, picking soft-bodied organisms from the bottom.

Some migrants, especially passerines, will stop to rest and may concentrate where mountain ranges converge and restrict their movement, around desert oases, or in the mouths of canyons offering cover and food.

Although winter finds the state depleted of all but its year-round residents (about a quarter of its total species), winter birding has its rewards. Some days it's reassuring simply to find something alive and moving in the cold and snow. Winter also brings some hardy species to the state like the Northern Shrike, Snow Bunting, and Lapland Longspur, which apparently find Utah's winter conditions not too dissimilar from those on their summer breeding grounds in northern Canada and Alaska.

On a diurnal scale, and especially during breeding season, the time to look for most species is between sunrise and about 10 a.m. This is the peak of activity for many birds as they come off of their nightly fast and begin the day's foraging and territorial defense. A second but smaller peak occurs just prior to nightfall, as the day cools and birds prepare to roost. This regimen does not apply to crepuscular or nocturnal species like most owls and members of the goatsucker family, which are abroad while those of us unadapted to the night flip on our flashlights and turn our thoughts to things besides birding.

After all these caveats you may still be wondering, *When is the best time to go birding?* The answer, in a nutshell, is when you have time. Just realize that the hour of the day and the time of year you choose will affect the kinds of birds you see.

WHAT TO WEAR

What you choose to wear will depend primarily on the season and elevation. In general you can expect cool temperatures after the sun goes down, even in summer. In winter expect subfreezing temperatures and a chance of snow. Whatever the season, the best strategy is to dress in layers which can be easily removed or replaced as the day goes on. Modern synthetics like polypropylene, capilene, synchilla, and polar fleece work wonders by shedding body moisture and retaining their insulating qualities even when wet. Wool is a second choice, having many of the beneficial qualities of the synthetics but tending to become heavy if it gets wet. An absolutely essential clothing item is a hat, or two. Sunburn should be a consideration, especially in winter, and a hat with a good brim is preferable to the alternative—skin cancer. A watch cap for those chilly morning hours feels good.

Although some of the locations in this book are literally a walk in the park, others are best pursued with a sturdy pair of boots that provide ankle support for scrambling over loose rocks or rambling off-trail.

Finally, a word about colors. If you have a choice, choose subtle earth tones. With more of us heading outdoors, we have something of an obligation to lessen our visual impact. It's difficult to say whether the birds care one bit about this, but muted colors seem less alarming to us and, thus, a good idea.

ESSENTIALS FOR A SUCCESSFUL BIRDING TRIP

Here are a few suggestions for items to fill your pack and the back seat of the car:

❑ This guide book
❑ Field guide to birds
❑ Utah highway map or gazetteer
❑ Other regional maps
❑ Binoculars
❑ Spotting scope
❑ Insect repellent
❑ Sunscreen
❑ Sunglasses

❑ Toilet paper
❑ Drinking water
❑ Food
❑ Travel money
❑ Pocket knife

Optional gear

❑ Journal for field notes
❑ Camera and film
❑ Water filter
❑ Cooler for drinks and food

If you're driving in winter, be prepared for a breakdown in cold weather. Take along enough water and high-energy food to get you and any companions through at least 24 hours in the outdoors. It's also a good idea to have a sleeping bag tucked in the back of the car. For winter travel, the list below should be heeded in addition to the list of items suggested above for a successful birding trip:

❑ Sleeping bag or wool blanket
❑ Extra clothing
❑ Boots
❑ Shovel
❑ Energy bars and/or chocolate bars

❑ Candles
❑ Waterproof matches and/or lighter
❑ Space blanket
❑ Charcoal-activated heat packets

WHERE TO STAY

Many of the birding sites in this book are within a short distance of a population center where options for a place to stay are plentiful. If hotel, motel, or bed-and-breakfasts are desired, the Utah Travel Council can help plan your trip (see Appendix C for address and phone number). In addition to providing information on lodging, the Utah Travel Council can connect you with regional chamber of commerce offices for additional help. Commercial campgrounds are frequently available near most large population centers and tourist destinations.

For those who prefer a short trip between bed and birds, camping is almost always an option. Some state parks and all national forests and national parks have at least one developed campground—usually several are available. Be forewarned that in busier months these campgrounds fill quickly and that some campgrounds do accept reservations (reservation lines for state and national park campgrounds are listed in Appendix C). Consult forest district offices, listed in Appendix C, for information on campground policies. Both the Bureau of Land

Management and the Forest Service allow dispersed, primitive camping on their lands, although regulations govern where you can establish a campsite and in some cases how long you can stay. Check with the appropriate USDAFS district office or the regional BLM office, as advised in "For more information" at the end of each site description. Addresses and phone numbers for these offices can be found in Appendix C. Once out in the field, practice low-impact camping techniques; if you must have a campfire, use dead and downed wood, carry out everything you take in, bury human waste at least 6 inches deep, and keep food securely stored in your vehicle.

Suggestions for places to camp appear at the end of each birding location description. In many cases the choices indicated won't be your only options, so keep your eyes open or ask locally for advice.

FIELD HAZARDS

For those who venture forth well equipped and well prepared, there are no field hazards, only delays and inconveniences. That said, it's probably not possible to be prepared for every contingency, and there are plenty of opportunities in Utah to get lost, stuck, sunburned, dehydrated, or hypothermic. The best defense is information about current travel conditions, and the best informants are people who live in the area you plan to visit. Ultimately, your best defense is a healthy dose of common sense, but should that fail you, the following suggestions can help you out of a potentially tight situation.

Spring squalls, like this one near Lucin, bring rain and often snow.

Equip yourself with a good map or maps covering your area of travel. Public lands in national forests and especially in the Great Basin Desert seem to be criss-crossed with a bewildering assortment of roads, some still in use, others long abandoned but still visible.

If you plan to travel off paved roads, call the appropriate land management agency to inquire about road conditions. Once on your way, inquire locally. Many clay-based, unpaved roads become impassable following spring thaw or after a rain.

Make sure you head into the backcountry with a full gas tank, and if you're headed to a very remote spot, carry an extra 5 or 10 gallons of gas in a container designed specifically for that job.

Keep in mind that four-wheel-drive vehicles allow you to get stuck farther away from help.

For summer travel, water is a valuable commodity; carry a gallon or so per person in case you get stuck or break down.

Hiking in the canyon country of southern Utah brings its own special set of concerns. Above all, be aware of the potential for deadly flash floods. These are most likely to occur in late summer and early fall, when isolated thunderstorms bring rain to the desert. Because southern Utah has little vegetation and little soil, rainfall quickly becomes runoff that can fill drainages with a viscous, murky gruel, often more mud and debris than water. In some narrow slot canyons, flood depth can reach 25 feet or more. Your best defense is knowledge; be aware of current weather conditions (remember that rain triggering a flash flood can fall many miles away). Be aware of potential escape routes as you hike in canyon bottoms and be sure to call or visit area land management agencies for a forecast of flash flood hazards where you plan to hike. Of the sites included in this guide, Fish Creek and Owl Creek are the most likely places to experience a flash flood, al-though birding is not at its best at these locations during flood season.

Utah is a dry state and insects aren't usually a problem, but they can be locally abundant. Depending on the time of year and even the time of day, some birding sites will expose you to hordes of mosquitoes or biting flies. A small bottle of insect repellent in your backpack can be the difference between sneering at the bloodsuckers and whimpering for mercy.

Although it's likely you'll never see one, Utah does have its share of rattle-snakes. Should you find yourself in close proximity to a "buzzer," back away slowly and gently, giving it a wide berth.

Utah has few large mammals that offer a threat. It's possible that you'll en-counter a moose, but highly unlikely a black bear or cougar. A moose will go out of its way to avoid you, but should you surprise one, back away slowly, talking in a calm voice; try to keep trees or brush between you and the moose. If you find yourself in close proximity to a bear or cougar, do the same—back slowly away, talking in a calm voice. Remember the *worst* thing you could do is turn and run, because that's exactly how deer or other potential prey would behave.

MAPS

Maps remind me of that aphorism that warns "If you don't know where you're going, then you probably won't get there." The corollary is that even if you know where you're going, if you don't take a map you probably won't get there the safest or easiest way.

Start with a state road map of Utah; no automobile should be without one. These are available for free from any chamber of commerce, welcome center at entry points to Utah along Interstate routes, or from the Utah Travel Council. Another useful resource is the *Utah Atlas and Gazetteer* (DeLorme Mapping), available from most bookstores in the state and at outfitting stores. This atlas contains 1:250,000 scale topographic maps of the entire state, and it's quite useful as a driving guide.

If you'd really like to expand your birding horizons, you should learn to read and use the USGS 1:24,000 series topographic maps. These fine-scale maps are widely available and perfect for hiking and exploring off-trail. You can find them at local outfitters and sporting goods shops as well as from the U.S. Geological Survey (see Appendix C).

BIRDING ORGANIZATIONS

For anyone with more than a passing interest in birds, there are many opportunities to get involved with bird-related organizations at either the state or national level. A birding group will help keep you apprised of travel possibilities, conservation concerns, organized field trips, and unusual sightings. You'll also be in touch with a host of like-minded individuals. Some of these organizations provide opportunities to become involved in conservation programs, monitoring projects, or habitat restoration efforts. The birds can use all the help we can give them.

Listed below are the major conservation organizations in the state with a voice in bird conservation and advocacy. A more extensive listing, including state and federal organizations, is included in Appendices B and C.

American Birding Association

The American Birding Association is the leading organization in the United States for amateur birders. The ABA offers a wonderful support network that can offer advice on birding opportunities, selecting optics, and finding field guides for birding trips to all reaches of the globe. Membership also includes a subscription to *Birding* magazine and ABA's *Winging It* newsletter. For more information, contact the ABA (see Appendix C).

National Audubon Society

Long associated with the welfare of North American birds, the National Audubon Society was founded in 1886 to prevent the extinction of a number of bird species by the millinery trade. Although the organization has expanded its horizons to take on a range of conservation battles, birds remain a major focus.

The National Audubon Society is organized into local chapters at the state level which conduct much of the grassroots efforts. These local chapters provide a great venue for involvement in the annual Christmas bird count, bird walks, hot lines, and educational meetings and field trips. For membership information, contact the national office or visit their web page (see Appendix C). Check Appendix B for more information on local Utah Audubon chapters.

The Nature Conservancy

The Nature Conservancy has contributed much to the preservation of sensitive lands in Utah, and some of their preserves have focused specifically on bird conservation. For more information, contact The Nature Conservancy at the address listed in Appendix C.

HawkWatch International

HawkWatch International has a research and educational scope far beyond the borders of Utah. But the organization is based in Salt Lake City and conducts vital research and monitoring projects here. Raptors are excellent barometers of environmental health, and HWI's primary goal is to obtain the most reliable raptor population trend data for western North America. Other efforts include conservation-based public education programs. To learn more, contact HawkWatch International at the address listed in Appendix C.

Utah Birdline

If you plan to grab your binoculars and head out the door for a birding trip, a call to the Utah Birdline is in order. The number is listed in Appendix C. The recorded message on the hot line is updated regularly with sighting information for unusual birds in the state and just may lead you to that once-in-a-lifetime discovery.

FOUR WAYS TO IMPROVE YOUR BIRDING EXPERIENCE

Ask people why they watch birds, and the reasons are likely as varied as the birds themselves. No matter your level of ability or commitment, here are a few suggestions for enhancing any day in the field.

Invest in a pair of binoculars that you will truly enjoy using. Although $1,000 binoculars are wonderful, an excellent pair can be had for $200 to $400. Keep in mind that binoculars are a bit like clothes: you want a pair that fits you physically, is comfortable to use, and meets your personal budget. A good pair of binoculars will actually make you *want* to go birding.

Learn some bird songs. I equate this with learning another language. You'll be surprised how much it will expand your birding horizons. A number of organizations sell recordings of bird songs. Re-record a small sample from the recording you purchase (which sometimes features more than 500 species) to a manageable list of perhaps 100 birds in your area of interest. Listen to the tape at least once a day. You'll soon be able to assign calls to families—readily distinguishing finches from sparrows from flycatchers—and soon enough you'll be identifying individual species. If you have a Walkman or personal tape player, you can verify songs right in the field.

Join a conservation organization. There's nothing quite like a vested interest to keep you focused and concerned. Many organizations have newsletters or magazines to keep you apprised of conservation developments.

Become proficient with a map and compass. Find someone who is competent at orienteering and have them spend a couple of days showing you the ropes. Good map and compass skills will allow you to leave the trail and look for birds where few others choose to wander.

AN ETHICAL APPROACH TO BIRDING

Birders have the opportunity to be model citizens in the community of outdoor enthusiasts. Birding for the most part is a very a low-impact activity, but we can still do damage, sometimes unwittingly. Our impact on the landscape and birds tends to be cumulative. One of us pushing into a clump of willows to admire a nesting flycatcher will have little impact, but by the time the tenth person has barged in, the bird may well have abandoned the nest.

Before going afield, ask yourself if you will be the only person along on that day or during that week or month. How will you and the people who come after you collectively change the land? How can you minimize your impact?

Respect private property owners' rights. Many landowners in Utah are still willing to share their land, but ask permission first. If you enter through a closed gate, close it behind you; if you find a gate open, leave it open. Be sure to carry out everything you brought in.

Don't drive on dirt roads that are saturated with water—you'll just tear up the road. Many of Utah's soils when wet turn into a gumbo that offers absolutely no traction; it's like trying to drive through a bottomless pit of grease. Those annoying souls who insist on charging down these roads anyway usually leave them so badly rutted that no one can drive over them again. If you're using a four-wheel-drive vehicle, where you *can* go and where you *should* go may be two different places.

Breeding birds are particularly vulnerable to disturbance and may abandon their nests. If a bird alters its behavior because of your presence, you're too close.

Wear clothing that does not draw attention to your presence; you'll see more, and the birds, other wildlife, and fellow birders will appreciate your deference.

The American Birding Association, the leading amateur bird-watching organization in North America, publishes and distributes a code of ethics to guide its members, reproduced on the next page. These points should be given thoughtful consideration before heading out the door with binoculars in hand.

American Birding Association Principles and Code of Ethics

Everyone who enjoys birds and birding must always respect wildlife, its environment, and the rights of others. In any conflict of interest between birds and birders, the welfare of the birds and their environment comes first.

1   Promote the welfare of birds and their environment.

1(a)   Support the protection of important bird habitat.

1(b)   To avoid stressing birds or exposing them to danger, exercise restraint and caution during observation, photography, sound recording, or filming.

Limit the use of recordings and other methods of attracting birds, and never use such methods in heavily birded areas or for attracting any species that is Threatened, Endangered, or of Special Concern, or is rare in your local area.

Keep well back from nests and nesting colonies, roosts, display areas, and important feeding sites. In such sensitive areas, if there is a need for extended observation, photography, filming, or recording, try to use a blind or hide, and take advantage of natural cover.

Use artificial light sparingly for filming or photography, especially for close-ups.

1(c)   Before advertising the presence of a rare bird, evaluate the potential for disturbance to the bird, its surroundings, and other people in the area, and proceed only if access can be controlled, disturbance can be minimized, and permission has been obtained from private landowners. The sites of rare nesting birds should be divulged only to the proper conservation authorities.

1(d)   Stay on roads, trails, and paths where they exist; otherwise keep habitat disturbance to a minimum.

2   Respect the law and the rights of others.

2(a)   Do not enter private property without the owner's explicit permission.

2(b)   Follow all laws, rules, and regulations governing use of roads and public areas, both at home and abroad.

2(c)   Practice common courtesy in contacts with other people. Your exemplary behavior will generate goodwill with birders and nonbirders alike.

3   Ensure that feeders, nest structures, and other artificial bird environments are safe.

3(a)   Keep dispensers, water, and food clean and free of decay or disease. It is important to feed birds continually during harsh weather.

3(b)   Maintain and clean nest structures regularly.

3(c)   If you are attracting birds to an area, ensure the birds are not exposed to predation from cats and other domestic animals, or dangers posed by artificial hazards.

4 **Group birders, whether organized or impromptu, require special care.** *Each individual in the group, in addition to the obligations spelled out in Items # 1 and #2, has responsibilities as a Group Member.*

4(a) Respect the interests, rights, and skills of fellow birders, as well as those of people participating in other legitimate outdoor activities. Freely share your knowledge and experience except where code 1(c) applies. Be especially helpful to beginning birders.

4(b) If you witness unethical birding behavior, assess the situation and intervene if you think it prudent. When interceding, inform the person(s) of the inappropriate action and attempt, within reason, to have it stopped. If the behavior continues, document it and notify the appropriate individuals or organizations.
Group Leader Responsibilities [amateur and professional trips and tours].

4(c) Be an exemplary ethical role model for the group. Teach through word and example.

4(d) Keep groups to a size that limits impact on the environment and does not interfere with others using the same area.

4(e) Ensure everyone in the group knows of and practices this code.

4(f) Learn and inform the group of any special circumstances applicable to the areas being visited (e.g., no tape recording allowed).

4(g) Acknowledge that professional tour companies bear a special responsibility to place the welfare of birds and the benefits of public knowledge ahead of the company's commercial interests. Ideally, leaders should keep track of tour sightings, document unusual occurrences, and submit records to appropriate organizations.

Additional copies of the Code of Ethics can be obtained from: American Birding Association (see Appendix C).

2. Utah's Varied Environments

For many species of birds, Utah's patchwork of habitats makes an ideal place to call home. But habitat variability, the very quality that makes Utah a wonderful birding destination, also makes sweeping descriptions impossible.

If you stand on the edge of the Great Basin Desert you are likely to declare, "There is nothing here but sagebrush and salt pans." What's needed here is an eye for subtleties. Likewise, if you stand on the brink of the Colorado Plateau and see nothing but slickrock and burning sand, you're overlooking the network of cottonwood-lined drainages that flow like blood vessels, supplying the region with life and a surprising variety of songbirds.

It's impossible to introduce the topic of habitats without considering the question of scale. At a state level, Utah has five ecoregions: the Wasatch-Uinta Mountains, the Great Basin Desert, the Uinta Basin, the Colorado Plateau, and the Mojave Desert. Each region, discussed in more detail below, has unifying characteristics such as rainfall, elevation, geology, and plant communities. These broad-scale characteristics certainly affect bird communities and determine why you're more likely to find, say, a Long-billed Curlew in the Great Basin than in the Uinta Mountains. Knowing something about these regionwide divisions will help you predict what type of climate and terrain you may encounter, but the scale is a little too coarse to lead you to a particular bird species.

A Violet-green Swallow perches on a fence wire.

For birds and other wildlife species, habitat is a much finer-scale issue. Many passerines, for example, exhibit strong nest site fidelity: the same individuals return each year to nest in nearly the same spot. For these species, maintaining a territory in a particular grove of trees or shrubs is more important than maintaining fidelity to a specific ecoregion.

If we back away just a little from a plant-by-plant inspection of the countryside, we can divide the landscape into a patchwork of plant community types that will be more helpful for locating birds—these divisions include lowland and upland desert shrub, desert steppe, lowland and mountain riparian, pinyon-juniper, spruce-fir, aspen, mountain meadow, and alpine communities.

THE UTAH LANDSCAPE

Topography

The state of Utah is 345 miles long at its maximum length and an average of 275 miles wide. Its highest and lowest points happen to be two of the state's more interesting birding spots—King's Peak in the Uinta Mountains reaches an elevation of 13,528 feet, while in the extreme southwest corner of the state Beaver Dam Wash lies at 2,200 feet. Utah's borders encompass 84,899 square miles. Only slightly more than three percent of that area is water (2,826 square miles), although, ironically, it is water that has shaped and defined the Utah landscape.

Utah is crisscrossed with active faults, and the relief in the modern landscape is largely the result of uplift and crustal deformation within these fault zones. The Wasatch Mountains, which divide the Great Basin from the Uinta Basin and the Colorado Plateau drainage, are a massive uplift 400 miles in length in Utah, which extends even farther to the north and south. The Wasatch Mountains harbor most of the state's trees. Meadows of wildflowers and groves of spruce, Douglas-fir, aspen, ponderosa pine, pinyon pine, and juniper, and streams provide valuable wildlife habitat and respite from the desert's heat.

The Uinta Mountains in northeast Utah are the oldest range in the state, having formed about 60 million years ago. The Uintas are also the longest east-west trending range in the contiguous United States. This range rises gradually out of the high sagebrush and desert steppe plains of Wyoming, crests in altitudes that support only low-growing alpine tundra, and drops more dramatically along its southern flanks into the parched Uinta Basin. Between these extremes lie extensive tracts of lodgepole pine, interspersed with meadows, streams, and mixed stands of aspens, fir, and spruce. The Uinta and the Wasatch mountains are the two regions in the state with visible evidence of glaciation. The Uintas in particular are dotted with hundreds of tiny lakes, all (except for a few more recent man-made lakes) the result of the advance and retreat of glaciers.

The Great Basin ranges are Utah's youngest mountains. These ranges began forming 10 to 15 million years ago as plates in the earth's crust began to spread. All of the ranges in this region formed along a north-south line, and superficially

Classic mountain riparian habitat in the Uinta Mountains.

each range appears to be identical to another, each separated from the other by a basin filled with angular rock tumbled from the mountains' flanks and topped with a thin veneer of sagebrush, shad scale, or creosote bush.

Utah's other desert region, the Colorado Plateau, is perhaps the landscape most people envision when they think of the state. This is the slickrock (or redrock) canyon country of dramatic, exposed geology, rock spires and arches, Anasazi cliff dwellings and petroglyphs, desert rivers, and vast unpeopled vistas. It's also the fodder of innumerable coffee-table books and postcards, Hollywood backdrops, and the inspiration of many writers, including Edward Abbey.

Ask someone to name some features that characterize Utah, and the Great Salt Lake is likely to be mentioned near the top of the list. The Great Salt Lake, along with Utah Lake and Rush Lake to the south, is actually a remnant of Lake Bonneville. Formed about 50,000 years ago, Lake Bonneville persisted in various configurations for about 10,000 years and at its zenith covered 20,000 square miles of Utah, Nevada, and Idaho. At its deepest the lake bottom lay 1,050 feet below the surface. Lake Bonneville actually held a number of stands—or depths— at various times in its history, and each of these stands left terraces, or "benches," along the shoreline. Today several of these stands are evident in terraces along the Wasatch Mountains and other Great Basin ranges; the most prominent of the benches is the Provo Terrace. Lake Bonneville broached an earthen dam of glacial origin in southern Idaho and lost much of its volume in episodic floods that may have lasted 300 years. These events, combined with a period of desertification and evaporation, created today's Great Salt Lake.

The Great Salt Lake ranges in salinity from about 15 to 30 percent—about four to eight times saltier than the ocean. Although the lake is too salty to nurture all but the hardiest life forms, it does support a simple but extraordinarily rich ecosystem. On an annual cycle the lake produces blooms of brine shrimp, which feed on algae enriched by dissolved nutrients. The brine shrimp, as well as brine flies, feed some of the largest flocks of migratory birds in the world. Lush marshes also flourish along parts of the shore and provide nesting sites and habitat for its remarkable array of bird species. An embarrassment of riches might be a good way to describe the Great Salt Lake's avifauna. The table below highlights some of the lake's resources and indicates why the area is so critical to the health of several North American bird species.

SELECTED BIRD SPECIES OF THE GREAT SALT LAKE

SPECIES	POPULATION	SIGNIFICANCE
Tundra Swan	60,000 in migration.	
Pintail	1,000,000 in migration.	
Gadwall	100,000 in migration.	
Cinnamon Teal	80,000 in migration.	
Mallard	500,000 in migration.	
Ruddy Duck	60,000 in migration.	
Green-winged Teal	600,000 in migration.	
Canada Goose	50,000 in mirgration.	
Redhead	150,000 in migration.	
Canvasback	50,000 in migration.	
Northern Shoveler	100,000 in migration.	
Wilson's Phalarope	500,000 seasonally.	Largest staging concentration in the world.
Red-necked Phalarope	280,000 in a single day.	
American Avocet	250,000 seasonally.	Many times greater than any other Pacific Flyway wetland.
Black-necked Stilt	65,000 seasonally.	Many times greater than any Pacific Flyway wetland.
Marbled Godwit	30,000 seasonally.	Only staging area in noncoastal states.
Snowy Plover	10,000 seasonally.	Largest assemblage in the world, representing 55% of the breeding population west of the Rocky Mountains.
Western Sandpiper	17,000 in one flock.	
Long-billed Dowitcher	32,000 single-day count.	
American White Pelican	18,000 breeding.	Among top 3 largest colonies in North America.
White-faced Ibis	7,500 breeding.	Largest breeding population in the world.
California Gull	160,000 breeding.	Largest breeding population in the world.
Eared Grebe	400,000	Second largest staging population in North America.
Peregrine Falcon	At least 11 active pairs.	

(CONTINUED ON NEXT PAGE)

SELECTED BIRD SPECIES OF THE GREAT SALT LAKE (CONTINUED)

SPECIES	POPULATION	SIGNIFICANCE
Bald Eagle	>500 wintering.	Among top 10 winter populations in lower 48.
Bank Swallow	>10,000 in single flock.	Great Salt Lake is one of the largest migratory corridors in western North America.

Climate

Deserts are predisposed to test the limits of every living thing. Precipitation in Utah falls primarily as snow. Little Cottonwood Canyon above Salt Lake City often records more than 500 inches of powder each year, thanks largely to moisture carried off the Great Salt Lake by storms. At the other extreme, the Uinta Basin receives only about 8 inches of rain a year; the statewide average works out to 13 inches per year.

Utah's average annual temperature is about 48 degrees F, but temperatures as high as 116 degrees F and as low as 50 degrees F below zero have been recorded. At lower elevations, daytime summer temperatures may surpass the 100-degree-F mark, although temperatures this high rarely persist. More typical summer daytime highs are in the 80 to 90 degrees F range, with higher altitudes anywhere from 10 to 20 degrees F cooler. Typical of desert climates, the difference between day and night temperatures can be dramatic, with the daytime sun prompting you to strip to T-shirt and shorts, and nighttime finding you snuggled into a down sleeping bag. Winter temperatures can likewise vary considerably with weather conditions and latitude. St. George, with a climate more closely resembling Arizona's Mojave Desert, is mild in the winter with daytime temperatures often in the 40 to 60 degrees F range. On the other hand, northern valleys usually experience a short cold snap each winter that sees temperatures hovering around zero degrees F. More typical daytime temperatures range from 20 to 35 degrees F.

The transitional seasons of spring and fall are a time of rapidly changing and highly variable weather. Thunderstorms may accompany rainfall, and temperatures can fall rapidly ahead of advancing fronts and produce snow at higher elevations. However, it is usually easy to change travel plans slightly and find more amenable weather. During an unusually cool year I drove an hour from a July snowstorm at 9,000 feet on the Wasatch Plateau to stand in shorts and T-shirt on a desert slickrock ledge overlooking the San Rafael River.

Habitats—Utah's Ecoregions

Based on a combination of factors such as bedrock, soil type, and annual rainfall, the USDA Forest Service has divided the United States into ecoregions. These divisions are useful for describing and categorizing large tracts of land; 14 ecoregions are recognized in Utah. For the purpose of directing you to birding sites while providing a sense of the Utah landscape, I have merged some ecoregions to produce five divisions.

Great Basin Desert—The Great Basin covers about a third of Utah and extends into Idaho to the north and Nevada to the west. This is an arid region of discrete, flat basins bounded by sharply rising, narrow mountain ranges, all of which have an approximate north-south trend. Whatever moisture falls in the region never reaches an ocean—the Great Basin has no outlet to the sea. Partly because of this feature, rain or snowfall in this region evaporates skyward, leaving behind minerals leached from the soil and creating the saline Great Salt Lake, the vast salt flats that surround the Great Salt Lake, and the alkaline and almost completely unvegetated basin floors at the lowest elevations.

Only a slight rise in elevation from the alkali beds provides adequate drainage to open the area to lowland and upland desert shrub and desert steppe communities. These cover the lower flanks of the mountains, grading into pinyon-juniper, and if the mountains are high enough and receive adequate water, pinyon-juniper gives way to spruce-fir and aspen, and in a few places even to isolated alpine vegetation. Although permanent water is rare, the area does contain examples of both lowland and mountain riparian communities.

Wasatch-Uinta Mountains—For those who are familiar with Utah as a landscape of dramatic but parched desert vistas, the lush, cool refuges of the high mountains may come as a surprise. The Wasatch-Uinta mountain complex is a spur range of the Rocky Mountains; these high mountains slow the passage of weather fronts and supply much of the state's water needs.

Evidence of glaciation in the northern portion of this ecoregion can be seen in its U-shaped valleys, cirques, and numerous glacial lakes. Patches of conifers, aspens, and meadows create a complex jigsaw puzzle of island habitats. There is at least one noteworthy exception to this pattern—the north slope of the Uinta Mountains contains Utah's most extensive monoculture of lodgepole pines. Still, even on the North Slope, there are enough meadows and aspen stands to draw an array of bird species.

Grass, often mixed with desert shrubs such as sagebrush, usually covers the open meadows and extends under ponderosa or pinyon-juniper stands. At lower elevations these interspersed glades and forests merge with adjacent desert steppe and upland desert shrub communities. Often at these lower elevations tall shrubs such as mountain mahogany are abundant; in much of the state these shrubs may be interspersed with stands of scrub oak. Along the border with the Colorado Plateau ecoregion, stands of ponderosa pine alternate with pinyon-juniper according to the aspect of the slopes.

Moving from the low shoulders of the mountains to their highest summits, the habitat types encountered in the Wasatch-Uinta Mountains ecoregion include upland desert shrub, pinyon-juniper, spruce-fir, aspen, mountain riparian, mountain meadow, and alpine.

Uinta Basin (Great Basin Desert, Eastern Division)—The eastern division of the Great Basin Desert is separated from its western counterpart by the spine of

The Pa'rus Trail follows this stretch of the Virgin River in Zion National Park.

the Wasatch Mountains, an area locally referred to as the "Uinta Basin." It's defined to the north by the east-west trending Uinta Mountains and to the south by the Colorado Plateau. The area is quite arid and receives only about eight inches of moisture annually. Aside from desert-tolerant species of birds, the region attracts a surprising array of shorebirds and ducks to its wetlands and scattered permanent drainages. Bird species more typically associated with the Great Plains and even east of the Mississippi River may occasionally be seen here.

Plant communities are typical of the western region of the Great Basin, although there is insufficient elevation to create montane plant communities.

Colorado Plateau—The Colorado Plateau is characterized by sedimentary tablelands eroded into rugged canyons and mesas. Arching canyon walls can range from 500 to 3,000 feet high. Mountains of volcanic origin rise several thousand feet above the plateau. Stream valleys are narrow and widely spaced. Several river drainages, all tributaries of the Colorado River, traverse the region, including the Green, Dolores, Dirty Devil, San Juan, and Escalante rivers.

Many areas in the Colorado Plateau lack topsoil and are completely devoid of vegetation. Life zones in this region include upland desert shrub, desert steppe, lowland and mountain riparian, pinyon-juniper, spruce-fir, aspen, and mountain meadow. The montane communities are restricted to higher elevations in the La Sal, Henry, and Abajo mountains.

Mojave Desert—An extension of the Mojave Desert edges into southwestern Utah, a region important for its ecological diversity. Unique birding opportunities exist here in the form of species more typically associated with Arizona and southern California.

Land forms in the Mojave Desert ecoregion are typical of the basin and range, with north-south trending ranges separated by extensive plains. The significant drainage in the region is the Virgin River, a tributary of the Colorado River. The dominant plant communities include lowland riparian, lowland and upland desert shrub, and pinyon-juniper.

Habitats—Utah's Community Types

To help you locate the birds of Utah, I have condensed the 37 plant communities identified by Utah State University's College of Natural Resources into the ten broader divisions described below.

Plant communities in Utah vary depending on the interplay of altitude, latitude, prevailing winds, slope exposure, and available moisture. You will also notice in your travels that a sharp, well-defined boundary between communities is rare. More often, a community blends gradually with its neighbor in what is called an ecotone. Ecotones are noteworthy because they can be richly rewarding to birders, who may find species from adjacent communities converging in these zones to exploit food resources.

The **lowland desert shrub** community lies at Utah's lowest and perhaps least hospitable elevations. The dominant plant in this community is shad scale but may also include winterfat, saltbush, and rabbitbrush. These low-growing shrubs have spiny stems and small gray-green leaves and can tolerate high soil salinity and low rainfall, generally less than 7 inches per year.

Even the slightest rise in elevation from the lowland desert shrub community will usually allow the **upland desert shrub** community to dominate. The added drainage that a little slope provides is usually sufficient to leach the salts from the soil that upland desert shrub plants cannot tolerate. Sagebrush, occasionally reaching 8 to 10 feet in height, dominates this community. Other plants include Mormon tea, rabbitbrush, blackbrush, bitterbrush, currant, snowberry, and in the Mojave Desert ecoregion, the Joshua tree.

Interspersed with the upland desert shrub community are expanses of **desert steppe**. These grasslands are dominated by bunchgrasses—wheatgrass, rice grass, and fescues. Examples of this community type are found in Skull Valley and Rush Valley, west of Salt Lake City, and around Golden Spike National Historic Site, north of the Great Salt Lake.

Two characteristics, elevation and plant species, distinguish **lowland riparian** communities from their montane counterparts. Generally, where a stream exits the mountains to enter the valley floor or where a spring bubbles up in a valley, lowland riparian communities are evident. These areas form critical habitat for a

Typical lowland desert shrub habitat.

variety of wildlife species and are vital to migrating birds. Lowland riparian zones are typically restricted to narrow corridors around streams or rivers but may form extensive wetlands and marshes in poorly drained or dammed channels. Lowland riparian areas are dominated by cottonwoods, willows, tamarisk, and Russian olive; the latter two are noxious exotics. Some lowland riparian areas, particularly those in the Great Basin Desert, may have no trees at all but support marsh plants such as cordgrass, cattails, and needle rush.

Located higher still from the desert shrub communities is the **pinyon-juniper** forest, the most extensive forest type in Utah. This plant community takes its name from the two dominant species: singleleaf pinyon (replaced along the eastern Great Basin by Colorado pinyon) and Utah juniper. Diminutive in stature with a canopy that rarely exceeds 30 feet in height, it covers more acreage in Utah than all other forests combined. Shrubs still appear interspersed with these trees, and common species include sagebrush, mountain mahogany, rabbitbrush, bitterbrush, Utah serviceberry, snowberry, and Mormon tea. Along much of the Wasatch Front, Gambel oak and Rocky Mountain maple may appear with or even dominate the pinyon-juniper zone.

The tall stands of evergreens that climb the mountain flanks above the pinyons and junipers are Utah's **spruce-fir** forests. Depending on your latitude, species in this zone include Douglas and subalpine fir (north of Logan), Douglas and white fir (south of Salt Lake City), along with blue and Engelmann spruce. On dryer sites ponderosa pine and limber pine are important species; a few isolated locations support bristlecone pine. As mentioned earlier, on the north slope of the Uintas, lodgepole pine is the dominant species. Common shrubs include Rocky Mountain maple, sagebrush, chokecherry, dwarf juniper, wild currant, and snowberry. Three other community types described below—aspen, mountain riparian, and mountain meadow—are interspersed within the spruce-fir community.

Aspen trees, those elegant, white-barked members of the forest, are commonly misidentified as birches. Aspen is a member of the poplar family and the most widely distributed tree in North America. Aspens tend to form discrete stands in a larger matrix of spruces, firs, and meadows.

The **mountain riparian** community is the high-altitude counterpart to the lowland riparian zone. At the heart of the riparian community is, of course, water. In the mountainous uplands, water usually comes in the form of a fast-moving stream, at least after the snow melts. Other focal points for the mountain riparian community include man-made and natural lakes, beaver ponds, and spring-fed marshes. Typical trees include box elder, cottonwood, willow, alder, water birch, and blue spruce.

The last part of the mountain mosaic is the **mountain meadow** community. These parks or glades are usually a blend of grasses and shrubs (sagebrush, rabbitbrush, snowberry, Utah serviceberry) in varying proportions. Only a small percentage of Utah's birds are specialized to this community, but it is an important foraging area for many species.

A grove of aspen trees.

Highest in altitude, and in Utah the rarest of all, is the **alpine** community. Lying above the timberline where short growing seasons, strong winter winds, and deep cold exclude taller vegetation, the alpine community grows as a low, tangled mat of woody vegetation on a few high peaks in Utah.

BIRDS OF UTAH'S VARIED ENVIRONMENTS

Many of Utah's bird species are capable of exploiting resources from more than one habitat. A Northern Flicker, a cavity nesting bird, may be dependent on a forest stand old enough to have developed tree cavities for rearing its young but will venture into nearby meadows or riparian zones to find food. A Red-tailed Hawk may stay aloft for hours waiting for a rabbit to venture into a meadow, but this same bird may return to a dense aspen stand to feed the rabbit to its young in the nest. Nonetheless, certain birds are more prevalent in association with certain plant communities, and the following list suggests locations for finding these species.

Lowland Desert Shrub

Golden Eagle	Horned Lark	Lark Sparrow
American Kestrel	Sage Thrasher	Black-throated
Say's Phoebe	Loggerhead Shrike	Sparrow

Upland Desert Shrub

White-faced Ibis
Swainson's Hawk
Red-tailed Hawk
Golden Eagle
American Kestrel
Prairie Falcon
Chukar
Ring-necked
  Pheasant
Gambel's Quail
California Quail
Sandhill Crane
Long-billed Curlew
Rock Dove
Common
  Nighthawk

Black-chinned
  Hummingbird
Say's Phoebe
Horned Lark
Black-billed Magpie
Verdin
Blue-gray
  Gnatcatcher
American Robin
Northern
  Mockingbird
Sage Thrasher
Loggerhead Shrike
European Starling
Green-tailed Towhee

Spotted Towhee
Brewer's Sparrow
Vesper Sparrow
Lark Sparrow
Savannah Sparrow
Western
  Meadowlark
Brewer's Blackbird
Brown-headed
  Cowbird
House Finch
American Goldfinch
House Sparrow

Desert Steppe

Northern Harrier
Golden Eagle
American Kestrel
Short-eared Owl

Ring-necked
  Pheasant
Long-billed Curlew
Horned Lark

Loggerhead Shrike
Western
  Meadowlark
Brown-headed
  Cowbird

Lowland Riparian

Pied-billed Grebe
Eared Grebe
Western Grebe
Clark's Grebe
American White
  Pelican
Great Blue Heron
Snowy Egret
Black-crowned
  Night-Heron
Tundra Swan
Canada Goose
Green-winged Teal
Mallard
Northern Pintail
Cinnamon Teal
Northern Shoveler
Gadwall

American Wigeon
Canvasback
Ring-necked Duck
Lesser Scaup
Common Goldeneye
Bufflehead
Ruddy Duck
Bald Eagle
Northern Harrier
Gambel's Quail
American Coot
Killdeer
Black-necked Stilt
American Avocet
Willet
Wilson's Phalarope
Franklin's Gull
California Gull

Forster's Tern
Mourning Dove
Common
  Nighthawk
Black-chinned
  Hummingbird
Ladder-backed
  Woodpecker
Downy Woodpecker
Hairy Woodpecker
Northern Flicker
Northern Rough-
  winged Swallow
Bank Swallow
Black-capped
  Chickadee
Canyon Wren
Marsh Wren

(CONTINUED ON NEXT PAGE)

Lowland Riparian (continued)

Hermit Thrush
American Robin
Plumbeous Vireo
Virginia's Warbler
Lucy's Warbler
Yellow Warbler

Common
  Yellowthroat
Wilson's Warbler
Black-headed
  Grosbeak
Blue Grosbeak
Lazuli Bunting

Savannah Sparrow
Song Sparrow
Red-winged
  Blackbird
Yellow-headed
  Blackbird
Bullock's Oriole

Pinyon-Juniper

Gambel's Quail
Gray Flycatcher
Ash-throated
  Flycatcher
Steller's Jay
Western Scrub-Jay
Pinyon Jay
Black-billed Magpie

Black-capped
  Chickadee
Juniper Titmouse
Bushtit
Bewick's Wren
Blue-gray
  Gnatcatcher
American Robin

Northern
  Mockingbird
Loggerhead Shrike
Plumbeous Vireo
Black-throated Gray
  Warbler
Spotted Towhee
House Finch
House Sparrow

Spruce-Fir

Cooper's Hawk
Blue Grouse
Ruffed Grouse
Great Horned Owl
Red-naped
  Sapsucker
Hairy Woodpecker
Northern Flicker
Hammond's
  Flycatcher

Cordilleran
  Flycatcher
Steller's Jay
Clark's Nutcracker
Black-capped
  Chickadee
Mountain Chickadee
Red-breasted
  Nuthatch
House Wren

Ruby-crowned
  Kinglet
Townsend's Solitaire
Swainson's Thrush
MacGillivray's
  Warbler
Western Tanager
Dark-eyed Junco
Cassin's Finch
Pine Siskin

Aspen

Cooper's Hawk
Blue Grouse
Ruffed Grouse
Great Horned Owl
Broad-tailed
  Hummingbird
Red-naped
  Sapsucker
Downy Woodpecker
Hairy Woodpecker

Northern Flicker
Olive-sided
  Flycatcher
Western Wood-
  Pewee
Dusky Flycatcher
Cordilleran
  Flycatcher
Tree Swallow
Violet-green Swallow

Mountain Chickadee
House Wren
Mountain Bluebird
American Robin
Hermit Thrush
Warbling Vireo
Yellow-rumped
  Warbler
MacGillivray's
  Warbler

Western Tanager
Chipping Sparrow

Dark-eyed Junco

Cassin's Finch

Mountain Riparian

Mallard
Northern Harrier
Spotted Sandpiper
Northern Flicker
American Dipper

Swainson's Thrush
American Robin
Orange-crowned
 Warbler
Yellow Warbler

Common
 Yellowthroat
Lazuli Bunting
Fox Sparrow
Lincoln's Sparrow

Mountain Meadow

Broad-tailed
 Hummingbird
Mountain Bluebird
American Robin

Green-tailed Towhee
Chipping Sparrow
Brewer's Sparrow
Fox Sparrow

Lincoln's Sparrow
White-crowned
 Sparrow

Alpine

White-tailed
 Ptarmigan
American Pipit
Broad-tailed
 Hummingbird

Calliope
 Hummingbird
Rock Wren
Lincoln's Sparrow

White-crowned
 Sparrow
Black Rosy-Finch

SEASONS

Utah experiences four distinct seasons, but latitude and altitude play a significant role in the timing and length of each. Across most of the state, winter is the longest season, bringing both cold temperatures and precious moisture in the form of snow. At the highest elevations snow may come at any time of year; snowfall that lingers to form snowpack begins as early as October and abates in late April. Lower elevations experience their severest snows from November through March, but snow rarely lingers once it reaches the ground.

Although most roads in Utah stay open throughout the year and the highway department is diligent in its snow removal duties, traveling during a storm is rarely worth either the hassle or the potential risk.

Birding in the winter can be surprisingly rewarding, although it pays to have good identification skills to pick out those species disguised in drab winter plumage. A number of species occur in Utah only in winter, including the Northern Shrike, Gyrfalcon, Snowy Owl, Common Redpoll, and Snow Bunting. It usually takes a strong cold front to push many of these species down into the northern portion of the state. Most winter birding in Utah is conducted at lower elevations; not only do the birds tend to congregate here, but travel is much easier for humans as well. Don't let this deter you, though, from strapping on skis or snowshoes and heading up a snowy drainage to seek birds in the heart of winter.

Little rain falls during a Utah summer. Nights can still be quite cool, even in the desert, and any birder planning to sleep beneath the stars should be prepared for temperatures as much as 40 degrees cooler than in daytime.

Spring is an excellent time to look for migrant species. Fall migration is not as spectacular as spring, but birding in certain locations can still reward the observant or push a new birder to develop identification skills. Few birds sing in the fall, and plumage is often ragged after breeding season. At this time of year, many birds do not announce their presence or give obvious clues to their identity. Spring and fall are particularly good times to look for waterfowl and shorebirds, especially around the Great Salt Lake.

MIGRATION

When it comes to forecasting the moves of a particular bird species, predicting migration can be tricky. Weather plays a role, with good weather hastening spring migration and delaying fall migration. Conversely, bad weather may delay the arrival of spring migrants and hasten the movement of birds in the fall. Depending on the species you are looking for and your latitude and altitude, spring migration occurs between March and May, while fall migration takes place beginning in August and continues into October and occasionally into early November. But for most birds, migration peaks around the months of April and September.

The American Goldfinch is a common visitor to bird feeders during the winter.

There are actually two types of migration, **latitudinal migration** and **altitudinal migration**. Most people are familiar with latitudinal migration, of which an extreme example is the Arctic Tern. This bird breeds in the high arctic and spends winters in Antarctica, a 25,000-kilometer round-trip journey. Warblers, hummingbirds, and flycatchers are among the many latitudinal migrants that summer here. Utah is also a stopover for many latitudinal migrants that summer elsewhere—most notably in the arctic. In contrast, altitudinal migrants move to lower elevations (in fall) to avoid harsh winter conditions upslope. Sometimes these migrations are brief and the birds move back to high elevations after a severe storm or deep cold front. Black Rosy-Finch, Dark-eyed Junco, Mountain Chickadee, and Townsend's Solitaire are some altitudinal migrants.

Migration offers great opportunities to find some of Utah's rare visitors. Common and Pacific Loons; Black-bellied Plover; Lesser Yellowlegs; Whimbrel; Dunlin; Nashville, Tennessee, and Townsend's Warblers; and Rufous Hummingbird are some species that can be seen by a birder in the right place at the right time.

Migration is also a time when certain species become easier to locate due to sheer abundance. Utah lies in the path of at least one significant hawk migration corridor. Along this route, species such as Northern Harrier, Sharp-shinned Hawk, Cooper's Hawk, Broad-winged Hawk, Golden Eagle, Merlin, and Peregrine and Prairie Falcons may be observed as they seek out rising columns of air to carry them toward their destinations. Another major migration involves the fascinating relationship between shorebirds and the Great Salt Lake. So extraordinary are the numbers of some species stopping over here that it has been designated a "Hemispheric" site in the Western Hemisphere Shorebird Reserve Network. To receive this designation a site must host more than 500,000 birds, or more than 30 percent of a flyway's population.

Congregations on the lake can include Eared Grebes numbering in the hundreds of thousands; more than 500,000 Wilson's Phalaropes; 1,000,000 Northern Pintails; and more than 250,000 American Avocets. Although none of us will ever witness the migration of millions of Passenger Pigeons that blocked the sun for days, the Great Salt Lake is one of the few places, perhaps the only place, where it is still possible to witness clouds of birds and imagine America at the time of the settlers.

3. Utah's Best Birding Areas

Whether you're on a business trip in Salt Lake City with a few hours to spare or exploring Utah's little-traveled back roads with days to burn, the following 112 site descriptions should lead you to memorable birding opportunities. The sites are organized according to ecoregions, and each of these regions is introduced by a map indicating site locations and major travel thoroughfares. Each site description is also accompanied by its own map, which shows in detail where you should focus your birding efforts. To navigate between the regional locator map and the individual site maps, a state of Utah highway map or gazetteer will almost always be required to complete your journey.

Each site description is written as an independent installment, and as a consequence, you will discover considerable repetition between sites when reading the list of species you might expect to encounter. You'll also detect a certain amount of repetition in the strategy I suggest for finding birds at each site; birding is ultimately about attentiveness and patience, qualities that will serve you well wherever you choose to bird watch.

In many cases, the description of the birding route outlines what I would consider the best birding opportunity in the area, and this information is often supplemented by additional suggestions for other areas to explore in the "general information" section. But keep an open mind while you're in the field, and be willing and ready to strike out and explore other interesting opportunities as they arise.

Great Basin Desert Region

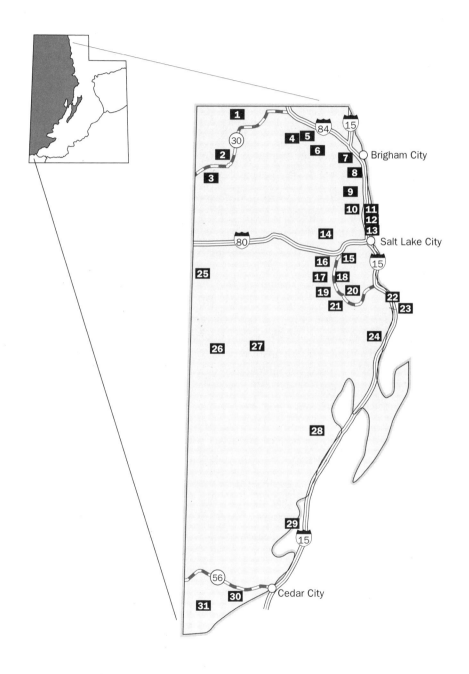

84
15
30
1
4 5
6
2
7 Brigham City
3
8
9
10 11
12
13
80
14
Salt Lake City
25
16 15
17 18
15
19 20
21
22
23
24
26 27
28
29
15
56
30 Cedar City
31

1 Johnson Creek

Habitats: Mountain riparian, pinyon-juniper, upland desert shrub, aspen
Specialty birds: Bald Eagle (fall); Sage and Blue Grouses; Western Screech-Owl; American Dipper; Townsend's Solitaire; Green-tailed and Spotted Towhees; Lazuli Bunting
Other key birds: Sharp-shinned and Cooper's Hawks; Black-chinned Hummingbird; Downy and Hairy Woodpeckers; Broad-tailed Hummingbird; Warbling Vireo; Western Scrub-Jay; House Wren; Hermit Thrush; Mountain Bluebird; Orange-crowned, Nashville (fall), Yellow, Yellow-rumped, Townsend's (fall), and MacGillivray's Warblers; Chipping, Brewer's, Lark, Song, Lincoln's, and White-crowned Sparrows
Best times to bird: May through June for breeding birds; September through early October for migrant warblers

The birding: From Yost to the end of the negotiable Forest Road 002, Johnson Creek slices through a variety of habitat types. At the lower elevation, the road passes through a dense pinyon-juniper forest, where Mountain Bluebirds, Western Scrub-Jays, and sometimes flocks of Pinyon Jays can be viewed from the road. Shortly after leaving Yost, the road crosses the Sawtooth National Forest boundary and begins to follow the stream.

Much of the activity in this canyon is from birds crisscrossing the narrow riparian zone. The grade is not particularly steep, so a good strategy here is to camp at one of the lower-canyon sites and take an early morning hike up the road the next day. The road often constitutes the border between the riparian zone, where the dominant species is alder, and the drier surrounding slopes covered in pinyon-juniper and sagebrush. In this drier zone you're more likely to find the towhees and other sparrows, while Warbling Vireos and most of the warbler species stick to the aspens, alders, and the few willows.

To hike from the Forest Service boundary to where the navigable road terminates at a steep stream crossing is a one-way distance of 3 miles.

Directions: Johnson Creek is south of the tiny community of Yost, which can be reached by driving around either the west or east end of the Raft River Range. From Yost, head south and west out of town, and in about a mile you'll reach an intersection with a small sign for Johnson Creek. This is the only road into and out of the drainage.

General information: The north slope of the Raft River Range is an anomaly in Utah. All streams exiting this area drain north into the Snake River and eventually to the Columbia River. The area may trap some interesting fall migrants; its association with a northerly watershed may attract breeding species more typical of states farther north.

In addition to the intriguing main canyon of Johnson Creek, there are a number of tributary canyons—some with intermittant streams and some dry—that beg for exploration.

1 Johnson Creek

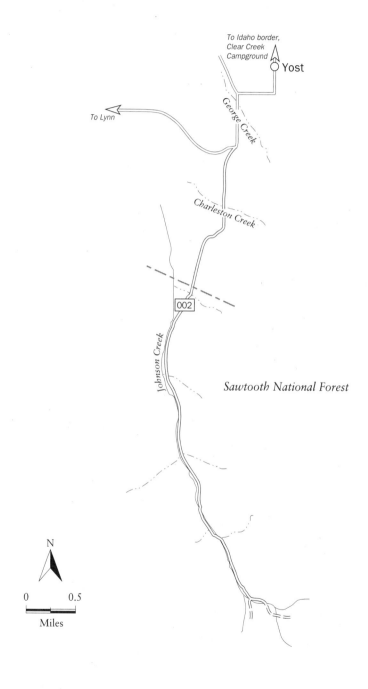

Dispersed camping is available at numerous spots along the length of this canyon if making the drive to Clear Creek Campground is unappealing.

ADDITIONAL INFORMATION

Map grid: 2B
Elevation: 6,300 to 6,900 feet.
Hazards: None. No drinking water available.
Nearest food, gas, and lodging: Brigham City.
Camping: Clear Creek Campground, Sawtooth National Forest.
For more information: Sawtooth National Forest.

2 Devil's Playground

Habitats: Pinyon-juniper, upland desert shrub
Specialty birds: Ferruginous Hawk; White-throated Swift; Gray Flycatcher; Pinyon Jay; Sage Thrasher; Green-tailed Towhee; Sage Sparrow
Other key birds: Swainson's Hawk; Golden Eagle; Barn and Great Horned Owls; Common Poorwill; Red-breasted and White-breasted Nuthatches; Black-throated Gray Warbler; Brewer's, Vesper, Lark, and Black-throated Sparrows
Best times to bird: Early mornings during breeding season, mid-May through June

The alcoves and caves in the rock outcrops of Devil's Playground provide nesting sites for hawks and owls.

2 Devil's Playground

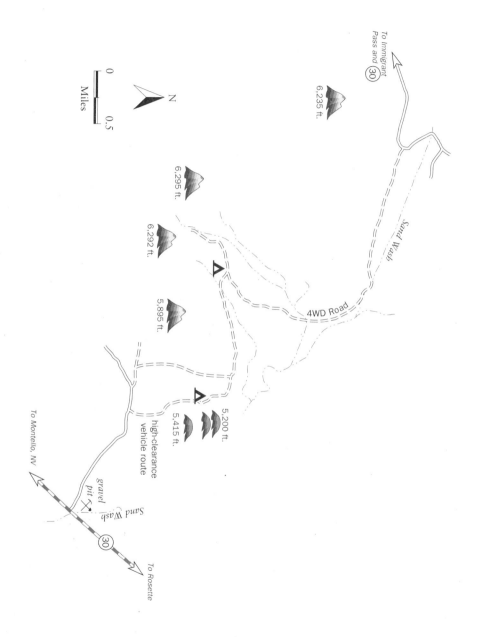

The birding: Although only a short distance off a paved road, this area has the feel of a remote and rugged wilderness. Long fins of granite descend from the surrounding peaks; the land between them is covered by a forest of pinyons and junipers. Along the approach and through the lower elevation of Sand Wash, sagebrush dominates.

There is no formal campground on this section of Bureau of Land Management land, though a few dispersed sites have been established through repeated use. The best way to bird this area is to camp at one of these spots and hike the area the following morning. Most of the area described here lies between two granitic fins. Both are pocked with cubby holes and overhangs stained with bird droppings. Explore the edges of these fins and the surrounding landscape. The road and its offshoots are convenient paths through the pinyon-juniper, and in this forest Gray Flycatchers, Juniper Titmice, Blue-gray Gnatcatchers, and White-crowned and Chipping Sparrows abound.

At the bottom of the slope below the scattered pinyon pines and junipers, the only thing that distinguishes Sand Wash from the surrounding terrain is a narrow gully. There is no riparian zone. However, the sagebrush is more extensive along the wash, and the vistas more open, so this is a good area to look for Sage Thrashers and Vesper, Brewer's, and Sage Sparrows.

The condition of the road deteriorates when you reach the westernmost campsite shown on the accompanying map. Unless you have a four-wheel-drive, high-clearance vehicle, it's best to park here, bird on foot, and return the way you came.

Directions: From the small community of Rosette, just west of Park Valley, follow UT 30 west and then southwest for 27.2 miles—mark your mileage carefully because there are few landmarks. After crossing a (usually) dry wash, you'll see an old gravel pit and a dirt road departing toward the rugged mountains off to the west. Follow the dirt road. If you have a high-clearance vehicle, turn right after 1.1 miles onto a dirt road that heads north through the sagebrush. Otherwise, continue west and bear onto the unimproved road that continues west for 1.2 miles. Take the next right into the sagebrush to the north, and you'll be traveling parallel to the earlier route taken by high-clearance vehicles. Both roads cross a low ridge and rejoin about a mile to the north. You can park, bird, or camp at a convenient spot on the north side of the ridge.

If you approach from the west on UT 30, the unsigned turnoff into the Devil's Playground is 34.8 miles east of Montello, Nevada, or about 15 miles east of Grouse Creek Junction, Utah.

General information: This is a very dry area; take plenty of water with you, especially if you plan to hike. Much of the road is impassable to passenger cars, but you can still camp and bird the area; just don't plan on making the complete drive from UT 30 west to the Immigrant Pass road. In this situation, your best approach would be to enter from the UT 30 side, sticking to the passable roads indicated on the map, and camp at either of the areas marked on the map. The section between the last campsite (where the road forks) and the intersection of Sand Wash is the worst.

ADDITIONAL INFORMATION

Map grid: 2B

Elevation: 5,500 feet.

Hazards: Remote location, no water, rough road, rattlesnakes.

Nearest food, gas, and lodging: Wendover.

Camping: Clear Creek Campground, Sawtooth National Forest.

For more information: Bureau of Land Management, Salt Lake Field Office.

■ 3 ■ Lucin

Habitats: Lowland riparian, lowland desert shrub, desert steppe

Specialty birds: Western Wood-Pewee; Willow Flycatcher

Other key birds: Cooper's Hawk; Golden Eagle; Sora; Killdeer; Great Horned Owl; Black-chinned Hummingbird; Ash-throated Flycatcher; Western Kingbird; Warbling Vireo; Tree Swallow; House Wren; Western Bluebird; Veery; Virginia's, Yellow, and Yellow-rumped Warblers; Northern Waterthrush (spring); Wilson's Warbler; Yellow-breasted Chat; Western Tanager; Lark, Fox, Lincoln's, and White-crowned Sparrows; Black-headed Grosbeak; Bullock's and Scott's Orioles; American Goldfinch

Best times to bird: May through June and September through October

These small ponds at Lucin attract a remarkable number of birds, especially in migration.

3 Lucin

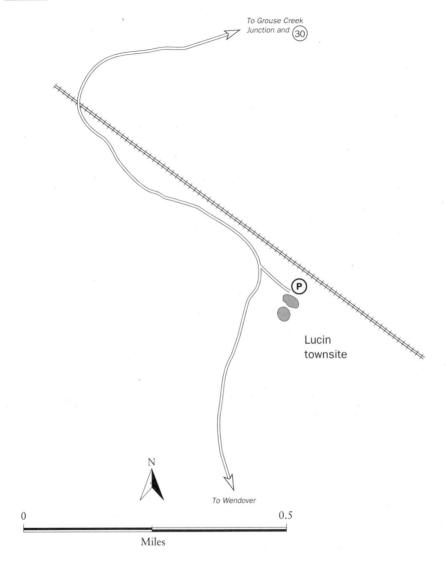

To Grouse Creek
Junction and (30)

P

Lucin
townsite

N

To Wendover

0   0.5

Miles

The birding: The town of Lucin, once an important stop on the Central Pacific Railroad, isn't even a ghost town anymore. The springs that once kept this town alive in the midst of the Great Basin Desert now feed two small pools and support a dense grove of willows and box elders. This oasis—visible for miles—forms a haven for birds. The area traps migrants on their spring and fall treks, and activity seems to continue unabated throughout the day. Birding Lucin during migration is a potluck—you never know what might show up.

The area is small, which makes all the diversity in species that much more remarkable. Park at the upper corner of the highest pond—there is so much scrap metal and so many scattered nails from the vanished town that you'll risk your tires if you drive any farther. From here, walk around both ponds, and be sure to spend some time strolling in the nearby desert, or simply sit where you've parked and observe the activity. There is an old wooden dam or retaining wall along the upper end of this top pond, and a Sora sometimes hangs out between the wall and the water. Soras are secretive birds, but the fact that there is no marsh to hide in makes them a little easier to detect.

The various warbler species spend most of their time hawking insects over the water. If you sit along the bank you'll see them swooping over the water and returning to the low branches overhanging the pools. Willow Flycatchers are both over the water and in the willows, but they also forage in the surrounding desert, where they're a little easier to see. Other birds such as Western Tanagers and Bullock's Orioles tend to work the higher branches. It's hard to get a view of these areas, but if you wander out into the desert you can look back and scan the tree-tops.

Directions: The turnoff for Lucin is about 8 miles east of the Nevada–Utah border on UT 30. The intersection is called Grouse Creek Junction, and the turn south is well signed. Follow the gravel road for 5 miles, and immediately after crossing the railroad tracks, turn left into the grove of trees surrounding the ponds at Lucin. Park at the edge of the first pond.

General information: Ownership of this old townsite is unclear, but it is not currently posted. This is one of the most interesting spots to bird in Utah, so it would be a shame if we lost it. Be on your best behavior and avoid disturbing any of the old homesites.

ADDITIONAL INFORMATION

Map grid: 1C
Elevation: 4,472 feet.
Hazards: Remote location, no drinking water.
Nearest food, gas, and lodging: Wendover.
Camping: Clear Creek Campground, Sawtooth National Forest.
For more information: Utah Travel Council.

4   Locomotive Springs Wildlife Management Area

Habitats: Lowland desert shrub, lowland riparian

Specialty birds: American White Pelican; Ferruginous Hawk; Sandhill Crane; Long-billed Curlew; Marbled Godwit; Snowy Plover; Northern Shrike (winter)

Other key birds: Eared and Western Grebes; Double-crested Cormorant; Snowy Egret; Black-crowned Night-Heron; Northern Pintail; Cinnamon Teal; Northern Shoveler; Gadwall; Golden Eagle; Northern Harrier; American Coot; Semipalmated Plover; Black-necked Stilt; American Avocet; Greater and Lesser Yellowlegs; Willet; Spotted Sandpiper; Sanderling; Western, Least, and Baird's Sandpipers; Dunlin; Long-billed Dowitcher; Wilson's and Red-necked Phalaropes; Franklin's, Bonaparte's, Ring-billed, and California Gulls; Caspian and Forster's Terns; Short-eared Owl; Common Nighthawk; Loggerhead Shrike; Common Raven

Best times to bird: Spring (April through mid-May) and fall migration (September through October)

The birding: Locomotive Springs lies in the midst of some of the driest and least hospitable terrain in Utah, but the contrasting landscapes are part of the experience. Nesting or migrating shorebirds and waterfowl abound on the marshes and open ponds, bounded by the salt flats of the northern Great Salt Lake. The surrounding country is dry and open, covered with expanses of saltbush. The existing springs have been deepened and diked to benefit waterfowl, and waterfowl production is the purpose of this management area. Some planting and growth of grasses and species other than saltbush have also been encouraged by the Division of Wildlife Resources.

A network of gravel roads passable to passenger cars connects all of the lakes, some of which are off-limits except during duck hunting season. As with most sites that focus on waterfowl and shorebirds, birding here during spring or fall migration will be most rewarding.

A visit to the wildlife management area should include a tour of all of the accessible ponds. I found that the northern ponds had very little vegetation and held few birds. This situation may change as habitat improvement efforts continue, and you may still find birds resting on these ponds, particularly during migration.

Birding to the south and east is a little more productive. A quick stop along the gated access road that departs between Baker Spring and the Bar M Spring will allow you to scan a heavily vegetated canal alongside the road. You may find ducks here (particularly during breeding season) and see Willets or Long-billed Curlews along the bank.

Be sure to check out the area around the Bar M Spring, the site of an old ranch (only the chimney is still standing). The spring is lush and green and you can see signs of an old basalt dam. The pond is shallow, a road traces its eastern side, and

Vegetation grows in the small canals at Locomotive Springs Wildlife Management Area, supporting waterfowl and other marsh-loving species.

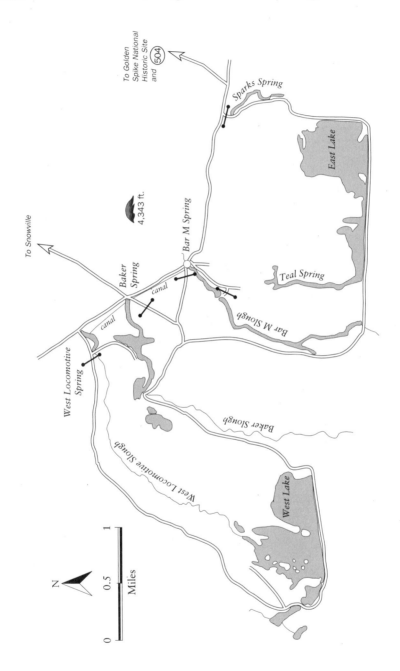

at the far end there is another seasonally locked gate. From the gate you can get a good view of the adjacent Bar M Slough and shallow pond. Approach slowly or you'll flush every bird on the pond.

Directions: From Golden Spike National Historic Site, continue westward on the West Grade Tour route, or drive northeast about a mile to the intersection with UT 504 where a sign directs you west to Locomotive Springs. Both of these routes join a short distance west of Golden Spike National Historic Site. Locomotive Springs lies about 24 miles away from Golden Spike. About a mile before you reach Locomotive Springs you'll encounter a well-signed intersection, where you'll turn south (left). Note that en route you will cross Salt Hills Flat, another site described in this guide.

General information: Access is possible year-round to some of the ponds at Locomotive Springs, while other areas, particularly those around West and East lakes, are open two weeks before and continuing through the day after duck hunting season, roughly mid-October to mid-January. If you have a compelling reason to explore these areas at other times of the year, consult with the refuge manager; depending on the nesting season, special access may be granted.

Locomotive Springs lies along the historic Central Pacific Railroad line—the western spur of the first transcontinental railroad line. If you're already touring the area with a railroad buff, the springs are a very short diversion off the tour route. Although the roads in this area are well maintained, they can become impassable when muddy. Use caution traveling here in early spring, after a heavy rain, or during winter—you may want to call ahead to the Utah Division of Wildlife Resources or the Golden Spike National Historic Site for information on road conditions.

There are no services in this area, so be sure to travel with plenty of water, gas, and at least one spare tire.

Although the nearest developed campground is far away, primitive camping is permitted on surrounding Bureau of Land Management lands.

ADDITIONAL INFORMATION

Map grid: 3B
Elevation: 4,210 feet.
Hazards: Remote location, lack of drinking water, biting insects.
Nearest food, gas, and lodging: Brigham City.
Camping: Clear Creek Campground, Sawtooth National Forest.
For more information: Utah Division of Wildlife Resources.

5 Salt Hills Flat

Habitats: Lowland riparian, lowland desert shrub
Specialty birds: Prairie Falcon, Snowy Plover, Long-billed Curlew, Marbled Godwit
Other key birds: Snowy Egret; White-faced Ibis; Northern Harrier; Semipalmated Plover; Lesser Yellowlegs; Willet; Western, Least, and Baird's Sandpiper; Long-billed Dowitcher; Wilson's Phalarope; Short-eared Owl; Loggerhead Shrike; Common Raven; Barn Swallow
Best times to bird: Migrations, both spring (April through May) and fall (September through October)

The birding: Salt Hills Flat is an alkali and salt-encrusted plain that supports seasonal tributaries draining into the northern most arm of the Great Salt Lake. There are stands of lush vegetation, some standing water and seeps, and tracts of shrubs adapted to the salty environment. An interesting array of birds uses this area, particularly during migration. It's a good spot for unobstructed viewing.

Dropping off the higher, drier slopes of the Great Basin Desert, Salt Hills Flat is an unmistakable bright white alkali flat. Within this short section of road there is no single place to look for birds; they are spread across the landscape or associated with intermittent pools of standing water.

As you cross this section of the road, scan both sides. Loggerhead Shrikes perch in the low shrubs, making the occasional foray to hawk a passing insect. If you pass through when seasonal tributaries do contain water, take time to stop and scan for ducks. There won't be many, but Mallards, Gadwalls, and Northern Pintails may be visible. The shorebirds tend to be grouped around the shallow water spread in the wash. It's worth stopping and scanning these areas; many species are well camouflaged in this environment, and you may not detect them until they scurry after a brine fly or some other delicacy.

Directions: Salt Hills Flat lies 10 miles west of Golden Spike National Historic Site and along the Central Pacific Railroad grade tour route between Golden Spike NHS and Locomotive Springs. From UT 504 northeast of Promontory, continue west following the route to Locomotive Springs. The flat is about 1.5 miles wide at the crossing point.

General information: The road crossing Salt Hills Flat is a lane-and-a-half track suitable for passenger cars. The road receives little traffic (except perhaps in duck hunting season), but if you meet another vehicle in a narrow spot, you'll need to back up or find a wide spot to let the vehicle through. **Do not pull off the road.** Read that sentence twice. Although the flat may look dry and solid, there is often a layer of gooey, saturated mud just beneath a very thin crust. If you decide to drive off the road, your vehicle could become a permanent part of the geologic record.

It's possible to make a long loop by recrossing Salt Hills Flat on the historic Central Pacific Railroad grade, which crosses just south of the road. However, this

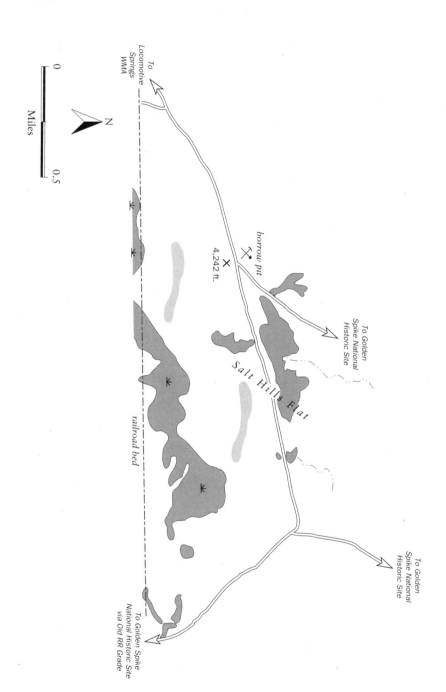

route is gated, so you'll either have to have a car at both ends or else be prepared for what could turn out to be a long, hot walk. A better way to extend the trip would be to park at one of the gates (but out of the way), walk a portion of the railroad grade, and retrace your steps to your car. A mountain bike would be another interesting approach to making a loop of this excursion.

ADDITIONAL INFORMATION

Map grid: 3B
Elevation: 4,240 feet.
Hazards: Isolated location, no drinking water, mosquitoes.
Nearest food, gas, and lodging: Brigham City.
Camping: Clear Creek Campground, Sawtooth National Forest.
For more information: Bureau of Land Management, Salt Lake Field Office.

6 Golden Spike National Historic Site

Habitat: Upland desert shrub
Specialty birds: Prairie Falcon; Chukar; Long-billed Curlew; Burrowing Owl; Northern Shrike (winter); Sage Thrasher
Other key birds: Northern Harrier; Swainson's and Rough-legged Hawks (winter); Golden Eagle; Ring-necked Pheasant; Barn and Short-eared Owls; Common Nighthawk; Common Poorwill; Black-chinned Hummingbird; Say's Phoebe; Ash-throated Flycatcher; Western Kingbird; Loggerhead Shrike; Barn Swallow; Black-billed Magpie; Common Raven; Rock Wren; Brewer's, Vesper, and Lark Sparrows; Brewer's Blackbird
Best times to bird: Early mornings May through June

The birding: There's not a high diversity of species here, though there are opportunities to see interesting birds in a high desert setting. Start at the visitor center, where you can obtain a current bird list and, if you catch the right ranger, information on recent bird sightings. There are usually Ash-throated Flycatchers nesting above the back porch of the visitor center, and Western Kingbirds, Barn Swallows, and Brewer's Blackbirds can usually be seen in the immediate vicinity.

Two other destinations are worth a visit. The West Grade Auto Tour begins at the visitor center and follows the historic railroad bed through sagebrush desert. Driving a few miles of this tour route often produces Short-eared Owls in abundance as well as hawks on the wing, Sage Thrashers, and sparrows.

The Big Fill Walk, along the East Grade and back in the direction of UT 83, is a 1.5-mile walk along another section of the railroad bed. Hiking this trail offers more opportunities for hawks, Chukars, flycatchers, Sage Thrashers, and sparrows. If you look upslope from the trail, you'll notice numerous shallow caves in the limestone cliffs—favored roosting sites of Barn Owls.

Upland desert shrub habitat dominates where the golden railroad spike was driven.

6 Golden Spike National Historic Site

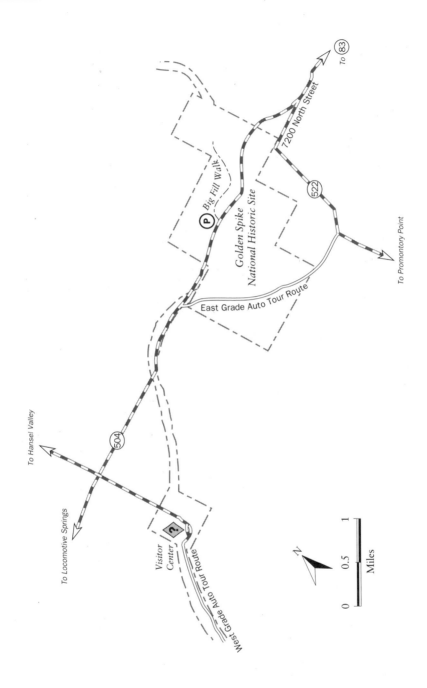

Burrowing Owls probably exist in modest numbers but are not easily detected at Golden Spike as they blend in with their surroundings. Two places where they have nested in past years include the intersection of UT 83 and UT 504—the junction where you first turn to enter the historic site—and at the opening of the canyon through which UT 504 passes, just west of the Big Fill Walk. Look for bare mounds of dirt alongside the road in these areas, and you may be lucky enough to see one of the owls perched on its burrow or on a nearby sagebrush plant. Unlike most owls, Burrowing Owls are active during daylight.

General information: Golden Spike National Historic Site is the location of the first meeting of the transcontinental railroad and the driving of the golden spike that united the Union Pacific and the Central Pacific lines. Two restored steam engines are on-site; in summer months re-enactments of the historic meeting of the two lines take place daily. Expect an entrance fee of about $6 per car when visiting Golden Spike NHS.

Directions: From I-15 near Brigham City, take Exit 368 and head west on UT 83. About 20 miles west of I-15, turn left and continue to follow the signs for Golden Spike NHS, about 8 miles distant. Your first stop is the visitor center, which lies at the end of this route.

ADDITIONAL INFORMATION

Map grid: 3B
Elevation: 4,900 feet.
Hazards: High temperatures, no drinking water on trails.
Nearest food, gas, and lodging: Brigham City.
Camping: Golden Spike RV Park, Brigham City.
For more information: Golden Spike National Historic Site.

7   Bear River Migratory Bird Refuge

Habitat: Lowland riparian

Specialty birds: Clark's Grebe; American White Pelican; Bald Eagle (winter); Peregrine and Prairie Falcons; Sandhill Crane; Snowy Plover; Long-billed Curlew; Marbled Godwit (spring and fall); Northern Shrike (winter); White-throated Swift; Sage Thrasher

Other key birds: Pied-billed, Eared, and Western Grebes; Double-crested Cormorant; Snowy and Cattle Egrets; Black-crowned Night-Heron; White-faced Ibis; Tundra Swan (November); Snow Goose (March); Green-winged Teal; Northern Pintail; Cinnamon Teal; Northern Shoveler; Gadwall; American Wigeon (spring and fall); Lesser Scaup (spring and fall); Common Goldeneye (spring and fall); Bufflehead (spring and fall); Common and Red-breasted Mergansers (spring); Ruddy Duck; Northern Harrier; Swainson's and Rough-legged Hawks (winter); Merlin (winter); Virginia Rail; Sora; Black-necked Stilt; American Avocet; Greater and Lesser Yellowlegs; Willet; Spotted, Western, Least (spring), and Baird's Sandpipers; Common Snipe; Wilson's Phalarope; Franklin's, Bonaparte's, Ring-billed, and California Gulls; Caspian, Forster's, and Black Terns; Common Nighthawk; Loggerhead Shrike; Tree, Violet-green (spring and fall), Northern Rough-winged (spring and fall), Bank (spring and fall), Cliff, and Barn Swallows; Common Raven; Marsh Wren; American Pipit (winter); Brewer's, Vesper, Savannah, and Song Sparrows; Lapland Longspur (winter); Snow Bunting (winter); Brewer's Blackbird

Best times to bird: February through early May or August through September for migrants; May through June for breeding birds

Birders stop for a sighting along the road in Bear River Migratory Bird Refuge.

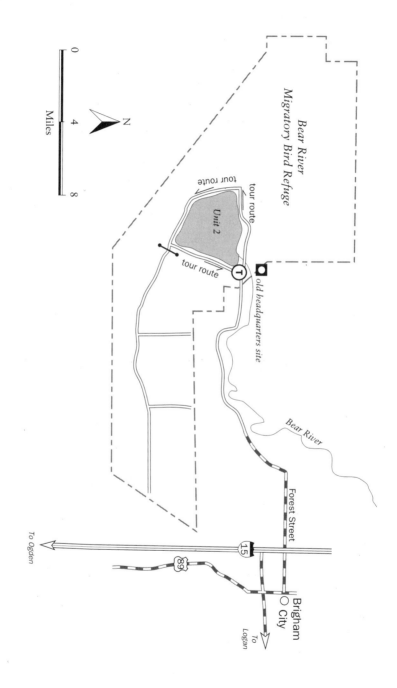

The birding: In the minds of most, this refuge is the crown jewel of Utah birding. Recognized as part of the Western Hemispheric Shorebird Reserve Network, the refuge is a critical staging area for millions of birds and host to no less than 221 species. The rhythms of the land and the annual cycle of bird immigration and emigration are exquisite, sometimes subtle, sometimes raucous; if we could each spend a year here with our binoculars and without watches, we'd all be better for the experience.

The slowest time of year on the refuge is likely to be June and July, when resident breeding birds are the only species on-site. But let's put this into perspective: these "slow" months offer the opportunity to see newly hatched stilts and avocets, downy puffballs perched on long, gangly legs; or young grebes riding on their parents' backs. Other species are still seen in great numbers at this time; more than 600,000 Wilson's Phalaropes have been recorded on the refuge in July.

The bird diversity is certainly at its richest and numbers at their highest during spring and fall migration. Depending on the species, migration can stretch into early spring (Snow Geese in early March) and late into fall with Tundra Swans reaching their peak in November.

You should definitely consider the drive to the refuge on Forest Street as part of the birding route. There are times when the birds in these farm fields and wet meadows will be greater in number and diversity than the birds on the refuge. Passerines are more abundant in this stretch as well, and the fence lines and trees are good places to look for Western Kingbirds, swallows, and shrikes. You're also likely to see herons, egrets, and White-faced Ibis in the wet meadows.

Forest Street terminates at the site of the old refuge headquarters and at the start of the refuge auto tour route. Before taking the tour, it's worth parking here to explore the short boardwalk through some of the marshes. You'll see many of the more common species here; Marsh Wrens are in particular abundance. At the northwest corner of this parking area, you'll see a shelter kiosk. This is a good area for swallows, with Cliff Swallows nesting under the kiosk and Bank Swallows in a nearby mound of sand used for road maintenance. Huge mixed-species flocks gather in this area beginning in August.

The 12-mile-long auto route takes you along the top of the dike surrounding Unit 2. Bear right and drive the route in a counterclockwise direction, scanning either side of the road. It's worth spending a little time at each of the pullouts listening to the sounds of the world around you and scanning for birds. The route passes through a mix of shallow marshes and open-water habitats with multitudes of shorebirds and waterfowl.

General information: The brief history of the Bear River Migratory Bird Refuge has been a lesson in humility for humans and a story of rebirth for this remarkable area. In 1983, after a series of particularly wet winters and cool summers, the Great Salt Lake rose some 10 feet above its historic level, inundating the refuge with hypersaline water and destroying the marsh, the few trees, and all of the refuge facilities. It wasn't until 1989 that the waters receded enough for restoration efforts to begin.

In an amazing tribute to the resiliency of nature, augmented by managerial efforts, much of the marsh has returned to its former glory, and waterfowl and shorebird populations are returning to their pre-flood levels. On the other hand, passerines, never particularly common on the refuge, are much rarer now because the few trees that provided perches and nesting sites are gone. Most songbirds found on the refuge are transients passing through in migration.

While the birds are doing better, visitors' needs have rightfully taken a back seat. Future efforts by the U.S. Fish and Wildlife Service will include a new visitor center and more displays, tour routes, and viewing stations. Plans are also on the books to expand the size of the refuge by purchasing easements in suitable surrounding habitat.

Massive outbreaks of avian botulism, which killed hundreds of thousands of waterfowl and shorebirds in the early 1900s, were the motivating factor behind establishing the refuge in 1928. Diked impoundments established on the refuge now allow managers to control water flow and depths, and this has helped control botulism outbreaks. Nonetheless, botulism continues to kill thousands of birds in late summer and fall, and the refuge is the site of ongoing, ground-breaking research into the nature of the epidemics and their control.

The auto tour route is open year-round—except during rare occasions when weather forces its closure—between sunrise and sunset.

Directions: From Main Street in Brigham City, head west on Forest Street—this turn is marked by an arch spanning Main Street that proclaims Brigham City to be the "Gateway to the Bear River Migratory Bird Refuge." The refuge and the auto tour route lie at the end of this road, about 15 miles away.

ADDITIONAL INFORMATION

Map grid: 4B
Elevation: 4,210 feet.
Hazards: Biting insects, no drinking water.
Nearest food, gas, and lodging: Brigham City.
Camping: Box Elder Campground, Wasatch-Cache National Forest.
For more information: U.S. Fish and Wildlife Service, Bear River Migratory Bird Refuge.

8 Willard Bay State Park

Habitat: Lowland riparian

Specialty birds: Clark's Grebe; American White Pelican; Bald Eagle; Western Wood-Pewee; Hammond's (spring and fall) and Dusky Flycatchers (spring and fall)

Other key birds: Eared and Western Grebes; Double-crested Cormorant; Snowy and Cattle Egrets; Black-crowned Night-Heron; Tundra Swan (November); Green-winged and Cinnamon Teals; Northern Shoveler; Osprey (winter and spring); Ring-necked Pheasant; Franklin's, Ring-billed (winter), California (winter), Herring (winter), Thayer's (winter), and Glaucous Gulls (winter); Caspian, Forster's, and Black Terns; Cliff Swallow; Black-billed Magpie; Common Raven; Orange-crowned (spring and fall), Yellow, Yellow-rumped, MacGillivray's (spring and fall), and Wilson's Warblers; Bullock's Oriole

Best times to bird: January through early March, 8 a.m. to 5 p.m., for Bald Eagles loafing in the cottonwoods. April through May and September through November to see other noted species during migration

The birding: Bald eagles are an unusual site in Utah in summer, but in the right area, they are relatively common in winter months. In fact, Utah has one of the highest concentrations of wintering Bald Eagles in the lower 48 states. Willard Bay is a great area for observing overwintering eagles because it is so accessible. The

A Bald Eagle occupies a roost overlooking Willard Bay.

8 Willard Bay State Park

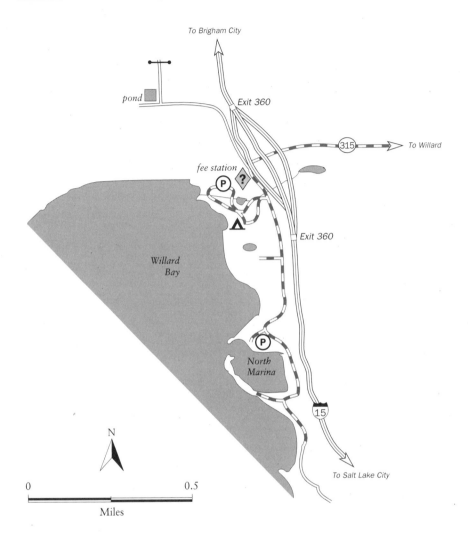

birds are easily visible from Interstate 15, where I have counted anywhere from 20 to 60 silhouetted against the winter sky. The eagles spend most of their time in the leafless cottonwoods that ring North Marina at Willard Bay, but occasionally they sweep across the open water, talons extended, to rake a fish from beneath the surface. There is little other bird activity in the area during winter, but the eagles alone are worth a trip.

A better angle on the eagles is achieved by taking your spotting scope and binoculars and strolling down any of the paved roads that wind to the marina, into the closed campground, or along the network of informal trails between the campground and marina.

Another worthwhile diversion in winter months is a small freshwater pond just to the north of the state park, a short drive or hike from the park entrance. It can be the only open water around during colder winter months. As such, it does attract quite a crowd of ducks, although when I've visited the species diversity has been low (Mallard, Northern Shoveler, Common Goldeneye, and Bufflehead). The pond is fenced off and it is on the property of a private hunting club, but it can be thoroughly scanned from the road. There is often a Bald Eagle or two in nearby cottonwoods, and other species such as Belted Kingfisher and Northern Harrier are possibilities around the pond.

Although the eagles are absent during other seasons, Willard Bay is still a choice birding spot during spring and fall migrations. During April, May, September, and October you'll likely see birds associated with lowland riparian areas, such as Bullock's Orioles, Yellow Warblers, Killdeers, Black-billed Magpies, and some of the open-water species like American White Pelicans, Ruddy Ducks, and Gadwalls. The added appeal of this spot, however, is that during these same months you stand a good chance of catching some species here which are not typical of this habitat type—western passerines such as MacGillivray's Warblers, Orange-crowned Warblers, and Dusky Flycatchers stop here on their annual migrations.

The best strategy for finding some of these migrating songbirds is to walk the roads in the park, scanning both the brush thickets as well as the higher branches of the cottonwoods. The area in and around the campground is full of hedgerows and, along with the small pond in the campground, can be productive for migrants.

Directions: Willard Bay is reached via Exit 360, 51 miles north of Salt Lake City or 5 miles south of Brigham City, on I-15. The exit is signed for Willard Bay, and the entrance gate and fee station are visible from the Interstate; turn west toward the Great Salt Lake upon exiting I-15, and then immediately turn left into the state park.

General information: Willard Bay is open for day use activities year-round, and there is a $4-per-vehicle entrance fee. The bay is actually an impoundment on the floodplain of the Great Salt Lake where levees slow the mixing of incoming freshwater with the highly saline (about 20 percent) waters of the Great Salt Lake. Avoid the area during the peak of summer, June through August, when the bay is used for water skiing, sailing, and fishing. Most facilities, including the campground, are closed during winter months.

If you go to view the eagles, remember that winter is a season of high stress for all animals. The loafing behavior of eagles is a strategy for conserving energy at a time when there is not much to eat; it's very important that the birds not be disturbed from their roosts. A spotting scope will allow you to keep a discrete distance.

It's likely that Willard Bay's appeal to migrating birds is due to its physiography. To the east, a steep dry escarpment of the Wasatch Mountains is visually dramatic but holds little appeal for any bird except a Peregrine Falcon. To the west, the wide-open expanse of the Great Salt Lake is equally inhospitable to passerines. To a migrating bird, the bay probably appears as an oasis situated in the narrow waist of an hourglass.

Expect an additional $10 fee if you intend to camp.

ADDITIONAL INFORMATION

Map grid: 4C
Elevation: 4,300 feet.
Hazards: Cold temperatures.
Nearest food, gas, and lodging: Brigham City.
Camping: On-site (closed seasonally).
For more information: Utah Division of Parks and Recreation.

9 Ogden Bay Waterfowl Management Area

Habitat: Lowland riparian
Specialty birds: Clark's Grebe; American White Pelican; Bald Eagle (winter); Ferruginous Hawk; Peregrine and Prairie Falcons (spring and fall); Snowy Plover; Marbled Godwit (spring and fall)
Other key birds: Pied-billed, Eared, and Western Grebes; Double-crested Cormorant; American Bittern; Snowy and Cattle Egrets; Black-crowned Night-Heron; White-faced Ibis; Tundra Swan (November); Snow Goose (February to March); Green-winged (spring and fall), Blue-winged, and Cinnamon Teals; Northern Shoveler; Gadwall; American Wigeon (spring and fall); Canvasback (spring and fall); Redhead; Ring-necked Duck (spring and fall); Lesser Scaup (spring and fall); Common Goldeneye (spring and fall); Bufflehead (spring and fall); Common (spring and fall) and Red-breasted Mergansers (spring and fall); Ruddy Duck; Northern Harrier; Sharp-shinned (spring and fall), Cooper's (spring and fall), Swainson's, and Rough-legged Hawks (winter); Gray Partridge; Ring-necked Pheasant; Black-bellied (spring and fall) and Semipalmated Plovers (spring and fall); Greater (spring and fall) and Lesser Yellowlegs (spring and fall); Solitary Sandpiper (spring and fall); Willet; Spotted, Western (spring and fall), and Least Sandpipers (spring and fall); Long-billed Dowitcher (spring and fall); Common Snipe; Red-necked Phalarope (spring and fall); Franklin's and California Gulls; Forster's Tern; Barn and Short-eared Owls; Downy Woodpecker; Western and Eastern Kingbirds; Tree, Violet-green, Northern Rough-winged, Bank, Cliff, and Barn Swallows; Black-billed Magpie; Common Raven; Marsh Wren; White-crowned Sparrow (winter); Bullock's Oriole
Best times to bird: Bird numbers typically peak in late March and April, and again in September. During this time of year, birding anytime during the day can be productive. In late spring and summer, early morning is best.

9 Ogden Bay Waterfowl Management Area

The birding: At nearly 20,000 acres, the Ogden Bay Waterfowl Management Area is the largest such management unit under the Utah Division of Wildlife Resource's stewardship. The area is critically important to waterfowl production, but it also hosts Peregrine Falcons, one of the largest known concentrations of nesting Snowy Plovers, and many other interesting species.

Much of the WMA is closed to human access through the nesting and brooding season, but a 2-mile section of dike that intersects extensive tracts of marsh, canal and riverbanks is available year-round for walking or biking visitors. From the parking area, head due north through the gate, cross the South Run of the Weber River, and continue straight on the gravel road. You'll note numerous side roads or paths off of this route, but all are closed from April 1 through September 1. Please respect the signs; they're for the benefit of all species of birds that nest here.

The habitat is fairly uniform as you hike this route. The expanse to the right of the trail has more open water, and it's in these areas that you'll likely glimpse waterfowl, including, grebes, swans, and ducks. After about 1.5 miles you'll see a long line of dead cottonwood snags following the course of the Weber River. These trees provide the only substantial perches around, and they're a great place to look for raptors and songbirds. Eastern Kingbirds abound here, and July through early September the branches of these trees can be covered with hundreds and sometimes thousands of swallows of all species.

Continuing even farther north, mud flats visible to the west of the boat launch are sometimes flooded in spring, providing habitat for migrating shorebirds. As always with these hard-to-identify species, a spotting scope is almost essential for positive identification.

Directions: From I-15 in South Ogden, take Exit 342 and head west into the town of Roy. In 0.3 mile you'll come to an intersection with UT 126 (also called 1900 West)—turn right (north) and travel another 0.6 mile, and then turn left on 4800 South. Follow this road west for 2 miles, and turn left again on 3500 West. Travel 0.8 mile on 3500 West, then turn right on 5500 South. Follow 5500 South to its terminus (5 miles) at a T intersection with 7500 West, and turn right. Stay on 7500 West through a couple of twists and turns, and you'll discover that the road dead-ends at the refuge, 0.9 mile from the T intersection. Proceed through the gate and head straight to the signed parking, another 0.6 mile from the entrance gate.

General information: The refuge gate is open from 8 a.m. to 5 p.m., so if you believe your birding will keep you later, park outside the gate and figure an additional 0.6 mile into your walk.

The WMA publishes both a bird list and a walking map of the refuge. Sometimes these are available at the information kiosk in the parking area; other times you have to make a special trip to the refuge office to obtain them. The office is back near the entrance gate—if you head back in that direction from the parking area, turn right just before crossing the refuge boundary and passing back through the gate; this will put you on the refuge office's driveway, and you can see the office compound from the driveway.

Another option for touring the refuge is to use a canoe and enter the refuge via the Weber River. A map illustrating this route is posted at the parking area kiosk, and the refuge office has additional information.

If you're in the area in March, September, or early October, the nearby Howard Slough Waterfowl Management Area is also worth a visit. Inquire at the refuge office for a map and information regarding access to this adjacent WMA, which receives fewer visitors.

ADDITIONAL INFORMATION

Map grid: 4C
Elevation: 4,200 feet.
Hazards: Biting insects.
Nearest food, gas, and lodging: Ogden.
Camping: Century RV Park, Westhaven.
For more information: Utah Division of Wildlife Resources.

10 Antelope Island Causeway and State Park

Habitats: Lowland riparian, upland desert shrub, desert steppe
Specialty birds: American White Pelican; Bald Eagle (fall and winter); Northern Goshawk (fall); Ferruginous Hawk; Prairie and Peregrine Falcons; Chukar; Long-billed Curlew; Marbled Godwit; Burrowing Owl; Northern Shrike (winter); Townsend's Solitaire (winter); Sage Thrasher; American Pipit (winter); Sage Sparrow; Black Rosy-Finch (winter)
Other key birds: Eared, Pie-billed, and Western Grebes; Snowy and Cattle Egrets; White-faced Ibis; Blue-winged, Green-winged, and Cinnamon Teals; Northern Shoveler; American Wigeon; Redhead; Lesser Scaup; Oldsquaw (winter); Surf (winter) and White-winged (winter) Scoters; Black-bellied and Snowy Plovers; Killdeer; Black-necked Stilt; American Avocet; Willet; Sanderling; Long-billed Dowitcher; Wilson's and Red-necked Phalaropes; Northern Harrier; Sharp-shinned (fall), Cooper's (fall), and Swainson's Hawks; Golden Eagle; Franklin's, Ring-billed, and California Gulls; Short-eared Owl; Common Nighthawk; Common Poorwill; Forster's and Black Terns; Western Kingbird; Say's Phoebe; Ash-throated Flycatcher; Loggerhead Shrike; Horned Lark; Northern Rough-winged, Barn, and Tree Swallows; Common Raven; Canyon and Rock Wrens; Blue-gray Gnatcatcher; Western Meadowlark; Red-winged, Yellow-headed, and Brewer's Blackbirds; Brown-headed Cowbird; Lapland Longspur (winter); Snow Bunting (winter); American Tree (winter), Brewer's, Vesper, and Lark Sparrows
Best times to bird: Year-round, although bird numbers and diversity are typically highest during spring and fall migrations, April through May and September through October; best viewing is mid-day. Summer birders should arrive early; the days get hot. Winter birding can reveal some interesting species.

A flotilla of Eared Grebes near the Antelope Island Causeway.

The birding: The 7.2-mile-long causeway to Antelope Island provides one of the state's more unique birding opportunities, including a view in cross section of life on the open lake and acres of waterfowl bobbing on the salty waters.

The greatest attraction on this route is the chance to see enormous flocks of waterfowl, but don't overlook the shorebirds. Immediately after passing the entrance gate, the causeway transects open mud flats. The extent of the flats will depend on the level of the Great Salt Lake, but this is the most likely spot for the shorebirds. Pull off on the ample shoulder of the road and scan the flats and the edge of the causeway, and be prepared to challenge your identification skills. Some highly unusual birds have been seen here, including a Hudsonian Godwit.

As you continue across the causeway, scan both sides for waterfowl. What you'll see depends largely on which species happen to be migrating through. You may also note that birds are far more numerous on one side than the other. The reason for this may be the differing salinity of the two water bodies, the prevailing wind, or some force altogether inscrutable. Keep an eye on the side of the road; although rare, such birds as the Lapland Longspur and Snow Bunting are occasionally seen here in winter, usually mixed with flocks of Horned Larks.

Two overpasses on the causeway allow water to flow between the two sides, and these spots seem to be particularly good for waterfowl. You'll come to the first after 2.1 miles, the second after an additional 4.1 miles. Birds congregate here because the current delivers brine shrimp like a revolving buffet table.

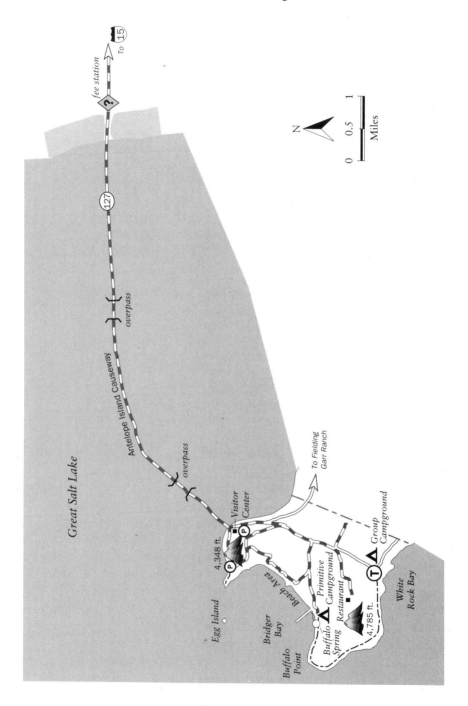

More than 100 species of birds can be found on Antelope Island. Though it appears parched and barren, the island supports scattered shrubs and a dry desert steppe. In this stark setting one might expect to see little life. The opposite is true.

A good place to start birding is the visitor center. Bear right upon reaching the island, then left as the road loops to the parking lot beside the visitor center. Not only can you obtain current information about the island, but several interesting species of birds surround you. The outcrop of rock by the visitor center frequently has Chukars perched on top and Rock Wrens around the boulders. The road leaving the visitor center and heading southwest passes through a Burrowing Owl colony. Look for the freshly excavated burrows within a 100 yards of leaving the parking lot; the birds perch at the mouths of their burrows, on nearby sagebrush, or even stand in the middle of the road. Long-billed Curlews may also be visible here.

If you return along the road you came in on and park in the lot at the northwest corner of the island, a short stroll will take you to a spit of land and a viewing point for Egg Island. This small, barren outcrop supports a dense mixed-species breeding colony of Double-crested Cormorants and California Gulls. Scan the shoreline in Bridger Bay and the open waters to the north for waterfowl; Eared Grebes are but one species that may be present in remarkable numbers.

A final suggestion involves a short hike. A trail leaves from the Group Campground by Buffalo Spring and travels around the perimeter of Buffalo Point. This is a great sunrise hike with striking views of the lake, and it will expose you to a length of shoreline as well as some upland areas where a great variety of shorebirds, waterfowl, raptors, and songbirds can be seen.

If you're in the area September through October, the best time to observe migrating raptors is between the hours of 10 a.m. and 3 p.m. Peak migration usually occurs around late September and early October. The best vantage point for this event is the southeast corner of the parking lot of the visitor center. Keep an eye to the north for birds flying south from the Promontory Mountains, then making their way over thermals rising off the Great Salt Lake. Migration peaks at the rate of about 20 birds per hour.

Directions: From I-15, take Exit 335 (in Layton) and proceed west on UT 108 (Antelope Road). The start of the causeway is about 7 miles west of I-15. Antelope Island is at the end of the causeway.

General information: The causeway gets you so close to most birds that binoculars are sufficient. The downside is that at such close range you can flush the birds, particularly if you get out of your vehicle. Unless you stop and walk from a discrete distance, viewing is best done from the car. A spotting scope can be handy, especially for those hard-to-identify shorebirds.

There is a $6 entrance fee to the causeway, which pays your passage to the state park. At 28,022 acres, Antelope is the largest island in the Great Salt Lake.

At present the park encompasses 2,000 acres; the remainder of the island is closed to the public. Plans are underway to expand visitor access, and undoubtedly, more interesting birds and birding sites will be found as people venture farther. The visitor center has an interpretive display that provides a look at the island's fascinating ecology. Stop in for a look and ask about access to the rest of the island and any recent sightings.

For nonbirders, the island also supports a large herd of bison, an antelope herd, a recently introduced band of bighorn sheep, bobcats, coyotes, badgers, and jackrabbits. The oldest continuously occupied residence in Utah can also be found on the island. This historic ranch house (the Fielding Garr Ranch) is periodically open on weekends for tours.

Camping is available for $8 per night. Reservations are highly recommended.

ADDITIONAL INFORMATION

Map grid: 4C
Elevation: 4,200 feet.
Hazards: Heat in summer months, cold in winter.
Nearest food, gas, and lodging: Layton.
Camping: Antelope Island State Park.
For more information: Utah Division of Parks and Recreation.

11 Layton Marsh Wetlands Preserve

Habitat: Lowland riparian
Specialty birds: American White Pelican; Peregrine Falcon; Sandhill Crane; Long-billed Curlew; Marbled Godwit; Snowy Plover; American Pipit (winter)
Other key birds: Eared Grebe; Double-crested Cormorant; Snowy and Cattle Egrets; Black-crowned Night-Heron; White-faced Ibis; Green-winged Teal; Northern Pintail; Cinnamon Teal; Northern Shoveler; Gadwall; American Wigeon; Red-breasted Merganser; Northern Harrier; Ring-necked Pheasant; Virginia Rail; Sora; Black-bellied Plover; American Golden-Plover; Semipalmated Plover; Black-necked Stilt; American Avocet; Greater and Lesser Yellowlegs; Willet; Spotted Sandpiper; Whimbrel; Red Knot; Sanderling; Western, Least, and Baird's Sandpipers; Dunlin; Long-billed Dowitcher; Common Snipe; Wilson's and Red-necked (spring and fall) Phalaropes; Franklin's, Bonaparte's, Ring-billed, and California Gulls; Caspian, Forster's, and Black Tern; Short-eared Owl; Loggerhead Shrike; Tree, Cliff, Barn, and Bank Swallow; Black-billed Magpie; Common Raven; Marsh Wren; Savannah Sparrow
Best times to bird: Spring and fall are best, March through April and September through mid-October. Breeding season, May through June, can also be interesting.

11 Layton Marsh Wetlands Preserve

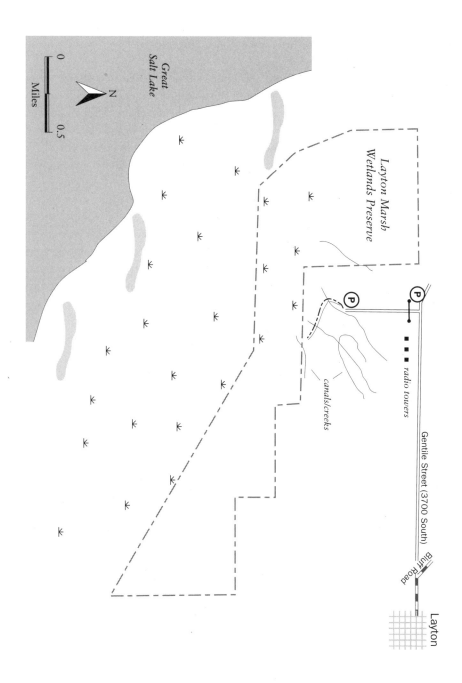

Great Salt Lake

N

Miles

0

0.5

Layton Marsh Wetlands Preserve

canals/creeks

radio towers

Gentile Street (3700 South)

Bluff Road

Layton

69

The birding: Like many areas set aside to protect habitat on the Great Salt Lake, the focus of this preserve is wildlife rather than people. Unlike other nearby areas managed by the Division of Wildlife Resources, people, while maybe not welcomed, are allowed to wander the marshes. The trade-offs are twofold: first, there are no trails or visitor facilities; and second, you must police yourself and not disturb nesting or brooding birds.

From the parking circle, an old and faint road does penetrate a short distance into the marshes. This is a good place to start, and if you walk through either of the gates in the fence, you'll be pointed in the right direction. After a short distance, this track crosses a small canal and forks. The left branch goes toward a slightly higher and therefore drier portion of the marsh and an unused corral. The right branch follows the canal in the opposite direction and shortly comes to an end in a very wet portion of the marsh.

The habitat is fairly homogeneous, at least around the parking area, so your opportunities for birding will be about the same wherever you wander on this short section of trail. The path does pass through mud flats, where you may find shorebirds, particularly in migration, and puts you within view of marshes, where you may hear more birds than you may actually see. You can expand your opportunities by wandering elsewhere in the marsh, but take plenty of insect repellent and don't get lost!

Peregrine Falcons have been hacked nearby, so keep an eye toward the sky for these exceptionally graceful and efficacious hunters.

Directions: From I-15 in Layton, take Exit 332 and head briefly toward town (east). Gentile Street takes off to the west—follow this road for about 6 miles. Three radio towers visible on the horizon are your landmark. Shortly before reaching the radio towers, the paved road veers right and actually becomes Bluff Road, while Gentile Road continues west and at this same intersection becomes a gravel road. Continue west toward the radio towers. Just beyond the third tower (less than 0.1 mile) another dirt road enters on the left. This is the entrance to the preserve. If the gate is closed, park on the road and walk through the turnstile. Otherwise, proceed through the gate and to the parking circle a short distance down this side road.

General information: The Layton Marsh Wetlands Preserve was The Nature Conservancy's first land acquisition in Utah. The management plan for the marsh takes a relatively hands-off approach, and water on the marsh is allowed to fluctuate in natural cycles in accordance with water levels on the Great Salt Lake. In wet cycles the marsh grows verdant, and ducks and ibis abound. When the Great Salt Lake inundates the marsh and salt waters reset the vegetation cycles, shorebirds become more numerous and can be seen wandering the mud flats.

ADDITIONAL INFORMATION

Map grid: 4C
Elevation: 4,205 feet.
Hazards: Biting insects, no drinking water.
Nearest food, gas, and lodging: Layton.
Camping: Century RV Park, Westhaven.
For more information: The Nature Conservancy, Utah Field Office.

12 Farmington Bay Wildlife Management Area

Habitat: Lowland riparian
Specialty birds: Clark's Grebe, American White Pelican, Bald Eagle (winter); Sandhill Crane; Marbled Godwit
Other key birds: Eared and Western Grebes; Double-crested Cormorant; Great Blue Heron; Snowy and Cattle Egrets; Black-crowned Night-Heron; White-faced Ibis; Green-winged Teal; Northern Shoveler; Lesser Scaup; Ruddy Duck; Northern Harrier; American Coot; Killdeer; Black-necked Stilt; American Avocet; Greater and Lesser Yellowlegs; Solitary Sandpiper; Willet; Spotted Sandpiper; Black-bellied Plover (spring); Western, Least, and Baird's Sandpipers; Long-billed Dowitcher; Wilson's and Red-necked (spring) Phalaropes; Red Knot; Franklin's, Ring-billed, and California Gulls; Caspian, Forster's, and Black Terns; Tree, Cliff, Barn, and Bank Swallows; Black-billed Magpie; Common Raven
Best times to bird: Generally good year-round. Species diversity is at its peak during spring and fall migrations; these are the best times to view shorebirds.

The Wasatch Range skirts the town of Centerville and the Farmington Bay WMA.

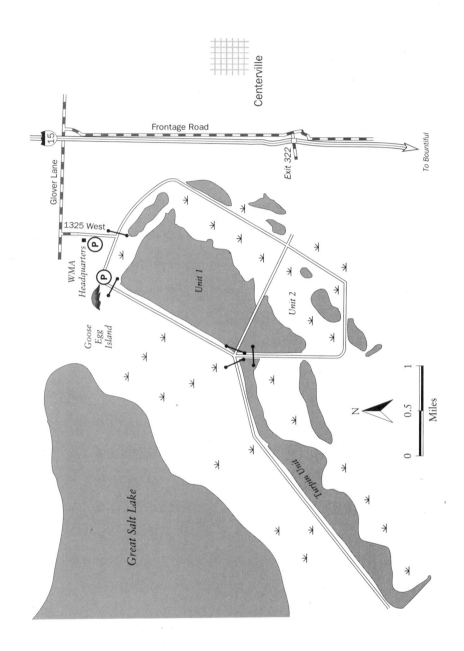

The birding: This management area is designed to provide quality birding whether you prefer to view from the car or a windswept dike. The only road into the refuge winds along the top of a dike, passing numerous small marshes and ponds. Most times of the year these contain waterfowl and shorebirds wading and foraging in the shallow waters. If there is not much traffic, you can pull to the side of the road and scan these flocks; this is a good way to find some of those more unusual migrants, especially the shorebirds. Many of the official pullouts are situated to provide views of these marshes.

The dike road is gated at Goose Egg Island, a prominent mound rising out of the marshes. Binoculars will suffice here, but if you hope to distinguish between Greater and Lesser Yellowlegs at a hundred yards, a spotting scope is essential. It is possible to continue on foot from Goose Egg Island as the dike continues more or less southwest across shallow impoundments. This area supports more of the open-water species; in migration you may be fortunate enough to see one or more species of duck associated with the Pacific Coast.

Directions: From I-15 in Centerville, take Exit 322 and proceed east. Immediately after descending from the overpass over the interstate, turn left (north) onto the frontage road, which is also signed as Market Place Drive. Proceed 3 miles to the intersection with Glover's Lane, and turn left (west). Go 1.4 miles and turn left again onto 1325 West Street just before passing under the high-tension power lines. The road soon turns to gravel at the entrance to the refuge.

General information: After suffering devastating damage from flooding in the mid-1980s, the refuge is recovering nicely, due in no small part to the efforts of the Division of Wildlife Resources. Interpretive signs at the numerous pullouts along the refuge drive enhance the experience. A visitor center is planned, along with boardwalks into some of the marshes.

ADDITIONAL INFORMATION

Map grid: 4D
Elevation: 4,200 feet.
Hazards: None.
Nearest food, gas, and lodging: Centerville.
Camping: Lagoon's RV Park and Campground, Farmington.
For more information: Utah Division of Wildlife Resources.

13 Jordan River Parkway

Habitat: Lowland riparian

Specialty birds: Bald Eagle (winter); Prairie Falcon; Western Wood-Pewee; Northern Shrike (winter); Green-tailed and Spotted Towhee; Lazuli Bunting

Other key birds: Sharp-shinned, Cooper's, and Swainson's Hawks; Ring-necked Pheasant; Franklin's, Ring-billed, and California Gulls; Common Nighthawk; Black-chinned and Broad-tailed Hummingbirds; Belted Kingfisher; Red-naped Sapsucker; Cordilleran Flycatcher; Say's Phoebe; Western Kingbird; Loggerhead Shrike; Plumbeous and Warbling Vireos; Western Scrub-Jay; Tree, Violet-green, Northern Rough-winged, Bank, and Cliff Swallows; Mountain Chickadee (winter); Bewick's, House, and Marsh Wrens; Ruby-crowned Kinglet; Western and Mountain Bluebirds; Hermit Thrush; Cedar Waxwing; Yellow, Yellow-rumped, and MacGillivray's Warblers; Common Yellowthroat; Wilson's Warbler; Western Tanager; American Tree (winter), Brewer's, Vesper, Savannah, Song, and Lincoln's Sparrows; Black-headed Grosbeak; Bullock's Oriole; Cassin's Finch (winter)

Best times to bird: Mid-April through May and September through mid-October for migrants; May through July for resident birds

The birding: This narrow avenue of cottonwoods and willows, often surrounded by city parks and golf courses, seems to attract a fair number of migrant songbirds in early spring and fall. The park is convenient for trips of varying length, from a half-hour lunch break to a half-day stroll. The birding experience from either of the two entrances described below is likely to be quite similar, so choose an entry point based on convenience.

Cottonwood Park is adjacent to the Utah State Fairgrounds, a short distance north of what I designate as the better riparian habitat. After parking along the road on 300 North and walking to the edge of the Jordan River, work your way along the river in either a north or south direction. There are frequent crossing points over the river—narrow footbridges—that provide good views down the river corridor. Take a few minutes at each of these crossings to scan the banks for foraging wrens, warblers, sparrows, or ducks sheltered beneath overhanging brush. If you head south from Cottonwood Park, bird only as far as the fairgrounds and North Temple Street. Heading north from Cottonwood Park, the river trail is hemmed between the steep banks of the river and residential property until it reaches the next park north, Riverside Park.

From the Rose Park Golf Course entrance you have similar choices. Head south and the mix of riparian habitat and parks becomes patchy; head north and you'll meander along the river as it passes through the golf course. If you'd like to link these walks together, from the southern terminus to the northern boundary is a modest hike of 2.3 miles (one-way).

Directions: To reach the Cottonwood Park entrance, drive west on North Temple Street from the city center. About 2 miles beyond the I-15 underpass, turn right on

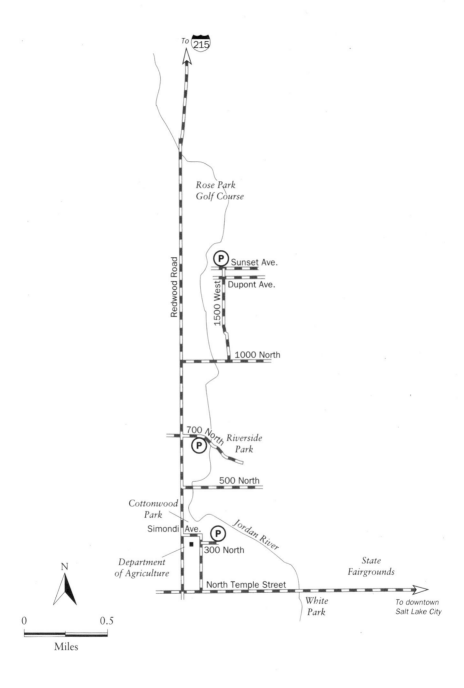

Redwood Road. After 0.5 mile, look for 300 North and turn right. The Department of Agriculture building on your left is surrounded by Cottonwood Park, and the river and walking path pass behind the building.

Continue north on Redwood Road to reach the Rose Park Golf Course entrance. At 1.5 miles north of the 300 North and Redwood Road intersection, turn right on 1000 North. Cross the Jordan River, and take the second left turn onto 1500 West. This residential street soon deadends at Sunset Avenue, where you should turn left and park at the hurricane fence and gate at the river's edge.

Parking is also available at Riverside Park, just east of Redwood Road on 700 North.

General information: There are numerous access points to the Jordan River corridor in Salt Lake City, and long portions of its length are popular for jogging, biking, or walking. Because of the fairly contiguous habitat, the section described here is probably the best for birders.

Habitat restoration along the Jordan River Parkway is an ongoing project. The area should continue to improve as a birding destination as vegetation becomes established. The river has been channelized and diked along its length and supports very little waterfowl and even fewer shorebirds. As you walk the footpath by the river, take a few minutes to reflect on how this flat plain might have looked when the river could flood its banks each spring and water the surrounding terrain; it's likely that the mix of bird species using this corridor between Utah Lake and the Great Salt Lake was quite different a century ago.

ADDITIONAL INFORMATION

Map grid: 4D
Elevation: 4,215 feet.
Hazards: None.
Nearest food, gas, and lodging: Salt Lake City.
Camping: Camp VIP, Salt Lake City.
For more information: Jordan River State Park.

14 Stansbury Island

Habitats: Lowland desert shrub, desert steppe, pinyon-juniper
Specialty birds: Prairie Falcon; Chukar; Northern Shrike (winter); Sage Thrasher; American Pipit (winter); Sage Sparrow
Other key birds: Swainson's Hawk; Short-eared Owl; Loggerhead Shrike; Common Raven; Rock and Canyon Wrens; Northern Mockingbird; Brewer's, Vesper, and Lark Sparrows; Black Rosy-Finch (winter)
Best times to bird: Early mornings for most species, May through June. Chukars are active at dusk.

The birding: Two canyons on Stansbury Island are accessible for exploration and offer a chance to find desert-adapted species. Stansbury Island has also traditionally been a good spot for locating Chukars, although the species is hunted here. The two canyons are adjacent to each other, one opening to the south and one to the west, and it is possible to connect the two in a long loop hike that would have you returning to your car by hiking along the road.

No matter which canyon you visit, expect to put in a mile or two hiking before you find many species; most birds in this harsh environment are widely scattered. If you're lucky, the Chukars may be foraging near the parking area; otherwise, look for them around rock outcrops in the hills along the trails.

Most other species that occur here are more visible along the access road, which passes through an expanse of sagebrush and other desert shrubs. It's worth hiking a section of the road, particularly near the mountain bike trailhead, in search of Sage Thrashers and the various species of sparrows that occur in the area.

Directions: From I-80 west of Salt Lake City, take Exit 84 and turn left onto the frontage road. After a hundred yards or so, follow the signed right turn across the railroad tracks and towards Stansbury Island. About 2 miles after crossing the railroad, the road forks—bear left. South Canyon lies above the gravel pit at the base of the mountain ahead, and both the pit and the canyon are visible on the approach road. About 3 miles past the fork, you'll see a rough access road heading right into the gravel pit. You can follow this route as far as your vehicle will take you, then park and continue following the road through the northeast corner of the gravel pit and up into Tabby's Canyon.

Another and more accessible birding area lies about a mile farther north on the main access road. This next canyon north has a parking area and trailhead for the Stansbury Island Mountain Bike Trail. You can park here and follow the trail for a good birding route.

General information: Some days you'll have this entire island to yourself; other days you'll be fighting hunters and off-road vehicles for elbow room. Hunting season is probably not the time to visit.

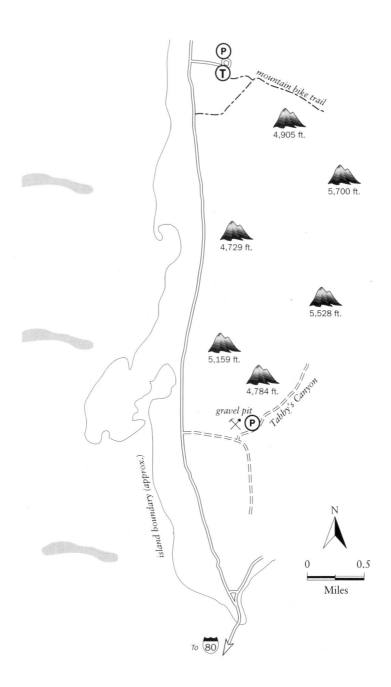

Most of the grass that you see here is cheatgrass, the scourge of all hikers. The less you wander off-trail and into this miserable stuff, the less time you'll have to spend picking seed heads out of your socks and flesh.

ADDITIONAL INFORMATION

Map grid: 4D
Elevation: 4,220 feet.
Hazards: Hot and dry, fairly remote, no drinking water.
Nearest food, gas, and lodging: Grantsville.
Camping: South Willow Canyon campgrounds, Wasatch-Cache National Forest.
For more information: Bureau of Land Management, Salt Lake Field Office.

15 Stansbury Lake

Habitat: Lowland riparian
Specialty birds: American White Pelican; Western Wood-Pewee; Willow, Hammond's, Dusky, and Gray Flycatchers; Green-tailed Towhee
Other key birds: Pied-billed and Eared Grebes; Black-crowned Night-Heron; American Wigeon; Canvasback; Redhead; Ring-necked Duck; Greater Scaup; Lesser Scaup; Common and Red-breasted Mergansers; California Gull; Caspian and Forster's Terns; Cordilleran Flycatcher; Orange-crowned, Yellow, Yellow-rumped, MacGillivray's, and Wilson's Warblers; Bullock's Oriole
Best times to bird: Interesting year-round, except perhaps in July and August

The birding: This artificial pond is fed by thermal springs, so even in winter there is usually open water to attract waterfowl. The remainder of the year you can expect to see waterfowl typical of the region during breeding season as well as a few passerines. Diversity increases markedly during migration, when many more species of waterfowl can be found and the majority of listed passerines may be seen.

After parking on the side of the entrance road, walk across the old ball field toward the arm of the pond approaching UT 138. There may not be a great diversity of songbirds in breeding season, but Barn Swallows, Yellow Warblers, Yellow-rumped Warblers, and Bullock's Orioles are a few of the more likely species you'll find in the trees surrounding the pond.

Walk the shore of the pond, scanning the water and the edges. The pond is a series of small fingers separated by peninsulas of land, and vantage points are numerous. From the ball field continue south across a footbridge and scan the body of water that lies before you.

Directions: From I-80 west of Salt Lake City, take Exit 99 and head south on UT 36. About 4 miles south of the interstate, turn right onto UT 138 (toward Grantsville). About 0.5 mile along UT 138 you'll see the Benson Historic Grist Mill on the right and a concrete monolith on the left indicating Stansbury Park.

15 Stansbury Lake

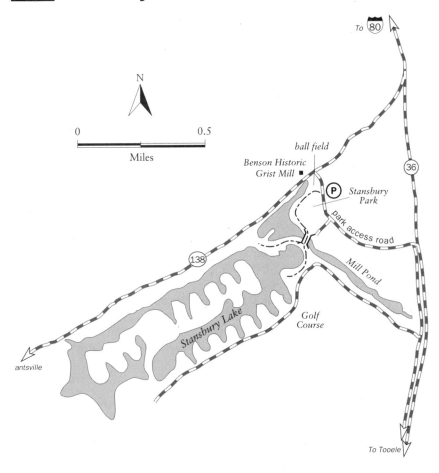

Turn left into Stansbury Park, park on the side of the road, and walk through the park and ball field on the right side of the road to reach an arm of the pond.

General information: The area around the pond is experiencing heavy residential development. As a result, only a small portion of the water body can be inspected by birders—the rest is wrapped up in private property.

ADDITIONAL INFORMATION

Map grid: 4D
Elevation: 4,300 feet.
Hazards: None.
Nearest food, gas, and lodging: Tooele.
Camping: South Willow Canyon campgrounds, Wasatch-Cache National Forest.
For more information: Utah Travel Council.

16 West Canyon in the Stansbury Range

Habitats: Lowland desert shrub, desert steppe, upland desert shrub, pinyon-juniper, spruce-fir

Specialty birds: Ferruginous Hawk; Prairie Falcon; Long-billed Curlew; Hammond's, Dusky, and Gray Flycatchers; Northern Shrike (winter); Townsend's Solitaire; Green-tailed Towhee; Lazuli Bunting

Other key birds: Swainson's Hawk; Short-eared Owl; Black-chinned and Broad-tailed Hummingbirds; Cordilleran Flycatcher; Loggerhead Shrike; Plumbeous Vireo; Western Scrub-Jay; Common Raven; Mountain Bluebird; Brewer's, Vesper, and Lark Sparrows

Best times to bird: May through June, early mornings; fall migration, September through early October, for passerines

The birding: The approach road to the West Canyon Trailhead cuts an interesting swath through a variety of desert habitats, from arid desert shrubland up to a well-watered canyon that supports a dense conifer forest.

After leaving UT 138 and starting the drive up to the canyon mouth, begin scanning either side of the road for raptors on the wing and for Long-billed Curlews, which frequent this grassland area. The area is also good for sparrows, and the most common bird here is probably the Horned Lark. The road is passable, but rough, and demands attention. If time allows, stop occasionally to walk short sections of this road and listen for bird activity.

The road climbs through a series of habitat types, eventually reaching a scattering of spruce and juniper along the watercourse out of the canyon mouth. In a short distance you'll reach a small parking area and the trailhead. From here, it's worth exploring both upstream and down for birds.

Walk back down the road for a short distance to get below the steepest part of the canyon, and then leave the road and walk east, exploring the creek gully and the scattered trees for Mountain Bluebirds, vireos, Green-tailed Towhees, and sparrows.

If you follow the West Canyon Trail from the parking area, you quickly pick up more complex vegetation communities with more trees. Even if you don't walk as far as the conifer forest that graces the hillside in the visible distance (where most of the flycatchers reside), it is worth walking about half a mile to a spring and grove of riparian vegetation on the north wall of the canyon. This is often an area of high bird activity, a good spot for Cordilleran Flycatchers.

Directions: From Grantsville, head west on UT 138. On the west edge of town, UT 138 bends sharply and turns north; from this bend, the well-signed turn to West Canyon Trailhead is 0.6 mile away. Turn left on West Canyon Road and start birding.

General information: The road to West Canyon is fair weather only, and a high-clearance vehicle is essential. Four-wheel drive is helpful but not required. If you

16 West Canyon in the Stansbury Range

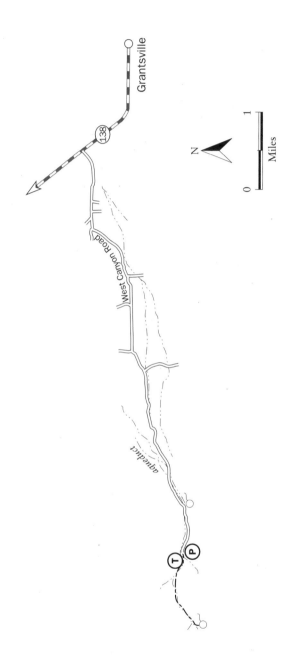

attempt to visit in foul weather, you might try birding nearby South Willow Canyon, which offers a similar but less remote experience.

ADDITIONAL INFORMATION

Map grid: 4D
Elevation: 6,000 feet.
Hazards: Rough road, no drinking water.
Nearest food, gas, and lodging: Grantsville.
Camping: South Willow Canyon campgrounds, Wasatch-Cache National Forest.
For More information: Wasatch-Cache National Forest, Salt Lake Ranger District.

17 South Willow Canyon

Habitats: Mountain riparian, spruce-fir, pinyon-juniper, aspen
Specialty birds: Ferruginous Hawk; Peregrine and Prairie Falcons; Long-billed Curlew; White-throated Swift; Gray Flycatcher; Western Wood-Pewee; Willow, Hammond's, and Dusky Flycatchers; Northern Shrike (winter); American Dipper; Townsend's Solitaire; Swainson's Thrush; Green-tailed and Spotted Towhees; Lazuli Bunting
Other key birds: Sharp-shinned, Cooper's, and Swainson's Hawks; Golden Eagle; Merlin (winter); Short-eared Owl; Black-chinned and Broad-tailed Hummingbirds; Red-naped Sapsucker; Downy and Hairy Woodpeckers; Cordilleran Flycatcher; Loggerhead Shrike; Plumbeous and Warbling Vireos; Steller's Jay; Western Scrub-Jay; Common Raven; Tree and Violet-green Swallows; Mountain Chickadee; Red-breasted and White-breasted Nuthatches; Brown Creeper; Rock, Bewick's, and House Wrens; Ruby-crowned Kinglet; Mountain Bluebird; Hermit Thrush; Orange-crowned, Virginia's, Yellow, Yellow-rumped, MacGillivray's, and Wilson's Warblers; Western Tanager; Chipping, Brewer's, Vesper, Lark, and Song Sparrows; Black-headed Grosbeak; Cassin's Finch; Pine Siskin; American Goldfinch
Best times to bird: May through June, early mornings; fall migration, September through early October, for passerines

The birding: This route offers a cross section of habitats and bird communities, from desert shrubs to a high montane forest. Begin scanning the roadside after turning onto the South Willow Canyon access road. This open country can be good for raptors and a few passerines, particularly sparrows. However, the best birding really starts after you enter the narrow canyon itself, which is heavily timbered on its north-facing slope. Shrubs, grasses, and pinyon-junipers grow on the south face.

Stop at points along the way and explore the various vegetation communities for bird activity. Hiking the loop through the campsites of the Boy Scout Camp-ground offers good birding, assuming there's not too much human activity. Look for American Dippers in the stream (here and at other stops along the creek as

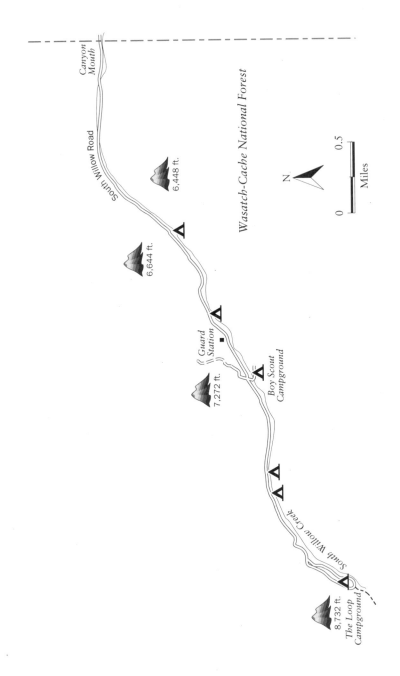

Canyon Mouth

South Willow Road

6,448 ft.

6,644 ft.

Wasatch-Cache National Forest

Guard Station

7,272 ft.

Boy Scout Campground

South Willow Creek

8,732 ft.

The Loop Campground

N

0   0.5

Miles

well), and vireos, nuthatches, and warblers in the streamside and campground forests. On the opposite side of the canyon from the Boy Scout Campground, a dirt road climbs the open slope and passes through scattered junipers. Hiking along this track offers a glimpse into the pinyon-juniper bird community and a chance to see Western Scrub-Jays, Juniper Titmice, Plumbeous Vireos, and various sparrows.

Continue up the road, stopping as the mood strikes. Be sure to save time for exploring Loop Campground at the end of the canyon road. A beautiful aspen-conifer forest surrounds the campsites. A walk here should produce Red-naped Sapsuckers, Hermit Thrushes, Warbling Vireos, and numerous warblers.

Directions: In Grantsville, turn south on 400 West. This turn is well signed for North and South Willow canyons. Continue south for about 5 miles, and then look for the right turn (again, well signed) for South Willow Canyon. Begin the birding route after turning onto this approach road, which you follow to its terminus at Loop Campground about 8 miles away.

General information: It's possible to extend this trip by hiking either of the trails that depart from the upper end of Loop Campground. Both the Deseret Peak Trail and the South Willow Lake Trail climb about 2,000 feet from the trailhead, and species you may add to your birding experience include Blue Grouse, Northern Pygmy-Owls, Northern Saw-whet Owl, White-throated Swift, Rufous Hummingbird (mid-July through August), flycatchers, and Clark's Nutcracker. Even if you don't make it all the way to the final destination of these trails, I recommend at least a short hike in this beautiful forest.

The road turns to gravel after crossing the national forest boundary but is passable to passenger cars. If you go early in the season before graders have worked the road, expect a slow drive.

ADDITIONAL INFORMATION

Map grid: 3D
Elevation: 5,800 to 7,418 feet.
Hazards: None.
Nearest food, gas, and lodging: Grantsville.
Camping: 6 Forest Service campgrounds in South Willow Canyon.
For more information: Wasatch-Cache National Forest, Salt Lake Ranger District.

18 Raptor Loop

Habitats: Lowland desert shrub, upland desert shrub, pinyon-juniper
Specialty birds: Bald Eagle; Ferruginous Hawk; Peregrine and Prairie Falcons; Pinyon Jay; Northern Shrike; American Pipit
Other key birds: Northern Harrier; Sharp-shinned, Cooper's, and Rough-legged Hawks; Golden Eagle; Merlin; Short-eared Owl; Loggerhead Shrike; Western Scrub-Jay; Common Raven; Mountain Bluebird; American Tree and Savannah Sparrows
Best times to bird: Any time during the day, mid-October through mid-March

The birding: With the opportunity to see more than 100 individuals representing up to a dozen species, this is one of the best areas for viewing raptors in the Intermountain West. The route, south of Great Salt Lake, leads you through a wide valley bounded on the east by the Oquirrh (pronounced "oak-er") Mountains and on the west by the Stansbury Mountains. The vegetation here is low growing, so views are expansive, and perched raptors are restricted to the few trees, telephone poles, and power lines that rise out of the valley floor.

This is a driving tour, so balance the need to keep the car in your own lane with scanning the sky and perches for raptors. There is not a lot of traffic on this route, particularly south of Tooele ("too-willa"), so bird watching is a relatively safe pastime from the road. But be sure to pull off when a great sighting beckons. The raptors can be spread anywhere or everywhere along the route. Your best chances for the jays, Townsend's Solitaire, and Mountain Bluebird will come in the limited amount of pinyon-juniper you'll pass through, particularly in the vicinity of Fivemile Pass.

Directions: From Exit 99 on I-80, head south on UT 36. About 5 miles south of Stockton, turn east on UT 73 and continue into Lehi, where you can return to a main highway, I-15. Total driving distance is about 60 miles.

General information: If you still can't get enough raptors after this trip, or if your direction of travel is westward, you can alter this route to include another interesting raptor area to the west. To include this extension, turn west on UT 199, south of the small community of Stockton. This route leads through the town of Rush Valley, over Johnson Pass, and north through Skull Valley on the west side of the Stansbury Range and finally back to I-80. It's about 58 miles from the turn off UT 36 through Skull Valley to I-80.

18 Raptor Loop

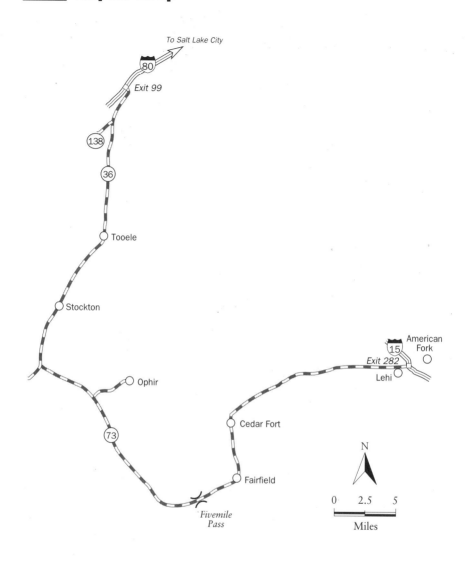

ADDITIONAL INFORMATION

Map grid: 4D, 4E
Elevation: 4,500 to 5,000 feet.
Hazards: None.
Nearest food, gas, and lodging: Tooele, Stockton, Cedar Fort, Lehi.
Camping: South Willow Canyon campgrounds, Wasatch-Cache National Forest, and Clover Spring Campground (Bureau of Land Management).
For more information: Utah Travel Council.

19 Clover Creek

Habitats: Lowland riparian, pinyon-juniper, upland desert shrub
Specialty birds: Northern Pygmy-Owl; Pinyon Jay; Townsend's Solitaire; American Dipper; Green-tailed and Spotted Towhees; Lazuli Bunting
Other key birds: Black-chinned and Broad-tailed Hummingbirds; Loggerhead Shrike; Plumbeous Vireo; Western Scrub-Jay; Mountain Bluebird; Warbling Vireo; Virginia's, Yellow, and Black-throated Gray Warblers; Western Tanager; Chipping, Song, and Lincoln's Sparrows; Black-headed Grosbeak; Lesser Goldfinch
Best times to bird: Mornings, May through June

The birding: This birding area focuses on a short but permanent stream draining an extensive pinyon-juniper forest in Utah's west desert. The stream supports a narrow riparian corridor with a tall canopy of cottonwoods and a shrubby understory of willow, hawthorn, and other natives.

About 2 miles of various points along the length of Clover Creek are accessible for birding. Choose a spot with a dirt access road leaving the paved UT 199, pull to the side, and spend some time exploring the riparian zone and the adjacent pinyon-junipers.

The easiest spot for accessing the creek is in Clover Spring Campground, a development surrounding the headwaters of the creek. The campground is divided into two loops. The loop to the left as you enter contains Clover Spring and Clover Creek, while to the right a loop has been pushed into the drier pinyon-juniper forest. Park near the spring, as described below, and take some time to explore the left campground loop. This walk will take you past the riparian zone and through some desert shrub habitat. Both species of vireo are visible along this route, along with sparrows, warblers, and both Green-tailed and Spotted Towhees. Northern Pygmy-Owls use the stream corridor and on rare occasions may be seen perched in the streamside cottonwoods, particularly in winter.

The right loop is shorter, but here you may see Black-chinned Hummingbirds, Plumbeous Vireos, and jays.

Directions: From the community of Rush Valley, head west on UT 199. About 3 miles west of town, the road begins to follow along the north side of Clover Creek. There are numerous access points in the form of dirt roads that head for the riparian corridor. The easiest access point is Clover Spring Campground on the left side of the road about 5 miles west of Rush Valley. Turn left after entering the campground and bear right on the campground loop. You can park near Clover Spring, which is signed, at the upper end of the loop.

General information: Continuing west on UT 199 will lead you into the heart of the pinyon-juniper forest and may provide an opportunity to find both species of jays mentioned. The Pinyon Jay in particular is an irruptive species, meaning it

19 Clover Creek

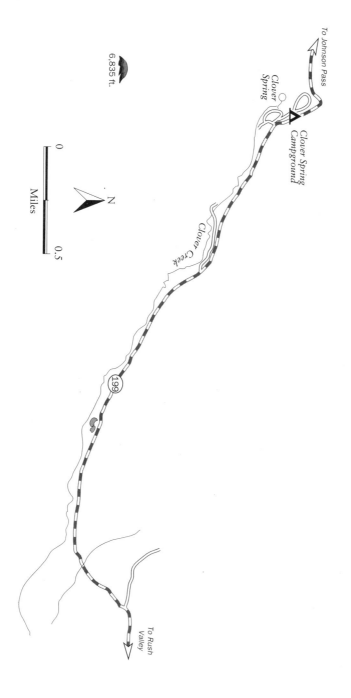

6,835 ft.

Miles
0
0.5
N

To Johnson Pass

Clover Spring

Clover Spring Campground

Clover Creek

199

To Rush Valley

occasionally moves out of its normal range. It travels widely in gregarious flocks. The more area you cover, the more likely you are to encounter it.

ADDITIONAL INFORMATION

Map grid: 3E
Elevation: 5,900 feet.
Hazards: None.
Nearest food, gas, and lodging: Tooele.
Camping: Clover Spring Campground.
For more information: Bureau of Land Management, Salt Lake Field Office.

20 Ophir Canyon

Habitats: Lowland riparian, mountain riparian, pinyon-juniper, upland desert shrub, aspen, spruce-fir
Specialty birds: Bald Eagle (winter); Western Screech-Owl; Northern Pygmy-Owl; Northern Shrike (winter); Clark's Nutcracker; American Dipper; Townsend's Solitaire; Sage Thrasher
Other key birds: Long-eared Owl; Northern Saw-whet Owl; Black-chinned and Broad-tailed Hummingbirds; Loggerhead Shrike; Warbling Vireo; Steller's Jay; Mountain Chickadee; Rock, Canyon, and House Wrens; Hermit Thrush; Western Tanager; Yellow, Yellow-rumped, and Black-throated Gray Warblers; Brewer's, Vesper, and Lark Sparrows
Best times to bird: Year-round

Main Street in the town of Ophir.

20 Ophir Canyon

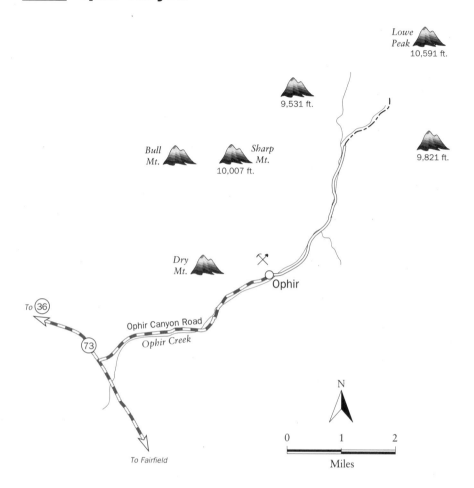

Lowe Peak
10,591 ft.

9,531 ft.

Bull Mt.

Sharp Mt.
10,007 ft.

9,821 ft.

Dry Mt.

Ophir

To (36)

Ophir Canyon Road

(73)

Ophir Creek

To Fairfield

N

0   1   2

Miles

The birding: Above the intersection with UT 73, Ophir Canyon Road climbs steeply up Ophir Canyon through an array of vegetation zones. At the turnoff you'll find yourself in distinctly desert terrain and a reasonably good area for Sage Thrashers, Loggerhead Shrikes, Northern Shrikes, and sparrows. The road quickly enters a mix of pinyon-juniper, pastureland, and riparian vegetation associated with Ophir Creek.

As the road climbs toward the community of Ophir, keep an eye out for Black-throated Gray Warblers, hawks (often Red-tailed Hawks), and in winter, Bald Eagles and Clark's Nutcrackers.

In winter, the town of Ophir holds many interesting montane species which descend from higher elevations. In summer, some of the most interesting birding lies beyond the eastern edge of the town. If you continue through Ophir, the road soon turns to dirt and the canyon opens up slightly to support a forest that grows around Ophir Creek. Above the canyon floor on the drier slopes oaks and maples dominate, while on wetter, north facing slopes, a mix of aspens and conifers grow. Drive up this valley, stopping occasionally to listen and look for birds. Expect to see typical montane species. Hermit Thrushes call from the drier upland slopes; Black-throated Gray Warblers are abundant in the oak thickets. In winter, this road is not maintained, although it is usually packed firm by snowmobile traffic. A short walk from the edge of town (and the end of the maintained road) at this time of year will often reveal owls roosting in the creek area.

The drive above Ophir requires four stream crossings—the first one coming just 0.3 mile beyond the pavement. The third crossing, 1.3 miles after the pavement ends, is impassable to passenger cars. The road ends completely 2.2 miles beyond the pavement, but it is possible to explore the aspen-conifer forest from here on foot.

Directions: From Toelle, head south on UT 36 for about 11 miles. At the intersection with UT 73, turn left. After 5.6 miles, turn left onto Ophir Canyon Road and begin watching for bird activity. From this intersection, it's another 3 miles to Ophir and an additional 1.3 miles to the end of the paved road.

General information: Like most mining towns, Ophir has suffered from a number of boom-and-bust periods. The town started as a mining town and became a ghost town. Then another mining boom hit, and more recently the mines closed for good. The town may live again in the future as a retreat for vacation homeowners and those lucky few who can telecommute from this remote outpost.

This is a popular snowmobile destination in winter. The road to Ophir is usually open all winter but may be impassable immediately after a storm.

ADDITIONAL INFORMATION

Map grid: 4E
Elevation: 5,498 to7,546 feet.
Hazards: None.
Nearest food, gas, and lodging: Tooele.
Camping: Clover Spring Campground.
For more information: Utah Travel Council.

21 James Walter Fitzgerald Wildlife Management Area

Habitats: Lowland riparian, lowland desert shrub
Specialty birds: American White Pelican, Sage Thrasher, Sage Sparrow
Other key birds: Pied-billed and Western Grebes; Ring-necked Pheasant; Virginia Rail; Sora; California Gull; Forster's Tern; Common Nighthawk; Western Kingbird; Northern Rough-winged, Cliff, and Barn Swallows; Brewer's, Vesper, Lark, and Black-throated Sparrows
Best times to bird: Spring (April) and fall (September) migration for waterfowl

The birding: Access to this small but productive wildlife management area is restricted from March 1 to August 1, so a September visit is arguably the best time to stop at this isolated desert water hole. It is possible to scan the lake from the parking area at other times of year and get a reasonable view of the species present. A spotting scope is required to make this worthwhile.

The parking area is essentially at the west end of the dam. Follow the road across the top of the dam, scanning the lake and the emerging marshes. This is a shallow body of water, appealing to many species of waterfowl and some shorebirds in migration.

Entrance is also possible from the south, but again the road is gated and restricted March 1 to August 1. This southern route passes through lowland shrub habitat and is worth driving or walking the short distance to look for Sage Thrashers and sparrows. This route is also good for viewing the marshes at the south end of the lake. It may be easier to approach from this direction and observe the lake without flushing the resident waterfowl.

Directions: From Tooele, head south on UT 36 for about 25 miles until you reach the Pony Express route. After driving 24 miles, look for a Utah Division of Wildlife Resources sign on the left that can only be read from the south. If you reach the intersection of the Pony Express route, you've driven 0.7 mile too far. The Utah Division of Wildlife Resources sign on the right indicates the WMA, and the entrance and parking area is just south of the refuge manager's house. Turn into the driveway and follow the signs to the parking area by the lake.

To reach the southern entrance, drive south on UT 36 for about 0.5 mile and turn left on Faust Road. After traveling 0.6 mile east, you'll see a rough dirt road on your left heading toward the refuge. From this turnoff, it's 0.3 mile to the WMA boundary.

General information: There seems to be some confusion over the name of this area—the lake appears on some topographic maps as "Astherly Reservoir." I have also heard this area referred to as the "Pony Express Wildlife Management Area," while the sign at the entrance indicates this is the James Walter Fitzgerald WMA.

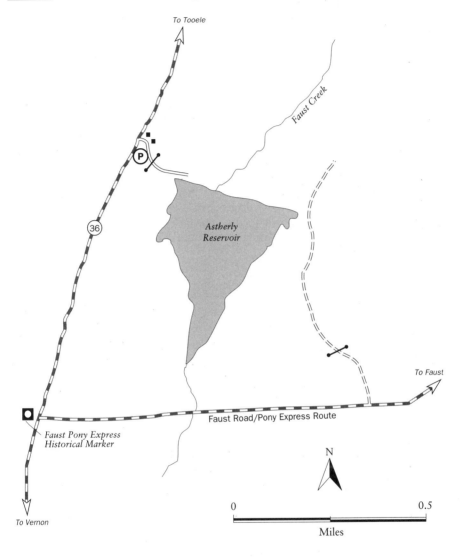

ADDITIONAL INFORMATION

Map grid: 4E
Elevation: 5,210 feet.
Hazards: None.
Nearest food, gas, and lodging: Tooele.
Camping: Clover Spring Campground.
For more information: Utah Division of Wildlife Resources.

22 Provo Bay

Habitat: Lowland riparian

Specialty birds: Bald Eagle (winter), Western Screech-Owl, Western Wood-Pewee, Willow Flycatcher

Other key birds: Snowy Egret; White-faced Ibis; Wood Duck; Cinnamon Teal; Gadwall; Lesser Scaup; Sharp-shinned and Cooper's Hawks; Ring-necked Pheasant; Franklin's, Ring-billed, and California Gulls; Barn and Long-eared Owls; Common Nighthawk; Black-chinned and Broad-tailed Hummingbirds; Belted Kingfisher; Red-naped Sapsucker; Cordilleran Flycatcher; Say's Phoebe; Western Kingbird; Loggerhead Shrike; Plumbeous and Warbling Vireos; Tree, Violet-green, Northern Rough-winged, Bank, and Cliff Swallows; Mountain Chickadee (winter); Bewick's, House, and Marsh Wrens; Western and Mountain Bluebirds; Hermit Thrush; Cedar Waxwing; Yellow, Yellow-rumped, and MacGillivray's Warblers; Common Yellowthroat; Wilson's Warbler; Western Tanager; American Tree (winter), Brewer's, Vesper, Savannah, Song, and Lincoln's Sparrows; Black-headed Grosbeak; Bullock's Oriole

Best times to bird: This privately owned property is open only during daylight hours. Birding is best for waterfowl during migration, spring (April through May) and fall (September through October). Breeding songbirds are best viewed mornings, May through June.

The birding: A mature forest of cottonwoods lines Hobble Creek and an adjacent canal as they end the last mile or so to Provo Bay. The cottonwood forest alone is often worthwhile with its share of warblers (particularly in fall migration), Willow Flycatchers, Warbling Vireos, Bullock's Orioles, House Wrens, thrushes, and Hairy and Downy Woodpeckers. However, as you follow the cottonwood forest out along the canal, you will also be hemmed on the north side by an extensive marsh complex and on the south by Provo Bay. Both feature a healthy share of birds. The marsh to the north hosts Marsh Wrens, sparrows, Snowy Egrets, and White-faced Ibis, while the arm of Provo Bay often shelters large numbers of waterfowl.

As you enter through the gate, the diked canal cuts straight across your path about 150 yards ahead. However, between the gate and the canal lies the densest part of the cottonwood grove, and you may want to take your time birding in this area before eventually intercepting the canal. Once you're ready to head for the marsh and waterfowl, begin following the canal as it flows toward the bay. This is a good place to use a spotting scope, but good binoculars will suffice.

Directions: From I-15, take Exit 265 (Springville) and head west. Instead of heading left (south) on the frontage road, turn right, cross a cattle guard, and immediately turn into a small graveled parking area on the left. A sign over the entrance gate reads "The Forest of Camelot."

22 Provo Bay

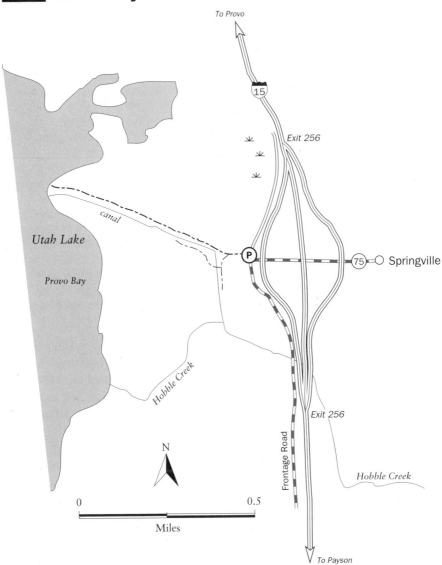

General information: This property seems to be set up to accommodate scout groups. There are proclamations nailed to trees, signs on the Camelot theme, and tree trunks carved into tables, watch towers, and other assorted furniture. The atmosphere is a little odd, but the birding is good.

Groups of seven or more need to call ahead for permission to use the facility. Anyone wishing to camp overnight will also require reservations.

ADDITIONAL INFORMATION

Map grid: 5E

Elevation: 4,500 feet.

Hazards: Biting insects.

Nearest food, gas, and lodging: Springville.

Camping: Utah Lake State Park.

For more information: For reservations or to reserve access for groups of seven or more, call number in Appendix C.

23 Provo River Parkway

Habitat: Lowland riparian

Specialty birds: Bald Eagle (winter); Prairie Falcon; Western Screech-Owl; Western Wood-Pewee; Northern Shrike (winter); Green-tailed and Spotted Towhee; Lazuli Bunting

Other key birds: Wood Duck; Sharp-shinned, Cooper's, and Swainson's Hawks; Ring-necked Pheasant; Franklin's, Ring-billed, and California Gulls; Barn and Long-eared Owls; Common Nighthawk; Black-chinned and Broad-tailed Hummingbirds; Belted Kingfisher; Red-naped Sapsucker; Cordilleran Flycatcher; Say's Phoebe; Western Kingbird; Loggerhead Shrike; Plumbeous and Warbling Vireos; Western Scrub-Jay; Tree, Violet-green, Northern Rough-winged, Bank, and Cliff Swallows; Mountain Chickadee (winter); Bewick's, House, and Marsh Wrens; Western and Mountain Bluebirds; Hermit Thrush; Cedar Waxwing; Yellow, Yellow-rumped, and MacGillivray's Warblers; Common Yellowthroat; Wilson's Warbler; Western Tanager; American Tree (winter), Brewer's, Vesper, Savannah, Song, and Lincoln's Sparrows; Black-headed Grosbeak; Bullock's Oriole; Cassin's Finch

Best times to bird: Year-round

The birding: This is a pleasant, level 2.5-mile walk along a mature cottonwood riparian corridor. The Provo River lies in its historic floodplain near its outlet at Utah Lake, although the river was long ago diked and thoroughly contained. The path that follows this section of the river is paved and accessible to every level of user. There are four access points with parking lots within this stretch, so the length of your walk is up to you.

This stretch of the river is fairly homogeneous for birding, so pick one of the parking areas and walk as much of the trail as holds your interest, birding the river, tree canopy, and adjacent fields. The trail stays almost entirely under the cottonwood canopy along the river. North of the trail lie farm fields, most under active cultivation for hay crops. Toward the east end of this stretch houses are growing faster than weeds, and this will ultimately affect the number and kinds of bird species one is likely to see.

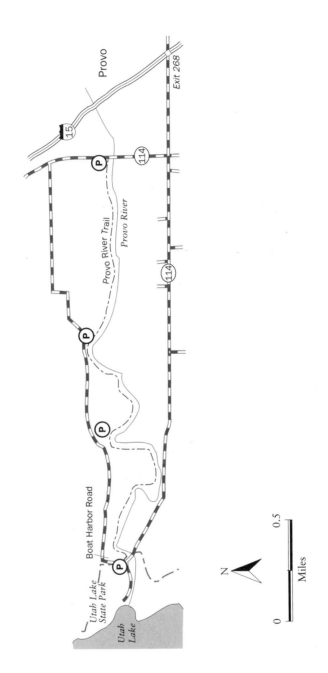

More than 70 species have been recorded here, although on any given outing you're more likely to see 25 to 30. Birding in the winter can yield various species of owls, Belted Kingfishers, sparrows, and ducks. In both spring and fall, migrants stop over; you'll likely find some interesting warblers, flycatchers, and other songbirds.

Directions: From I-15 in Provo, take Exit 268 and head west toward Utah Lake State Park, about 2 miles from the interstate. You'll cross the Provo River and the state park will appear immediately ahead; instead of going to the park, after crossing the bridge turn right onto Boat Harbor Road and proceed about 100 yards— pull into the parking lot on your right, just before the park ranger's residence. This is the west end of the Provo River Trail.

General information: This trail is open to a variety of recreationists, including cyclists and roller bladers. Be aware of these other users as your attention focuses in on some cryptic bird calling from the undergrowth. Don't get run over.

The Provo River Parkway is actually a long municipal trail that climbs well up into the city of Provo. The section described here is probably the most interesting for birders.

ADDITIONAL INFORMATION

Map grid: 5E
Elevation: 4,500 feet.
Hazards: Biting insects.
Nearest food, gas, and lodging: Provo.
Camping: Utah Lake State Park.
For more information: Utah Travel Council.

24 Warm Springs Wildlife Management Area

Habitats: Lowland riparian, upland desert shrub
Specialty birds: Prairie Falcon; Chukar; Sage Thrasher
Other key birds: Pied-billed and Eared Grebes; American Bittern; Snowy Egret; Green-winged Teal; Northern Pintail; Cinnamon Teal; Gadwall; American Wigeon (spring and fall); Lesser Scaup (spring and fall); Common Goldeneye (spring and fall); Ruddy Duck; Northern Harrier; Sharp-shinned and Cooper's Hawks; Ring-necked Pheasant; Virginia Rail; Sora; Greater (spring and fall) and Lesser (spring and fall) Yellowlegs; Long-billed Dowitcher (spring and fall); Red-necked Phalarope (spring and fall); Franklin's and California Gulls; Common Nighthawk; Western Kingbird; Violet-green, Cliff, and Barn Swallows; Rock and Marsh Wrens; Yellow Warbler; Brewer's and Lincoln's Sparrows
Best times to bird: Spring and fall are best, April through mid-May and September through mid-October. Early mornings in late spring and summer can be interesting.

24 Warm Springs Wildlife Management Area

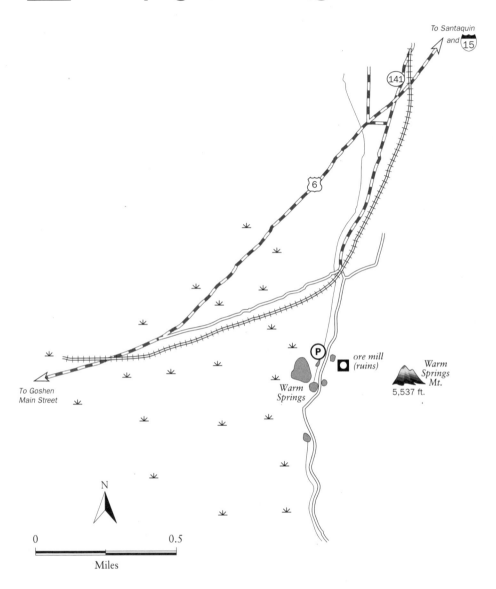

The birding: This area features a series of pools and shallow ponds surrounded by a lush marsh complex and dense stands of Russian olives. The area is best during spring and fall migration, when it attracts a great diversity of waterfowl, shore-birds, and passerines.

There are no official trails; pick your way along the dikes and banks, and explore the drier parts of the marshes. From the parking area you can either continue to follow the gravel road along the marshes or depart immediately to the right (west) and cross the small canal. Either way you'll probably want to make a loop out through the marshes and then return to the parking area. The Russian olive groves are not particularly interesting—this invasive exotic doesn't seem to support much bird activity.

Be sure to investigate the dry, sagebrush-covered slope rising from the road for Sage Thrashers and sparrows.

Directions: From I-15, take the Santaquin Exit 248 and head west on US 6 for 4.4 miles. After crossing a set of railroad tracks, turn left onto a paved road and continue for 0.6 mile. The road turns to gravel and splits; turn left and re-cross the railroad tracks. Immediately after crossing the tracks turn right—this road is below the railroad grade and not even visible on the approach. You'll see the signed entrance to the Warm Springs Wildlife Management Area immediately ahead. Continue along this road for about 0.5 mile to a parking area above a small pond.

From the west, head out of Goshen on Main Street (US 6) for 1.9 miles. As the highway swings northeast, a gravel road continues straight along the railroad tracks. Follow this gravel road until you reach pavement and turn right, crossing the tracks. The remaining directions are the same as those indicated above.

General information: If you're approaching this area from the west (Goshen), a prominent landmark is the abandoned ore-processing mill on the side of the mountain to the east. Warm Springs WMA is directly beneath it.

ADDITIONAL INFORMATION

Map grid: 5E
Elevation: 4,500 feet.
Hazards: Biting insects.
Nearest food, gas, and lodging: Goshen.
Camping: Maple Bench Campground, Uinta National Forest.
For more information: Utah Division of Wildlife Resources.

25 Blue Lake

Habitats: Lowland riparian, lowland desert shrub, upland desert shrub
Specialty birds: Ferruginous Hawk; Prairie Falcon; Sandhill Crane; Sage Thrasher
Other key birds: Pied-billed and Eared Grebes; American Bittern; Snowy Egret; Black-crowned Night-Heron; Northern Pintail; Cinnamon Teal; Northern Shoveler; Gadwall; Canvasback; Northern Harrier; Swainson's Hawk; Virginia Rail; Sora; Semipalmated and Mountain Plovers; Black-necked Stilt; American Avocet; Greater and Lesser Yellowlegs; Willet; Short-eared Owl; Common Nighthawk; Loggerhead Shrike; Northern Rough-winged Swallow; Rock and Marsh Wrens; Northern Mockingbird; Yellow-rumped Warbler; Common Yellowthroat; Lark Sparrow; Bullock's Oriole
Best times to bird: During migration is best, March through mid-May and September through October. Few species seem to nest at this site.

The birding: Lying on the edge of a vast, dead-level desert plain that seems to touch the horizon, Blue Lake is the kind of startling oasis that makes you rub your eyes and wait for the sting of mosquito bites before you believe it's real. Although the lake is slightly saline, it does support a lush marsh and is an important stopover for numerous species of migrating birds.

There are few trees at Blue Lake, so passerines make do with the few desert shrubs that surround the lake. It's odd to see warblers and Bullock's Orioles foraging in sagebrush or saltbush but that's exactly what they do here. Shorebirds and waterfowl use the marshes and small bodies of water scattered across the area.

One of the first things you'll notice as you arrive is a rock outcropping rising about 10 feet above the road on the west side of the lake. There is a good level spot behind the rock for camping and the rock provides an excellent place to sit and scan the marsh. From this vantage you see a swath of desert shrubs, a good chunk of marshland, and some of the open water. A spotting scope is helpful but not required.

A second strategy is to head into the marsh along one of the many short trails left by previous users. A third option is to simply start hiking east on the south side of the pond immediately below the aforementioned rock. Because water level fluctuates seasonally, I can't advise you specifically on where to walk. But you needn't go far in this direction before finding some less-impacted terrain where you'll likely see both shorebirds and waterfowl, and possibly a Northern Harrier or Short-eared Owl hunting the marsh. Again, that rock face comes in handy, this time as a landmark for making your way back.

Take a little time to explore along the road through some of the upland desert shrub habitat. Birds are not numerous here, but this is the best area for Sage Thrashers, Rock Wrens, and Lark Sparrows.

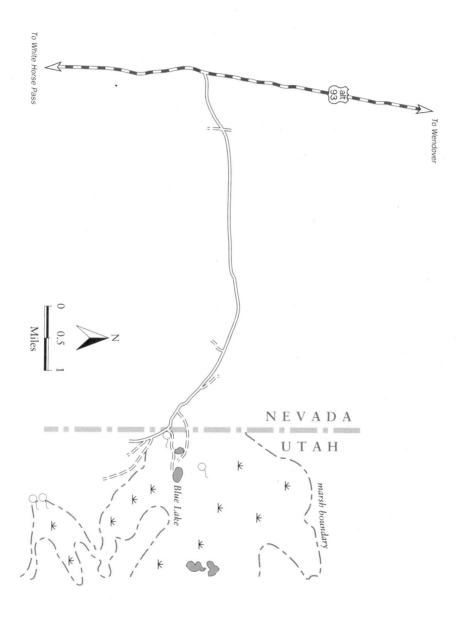

Directions: From Wendover, head south on NV Alt-93. About 17 miles south of the railroad crossing (just on the outskirts of Wendover), you'll see a small sign pointing east to Blue Lake. The road turns to gravel as soon as you leave NV Alt-93 and proceeds steadily downhill toward the alkali desert flat. Blue Lake lies at the terminus of this road, about 5 miles away.

General information: Blue Lake is surrounded by military lands under active use; you'll see plenty of boundary signs and dire warnings not to violate the boundary. Heed them. If you think you're alone, try going for a stroll in the restricted area: people will appear out of nowhere just like in the movies. It's eerie, and there is unexploded ordnance and who-knows-what-else on the military lands, so it's best to hang with the birds.

One other word of caution. This is a popular destination for scuba divers. During the week you're likely to have Blue Lake to yourself, but on weekends the lake is anything but quiet and isolated, especially in hotter months. In the cooler months during bird migration, relative calm may prevail through the weekends.

The stretch of gravel road that leads to this site is often badly washboarded but passable to any car—just take it slow.

Primitive camping is the rule here, with plenty of open spots (except maybe on those crowded weekends) to pitch a tent or park a camper. The closest developed campground is in Wendover (State Line RV Park); it does not accommodate tents.

ADDITIONAL INFORMATION

Map grid: 1E
Elevation: 4,450 feet.
Hazards: Heat, biting insects, no drinking water.
Nearest food, gas, and lodging: Wendover.
Camping: State Line RV Park, Wendover.
For more information: Bureau of Land Management, Salt Lake Field Office.

26 CCC Campground, Tom's Creek, and Granite Creek

Habitats: Lowland riparian, lowland desert shrub, mountain riparian, pinyon-juniper, upland desert shrub

Specialty birds: Ferruginous Hawk; Prairie Falcon; Burrowing Owl; Willow Flycatcher; Pinyon Jay; Sage Thrasher; Green-tailed and Spotted Towhees; Lazuli Bunting

Other key birds: Turkey Vulture; Sharp-shinned, Cooper's, and Swainson's Hawks; Golden Eagle; Common Nighthawk; Black-chinned and Broad-tailed Hummingbirds; Cordilleran Flycatcher; Say's Phoebe; Western Kingbird; Plumbeous and Warbling Vireos; Western Scrub-Jay; Black-billed Magpie; Common Raven; Violet-green Swallow; Black-capped Chickadee; Bushtit; Rock, Canyon, and House Wrens; Mountain Bluebird; Nashville (fall), Yellow, Yellow-rumped, and Townsend's (fall) Warblers; Common Yellowthroat; Wilson's Warbler; Western Tanager; Chipping, Brewer's, Lark, and Black-throated Sparrows; Black-headed Grosbeak; Brewer's Blackbird; Bullock's and Scott's Orioles; Cassin's Finch

Best times to bird: Early mornings May through June and September through October

The birding: This small Bureau of Land Management campground with maturing riparian-associated trees lies downstream of a narrow but dense riparian corridor along Tom's Creek. Birding in the surrounding desert shrub community can also produce some interesting species, particularly sparrows.

Birding is often best in the campground. There are some scattered cottonwoods there and the vegetation along Tom's Creek forms the end of the short riparian zone. Spotted Towhees, orioles, and Western Kingbirds are probably the most visible species in this area. Look in the surrounding shrub community for Burrowing Owls. A telltale sign would be freshly excavated burrows and, best of all, an owl perched on the burrow or in the top of a nearby saltbush.

If you cross the road at the entrance to the campground and continue west, a track follows along the south side of Tom's Creek. This is an easy walk on a gentle grade with views of the riparian corridor and the surrounding shrub community. Birding for sparrows is often at its best just as you enter this trail and along the main access road. Continue to the end of this trail, about a mile up the stream, where a tributary enters Tom's from the south. Tom's Creek itself becomes too narrow above this point to follow comfortably.

To explore the nearby higher-elevation habitats, head south on Deep Creek Mountains Road and then west into the Granite Creek drainage. The approach road to Granite Creek climbs gradually through an expanse of desert shrub before reaching the mouth of Granite Creek Canyon. The riparian zone exits the canyon and follows the grade down the sloping flank of the mountain. It's clearly visible even from the Deep Creek Mountains Road. In the riparian corridor, the dominant species is the cottonwood, which forms a tall canopy over the rushing creek.

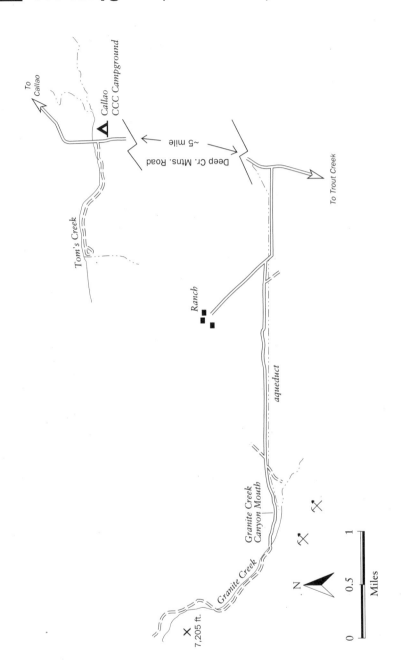

To Callao

Callao
CCC Campground

Tom's Creek

Deep Cr. Mtns. Road

~5 mile

To Trout Creek

Ranch

aqueduct

Granite Creek
Canyon Mouth

Granite Creek

7,205 ft.

N

Miles

0   0.5   1

Once the road enters the canyon, you can stop at any of the available pullouts and informal campsites and walk the short distance down to the cottonwoods. Follow the stream either up or down, depending on where you've parked. In spring it can be difficult to hear birds singing over the creek's effusive babble. At this time of year, you may want to try walking a short distance away from the stream banks—say 50 yards or so. There is no trail in the area; you can either walk the road or blaze your own trail through the sagebrush.

As the elevation increases, the canyon becomes narrower and the surrounding sagebrush gives way to a pinyon-juniper forest. If you're in a passenger car, you'll have to find a place to park before the road crosses the stream—this ford requires a high-clearance vehicle and, in spring runoff, probably four-wheel drive. The creek is easy to cross by foot, even in spring—just look for a convenient spot upstream from the road crossing.

Warbling Vireos seem to be particularly numerous in the cottonwood canopy. Listen for their song and then look for the birds as they forage at the ends of branches. Lazuli Buntings sing in the brush along the creek with various warbler species.

As with Tom's Creek, this area may be most interesting, at least for warblers, during fall migration.

Directions: From Callao, drive southwest toward Trout Creek on the Deep Creek Mountains Road. After about 4 miles, the road turns sharply south and crosses Tom's Creek, and a large Bureau of Land Management sign indicates the Callao CCC Camp. Park in the campground or in the pullout on the opposite side of the road.

To get to Granite Creek from the CCC Campground, continue south on the Deep Creek Mountain Road, again heading toward Trout Creek. The right turn onto the Granite Creek approach road is marked with a BLM sign, and it comes about 6 miles after leaving the campground. You'll encounter one more fork in this road, which is well signed; take the left fork toward the canyon mouth, clearly visible from this intersection.

General information: It's possible to continue hiking up Granite Canyon over the ridge and into the basin on the west side. This would be quite a trek and certainly beyond the expectations of your average birding trip. But the higher you go the wetter the habitat, and you'll encounter more montane species such as Clark's Nutcrackers and Blue and Ruffed Grouse.

ADDITIONAL INFORMATION

Map grid: 2F
Elevation: 4,800 to 7,200 feet.
Hazards: Remote location.
Nearest food, gas, and lodging: Wendover.
Camping: Callao CCC Campground.
For more information: Bureau of Land Management, Fillmore Field Office.

27 Fish Springs National Wildlife Refuge

Habitats: Lowland riparian, lowland desert shrub
Specialty birds: Snowy Plover, Long-billed Curlew, Willow Flycatcher
Other key birds: Pied-billed, Eared, and Western Grebes; Great and Snowy Egrets; Black-crowned Night-Heron; White-faced Ibis; Tundra (fall and winter) and (winter) Trumpeter Swans; Green-winged Teal; Northern Pintail; Cinnamon Teal; Northern Shoveler; Gadwall; American Wigeon (fall and winter); Redhead; Ring-necked Duck (fall and winter); Lesser Scaup (fall and winter); Ruddy Duck; Northern Harrier; Ring-necked Pheasant; Virginia Rail; Sora; Greater Yellowlegs (spring); Willet; Spotted Sandpiper; Wilson's Phalarope; Ring-billed Gull; Caspian and Forster's Terns; Tree (spring) and Northern Rough-winged (spring) Swallows; Common Raven; Marsh Wren; Yellow and Yellow-rumped Warblers; Lark, Black-throated, Savannah, Song, and White-crowned (spring) Sparrows; Brewer's Blackbird
Best times to bird: Spring and fall migration are best; during summer, bird activity peaks in the early morning.

The birding: Over 250 species of birds have been recorded here. Although a number of species, mostly waterfowl and shorebirds, are residents, diversity is greatest during spring and fall migration, which peaks about mid-April and again in late September. The weather at those times is far more hospitable than in summer months, which can be painfully hot.

The refuge encompasses just under 18,000 acres. Lying at the southern end of the Great Salt Lake Desert and bounded by rugged and virtually barren mountains, the refuge appears as a welcome oasis for birds and birders alike. Start your tour at the information kiosk by the refuge headquarters, where you should pick up an auto tour route map and a current bird list. Proceed to the start of the tour route, but detour slightly into the picnic area. This area supports a few mature cottonwood trees, and you should take a few minutes to scan for flycatchers, warblers, tanagers, and any other songbird that might be foraging in the branches. This early section of the drive—up to and around the picnic area—passes through desert shrubs. Keep an eye open for Sage Thrashers and various species of sparrows.

From the picnic area, proceed to the nearby start of the auto tour route and begin the drive. The road follows a dike network, exposing you to both open waters where waterfowl forage and loaf, as well as to marsh expanses where you may see shorebirds, Marsh Wrens, and the more common marsh species such as Red-winged and Yellow-headed Blackbirds. Take your time, scanning each side of the road.

The best spot for passerines is in the trees surrounding refuge headquarters. However, these are the private residences and facilities for the refuge, so be sure to ask for permission at refuge headquarters before entering this area.

Directions: Fish Springs National Wildlife Refuge is 104 miles southwest of Tooele and 78 miles northwest of Delta. From Tooele, head south on UT 36 for about 25 miles until you reach the Pony Express route. This intersection is signed and a

27 Fish Springs National Wildlife Refuge

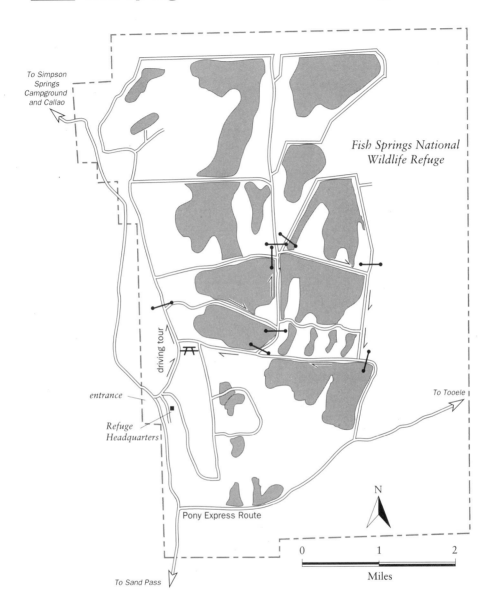

historical marker stands on the right side of the road. Turn right on the Pony Express route (a gravel road) and follow it to the refuge, about 79 miles away.

For an alternative route, about 9 miles northeast of Delta on US 6, turn west onto UT 174. Follow this route for 58 miles, at which point you'll reach an intersection with the Pony Express route. Turn left, and proceed the remaining 20 miles to the refuge headquarters.

An information kiosk at refuge headquarters provides a current bird list and driving map for the auto tour route.

General information: All of the refuge except the picnic area and the driving route are closed to protect breeding populations between May 15 and about September 1. Some species, particularly Long-billed Curlew, prefer the north end of the refuge, so spring birding may be most rewarding just prior to the May 15 closure.

One of the fun things about birding here is that you can never really predict what you'll find, and oddities do show up. Although I have listed the most common species associated with this site, it's also possible to find species like the Bald Eagle, Rough-legged Hawk, Short-eared Owl, Western Wood-Pewee, Eastern Kingbird, Western and Mountain Bluebirds, Sage Thrasher, and Brown Thrasher if you visit during the appropriate season. And the list gets stranger. For example, in the summer of 1997, researchers mist-netting at refuge headquarters caught a Phainopepla—a Mojave and Sonoran desert species well out of its range.

This is a remote, rugged, and beautiful part of the state; travel here warrants preparation. The Pony Express route is usually in poor condition and best taken at a slow pace. The route from Delta, though circuitous if you're traveling from the north, is over gravel roads that seem to be in better condition. Bring plenty of water (there is potable water at the refuge), at least one spare tire, and adequate gas for the round trip. Both roads are suitable for passenger cars when they're dry, but inquire locally about road conditions.

ADDITIONAL INFORMATION

Map grid: 2F
Elevation: 4,325 feet.
Hazards: Remote location, biting insects.
Nearest food, gas, and lodging: Delta.
Camping: Simpson Springs Campground (BLM).
For more information: U.S. Fish and Wildlife Service, Fish Springs NWR.

28 Clear Lake Wildlife Management Area

Habitats: Lowland riparian, lowland desert shrub, upland desert shrub
Other key birds: Pied-billed and Eared Grebes; Snowy Egret; White-faced Ibis; Snow Goose; Cinnamon Teal; Northern Shoveler; Redhead; Ruddy Duck; Northern Harrier; Virginia Rail; Sora; Black-necked Stilt; American Avocet; Greater and Lesser Yellowlegs; Forster's Tern; Marsh Wren; White-crowned Sparrow; Brewer's Blackbird
Best times to bird: February through March for Snow Goose; for other species spring and fall migration are best, mid-March through April and September through mid-October

A canal and pond at Clear Lake Wildlife Management Area.

The birding: The great attraction at Clear Lake is the annual spring migration of Snow Geese. Each year this phenomenon takes place during a narrow window of time, usually lasting about three weeks, between the end of February and the beginning of March. This particular migrating flock numbers about 20,000 geese, and they all land at some point in the relatively small confines of the Clear Lake Wildlife Management Area. During the day the flock splits its time between Clear Lake and nearby Gunnison Reservoir, about 10 miles to the north in the town of Delta. In spite of the often inhospitable weather, this is a hot time at the refuge. Numerous birders make the pilgrimage and the refuge is well prepared to handle birds and birders alike.

The remainder of the year the refuge assumes a quieter but vital roll as a stop-over point for other less numerous spring and fall migrants as well as hosting breeding populations of waterfowl, shorebirds, and passerines. The area is a series of shallow ponds surrounded by a marsh complex and a few scattered cotton-woods, all surrounded by a vast expanse of desert shrubs and, farther away still, sparse stands of junipers.

The area also plays host to duck hunters, and access is usually limited to walk-ins except during hunting season. The main access road cuts across the center of the marshes and ponds on a causeway. This provides for good viewing, and it's a good place to get an introduction to Clear Lake. As you drive across this causeway, stop frequently to scan the ponds and to listen for calling birds. The pond to the north is shallow and seems to be preferred by shorebirds, while the pond to the

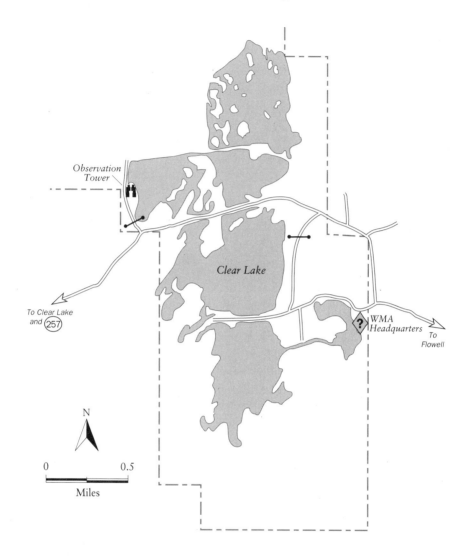

south holds only waterfowl. If you visit during low water, you may find shorebirds on both sides of the road.

On the west side of this causeway before you cross the pond is a gated road with a turnstile for walk-in access. If you head in here, a quarter-mile hike will lead you to the viewing tower visible from the parking area. This tower provides a view of several adjacent ponds. Binoculars are adequate but if you have a spotting scope this is the place to use it.

At the southeast corner of the refuge another minor road enters the wetland. This road is gated. About a quarter of a mile beyond the gate, the road ends at a boat launch and two adjacent ponds, but you can continue walking from here. A path leads across another gravel causeway before ending on the west side of these lower ponds. This is a pleasant walk with more good birding to the north and south of this road and trail.

Directions: From Delta, drive about 10 miles south on UT 257 until you reach Clear Lake and a sign indicating the left turn to the refuge; from here it's another 6 miles on a graded dirt road.

The approach from Fillmore is a little more confusing. Exit from I-15 into the town of Fillmore, and proceed to 500 North Street—a small sign will point toward the town of Flowell. Take this road west until you reach a T intersection with 4600 West, about 6.3 miles from Fillmore. Turn north (right), drive 1.1 miles to the next T intersection, this one with 1200 North. Turn left, and stick to this road, which soon turns to gravel and bears northwest to the wildlife management area 13 miles away.

Gunnison Reservoir in Delta is located near the intersection of 500 North and 2000 West Streets.

General information: Clear Lake is one of many small, isolated, desert oases that plays a vital role in the migration of dozens of species. These little oases attract and concentrate whatever species are passing through, which makes for great birding. This area is relatively isolated and visitors should be prepared. The road through the WMA receives a surprising amount of traffic, but if you forget water, the wait for help will be a long one.

ADDITIONAL INFORMATION

Map grid: 3G
Elevation: 4,600 feet.
Hazards: Remoteness, lack of water, extreme temperatures.
Nearest food, gas, and lodging: Delta or Fillmore.
Camping: Wagons West RV Park, Fillmore.
For more information: Utah Division of Wildlife Resources.

29 Minersville State Park

Habitats: Lowland riparian, upland desert shrub

Specialty birds: American White Pelican (spring and fall); Bald Eagle (winter); Peregrine and Prairie Falcons; Gray Flycatcher; Northern Shrike (winter); Pinyon Jay; American Pipit (winter); Spotted Towhee; Lazuli Bunting

Other key birds: Common Loon (April to May); Pied-billed (April to May), Eared (April to May), Western, and Clark's Grebes; Snowy and Cattle Egrets; Double-crested Cormorant; Black-crowned Night-Heron; White-faced Ibis; Turkey Vulture; Snow Goose (February to March); Gadwall; Northern Pintail; American Wigeon (April to May); Northern Shoveler; Green-winged (winter) and Cinnamon Teals; Redhead; Ring-necked Duck (winter); Lesser Scaup (fall to spring); Common Goldeneye (spring and fall); Bufflehead (spring and fall); Ruddy Duck; Common (spring and fall) and Red-breasted (fall to spring) Mergansers; Osprey (spring); Northern Harrier; Sharp-shinned, Cooper's, and Swainson's Hawks; Golden Eagle; California, Ring-billed (winter), and Franklin's Gulls; Forster's and Common (fall and spring) Terns; Wild Turkey; Willet (fall); Spotted and Western (fall) Sandpipers; Black-chinned Hummingbird; Belted Kingfisher; Downy and Hairy Woodpeckers; Western Kingbird; Say's Phoebe; Loggerhead Shrike; Tree, Violet-green, Northern Rough-winged, Bank, Cliff, and Barn Swallows; Black-billed Magpie; Mountain Chickadee (winter); White-breasted (winter) and Red-breasted (winter) Nuthatches; Rock and Bewick's Wrens; Hermit Thrush; Mountain Bluebird (winter); Cedar Waxwing (winter); Virginia's, Yellow, and Yellow-rumped Warblers; Great-tailed Grackle; Bullock's Oriole; American Tree (winter), Chipping, Brewer's, Vesper, Lark, Black-throated, Savannah, Fox, Song, White-crowned, and Harris's (winter) Sparrows; Cassin's Finch; Lesser and American Goldfinches; Evening Grosbeak

Best times to bird: Spring and fall migration, April through May and September through October

The birding: In many places around the perimeter of Minersville State Park the sagebrush comes right down to the water's edge. Couple this with a water level that fluctuates according to available runoff and the demands of farmers and towns far away, and you can begin to appreciate why there are no marshes, and therefore few or no wading birds, around this lake. However, the reservoir is an important stopover for migrating waterfowl and passerines, and at the right time of year you can encounter some interesting species in this arid setting.

The greatest habitat diversity, and therefore the most bird diversity, occurs in the area of the Minersville State Park campground and headquarters along the southeast corner of the lake, just a little above the dam. Head to the boat launching area, where you can scan most of the lower region of the lake. Look for Common Loons scattered across the lake, diving frequently to search for fish, as well as Western Grebes and Double-crested Cormorants. Other waterfowl may be sticking

29 Minersville State Park

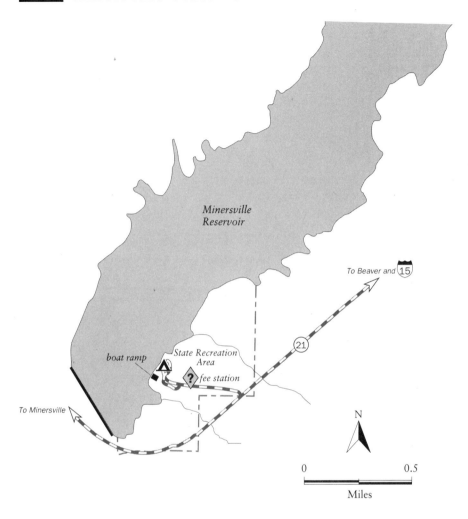

closer to shore, but sometimes rafts of grebes bob on waves far from shore. If you're both lucky and intrepid, you might encounter a Surf Scoter or White-winged Scoter in late October and early November. If the water is high enough, a small arm of the lake juts into the shoreline just south of the boat dock and adjacent to one of the overflow campgrounds. This is a good area for Forster's Terns, particularly if a steady wind is whipping up a chop on the rest of the lake.

To the north of the campground lies a copse of cottonwood trees. Follow the dirt road that departs north from the corner of the boat ramp/campground area. This track passes through a corner of the sagebrush habitat, where you're likely to encounter Lark Sparrows, and cuts across the top of the cottonwood grove before continuing north. As the road reaches the cottonwoods, leave the track and make your way down toward the water, keeping an eye on the cottonwoods for war-blers or other passerines. The cottonwood grove is also a rookery for Great Blue Herons and, sometimes, Black-crowned Night-Herons. Be sure to avoid disturb-ing these species during spring and early summer.

Directions: From I-15 (Exit 112) in Beaver, head west on UT 21. (The route is well signed.) Minersville Reservoir and Minersville State Park are about 12 miles from I-15.

General information: Although the area lacks habitat diversity, there is a surpris-ing amount of bird diversity. The state park caretakers, who had arrived only seven months before my visit, already had a list of 114 species. A large component of this diversity appears to be migrating birds, and it seems unlikely that you'll encounter large numbers of any single species. But if you're already passing through on I-15 you can come up with some interesting species on a quick side trip. If you're planning on staying the night, the state park facilities are fairly new and comfortable, and the best birding will be right outside your tent or camper.

Minersville Reservoir is designed primarily to meet the needs of anglers and does accommodate motorboats.

ADDITIONAL INFORMATION

Map grid: 3I
Elevation: 5,493 feet.
Hazards: Exposed area—can be cold and windy.
Nearest food, gas, and lodging: Beaver.
Camping: Minersville Reservoir State Park.
For more information: Utah Division of Parks and Recreation.

30 Newcastle Reservoir and Pinto Creek

Habitats: Lowland riparian, pinyon-juniper, upland desert shrub
Specialty birds: Pinyon Jay; Green-tailed and Spotted Towhees
Other key birds: Common Loon; Eared Grebe; Black-chinned and Broad-tailed Hummingbirds; Black Phoebe; Bank Swallow; Western Scrub-Jay; Rock Wren; Yellow-rumped and Black-throated Gray Warblers; Yellow-breasted Chat; Lark Sparrow; Western Meadowlark; Brewer's Blackbird; Great-tailed Grackle; Bullock's Oriole
Best times to bird: Spring and fall migration for waterfowl; May through June for breeding birds

The birding: This site covers a mid-elevation reservoir in southern Utah and its major tributary. Newcastle Reservoir has little habitat other than open water to attract waterfowl, but the scarcity of this resource in the Desert Southwest means

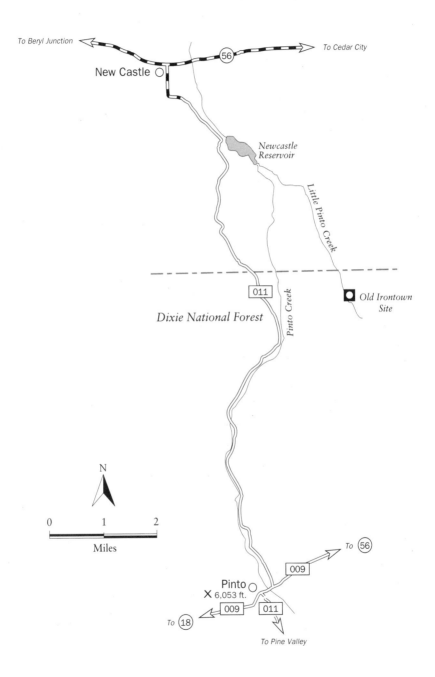

To Beryl Junction

To Cedar City

56

New Castle

Newcastle Reservoir

Little Pinto Creek

011

Dixie National Forest

Pinto Creek

Old Irontown Site

N

0   1   2

Miles

To 56

Pinto
X 6,053 ft.

009

To 18   009   011

To Pine Valley

that a fair number of ducks, grebes, and loons use the area during migration. The species of waterfowl you'll find here will likely be the same as those found on other reservoirs in the vicinity, like Enterprise Reservoirs and Minersville Reservoir, both a short flight away and on the same migration path.

Like many of those other relatively new reservoirs, there is little or no riparian vegetation surrounding Newcastle Reservoir. The lake is open and exposed, with sagebrush or bare rock descending right to the waterline. As you approach from the town of New Castle, the road tops a rise just above the dam face. At this point a single-lane dirt road departs from the main road and ends in an informal parking area overlooking the lake. Because most of the other access points to the lakeshore are on very rough roads, this is a good place to pull off and scan the lake for waterfowl. What you'll see will depend on what species happen to be migrating through at the time of your visit, but Common Loons and Western, Clark's, Pied-billed, and Eared Grebes are among a few of the possibilities. A few other species make their homes in the sagebrush and pinyon-juniper forest surrounding the reservoir, and you may also see Rock Wrens, Canyon Wrens, Blue-gray Gnat-catchers, Western Scrub-Jays, Lark Sparrows, White-crowned Sparrows, and Brewer's Sparrows around the lake's perimeter.

Continuing southward on the Newcastle Reservoir Road, you'll pass through an extensive stand of pinyon-juniper forest. The road starts losing elevation, enters the Dixie National Forest, at which point it becomes FR 011, and shortly thereafter intersects the Pinto Creek Valley and begins following the creek to its origin. Pinto Creek supports an interesting willow-cottonwood riparian zone, again bordered by sagebrush, pinyon-juniper, and Gambel oak. Along the length of the creek a few informal access roads have been forged to the creek's edge by folks looking for a place to camp, and each of these is a good spot to stop and walk to the creek and listen for birds. You're likely to find both Green-tailed and Spotted Towhees, hummingbirds, warblers, and sparrows at any of these stops; Yellow-breasted Chats in particular seem to be common along the creek.

Two other spots along the creek are worth a brief visit. About halfway between the reservoir and the little community of Pinto, the road crosses the creek for the first time. This crossing is beside a small farm and pasture, and the combination at the bridge of the riparian zone, open field, pinyon-juniper, and a grove of oaks above the creek makes for great habitat diversity in a short section of the creek. It's worth spending a few minutes walking this section of road. In addition to the possibility of seeing any of the aforementioned passerines, Black Phoebes have been seen in this stretch, and Black-throated Gray Warblers can be found among the oaks.

Farther upstream the riparian zone gives way to deeply eroded banks along the creek. Watch for the rodent-sized holes in these mud cliff faces which indicate the presence of Bank Swallows. There is at least one colony of these birds a short distance downstream from the town of Pinto.

Directions: In New Castle, proceed south on Main Street for 0.3 mile. Turn left on 200 south, where a small Forest Service sign indicates the direction to the reservoir, 1 mile distant. Continue on this route past Newcastle Reservoir and to the town of Pinto.

General information: Aside from the attraction of birds, this is a picturesque part of the state with an interesting mining history. The nearby ghost town of Old Irontown lies on Little Pinto Creek and is accessible from UT 56 and via FR 012. The town of Pinto also has an interesting pioneer past. It has recently experienced a small revival and there is a lot of new home construction. The stately old cottonwoods in Pinto house woodpeckers, warblers, Bullock's Orioles, and Red-tailed Hawks. It's a pleasant place to get out and stretch your legs after the drive up Pinto Creek.

Rather than retracing your steps, it is possible to turn west in Pinto on Pinto Road (FR 009) and continue to Enterprise Reservoirs. You can also continue south on FR 011 and end up in Pine Valley, a great spot for montane bird species. This latter route is on a fair-weather road and should only be attempted after all local roads have thawed and dried out.

ADDITIONAL INFORMATION

Map grid: 2J
Elevation: 6,000 feet.
Hazards: none.
Nearest food, gas, and lodging: New Castle.
Camping: Pine Valley campgrounds, Dixie National Forest.
For more information: Dixie National Forest, Pine Valley Ranger District.

31 Enterprise Reservoirs

Habitats: Lowland riparian, upland desert shrub, pinyon-juniper, spruce-fir

Specialty birds: American White Pelican (spring and fall); Bald Eagle (winter); Peregrine and Prairie Falcons; Flammulated Owl; Gray Flycatcher; Cassin's Kingbird; Northern Shrike (winter); Pinyon Jay; American Pipit (winter); Green-tailed and Spotted Towhees; Lazuli Bunting

Other key birds: Common Loon (April to May); Pied-billed (April to May), Eared (April to May), and Western Grebes; Snowy and Cattle Egrets; Double-crested Cormorant; Black-crowned Night-Heron; White-faced Ibis; Turkey Vulture; Gadwall; Northern Pintail; American Wigeon (April to May); Northern Shoveler; Green-winged (winter) and Cinnamon Teals; Redhead; Ring-necked Duck (winter); Lesser Scaup (fall to spring); Common Goldeneye (spring and fall); Bufflehead (spring and fall); Ruddy Duck; Common (spring and fall) and Red-breasted Mergansers (fall to spring); Osprey (spring); Northern Harrier; Sharp-shinned, Cooper's, and Swainson's Hawks; Golden Eagle; Franklin's, Ring-billed (winter), and California Gulls; Forster's and Common (fall and spring) Terns; Wild Turkey; Willet (fall); Spotted and Western (fall) Sandpipers; Black-chinned Hummingbird; Belted Kingfisher; Downy and Hairy Woodpeckers; Western Kingbird; Say's Phoebe; Loggerhead Shrike; Tree, Violet-green, Northern Rough-winged, Bank, Cliff, and Barn Swallows; Black-billed Magpie; Mountain Chickadee (winter); White-breasted and Red-breasted (winter) Nuthatches; Rock and Bewick's Wrens; Hermit Thrush; Mountain Bluebird; Cedar Waxwing (winter); Virginia's, Yellow, and Yellow-rumped Warblers; Bullock's Oriole; Chipping, Brewer's, Vesper, Lark, Black-throated, Savannah, Song, White-crowned, and Harris's (winter) Sparrows; Cassin's Finch; Lesser and American Goldfinches; Evening Grosbeak

Best times to bird: Spring and fall for migrating waterfowl and passerines; other species are best May through June

The birding: Neither the Lower nor Upper Enterprise Reservoir has any significant riparian zone, so these open bodies of water attract primarily waterfowl during migration. Of the two, Lower Enterprise, which is the first body of water you encounter on the drive up from the town of Enterprise, is likely to have the most birds and the greatest diversity. Both reservoirs are visible from the paved access road, so the best initial approach is to scan each body of water from the road. As you near the reservoirs on FR 006, the road rises sharply to climb the short distance out of the riparian corridor to the top of the dam. There is a good pullout right above the dam, so pull off to the right and scan the lake.

FR 006 continues along the eastern edge of Lower Enterprise, then turns above the lake and climbs a short distance to an overlook of Upper Reservoir. Upper Enterprise is far more exposed, and the more sheltered nature of Lower Enterprise

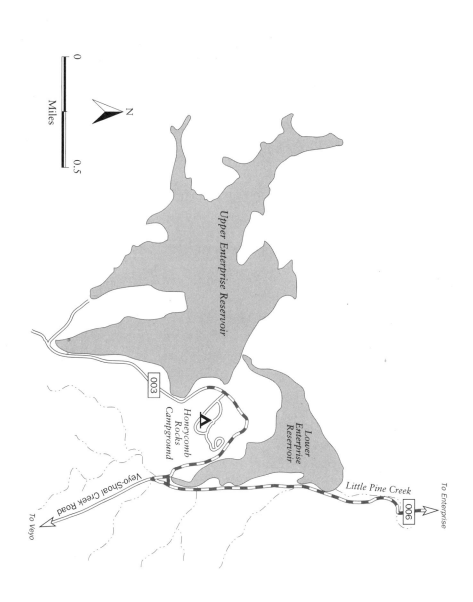

may be one reason it seems to hold more appeal to birds. Nonetheless, from this overlook of the upper reservoir, take a few minutes to scan the lake's surface.

Whether or not there is much waterfowl activity, there are a few other spots around the reservoirs worth checking out. Honeycomb Rocks Campground lies between the two reservoirs. It's one of the more intriguing Forest Service campgrounds I've seen—integrated into ridges of rock outcrops. There are several Cliff Swallow colonies in the campground, and sparrows, Spotted Towhees, and Cassin's Kingbirds all frequent the area.

Surrounding the reservoirs is a landscape of open ponderosa pine forests along with some interspersed junipers. If you choose to stay overnight in this area, the ponderosas would be an excellent place to listen and look for Flammulated Owls.

Finally, the riparian zone below the dam—the area you probably drove through to reach the reservoirs—can be an interesting birding area. There aren't many pullouts, but the few that exist provide a chance to explore this narrow canyon. Warblers and sparrows common to this habitat should be easily found.

Directions: From Enterprise, head west on Main Street. About 6 miles from town the route bears left and follows Little Pine Creek, which drains the reservoirs. This intersection is signed, the road becomes FR 006 at the turn, and Lower Enterprise Reservoir lies 5 miles from the intersection.

General information: Enterprise Reservoirs is a popular fishing destination, so you may have to compete with anglers for the area's resources. However, only Upper Enterprise has a boat dock, so Lower Enterprise is typically quieter, perhaps another reason why the birds prefer Lower Enterprise.

ADDITIONAL INFORMATION

Map grid: 1J
Elevation: 5,700 feet.
Hazards: None.
Nearest food, gas, and lodging: Enterprise.
Camping: Honeycomb Rocks Campground, Dixie National Forest.
For more information: Dixie National Forest, Pine Valley Ranger District.

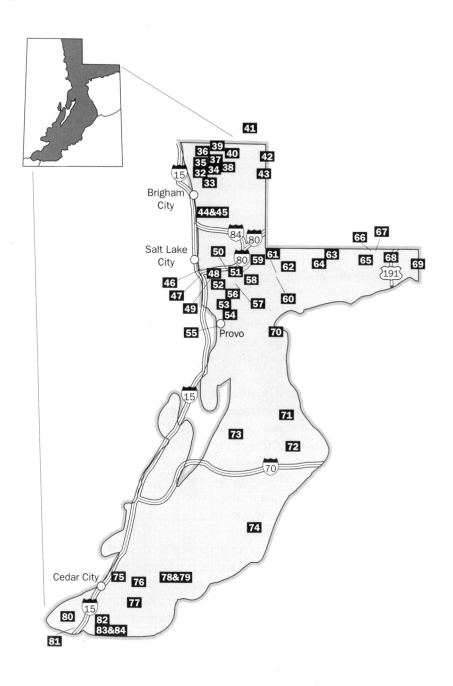

Brigham
City

Salt Lake
City

Provo

Cedar City

32 Deep Creek Trail and Stewart Pass, Wellsville Mountains

Habitats: Spruce-fir, aspen, pinyon-juniper, mountain meadow, desert steppe

Specialty birds: Bald Eagle (fall); Northern Goshawk; Ferruginous Hawk (fall); Peregrine and Prairie Falcons; Blue Grouse; Northern Pygmy-Owl; Hammond's and Dusky Flycatchers; Pinyon Jay (fall); Green-tailed Towhee; Lazuli Bunting

Other key birds: Osprey (fall); Northern Harrier; Sharp-shinned (fall), Cooper's, Broad-winged (fall), Swainson's, Red-tailed, and Rough-legged Hawks; Golden Eagle; American Kestrel; Merlin; Ruffed Grouse; House Wren; Ruby-crowned Kinglet; Mountain Bluebird; Hermit Thrush; Nashville (fall), Yellow, Yellow-rumped, and Townsend's (fall) Warblers; Western Tanager; Evening Grosbeak; Cassin's Finch; Pine Siskin

Best times to bird: May through July for breeding birds; September through mid-October for migrants and raptors. Raptors are best viewed on the wing in early afternoon, from about noon until 4 p.m.

The birding: There is no trail access to the Wellsville Mountains ridge from the west, so visitors need to enter the Cache Valley area to reach one of the two trailheads that are the gates to the Wellsvilles. Both trails offer essentially the same birding, but Deep Creek Trail at the north end of the range is best in September and October because it leads to HawkWatch International's lookout station. Time permitting, volunteers from HawkWatch can be very helpful in locating and identifying raptors.

The Deep Creek Trail departs from the end of a gravel road and begins a gradual climb through a dense maple and aspen forest. Not long after departing the parking area, the trail begins a series of switchbacks and trends southward. From the saddle (elevation 8,120 feet), the HawkWatch lookout is about another half a mile northwest along a well-worn trail.

Although the Wellsville Mountains are only about 5 miles wide and 14 miles long, they are the steepest mountain range in the United States; the average rise on their sloping shoulders is about 40 percent. The hike to the top is strenuous, but the payoff is spectacular. The mountains fall away so abruptly on either side that you feel as if you are sitting on the roof of the world. Views of both Cache Valley to the east and the Salt Lake Valley to the west are unforgettable. Wildflowers in June and July carpet the mountainside, and in late September aspens and canyon maples set the mountains ablaze with color. Perhaps the most memorable experience is watching the migrating hawks riding air currents, often at or below eye level. Keep in mind that you needn't reach the summit to see raptors, but the higher vantage will allow you to observe them on both sides of the range. If you lack either the time or energy to reach the saddle, it's possible to see raptors at almost any level along the mountains' flanks. The birds often fly fairly close to the

32 Deep Creek Trail and Stewart Pass, Wellsville Mountains

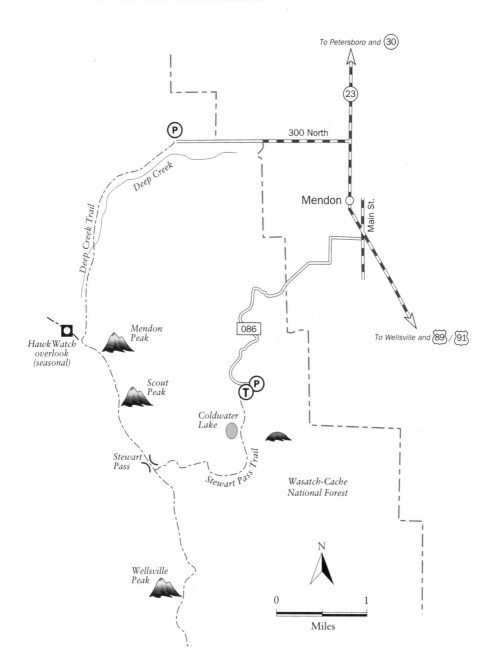

To Petersboro and (30)

(23)

(P)   300 North

Mendon

Main St.

To Wellsville and (89)/(91)

Deep Creek

Deep Creek Trail

Hawk Watch
overlook
(seasonal)

Mendon
Peak

Scout
Peak

086

(T)(P)

Coldwater
Lake

Stewart
Pass

Stewart Pass Trail

Wasatch-Cache
National Forest

Wellsville
Peak

N

0   1
Miles

tops of the trees or open sides of the mountain, so keep an eye toward the sky as you hike the trail.

Most songbirds are scattered throughout the forest that lines the lower portion of the trail. As you approach the saddle, the trees become more scattered and give way to meadow, and the balance of the species listed above may be seen in this area. One particular spot for passerines is worth noting. About three quarters of the way up the trail you'll cross a ravine filled with mountain ash and surrounded by maples. This ravine seems to attract a lot of birds, particularly warblers, and it is worth spending a few minutes scanning the area and listening for calls.

A hike to the top is a serious undertaking, and hikers should bring ample water (at least two quarts per person) and be prepared for a steep ascent and weather that can change rapidly and dramatically, especially in the fall.

The hiking and birding experiences along Stewart Pass Trail are similar to those on the Deep Creek Trail. This hike is also quite steep and there's no potable water along the way. The ascent to Stewart Pass is shorter because you drive to a higher elevation to find the trailhead. On the other hand, the chances are greater for seeing migrating warblers on the Deep Creek Trail, and unless you hike some distance north along the ridge, you won't encounter any of the HawkWatch International folks on the Stewart Pass Trail.

After leaving the parking area, the trail to Stewart Pass climbs gradually through a beautiful forest of maple, aspen, and firs to reach Coldwater Lake. There is no warning that you are approaching the lake—it appears suddenly after a short, steep climb. If your sudden presence doesn't flush them, the small lake sometimes contains a pair of ducks or a raptor perched over the water. There's not as much bird activity at the lake as one would expect, but the surrounding forest is a good area for House Wrens, warblers, and Hermit Thrushes.

After leaving the lake, the trail climbs rapidly through mixed terrain with dry, open meadows, areas of maple, mountain ash, and chokecherry, and conifers on north-facing drainages. Bird activity seems to be spread uniformly along the trail, and the numerous stops required for resting provide ample time for birding.

At Stewart Pass, sitting on the narrow ridge and scanning both sides of the range is often productive. Not only can you see a lot of soaring raptors, but all birds seem to prefer this low point in the range for moving from one side to the other.

The steep and essentially waterless terrain dictates that this trail is best completed as a day hike.

Directions: To reach the Deep Creek Trailhead, drive west on 300 North in the town of Mendon. The road turns to gravel after about 3 miles, and there is parking at the end of the road, at the Forest Service sign marking the beginning of "TH39" (Trailhead 39).

To reach the trail to Stewart Pass, head south on UT 23 in Mendon. At the intersection with Main Street, turn right onto FR 086. The road turns immediately to gravel and begins a steep ascent. Follow this road for about 3 miles to its termination at the Stewart Pass Trailhead.

General information: In the early 1970s, HawkWatch International founder Steve Hoffman began a search for a natural resource treasure that he knew existed only by instinct. Hawk Mountain in Pennsylvania had long been known for its spectacular annual congregation of thousands of migrating raptors. Hoffman reasoned that similar migrations should take place in the western United States, though none had ever been identified. Since those early days HawkWatch International has become a significant conservation organization. Eight raptor migration corridors have been identified in the West, and Hoffman and his staff continue their search for more. One of the corridors Hoffman identified and monitors annually passes over northern Utah's spectacular Wellsville Mountain Wilderness Area.

After 13 seasons of research in the Wellsvilles, HawkWatch International has pretty well defined raptor use of the area. Migrating hawks use rising columns of air to generate lift and minimize energy use. As a consequence, very little raptor activity occurs before noon, and daily migration peaks between 2 to 5 P.M. Hawks also favor warm, sunny days with a southwest breeze; peak migrations often occur ahead of a storm front. Once storms hit, hawks tend to hunker down and wait out the bad weather. HawkWatch has recorded 16 species of raptors in the Wellsvilles. Listed in decreasing order of abundance, these are American Kestrel (approximately 1,000 per year), Sharp-shinned Hawk (approximately 1,000 per year), Red-tailed Hawk (approximately 1,000 per year), Cooper's Hawk (approximately 200 per year), Northern Harrier (approximately 200 per year), Golden Eagle (approximately 200 per year), Peregrine Falcon, Merlin, Prairie Falcon, Broadwinged Hawk, Osprey, Swainson's Hawk, Northern Goshawk, Rough-legged Hawk, Bald Eagle, and Ferruginous Hawk.

The Stewart Pass Trail is also referred to as the Maple Bench Trail, and it offers the most direct route to the top. In dry conditions a patient and careful driver can negotiate the road to the trailhead in any two-wheel-drive vehicle; high clearance is recommended and four-wheel drive is essential in muddy conditions.

The Wellsvilles are capped by the 23,750 acre Wellsville Mountain Wilderness Area, and certain use restrictions apply. No motor vehicles, motorized equipment, hang gliders(!), or bicycles are allowed, and no-trace hiking and minimum impact camping techniques are encouraged. Also prohibited are groups of more than ten for overnight camping; camping within 200 feet of trails, lakes, or other sources of water; camping for three or more days at the same site; shortcutting trails; and disposing of garbage.

A locally available guidebook provides more details on hikes in this area. The book, *Cache Trails* by J. Wood (published by Bridgerland Audubon Society) is available from bookstores and outfitters in downtown Logan.

ADDITIONAL INFORMATION

Map grid: 4B

Elevation: 5,000 to 8,400 feet.

Hazards: Lack of water, steep terrain, unpredictable fall weather.

Nearest food, gas, and lodging: Logan.

Camping: Dispersed, primitive car camping on the Stewart Pass approach. Other developed Forest Service campgrounds are in Logan Canyon on US 89, a 15 to 20 mile drive. ·

For more information: Wasatch-Cache National Forest, Logan Ranger District.

33 Hyrum State Park

Habitats: Lowland riparian, upland desert shrub

Specialty birds: Clark's Grebe, American White Pelican, Bald Eagle (winter), Sandhill Crane

Other key birds: Common Loon (spring); Western Grebe; White-faced Ibis; Oldsquaw; Surf (winter) and White-winged (winter) Scoters; Common and Red-breasted Mergansers (winter to April); Osprey; Franklin's Gull; Caspian and Forster's Terns; Bank Swallow; Black-billed Magpie; Spotted Towhee (winter); Western Meadowlark; Yellow Warbler

Best times to bird: Throughout daylight hours during winter and during spring and fall migration, or for any of the waterfowl viewing opportunities. Sunrise to noon for nesting songbirds, late April through June

The Bear River Range provides a snowy backdrop to Hyrum Reservoir.

33 Hyrum State Park

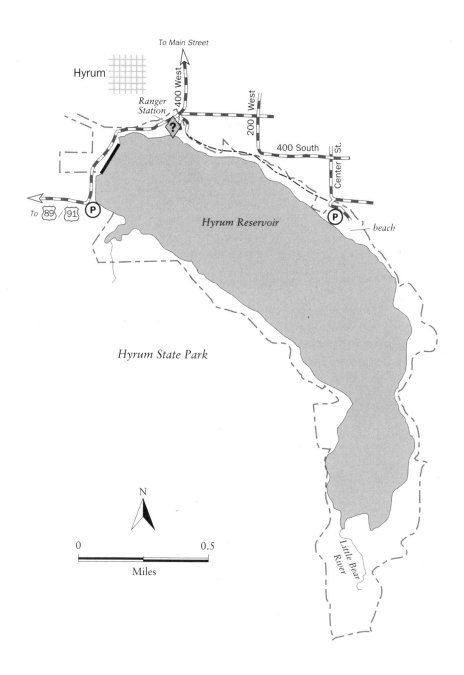

Hyrum

To Main Street

400 West

200 West

Ranger Station

To 89 / 91 P

400 South

Center St.

Hyrum Reservoir

beach

P

Hyrum State Park

N

0   0.5
Miles

Little Bear River

The birding: The focus of this birding site is 405-acre Hyrum Reservoir. This body of water and its surrounding habitat host a wide array of species adapted to the riparian and upland desert shrub communities. In addition to the species you'd expect to find in these habitats, Hyrum Lake tends to attract more than its share of unusual migrants. Both species of scoter mentioned in the list above are fairly uncommon but can be found in winter or during migration. Another recent surprise included a Pacific Loon during fall migration.

Probably the best all-around destination for bird watching on the reservoir is a developed beach area to the east of the campground and ranger station. Before entering this day use area, stop at the pullout and scan the water for rafts of gulls, waterfowl, or (in winter) Bald Eagles perched in lakeshore trees. Once at the beach parking area, find the signed foot trail that begins behind the bathroom. This rough but easily followed trail leads back toward the park headquarters, straddling the mid-level elevation along the bench and exposing you to views of both the reservoir and cottonwood canopy along shore. You'll likely encounter Ring-Necked Pheasants on this walk as well. During spring and fall migration, loons, mergansers, and other waterfowl can be easily viewed along this trail. During the breeding season, you'll have the added benefit of a variety of passerines foraging along this riparian corridor.

Another spot worth a quick inspection is the dam area. The pullout at the southwest corner of the reservoir (on the dam face) provides a good vantage point to scan for waterfowl, although a spotting scope would be a great asset.

For those equipped with a canoe, a great opportunity occurs during a few short weeks in early spring. When the water is up in the Little Bear River, which feeds the reservoir, it is possible to canoe south from the beach to the head of the reservoir and then a short distance up the flooded marshes of the river. This short trip not only provides great viewing of passerines and waterfowl, but you may also encounter Western Grebes, Great Blue Herons, White-faced Ibis, and Sandhill Cranes in the quieter backwaters of the Little Bear.

Great birding opportunities may be available in the wonderful mixed riparian/cottonwood-maple grassland area below the dam, but as of this writing, the area is not open to the public. The park is working to incorporate this area into its publicly accessible lands, and you should check at the office to see if these plans have come to fruition. This area should substantially increase the diversity of species available to birders, especially warblers, finches, and sparrows.

Directions: Turn east off US 89/91 onto UT 101 (also signed as Wellsville's Main Street). This turn is clearly signed on US 89/91 with a brown state park sign, and there is also a traffic light at this intersection. Follow the signs 3.3 miles to Hyrum State Park, eventually turning right on 400 West in Hyrum. This road forks at the entrance gate to the park, with the right fork going 0.5 mile to the dam, and the left fork leading you 1 mile to the developed beach.

General information: The focus of human activities on Hyrum Reservoir is boating, water-skiing, jet skiing, and fishing. Birders seeking solitude might consider early morning jaunts during summer or avoiding the area altogether during the busier summer months when bird activity is low anyway.

The park does have well-developed, modern camping facilities available for a fee of about $10. And as with all state parks, an entrance fee is required: $4 to access the boat ramp or $1 to use the developed beach.

ADDITIONAL INFORMATION

Map grid: 4B
Elevation: 4,670 feet.
Hazards: Motorboats and water-skiers.
Nearest food, gas, and lodging: Hyrum.
Camping: Hyrum State Park.
For more information: Utah Division of Parks and Recreation.

34 20-20 Ponds

Habitat: Lowland riparian
Key birds: Trumpeter and Mute Swans; Green-winged Teal; Northern Pintail; Northern Shoveler; Gadwall; American Wigeon; Canvasback; Ring-necked Duck; Common and Barrow's Goldeneyes; Bufflehead; Northern Harrier; Marsh Wren
Best times to bird: Anytime during daylight hours in winter, mid-November through February. Mornings are probably best on sunny days since the pond is backlit in the afternoon.

The birding: These small ponds are a great place to look for waterfowl in cold winter months, particularly during the deepest cold snaps when it is often the only open water around. At these times the ponds can be chock-full of ducks grateful to be paddling around. As a waterfowl magnet, these ponds also tend to attract any of the more unusual species that may be overwintering in the area or taking their time heading south. The ponds also attract some semidomestic hybrid waterfowl and Mute Swans (a European exotic). The swans might be the pets of nearby residents. At any rate, the presence of hybrids and exotics makes for difficult identification.

The ponds are entirely surrounded by private land, so birding from the roadside is the only option. Nonetheless, the road does provide a good vantage point, and there is an adequate shoulder for parking. The southeast corner of the ponds approach the road close enough that you can identify birds without the aid of binoculars, but you may find this vantage to be too close, and the birds may flush or swim to the other end of the ponds. Try birding from a spot about 50 yards farther north to avoid spooking the birds. Be adequately dressed for the weather

131

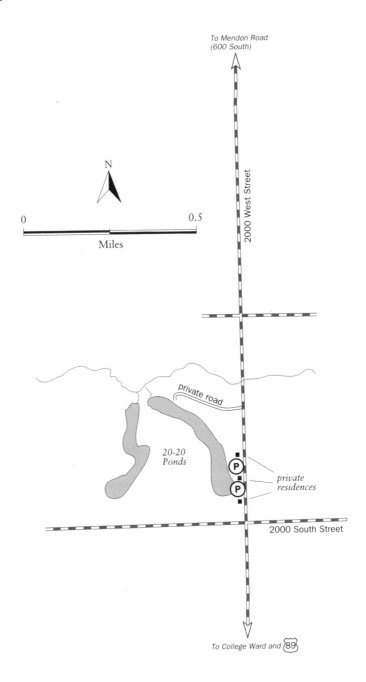

so you can set up a spotting scope and spend an half hour or so scanning the entire length of the ponds as the waterfowl mill about.

The habitat surrounding the ponds is primarily fallow fields, although there are a few slivers of marsh lining parts of the shoreline. It's often worth taking a few minutes to scan these areas for sparrows, wrens, or blackbirds.

Directions: From Main Street in Logan, head west on 200 North and proceed to 1000 West, and turn left (south). Continue to 600 South (Mendon Road), and turn right (west). In about 1.5 miles you'll cross the Logan River, turn left immediately onto 2200 West Street, and drive 1.8 miles to the ponds, which will be on the right (west) side of the road.

General information: These ponds actually have no official name appearing on any map. It has been named "20-20 Ponds" by local birders, because under Utah's grid system of naming streets, the ponds lie at the intersection of 2000 South and 2000 West streets.

ADDITIONAL INFORMATION

Map grid: 4B
Elevation: 4,440 feet.
Hazards: Cold temperatures.
Nearest food, gas, and lodging: Logan.
Camping: Logan Canyon campgrounds, Wasatch-Cache National Forest.
For more information: Utah Travel Council.

35 Cutler Marsh

Habitat: Lowland riparian
Specialty birds: Clark's Grebe; American White Pelican; Sandhill Crane; Willow Flycatcher
Other key birds: Western Grebe; American Bittern; Snowy Egret; Black-crowned Night-Heron; White-faced Ibis; Wood Duck; Green-winged and Cinnamon Teals; Northern Shoveler; Gadwall; Redhead; Northern Harrier; Swainson's Hawk; Virginia Rail; Sora; Black-necked Stilt; American Avocet; Willet; Franklin's Gull; Cliff and Barn Swallows; Marsh Wren; Black-headed Grosbeak
Best times to bird: Year-round, depending on desired species

The birding: Birding for waterfowl, shorebirds, birds of prey, and passerines is often highly rewarding in this area. In addition to supporting a diverse community of breeding birds, the area also attracts migrants; in the winter, many species of birds still forage in the area or seek refuge in the senescent cattails and rushes.

The best access to this area requires a canoe or other shallow-draft boat, but viewing from the road is also popular and often successful. If you do choose the roadside viewing option, be forewarned that Valley View Highway can be busy,

A canoe provides the best means of exploring Cutler Marsh and enjoying a view of the Wellsville Mountains.

and you'll want to avoid causing traffic congestion or endangering yourself and others.

If you're without a boat, the best approach may be to park at the boat ramp or the wide road shoulder west of the bridge crossing the marsh, and from either of these vantages, scan the marsh for birds. The road here perches high above the marsh, so the view is good in all directions. There isn't much along the bank near the boat ramp, but a good marsh lies directly across the river. The surrounding farms and pastureland often hold shorebirds, ducks, Sandhill Cranes, and White-faced Ibis.

If you're equipped with a boat, the marshes to the north and south of the highway offer slightly different opportunities, but the marsh complex is confusing and it's easy to get disoriented if you explore away from the areas described below, especially during periods of low water, when the direction of flow can be indiscernible. If you pay careful attention to your route as you paddle and use the bridge bisecting the area as a landmark, you should have no trouble navigating.

On the south side of the highway, follow the western edge of the marsh for a mile or two toward the south, where you'll see Northern Harriers, Marsh Wrens, blackbirds, and possibly hear rails or Soras. In open water, look for numerous species of ducks as well as American White Pelicans. A variety of birds also forage in visible farm pastures, including Sandhill Cranes, White-faced Ibis, Willets, and any other shorebirds that may be in the area.

The north side of the highway is predominantly marshes and meandering river. If you again follow the western edge of the waterway, there is a small arm of the Cutler Reservoir where pasture meets water, and this area often supports a large mixed-species flock of waterfowl. Look for American White Pelicans here as well.

Whether you head north, south or choose to do both, the current is not swift and the return route is via the same course you paddled in, unless your sense of direction and adventure lead you elsewhere.

Directions: From Main Street in Logan, proceed west out of town on 200 North. This route becomes Valley View Highway, and after crossing several marshes and bends in the Logan River, you'll cross one final bridge before beginning the climb out of Cache Valley. About 200 yards after this bridge crossing, you'll see the entrance to the Utah Division of Wildlife Resources boat ramp on the south side of the road—total distance from Main Street is about 5.5 miles.

General information: Local birders in Cache County will be quick to point out that the Little Bear and Logan rivers, both of which feed Cutler Reservoir to create an intricate marsh complex, attract almost all of the same species as the more famous Bear River Migratory Bird Refuge to the west, but in a more visually appealing setting. With the spectacular Wellsville Mountains towering as a backdrop to this area, it would be hard to dispute that point. You certainly won't, however, encounter the huge flocks that settle onto the Bear River Migratory Bird Refuge.

Birding from the road and the boat launch area is popular for those with limited time, and this approach can be quite rewarding. There is little doubt, though, that canoeing the area will open up substantially more opportunities. Canoes can be rented for a reasonable fee in Logan—inquire at local outfitters for more information.

If you discover that DWR has locked the gate at the boat ramp, you can retrace your route back to the bridge crossing and launch a canoe from the roadside. There is ample room for pulling off the road, and the northwest corner of the bridge seems to be the easiest place to put in.

ADDITIONAL INFORMATION

Map grid: 4B
Elevation: 4,400 feet.
Hazards: None.
Nearest food, gas, and lodging: Logan.
Camping: Western Park Campground, Logan.
For more information: Utah Division of Wildlife Resources.

Benson Bridge and Bear River Oxbow

Habitat: Lowland riparian

Specialty birds: Clark's Grebe; American White Pelican; Sandhill Crane; Spotted Towhee (winter)

Other key birds: Western Grebe; Black-crowned Night-Heron; White-faced Ibis; Trumpeter Swan (spring); Greater White-fronted (spring), Snow (April), and Ross's (April) Geese; American and Eurasian (winter) Wigeons; Cinnamon Teal; Redhead; Ruddy Duck; American Coot; Virginia Rail; Sora; Black-bellied Plover (spring); Black-necked Stilt; Greater (spring) and Lesser (spring) Yellowlegs; Red-necked Phalarope (spring); Franklin's and California Gulls; Forster's Tern; Great Horned and Long-eared Owls; Black-chinned Hummingbird; Western Kingbird; Cliff and Barn Swallows; Mountain Chickadee (winter); Bushtit; Marsh and Bewick's Wrens; Yellow-throated Warbler; Common Yellowthroat; Song Sparrow

Best times to bird: Mid-morning and early evenings in winter for owls and unusual winter visitants at Benson Bridge. Spring through fall, although spring is probably best, at the Oxbow. At both sites, mornings until about noon are good, because the afternoon sun back-lights the birds and makes for uninteresting viewing and challenging identification.

In years of plentiful snow, the Oxbow area floods extensively, but usually dries by early summer.

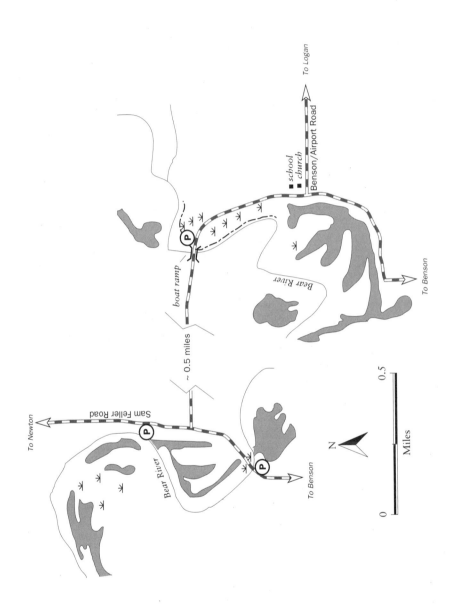

The birding: The Utah Division of Wildlife Resources recently improved the parking at Benson Bridge with boaters and hunters in mind. You'll see a parking area with pit toilet facilities and a boat ramp off the northwest corner of the bridge—park here. The informal trail starts on the southeast side of the bridge, so hike back over the paved road and drop down the embankment; you'll be able to see the track from the road. Follow this path south through the cottonwood stand, birding the marsh to the east, the brush and cottonwoods you're passing through, and the river corridor to the west. The trail is short, only a few hundred yards, so take it slow and let bird activity reveal itself.

In summer months the marsh will be full of Red-winged and Yellow-headed Blackbirds, and along with Franklin's Gulls or the occasional Forster's Tern, these species will be easy to spot. The challenge is to find the more furtive Virginia Rail or a Sora, which you may be lucky enough to see (but will more likely hear) patrolling the interface between marsh and woods. Many of the cottonwoods have large, messy platform nests made of tangled twigs; these were probably made by Black-billed Magpies which you'll likely see. These nests are sometimes taken over by owls, either as active nests or as convenient roosts, and it's worth scanning each nest carefully to see if it's occupied by an owl.

A short distance down the road from Benson Bridge you'll find an excellent spot for scanning a large oxbow on the Bear River. This sweeping bend is protected from winds and offers birds an expanse of flooded pasture during spring runoff. The great attractions at this site are waterfowl and shorebirds, some of which are only brief visitors during spring migration (April to May). Although the roadside pullout provides a commanding view, a spotting scope would be extremely useful. There is not a lot of cover so you should get a thorough accounting of the birds in the area.

Outside of the spring migration, large flocks of American White Pelicans gather in this area. Sandhill Cranes and White-faced Ibis are good bets, and if you linger around sunset, you should see numerous flocks of the latter species flying south toward evening roosts.

Directions: Follow US 91 (Main Street) north out of Logan. Measuring from the intersection with 1400 North, drive 1.2 miles and then turn left onto Benson/Airport Road (you'll see a sign directing you to the Logan Airport). Follow this road 6.8 miles to a T intersection in Benson, and turn right. You'll find yourself descending from a bench overlooking the Bear River on your left, and soon the road curves left to cross the river—the parking area for Benson Bridge is on the right, before the Bear River.

If you cross the bridge and continue west for about a mile you'll reach another T intersection. Turn right, and in about 0.1 mile [Looking] you'll see a narrow pullout on the west side of the road overlooking the oxbow in the Bear River.

General information: The area at Benson Bridge is small and your choices for walking are restricted to the cottonwood grove. As a result, it can be hard to bird here without spooking whatever you're after, particularly if you're looking for owls. Walk slowly and scan the trees for silhouettes, and if you manage to spot an owl, give it a wide berth. This is especially important in winter, when forcing the birds to fly wastes valuable energy reserves. You may also want to spend a little time here exploring the marsh complex to the east of the parking area. Scan it from the road, or walk the gated dirt road that heads north to the parking area.

Both the bridge area and the oxbow are surrounded by privately held farmland in active cultivation. Please don't use private driveways or walk across fields, no matter how intriguing that distant bird looks.

If you don't like gawking from a distance, explore the area by canoe. Check with outfitters in Logan for advice on where to put in, take out, and rent a canoe. There is also a locally published guidebook called *Boating the Bear*, available in Logan, which describes the section of the river between the bridge and the oxbow.

ADDITIONAL INFORMATION

Map grid: 4B
Elevation: 4,410 feet.
Hazards: Mud in spring (at Benson Bridge).
Nearest food, gas, and lodging: Logan.
Camping: Benson Marina, or Logan Canyon campgrounds, Wasatch-Cache National Forest.
For more information: Utah Travel Council.

37 Green Canyon

Habitats: Pinyon-juniper, aspen, spruce-fir, upland desert shrub
Specialty birds: Northern Goshawk; Blue Grouse; Chukar; Northern Pygmy-Owl; Clark's Nutcracker (winter); Townsend's Solitaire (winter); Spotted Towhee; Lazuli Bunting
Other key birds: Merlin (winter); Ruffed Grouse; Common Poorwill; Black-chinned and Broad-tailed Hummingbirds; Warbling Vireo; Black-billed Magpie; Bushtit (winter); Canyon Wren; Golden-crowned and Ruby-crowned Kinglets; Hermit Thrush; Nashville (fall), Virginia's, Yellow, Yellow-rumped, Black-throated Gray, and Townsend's (fall) Warblers; Western Tanager; Chipping Sparrow; Black-headed and Pine (winter) Grosbeaks
Best times to bird: Mornings, May through mid-July

The birding: Green Canyon provides numerous year-round recreational opportunities, including access to the Mount Naomi Wilderness Area. The habitat is fairly uniform up to the wilderness boundary—the mouth of the canyon supports drier, lower altitude species, while the upper canyon gives way to montane species. At the canyon mouth you'll encounter pinyon-juniper, some scattered sagebrush, and, on the north-facing slope, mountain maples. The road follows the narrow canyon

140

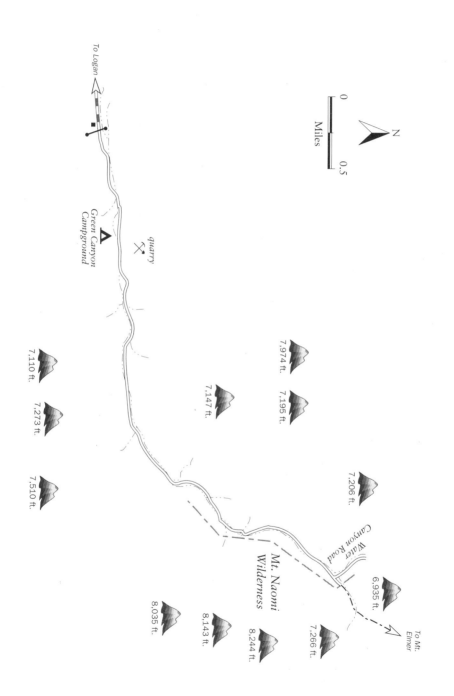

To Logan

0
Miles
0.5

N

Green Canyon
Campground

quarry

7,974 ft.

7,195 ft.

7,147 ft.

7,206 ft.

7,110 ft.

7,273 ft.

7,510 ft.

Water Canyon Road

Mt. Naomi
Wilderness

6,935 ft.

To Mt.
Elmer

7,266 ft.

8,035 ft.

8,143 ft.

8,244 ft.

141

bottom and a creek bed that is usually dry—the water is diverted higher up in the canyon and used to supply municipalities in the Cache Valley. The canyon bottom is a mixture of aspen, box elder, and mountain maples, and occasionally spruce and fir descend from the north slope to reach the canyon floor. At the wilderness boundary, spruce-fir becomes dominant.

The way you choose to bird Green Canyon will depend on how much time you have. It is possible (spring through fall) to drive to the end of the road, although a high-clearance vehicle would make the drive less nerve-racking. If you're short on time, this is a reasonable approach. Make sure to stop periodically and spend 15 or 20 minutes walking around. There are a number of meadows along the route, and I particularly like to bird these areas where the visibility is a little better.

Walking will allow you to see and hear the greatest diversity of birds. You can park at the gate at the canyon mouth and start following the road up the canyon. The road climbs gradually over the 4 miles to the wilderness boundary. Take time to explore the canyon mouth as you start walking—this is a good area for pinyon-juniper species such as Black-throated Gray Warblers and Bushtits (in winter), as well as Lazuli Buntings and Spotted Towhees.

The mouth of the canyon is open and vegetated mostly with grasses and shrubs. Just before moving out of this area and crossing the creek bed, a path takes off to the right and goes through a gap in the split-rail fence. I'd recommend this trail over the road because you'll have a little more solitude and won't have to deal with any vehicle traffic. The path parallels the road but follows the south side of the creek, rejoining the road about a mile up the canyon. You should begin to pick up warblers in this area, as well as sparrows, wrens, Western Tanagers, and more Lazuli Buntings. Canyon Wrens can be heard year-round, calling from the canyon walls.

As you continue to climb you may notice some subtle changes in the bird communities. Hermit Thrushes can be heard singing on the dry slopes; they seem to prefer the upper half of the canyon. A resident pair of Northern Goshawks nests in the canyon and may be seen year-round. In spring and summer they too seem to be in the upper half of the canyon. Although this route does not expose you to much of the montane community, as you near the wilderness boundary you may encounter Clark's Nutcrackers or Pine Grosbeaks or possibly Steller's Jays; these species are more prevalent at this altitude in winter. If you have a real hankering for these species and boundless energy, you can continue on the trail that departs from the wilderness boundary and climbs to Mount Elmer, with a summit just under 10,000 feet. Be prepared for a long hike, and equip yourself with the appropriate topographic maps if you decide to continue.

Green Canyon is open to ski and snowshoe travel in winter, but bird diversity and abundance tend to be fairly low. You are more likely to encounter Clark's Nutcrackers, Steller's Jays, Townsend's Solitaires, and other altitudinal migrants, but there are rarely many birds present at this time of year. Merlins have been known to hang out around the canyon mouth in winter.

Directions: From Main Street (US 91) in Logan, turn east onto 1800 North. This road winds through mixed farmland, residential areas, and businesses before jogging to the left and becoming 1900 North. Continue east on 1900 North, which leads directly into Green Canyon.

General information: In winter the road is closed to snowmobiles and the Forest Service sets a track for cross-country skiers. The rest of the year the gate at the mouth of the canyon is open, and vehicles may travel to the wilderness boundary 4 miles away. After the snow melts and the road has a chance to dry, mountain biking is popular.

There are numerous dispersed camping sites in Green Canyon, and the Forest Service may upgrade the one existing walk-in campground which lies fairly close to the mouth of the canyon. Because the road is narrow and rough in places, this is not a good place for RVs or trailers.

As with other east-west canyons in the Wasatch Range, winds can be prevalent and persistent here. If you encounter these conditions, you may want to bird another Cache Valley site. Canyon winds make birding difficult; it's hard to hear birds, and the trees whip around enough that detecting them by motion is nearly hopeless.

ADDITIONAL INFORMATION

Map grid: 5B
Elevation: 5,086 to 6,200 feet.
Hazards: None.
Nearest food, gas, and lodging: Logan.
Camping: Green Canyon Campground, Wasatch-Cache National Forest.
For more information: Wasatch-Cache National Forest, Logan Ranger District.

38 **Spring Hollow**

Habitats: Mountain riparian, pinyon-juniper, spruce-fir, upland desert shrub

Specialty birds: Blue Grouse; Northern Pygmy-Owl; Hammond's and Dusky Flycatchers; American Dipper; Townsend's Solitaire; Swainson's Thrush; Green-tailed and Spotted Towhees; Lazuli Bunting

Other key birds: Common (winter) and Barrow's (winter) Goldeneyes; Bufflehead (winter); Golden Eagle; Cooper's Hawk; Ruffed Grouse; Belted Kingfisher; Broad-tailed Hummingbird; Common Raven (winter); Cordilleran Flycatcher; Warbling Vireo; Mountain Chickadee; Red-breasted Nuthatch; Brown Creeper; Canyon, Winter (winter), and Marsh Wrens; Golden-crowned and Ruby-crowned Kinglets; Hermit Thrush; Gray Catbird; Yellow Warbler; Fox and Lincoln's Sparrows; Cassin's Finch

Best times to bird: Winter mornings until around noon, although waterfowl are usually present throughout the day. During spring and early summer, mornings are most productive. During summer there may be little bird activity on Third Dam due to heavy use by people.

The birding: Spring Hollow often has the greatest species diversity of any birding destination in the area, offering numerous year-round options and a chance for some interesting finds. The small reservoir on the Logan River, known as Third Dam, is the starting point for this walk. It's a popular recreation destination, particularly for fishing; if there are too many people around the lake for productive birding, there are plenty of other options accessible via short walks. In winter, the water is open except in the deepest cold snap, and there are often a half dozen species of waterfowl swimming about, including on rare occasion, a Common Loon. If snows have been heavy, access to other birding opportunities may be limited, but most of the time you can walk around the Spring Hollow Campground or explore below the dam. Also in winter, both Golden Eagles and, more rarely, Bald Eagles use the river corridor. Keep your eyes peeled to see if one of these impressive birds is soaring or perched on a tree overlooking the river.

Check below the dam for Northern Pygmy-Owls, which sometimes perch in trees lining the river. American Dippers have a territory in the stretch of river immediately below the dam, and one or more of these birds can frequently be seen flying just above the water, or bobbing on a boulder in the middle of the river before plunging beneath the surface to forage. You may encounter warblers in this stretch as well; keep your eyes on the brush along the riverbank and the branches of the cottonwoods overhead.

Upstream from the reservoir is a small marsh complex that attracts a variety of sparrows, as well as Marsh Wrens and, in winter, an occasional Winter Wren. This area is probably best viewed from the Riverside Trail, which offers a quiet 2-mile hike to the Guinavah and Malibu campgrounds farther upstream. In addition to

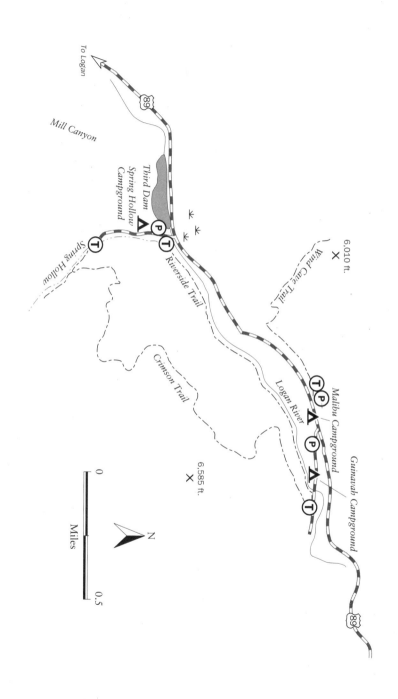

sparrows and wrens, you can expect to encounter Warbling Vireos, Gray Catbirds, flycatchers, and Lazuli Buntings along the Riverside Trail.

Two trails leave from the Spring Hollow area and climb at least partway up the north and south walls of the canyon. Each trail offers access to different communities of forest birds. After crossing the bridge over the upper end of Third Dam and entering the Spring Hollow Campground/Picnic Area, the paved road continues straight up the drainage to the group camping area. This is where you'll find the trailheads for Spring Hollow Trail and Crimson Trail. The Crimson Trail climbs steeply through junipers and shrubs to reach the top of China Wall—an impressive cliff face exposed in either side of the canyon walls. Once on top, the trail heads east through spruce and firs interspersed with a few open meadow areas, then descends to the river. Once back at the river, it's a level walk on the Riverside Trail back to Spring Hollow. Though steep, the hike is relatively short and typically takes 2 to 4 hours.

In addition to forest-adapted species, this route provides an opportunity for you to challenge your birding skills. The Dusky Flycatcher is often encountered in the vicinity of the Spring Hollow Campground and up to the trailhead. Hammond's Flycatcher, which is notoriously difficult to distinguish from the Dusky Flycatcher, is associated with the conifers at elevations above the trailhead. In some years, these species are numerous enough during breeding that you can stand in the area of the trailhead and hear both species calling—one of the few reliable ways to tell them apart, if you know what to listen for!

Farther north in the canyon, just opposite the Guinavah and Malibu campgrounds, you'll see the trailhead for Wind Cave. This is another short but steep hike. With its southern aspect, this slope is drier and dominated by junipers; you're more likely to encounter the Green-tailed Towhee on this hike. In winter this trail provides good views of soaring birds, and Blue Grouse may be encountered in the area around and above Wind Cave.

Directions: From Logan, continue west on US 89 (400 North in Logan). The road soon enters Logan Canyon, and after 6.5 miles arrives at Third Dam and Spring Hollow, both well marked with Forest Service signs. Take the Spring Hollow turn, cross the small reservoir, and turn immediately (right) into the parking area. If you plan to hike the Wind Cave Trail, it's worth driving another half a mile to the Wind Cave Trail parking area, which is on the left (north) side of the road.

General information: This is a good destination for "mixed groups," those in which not everyone is interested in birding, because there are plenty of opportunities for other types of outdoor recreation. There are plenty of hiking trails in the area, as well as places for fishing, rock climbing, and mountain biking. Wildlife is also fairly abundant. One can often find signs of bobcat, moose, mule deer, pika, and many other species.

You'll be limited in Spring Hollow only by your willingness to hike and explore. Two other options, for example, would be to explore the Spring Hollow

Trail or to find your way into Mill Canyon, which is the side canyon entering just above the south side of the dam.

Forest Service campgrounds abound here and if you can't find a spot at the small Spring Hollow Campground, continue up the canyon to Guinavah and Malibu campgrounds.

ADDITIONAL INFORMATION

Map grid: 5B
Elevation: 5,100 to 6,000 feet.
Hazards: Rattlesnakes occasionally along Crimson and Wind Cave trails.
Nearest food, gas, and lodging: Logan.
Camping: Spring Hollow Campground, Wasatch-Cache National Forest.
For more information: Wasatch-Cache National Forest, Logan Ranger District.

39 High Creek Ridge

Habitats: Desert steppe, upland desert shrub
Specialty birds: Black Rosy-Finch (winter)
Other key birds: Sharp-tailed Grouse; Black-billed Magpie; Common Raven (spring); Savannah and Grasshopper Sparrows
Best times to bird: Sunrise to about 10 a.m., mid-March through mid-May, for Sharp-tailed Grouse. Early mornings before noon from late April through June for other seasonal species

The birding: After hiking to the top of the ridge north of the access road, you'll find the only limits to your birding options here are your time and energy. An expansive grassland follows the ridge, drops away to the north, and is all fair game for birding. Your best opportunities, however, probably lie along the ridgeline which proceeds west. Walking the ridge provides a view down into the canyon you drove up to reach the trailhead, as well as a view across a good portion of the grasslands to the north. Red-tailed Hawks, Northern Harriers, Common Ravens, Crows, and perhaps a Golden Eagle may be surfing the thermal waves rising from the ridge. As you walk, listen attentively for bird songs and scan the top of the shrubs and the few scattered trees for sparrows, Western Meadowlarks, and Black-billed Magpies. The Sharp-Tailed Grouse are most likely to occupy the gentler northern slope with more grass and fewer shrubs. Another game bird you may see is the Ring-Necked Pheasant.

Only a faint game trail follows the crest of the wide-open ridge which is your destination, but the walking, once you gain the ridge, is easy. Spotting birds can be surprisingly hard because many of the species blend in with the tapestry of sagebrush and last year's grass. It's often best to walk slowly and let your ears guide you to singing sparrows, meadowlarks, or the whir of retreating grouse.

39 High Creek Ridge

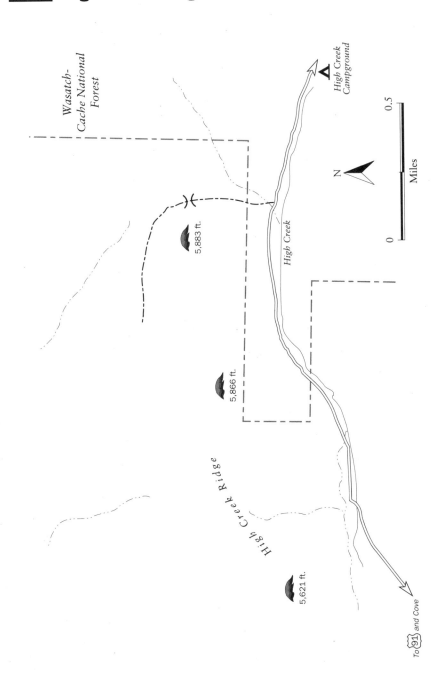

Wasatch-
Cache National
Forest

High Creek
Campground

5,883 ft.

High Creek

N

0.5

Miles

0

5,866 ft.

High Creek Ridge

5,621 ft.

To 91 and Cove

148

Directions: From Richmond, head north on US 91 (Main Street). About a mile north of town, you'll see a Forest Service sign indicating a right turn and pointing you in the direction of High Creek. Follow this route up the drainage and to the forest boundary, which is marked with a cattle guard and a Forest Service sign. The ridge you'll hike rises steeply on your left—the easiest access is another 0.7 mile farther up the canyon. As you continue, you'll note that the road climbs some and the ridge descends slightly to meet the face of the Bear River Range. Just as the road enters a grove of maples and starts into High Creek Canyon, an old road takes off to the left and climbs to the top of the ridge. The Forest Service has blocked this old road trace with a sign that prohibits motorized use. Park at one of the nearby pullouts, and hike either the old road or the route of your choice to reach the ridge to the north.

General information: The desert steppe habitat type and its associated plant and animal communities have declined precipitously because of grazing practices, fire suppression, and conversion to cropland or housing developments. This long, wind-swept ridge at the mouth of High Creek Canyon holds one of the best remaining examples of desert steppe, and it still supports small populations of the various bird species associated with this habitat.

Species diversity is not very high in the desert steppe, nor are any species particularly numerous. This spot will test both your physical stamina and your visual acuity, but you're guaranteed a breathtaking view of the surrounding valley and an array of wildflowers if you visit in spring.

A word of caution. It is possible that grouse are on their lek in this general area. Should you be fortunate enough to discover this extraordinary display, you should be extremely careful not to disturb the birds. Sit quietly at a distance of 100 yards and watch their performance through binoculars or a spotting scope. A few people spooking a flock of grouse from their lek might be all that is required for the birds to abandon the area and perhaps fail to reproduce.

This area does attract occasional flocks of Black Rosy-Finches in the winter, but access may be difficult or possible only after a long ski, as the access road is not maintained in winter.

ADDITIONAL INFORMATION

Map grid: 5B
Elevation: 5,900 feet.
Hazards: Strenuous climb.
Nearest food, gas, and lodging: Richmond.
Camping: High Creek Campground, Wasatch-Cache National Forest.
For more information: Wasatch-Cache National Forest, Logan Ranger District.

▮40▮ Tony Grove Lake

Habitats: Mountain riparian, spruce-fir, aspen, mountain meadow
Specialty birds: Williamson's Sapsucker; Three-toed Woodpecker; Western Wood-Peewee; Clark's Nutcracker; Townsend's Solitaire; Pine Grosbeak; Red Crossbill (irregular)
Other key birds: Golden Eagle; Ruby-throated, Calliope (August), Broad-tailed, and Rufous Hummingbirds; Purple Martin; Gray and Steller's Jays; Mountain Chickadee; Red-breasted and White-breasted Nuthatches; Brown Creeper; Ruby-crowned Kinglet; Mountain Bluebird; Townsend's Warbler (fall); Brewer's and Lincoln's Sparrows
Best times to bird: Early morning to noon during breeding season, mid-May through mid-July; September through mid-October for migrating warblers

The birding: Tony Grove is a gateway to a variety of montane habitat types. The area is a mix of spruce-fir stands, aspen groves, mountain meadows, and mountain riparian zones. A hike along any of the numerous trails leaving from Tony Grove will be sure to yield rewards. The mountain meadows that dot the landscape are filled with wildflowers, which usually peak in late July. I'll suggest three trails from among the many possibilities.

The 1-mile Tony Grove Lake Trail starts from the day use parking area and circles the lake. There is no elevation change, and much of the trail is visible from the parking lot. The trail can be crowded with anglers and day hikers, so early morning and late evening tend to be the best times for birding. You can hike in either direction, but if you start walking in the direction opposite from the dam, you can pick up a brochure at the trail board and also take in the self-guided walk. Birds along this route include Pine Siskins, Mountain Chickadees, Mountain Bluebirds, and Lincoln's Sparrows. The wildflower meadows along this trail, particularly the area around the trail board, teem with Broad-tailed Hummingbirds, and this is a good spot for Calliope Hummingbirds in late summer.

The 1.1-mile-long Coldwater Spring Trail climbs through the mature spruce-fir forest above the campground, through a low saddle above the lake, and eventually into an open aspen forest near Coldwater Spring. Total elevation gain is a modest 400 feet. This trail is excellent for locating some of the more forest-dependent species, such as Ruby-crowned and Golden-crowned Kinglets, Hairy and Downy Woodpeckers, Warbling Vireo, Western Wood-Peewee, and Yellow-rumped Warbler. You can start at the upper end of the campground or at the backcountry trailhead, about an eighth of a mile before the campground.

The Mount Naomi Trail starts at the day use parking area and heads north into the high country. Mount Naomi at 9,980 feet is the highest point in the Bear River Range, but the total elevation gain is not strenuous. The trail passes through high mountain meadows, follows intermittent tumbling streams that drain the snow banks, and crosses through limber pine, Douglas-fir, and spruce communities.

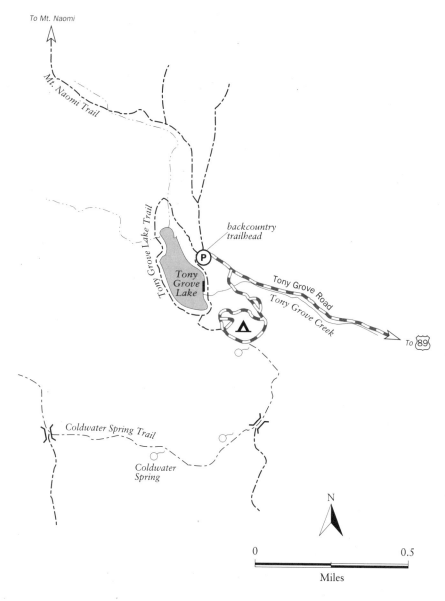

To Mt. Naomi

Mt. Naomi Trail

Tony Grove Lake Trail

backcountry trailhead

P

Tony Grove Lake

Tony Grove Road

Tony Grove Creek

To 89

Coldwater Spring Trail

Coldwater Spring

N

0   0.5

Miles

A hike on this trail should lead you to Clark's Nutcrackers (foraging in pinyon pines), Gray and Steller's Jays, Cassin's Finches, Pine Siskins, Townsend's Solitaires, Williamson's Sapsuckers, and White-breasted Nuthatches. Shortly after climbing out of the cirque the trail passes open meadows. If wildflowers are in bloom this area is excellent for hummingbirds. Keep your eyes open for Purple Martins, which may be on the wing along this trail.

Directions: From Main Street in Logan, turn east on 400 North/US 89. The Tony Grove turnoff is a left turn 19.2 miles from Logan, clearly marked with a Forest Service sign. If you continue for a couple hundred yards along this road you'll reach the Lewis M. Turner Campground. Instead, turn left immediately after leaving the highway and drive 7 miles to Tony Grove Lake.

General information: Tony Grove is usually accessible by car from mid-May through October, although road conditions may be marginal at either end of this time slot. Tony Grove is a natural lake which sits cradled in a picturesque glacial cirque. The natural outlet to the lake has been augmented with a short stone dam that increases the lake's depth and surface area. Tony Grove is a popular summer destination for both tourists and locals: it's aesthetically appealing, and the high altitude provides relief from summer's heat. Summer nights at Tony Grove can be remarkably cool, so overnight visitors should be prepared for temperatures which can dip into the 40s. Tony Grove is a great destination if there are nonbirding members in your party because there are plenty of opportunities for hiking, fishing, swimming, and boating. A Forest Service campground provides ready access to the great birding but tends to fill quickly.

The Tony Grove Lake Trail has been widened and leveled, making it wheelchair-accessible.

ADDITIONAL INFORMATION

Map grid: 5B
Elevation: 8,000 to 9,980 feet.
Hazards: High altitude, cold weather.
Nearest food, gas, and lodging: Logan or Garden City.
Camping: Tony Grove Lake Campground, Lewis M. Turner Campground.
For more information: Wasatch-Cache National Forest, Logan Ranger District.

41 Bear Lake National Wildlife Refuge

Habitat: Lowland riparian
Specialty birds: Sandhill Crane
Other key birds: Eared and Western Grebes; Double-crested Cormorant; American Bittern; Snowy Egret; Black-crowned Night-Heron; White-faced Ibis; Tundra (spring and fall) and Trumpeter (spring and fall) Swans; Blue-winged and Cinnamon Teals; Northern Shoveler; Gadwall; Canvasback; Redhead; Lesser Scaup; Common Goldeneye (winter); Hooded (winter) and Common (winter) Mergansers; Ruddy Duck; Northern Harrier; Gray Partridge; Virginia Rail; Sora; Black-necked Stilt; American Avocet; Willet; Wilson's Phalarope; Franklin's and California Gulls; Caspian, Forster's, and Black Terns; Northern Rough-winged, Bank, Cliff, and Barn Swallows; Marsh Wren; Savannah and Song Sparrows; Bobolink
Best times to bird: Usually good throughout the day during spring and fall migration and during breeding season

Wetlands at Bear Lake National Wildlife Refuge.

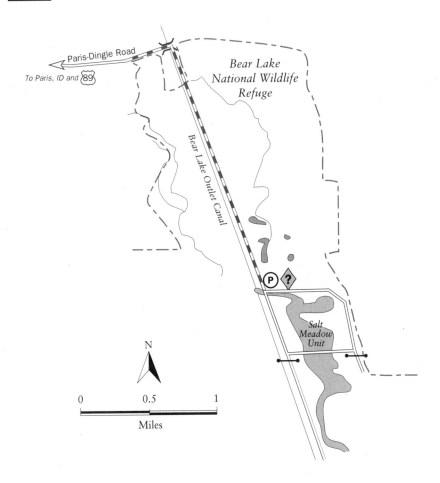

The birding: As with many of the refuges and wildlife management areas set aside for the enhancement of waterfowl and shorebirds, a large portion of this refuge is off-limits to visitors the majority of the year. A 2.5-mile-long viewing loop is open all year and provides excellent birding. The refuge is located in the low, marshy floodplain of Bear Lake, in the middle of Bear Lake Valley.

Because travel on the refuge is essentially restricted to the dike that constitutes the viewing route, your options are clear and limited. However, the southern (and much larger) portion of the refuge is open to boat travel from September 25 through January 15—a good possibility for those wishing to expand their viewing options during fall migration. The dike is open to vehicle, foot, or bicycle traffic, and all of these approaches will provide for good viewing.

As you leave Paris, Idaho, for the drive to the refuge, be sure to scan the farm fields on either side of the approach road. These fields can be marshy or even flooded in spring, and waterfowl or shorebirds may be about, as well as flocks of Yellow-headed Blackbirds, Northern Harriers, and Bobolinks. Be sure to stop at the first information board as you enter the refuge to pick up a current brochure and map. Shortly after that first information board, you'll come to a kiosk situated where the route divides at the start of the Salt Meadow Unit Wildlife Observation Viewing Route. This is also a good stop, and the site gives you your first view of the impounded Salt Meadow Unit.

There is room to park near the kiosk if you'd like to walk or cycle the route; otherwise proceed to the right of the kiosk and onto the dike road. Depending on when you visit you could be the only person here. Otherwise, be aware that there are pullouts along the route where you can stop and allow traffic to continue around you. It's worth taking your time around this route anyway, and sitting on the side of the dike and listening to all the bird activity is rewarding and revealing. Be sure to take time to scan flocks of foraging American Avocets and Black-necked Stilts (these tend to be in the shallower water on the east side of the loop). There are often more unusual and more cryptic shorebirds (Short-billed or Long-billed Dowitchers, Greater or Lesser Yellowlegs) mixed in with these flocks.

Like most area wetlands, bird diversity is greatest during spring and fall migration. Spring can be the easiest time to view birds here because the marsh vegetation is sparser. Birding in breeding season and even during winter can also be rewarding. In spring and summer, the refuge produces about 4,500 ducks and 1,800 geese. The refuge also hosts about 5,000 White-faced Ibis, one of the largest breeding colonies in the country.

Directions: In Paris, Idaho, turn east from Main Street (US 89) onto 200 North—signs here point to the refuge and to the local airport. Continue to follow the refuge signs, turning right onto the refuge immediately after crossing the narrow trestle bridge over the Bear Lake Outlet Canal. The Salt Meadow Unit Wildlife Observation Route begins a few hundred yards down this road.

General information: Managing a dynamic marsh is a constant battle. Refuge literature indicates that habitat quality here began declining around the turn of the century due to human activities. Management has reversed this trend by controlling water levels, reducing sediment inputs from the Bear River, and excluding carp. As you travel you'll notice raised platforms a few feet above the marsh. These were built for breeding Canada Geese, but recent muskrat activity has provided geese with natural islands or mats of vegetation they seem to prefer.

Another program at the refuge includes the production of crops to attract Sandhill Cranes and Canada Geese in fall, with the purpose of keeping them out of farmers' crops. Several thousand geese and a few hundred cranes take advantage of this resource in late September and early October.

ADDITIONAL INFORMATION

Map grid: 5A

Elevation: 5,925 feet.

Hazards: Biting insects, cold in winter.

Nearest food, gas, and lodging: Paris, Idaho.

Camping: Paris Spring Campground, Wasatch-Cache National Forest.

For more information: U.S. Fish and Wildlife Service, Bear Lake NWR.

42 Six Mile Reservoir

Habitats: Lowland riparian, upland desert shrub
Specialty birds: Ferruginous Hawk; Sandhill Crane
Other key birds: Common Loon; Northern Pintail; Cinnamon Teal;
Northern Shoveler; Gadwall; Common Goldeneye (fall); Bufflehead
(fall); Northern Harrier; Swainson's Hawk; Golden Eagle; Loggerhead
Shrike; Northern Rough-winged and Barn Swallows
Best times to bird: Early mornings mid-April through June for
waterfowl and hawks. September through October for Sandhill
Cranes

The birding: While the barren shore of this small reservoir doesn't offer much cover for waterfowl or passerines, this is a good spot for finding two interesting species. In the field occupying the narrow valley below the dam, Sandhill Cranes congregate in fall in such numbers that they damage grain crops. Cranes may be seen throughout summer but their numbers peak in early fall, with several hundred sometimes visible in this field.

The other species of interest is the Common Loon. This northernmost corner of Utah is at the extreme southern limit of the loon's summer range, or just slightly out of it, depending on who you ask. It's the only place I have consistently found Common Loons in Utah in the summer. Other than the loons, you can expect to see a few of the more common breeding waterfowl; these other species seem to prefer the upper end of the small reservoir (away from the dam).

You can easily scan the lake from the road, which passes along the north side of the reservoir. Park off the side of the road just below the dam, then quietly walk up the road until you can scan the lake.

Directions: From the intersection of UT 16 and UT 30 (Sage Creek Junction) head north on UT 16 for 6 miles. Immediately before the road climbs up a short knoll, Six Mile Road heads off to the left. Take this turn and proceed about a mile to the reservoir.

General information: Six Mile Reservoir is clearly marked as private land. Please respect the property owner's wishes and stick to the road for viewing. Because the lake is long and narrow, it's relatively easy to take in all the activity with a pair of binoculars, although a spotting scope would be handy.

42 Six Mile Reservoir

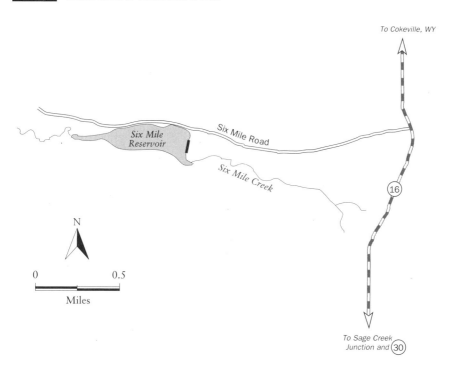

ADDITIONAL INFORMATION

Map grid: 6B
Elevation: 6,300 feet.
Hazards: None.
Nearest food, gas, and lodging: Cokeville, Wyoming.
Camping: Rendezvous Beach, Bear Lake State Park.
For more information: Utah Travel Council.

43 Randolph Viewing Area

Habitat: Lowland riparian

Specialty birds: Prairie Falcon; Sandhill Crane; Long-billed Curlew; Green-tailed Towhee

Other key birds: American Bittern; Snowy and Cattle Egret; Black-crowned Night-Heron; White-faced Ibis; Cinnamon Teal; Northern Shoveler; Gadwall; American Wigeon (spring and fall); Redhead; Lesser Scaup (spring and fall); Ruddy Duck; Northern Harrier; Swainson's Hawk; Golden Eagle; Ring-necked Pheasant; Virginia Rail; Sora; Willet; Spotted Sandpiper; Common Snipe; Franklin's and California Gull; Short-eared Owl; Black-chinned and Broad-tailed Hummingbird; Belted Kingfisher; Western Kingbird; Loggerhead Shrike; Violet-green, Northern Rough-winged, Cliff, and Barn Swallow; Black-billed Magpie; Mountain Bluebird; Orange-crowned and Yellow Warbler; Common Yellowthroat; American Tree (winter), Brewer's, Vesper, Savannah, and Song Sparrow; Brewer's Blackbird

Best times to bird: April through October; early mornings are best

The birding: This route takes you across the Bear River Valley at a point where the river is a shallow, meandering watercourse surrounded by wet meadows, marshes, and willow thickets. The area can be particularly wet in spring when the river floods adjacent fields.

Scan the surrounding fields, oxbow ponds, and the meandering river channel for bird life. Waterfowl nest in the area and use it as a stopover during spring and fall migration. Sandhill Cranes also nest in the area, and the fields are used by herons, egrets, and White-faced Ibis. All of these species can be seen by scanning from your vehicle.

When you approach the narrow corridors of willows that line the river channel and isolated ponds, it's worth stopping for a short stroll along the road. Investigate these areas for flycatchers and warblers, particularly during spring and the early months of summer.

After crossing the narrow valley on this 5-mile-long route, you can backtrack to UT 16, or explore the east side of the valley from the dirt road that travels north and south along the base of the Crawford Mountains.

Directions: From Randolph, travel about 1.5 miles north on UT 16 and turn right onto Crawford Mountain Road. This is the start of the viewing route—from here, proceed across the valley.

If you're approaching from the north, turn south onto UT 16 from UT 30 at Sage Creek Junction. The left turn to Crawford Mountain Road is signed from this direction as a wildlife viewing route. The turnoff lies about 6.5 miles from the intersection of UT 16 and UT 30.

General information: This entire route is surrounded by private property. Confine your viewing to the roadside.

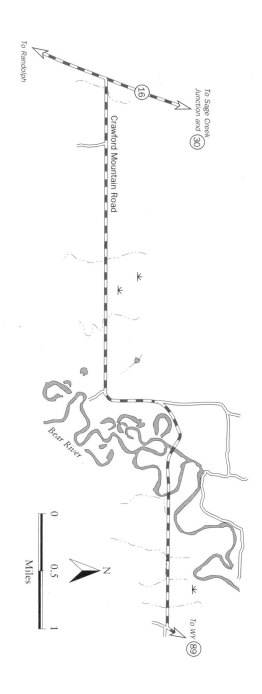

ADDITIONAL INFORMATION

Map grid: 6B
Elevation: 6,300 feet.
Hazards: None.
Nearest food, gas, and lodging: Randolph.
Camping: Rendezvous Beach, Bear Lake State Park.
For more information: Utah Travel Council.

44 Ogden Nature Center

Habitats: Lowland riparian, upland desert shrub
Specialty birds: Bald Eagle (winter); Ferruginous Hawk (winter); Prairie Falcon; Western Screech-Owl; Western Wood-Pewee; Northern Shrike (winter); Green-tailed and Spotted Towhees; Lazuli Bunting
Other key birds: Wood Duck; Sharp-shinned, Cooper's, and Swainson's Hawks; California Quail; Sora; Spotted Sandpiper; Common Snipe; Franklin's, Ring-billed, and California Gulls; Caspian and Forster's Terns; Barn, Great Horned, and Long-eared Owls; Common Nighthawk; Black-chinned, Calliope, Broad-tailed, and Rufous (fall) Hummingbirds; Red-naped Sapsucker; Cordilleran Flycatcher; Say's Phoebe; Western Kingbird; Loggerhead Shrike; Plumbeous and Warbling Vireos; Western Scrub-Jay; Mountain Chickadee (winter); Red-breasted and White-breasted Nuthatches; Brown Creeper; Bewick's, House, and Marsh Wrens; Western and Mountain Bluebirds; Hermit Thrush; Bohemian Waxwing (winter); Yellow, Yellow-rumped, and MacGillivray's Warblers; Common Yellowthroat; Wilson's Warbler; Western Tanager; Brewer's, Vesper, Lark, Savannah, and Song Sparrows; Black-headed Grosbeak; Cassin's Finch
Best times to bird: Throughout the day in spring; summer mornings until about noon. Evenings can be good, but the center closes about the time owls start calling.

The birding: The Ogden Nature Center hosts a variety of birds and it would be hard to imagine a place better designed for ease of human access. At just around 200 acres, the Nature Center features a diverse mix of regenerating fields, canals, ponds, and marshlands, and stands of mature cottonwoods and box elders with dense, tangled understories of shrubs. The result is a haven for birds and, because level trails have been carefully and unobtrusively installed, a haven for birders. Numerous nest boxes for passerines, owls, and ducks have been placed throughout the park. Remember to check these boxes with your binoculars as you're out walking. You never can predict what might poke its head out to look at you.

Begin at the visitor center where you'll pay your fee, obtain a current map, and get the latest information on sightings. The walking trails total about 1.5 miles and originate near the visitor center. You also may want to spend a few minutes observing what is coming and going from the feeders behind the visitor center.

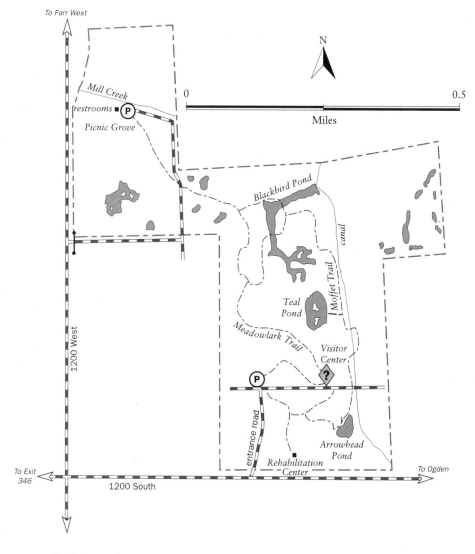

All of the trails provide access to a variety of birding. The riparian corridor along the Moffet Trail offers a good opportunity for owls among the cottonwoods, and the small side trail to the Teal Pond is worthwhile; there are often ducks on the pond and gulls and terns overhead. Wherever a trail crosses a canal or pond, be sure to scan for ducks. The Meadowlark Trail passes through more open terrain and you can hike at least part of this while returning from the Moffet Trail. This area is drier and you're more likely to see sparrows, finches, and bluebirds on perches in this regenerating field.

The Nature Center's bird list contains 136 species, and what you'll encounter depends as always on a certain amount of luck. The most unusual birds are likely to be seen in migration, including Northern Goshawk, Rough-legged Hawk, and Merlin, all of which have been recorded here.

Directions: From I-15, take the 12th Street Exit (347) and head east towards Ogden. The Nature Center's property is surrounded by a high fence and the entrance is through a well-signed gate on 12th Street. The center is on the left as you head towards Ogden, about 1.5 miles after leaving I-15.

General information: The Nature Center has varied hours: Saturday 7 A.M. to 4 P.M.; Tuesdays and Thursdays from 10 A.M. to 7 P.M.; Monday, Wednesday, and Friday 10 A.M. to 4 P.M.; closed Sundays, holidays, and December 23 to January 2. It is possible, particularly with a small group, to arrange for evening or overnight use of the facilities, or to arrange for a guided tour. Contact the Nature Center for more information and for their modest fee schedule. The Nature Center charges $1 for admission—a pittance for what you get in return.

The center, already well designed to provide a great birding experience, has plans to expand opportunities to include more interpretive displays, and best of all, some strategically placed wildlife viewing blinds.

ADDITIONAL INFORMATION

Map grid: 4C
Elevation: 4,300 feet.
Hazards: None.
Nearest food, gas, and lodging: Ogden.
Camping: Century RV Park, Westhaven.
For more information: Ogden Nature Center.

45 Ogden River Parkway

Habitats: Lowland riparian
Specialty birds: Lazuli Bunting
Other key birds: Cooper's Hawk; Great Horned, Long-eared, and Northern Saw-whet Owls; Downy Woodpecker; Western Scrub-Jay; Black-billed Magpie; Brown Creeper (winter); Ruby-crowned Kinglet; Common Yellowthroat; Yellow-breasted Chat; Spotted Towhee; Song and White-crowned Sparrows; Black-headed Grosbeak
Best times to bird: Mid-April through May and September through mid-October for migrants. Early mornings, May through July for breeding birds

The birding: This birding route is a pleasant walk along a riparian corridor in an urban park. The trail, which is paved along its length and has numerous access points, is bounded on one side by the Ogden River and on the other by a golf course, city parks, and low-density developments. The Wasatch Range forms a dramatic backdrop to it all.

45 Ogden River Parkway

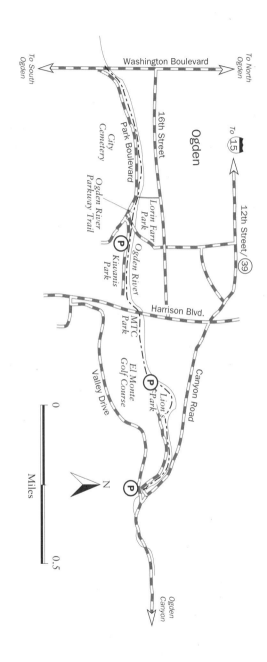

To South Ogden

Washington Boulevard

To North Ogden

City Cemetery

Park Boulevard

16th Street

Ogden

To 15

Ogden River Parkway Trail

Lorin Farr Park

P

Kiwanis Park

Ogden River

12th Street (39)

Harrison Blvd.

MTC Park

El Monte Golf Course

Valley Drive

P Lion's Park

Canyon Road

0

N

Miles

0.5

P

Ogden Canyon

From the mouth of Ogden Canyon, the paved hiking path extends west beneath an underpass, emerges on the opposite side of Harrison Boulevard, and follows the river corridor to the MTC Learning Park. The trail is well-signed and leads through the long, narrow grove of cottonwoods lining the river.

Although this can be a pleasant walk in any season, bird diversity is at its highest during migration. For birds and birders the attraction is the lane of stately cottonwoods along the Ogden River and the associated undergrowth. The MTC Learning Park, at the terminus of this walk, is a good place to move off the path and explore brush and vegetation away from the river. In this slightly drier area, you may find more sparrows and the occasional Spotted or Green-tailed Towhee.

The corridor becomes narrow with considerably more development west of the MTC Learning Park, a small greenspace with a botanical garden and visitor center with interpretive displays. If the birding seems fruitful continue the walk for another 0.75 mile past the park along the river, returning along the same route.

Directions: The park and riparian corridor begin at the mouth of Ogden Canyon, and end at MTC Learning Park at the intersection of Park Blvd. and Monroe Blvd. From I-15, take the 12th Street exit (#347) and head east through Ogden. About 100 yards before entering Ogden Canyon, turn right onto an unsigned, paved road. Although the road is not named, there is a sign for the "Dinosaur Park." The road crosses the Ogden River, where the Animal Shelter Road enters immediately on the right. Take this turn and park—the Ogden River Parkway starts at this intersection and is on your right, to the north.

General information: Lying at the mouth of Ogden Canyon and surrounded by other city greenspace, this park attracts a reasonable number of birds, given its restricted size and urban surroundings.

The entire Wasatch Front is affected by a phenomenon known as canyon winds. As weather systems pass across the state, they create a pressure gradient where a low pressure system lies to the east of the range and a high pressure system to the west. The result is state-sized parcels of air trying to force their way through the narrow canyons that dissect the Wasatch Mountains, and the winds exiting the canyon mouths can be impressive. If you find yourself trying to bird in such conditions (which is impossible), come back later (the winds abate through the course of the day), or choose another destination away from any canyon outlets.

ADDITIONAL INFORMATION

Map grid: 4C
Elevation: 4,425 feet.
Hazards: None.
Nearest food, gas, and lodging: Ogden.
Camping: Century RV Park, Westhaven.
For more information: Utah Travel Council.

46 City Creek Canyon

Habitats: Lowland riparian, spruce-fir, pinyon-juniper
Specialty birds: Blue Grouse; Western Screech-Owl; Northern Pygmy-Owl; American Dipper; Townsend's Solitaire; Lazuli Bunting
Other key birds: Sharp-shinned and Cooper's Hawks; Ring-necked Pheasant; Ruffed Grouse; California Quail; Great Horned, Long-eared, and Northern Saw-whet Owls; Common Poorwill; Broad-tailed Hummingbird; Warbling Vireo; Steller's Jay; Western Scrub-Jay; Mountain Chickadee; Red-breasted Nuthatch; Brown Creeper; Golden-crowned and Ruby-crowned Kinglets; Bohemian (winter) and Cedar Waxwings; Virginia's and Yellow-rumped Warblers; Song Sparrow; Black-headed Grosbeak
Best times to bird: Mornings in spring and summer are best for breeding birds. Other seasons can be productive, but you may not find much diversity. Evenings around dusk are best for owls and Common Poorwills, more likely heard than seen.

The birding: This is a pleasant hike through a narrow riparian corridor which meanders out of the north end of Salt Lake City. The primary trail is paved and wide enough to accommodate the mix of walkers, joggers, and cyclists. In the lower section a dirt path also parallels each side of the paved trail, taking you through a greater variety of habitats, including dense brush and some of the more open fields above the creek. There are also numerous access points to these side trails, so you have many opportunities to rejoin or leave the main trail as you hike the canyon.

The entrance to Memory Grove in City Creek Canyon.

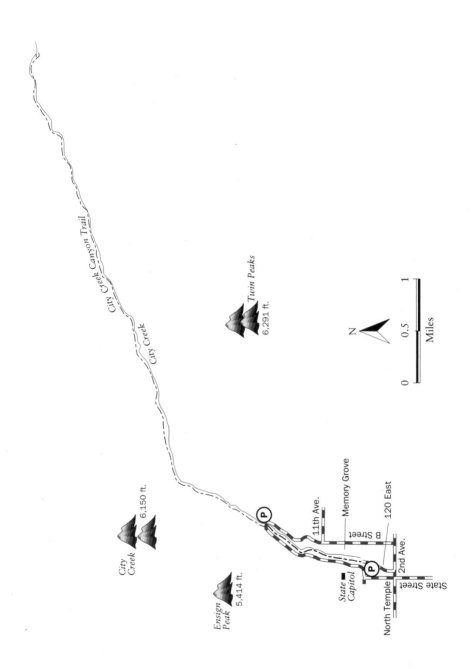

The lower stretch of Memory Grove contains numerous conifers. It's worth spending a little time in this area looking and listening for kinglets, Steller's Jay, Brown Creeper, and any of the owl species. The conifers are preferred roosts for owls in the winter, so walking under each conifer and looking up through the branches just might reveal an owl. In snow-free months look for owl pellets under the trees; these may reveal a roost and perhaps an owl perched quietly above.

As you climb the canyon, the surrounding terrain becomes drier and the vegetation changes noticeably. The riparian zone narrows; cottonwoods become sparse and eventually give way to maples and Gambel oak, which yield to grasses and meadows. As you climb even higher, conifers again begin to appear on the north-facing slope.

You're more likely to find the grouse, Common Poorwills, and Ring-Necked Pheasants in the upper reaches of the canyon. Check the creek periodically for American Dippers, and work your way into areas where you can inspect the grassland/forest interface for sparrows.

Directions: The Memory Grove entrance is an easy walk from downtown Salt Lake City. Proceed east on North Temple Street, also known as Second Avenue; then turn north onto Canyon Road (120 East). Travel another 0.3 mile to the gate at Memory Grove.

To reach the City Creek Canyon entrance, continue a short distance east on Second Avenue and turn left on B Street. The canyon road continues northward from the corner of 11th Avenue and B Street. After 0.7 mile, the road crosses City Creek and turns back down the canyon; turn right into the parking area at the canyon gate immediately after crossing the creek and before heading back toward the city.

General information: There are actually two adjacent parks in this corridor, which makes for one long park corridor. Memory Grove closes at 10 p.m. and City Creek at 11 p.m., so if you're out for a little early evening owling, make sure you allow yourself sufficient time to get back to your vehicle.

The two access points mean that you can tailor this hike to fit your time constraints. From Memory Grove to the City Creek parking area is a walk of 1 mile; to reach the end of the trail in City Creek Canyon is an additional 5.5 miles.

ADDITIONAL INFORMATION

Map grid: 4D and 5D
Elevation: 4,440 to 6,044 feet.
Hazards: None.
Nearest food, gas, and lodging: Salt Lake City.
Camping: Camp VIP, Salt Lake City.
For more information: Utah Travel Council.

47 City Cemetery

Habitat: Spruce-fir
Specialty birds: Western Screech-Owl; Hammond's (spring) and Dusky (spring) Flycatchers; Townsend's Solitaire; Green-tailed Towhee (spring)
Other key birds: Sharp-shinned and Cooper's Hawks; Red-naped Sapsucker (spring); Steller's Jay; Western Scrub-Jay; Black-billed Magpie; Mountain Chickadee; Red-breasted Nuthatch; Brown Creeper; Golden-crowned Kinglet; Bohemian (winter) and Cedar Waxwings
Best times to bird: A good year-round site. Late summer is probably the slowest time. Winter days can be productive, while birds are most active mornings during spring and summer.

The birding: The cemetery is an island of manicured greenspace isolated in a sea of stately old houses. The predominant tree in this landscape of exotic imports is the conifer, but a few deciduous species such as birch and willow add diversity.

The birds don't seem to mind the controlled environment. This is a good year-round spot for species often associated with suburbia, as well as more montane species which actually have not strayed too far away from more pristine habitat. In winter, altitudinal migrants descend from the surrounding mountains to congregate here. These colder months can bring in Bohemian and Cedar Waxwings, Steller's Jays, and Townsend's Solitaires. You're likely to see Sharp-shinned and Cooper's Hawks patrolling the trees.

The cemetery is also a good place to observe spring migrants. Among the possibilities are Red-naped Sapsuckers, Green-tailed Towhees, Dusky and Hammond's Flycatchers, and various warblers and sparrows.

There is no particular hot spot—it's all pretty much the same. In the center of the cemetery is an area used by maintenance staff, which contains a small amount of brush along the banks of a shallow wash. This cover is worth visiting for a chance to discover sparrows or warblers, foraging in the undergrowth. Although you can drive any of the roads (at least in snow-free months), you'll discover more birds by parking outside the cemetery and walking in.

Directions: The City Cemetery is extensive and has numerous entrances, not all of which may be open. The cemetery lies between N Street (on the west) and U Street (on the east), and 11th Avenue (on the north) and Fourth Avenue (on the south). From Main Street in Salt Lake City, proceed east on North Temple (which immediately becomes Second Avenue). Turn left on B Street and continue to 11th Avenue, where you should turn right. Proceed 1.2 miles and enter the cemetery by car or foot at one of the numerous gates.

General information: The City Cemetery is an oasis of calm in the midst of Salt Lake City and well worth a couple of hours if you're in town.

Birding at the City Cemetery in Salt Lake City.

47 City Cemetery

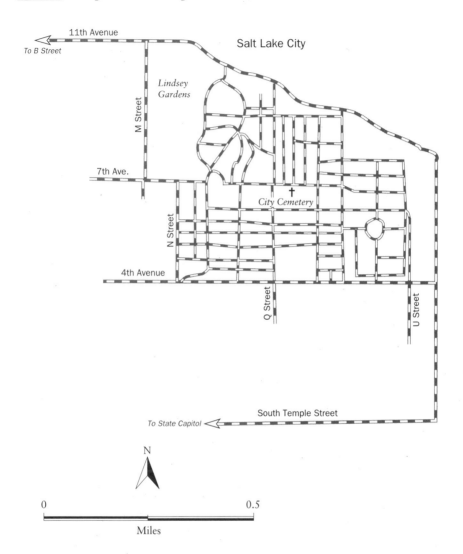

ADDITIONAL INFORMATION

Map grid: 5D
Elevation: 4,800 feet.
Hazards: None.
Nearest food, gas, and lodging: Salt Lake City.
Camping: Camp VIP, Salt Lake City.
For more information: Utah Travel Council.

48 Parley's Historic and Nature Area

Habitats: Lowland riparian, pinyon-juniper, upland desert shrub
Specialty birds: Western Screech-Owl; Western Wood-Pewee (spring
and fall); Willow (spring and fall), Hammond's (spring and fall), Dusky
(spring and fall), and Gray (spring and fall) Flycatchers; Northern
Shrike (winter); American Dipper
Other key birds: Sharp-shinned and Cooper's Hawks; California Quail;
Black-chinned, Calliope (fall), Broad-tailed, and Rufous (fall)
Hummingbirds; Red-naped Sapsucker (spring and fall); Downy and
Hairy Woodpeckers; Cordilleran Flycatcher (spring and fall); Cliff and
Barn Swallows; Western Scrub-Jay; Black-billed Magpie; Mountain
Chickadee (winter); Bewick's and House Wrens; Blue-gray
Gnatcatcher; Orange-crowned (spring and fall), Nashville (spring and
fall), Yellow, and Virginia's (spring and fall) Warblers; Western
Tanager; Lincoln's, Harris's (winter) Sparrows; Black-headed
Grosbeak; Bullock's Oriole
Best times to bird: Diversity is greatest during spring and fall
migration, April through May and September through mid-October;
interesting during breeding season (May through mid-July) as well.

The birding: This is a remnant of natural habitat saved from development, which
encroaches from all sides. Parley's Creek empties from the mouth of its namesake
canyon and flows through this park, nurturing the riparian zone and providing a
stopover for numerous species of passerines.

From the parking area, walk downhill onto the valley floor. You'll descend
through a few Gambel oaks (which here constitute the "pinyon-juniper" zone)
before reaching groves of box elder and cottonwood trees. In this drier upland
zone, Black-billed Magpies and Western Scrub-Jays are two of the noisier, if not
most common, species.

The habitat in this valley is a patchwork of sagebrush, brushy oak, and riparian; you're as likely to see a species in one place as another. One exception, of
course, is the American Dipper, which will be somewhere in the creek corridor.
These birds need exposed perches (rocks) in the creek, so if the water is running
too high and covers the perches, the birds will be elsewhere in the watershed.
Spend some time lingering on one of the bridges crossing the creek. Sooner or
later, a dipper should fly up or down the creek.

The park is not large, so a good strategy is to spend an hour or two strolling
around the major trail looping through the area. This will take you along the creek
in several places as well as through more upland habitat. Listen for bird activity,
and take advantage of the numerous informal trails penetrating the vegetation to
try to get closer to the birds.

Directions: From I-80 east in south Salt Lake City, take Exit 171 (2300 East Street
exit). Immediately after the exit ramp curves right, turn left onto Heritage Way
(2760 South), and proceed to the intersection with 2700 East. There is a stop sign
here, and on your left is a small parking area and the gated road leading into the

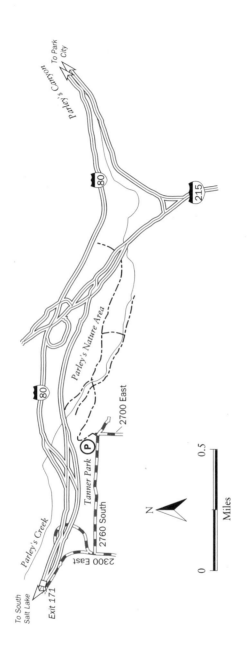

nature area. If this lot is full, backtrack a few feet and park in one of the Tanner Park parking lots.

General information: The park is open from 8 A.M. to 11 P.M., not exactly optimal birding hours, so plan your visit accordingly. The park is also a popular after-work destination for dog owners, mountain bikers, and anyone looking for a place to stretch their legs, so don't expect a wilderness experience.

ADDITIONAL INFORMATION

Map grid: 4D
Elevation: 4,722 feet.
Hazards: none.
Nearest food, gas, and lodging: Salt Lake City.
Camping: Tanner's Flat Campground, Wasatch-Cache National Forest.
For more information: Utah Travel Council.

49 Desolation Trail, Mill Creek Canyon

Habitats: Spruce-fir, pinyon-juniper, mountain riparian
Specialty birds: Northern Goshawk; Blue Grouse; Flammulated Owl; Northern Pygmy-Owl; White-throated Swift; Olive-sided and Dusky Flycatchers; Clark's Nutcracker; American Dipper; Townsend's Solitaire; Swainson's Thrush; Green-tailed Towhee
Other key birds: Golden Eagle; Northern Saw-whet Owl; Black-chinned and Broad-tailed Hummingbirds; Warbling Vireo; Steller's Jay; Western Scrub-Jay; Violet-green Swallow; Mountain Chickadee; Ruby-crowned Kinglet; Hermit Thrush; Orange-crowned, Yellow, and Yellow-rumped Warblers; Western Tanager; Black-headed Grosbeak
Best times to bird: May through mid-July

The birding: Mill Creek Canyon is one of several heavily vegetated and well-watered canyons descending from the Wasatch Mountains into Salt Lake City. A popular year-round destination for a variety of recreationists, the entire canyon can make for interesting birding. Desolation Trail, described here, is just one of many possibilities.

Before hitting the trail, take time to explore the parking area. It's adjacent to Mill Creek, and the box elders and spruces here can be full of bird activity. It's also worth crossing the road to explore a short section of the creek, looking in particular for American Dippers. To do this, walk through the South Box Elder Picnic Area, where paved trails meander through the forest and along the stream. If you fail to find dippers here, consider driving a mile or two up the canyon and search from other pullouts upstream.

Desolation Trail climbs gently at first through a mature conifer forest, then rises more steeply through mixed fir and oaks, and crosses into the Mount Olympus

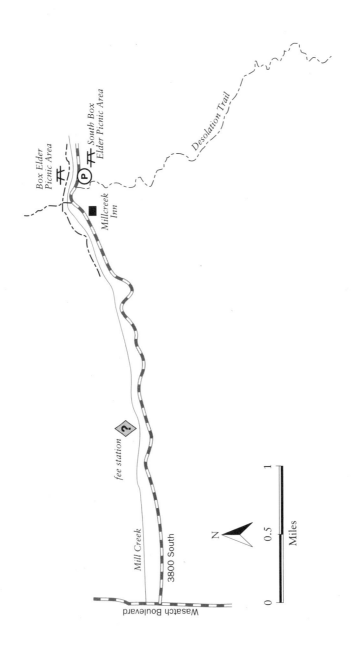

Wilderness Area. The trail is quite long—almost 18 miles—but you need only travel the first 2 miles for a good experience. This is where you'll likely find little pockets of high bird activity. Take some time to listen and observe in these hot spots, moving on as the birds move to forage elsewhere. Keep an eye on the ridgetops for raptors riding the thermals, and to the cliff face on the opposite canyon wall where swifts and swallows hunt insects.

Directions: From I-215 in Salt Lake City, take Exit 3 and proceed south on Wasatch Boulevard. Turn left on 3800 South and proceed into Mill Creek Canyon. From the fee station, South Box Elder Picnic Area and the Desolation Trailhead lie 2.6 miles away, near milepost 3. The parking area is well signed, on the right side of the road just a few yards beyond Millcreek Inn.

General information: Mill Creek provides part of Salt Lake City's drinking water needs. Consequently there are restrictions on use of the area, particularly for dogs and horses. You can also expect to pay a modest user fee of about $2.25 per car, which is sometimes collected as you leave the area and sometimes when you enter.

ADDITIONAL INFORMATION

Map grid: 5D
Elevation: 5,800 feet.
Hazards: none.
Nearest food, gas, and lodging: Salt Lake City.
Camping: The Spruces Campground, Wasatch-Cache National Forest.
For more information: Wasatch-Cache National Forest, Salt Lake Ranger District.

50 The Spruces Campground

Habitats: Spruce-fir, aspen, mountain riparian, mountain meadow
Specialty birds: Hammond's and Dusky Flycatchers; Western Wood-Pewee; Olive-sided Flycatcher; American Dipper; Townsend's Solitaire; Swainson's Thrush; Green-tailed Towhee; Pine Grosbeak; Lazuli Bunting
Other key birds: Turkey Vulture; Cooper's Hawk; Golden Eagle; Black-chinned, Broad-tailed, and Rufous (mid-July to August) Hummingbirds; Red-naped Sapsucker; Hairy and Downy Woodpeckers; Cordilleran Flycatcher; Warbling Vireo; Steller's Jay; Tree, Violet-green, and Cliff Swallows; Mountain Chickadee; Red-breasted and White-breasted Nuthatches; Ruby-crowned Kinglet; Mountain Bluebird; Hermit Thrush; Orange-crowned, Virginia's, Yellow, Yellow-rumped, and MacGillivray's Warblers; Western Tanager; Chipping, Fox, Song, and Lincoln's Sparrows; Black-headed Grosbeak; Cassin's Finch; Pine Siskin; American Goldfinch
Best times to bird: Late May through mid-July

50 The Spruces Campground

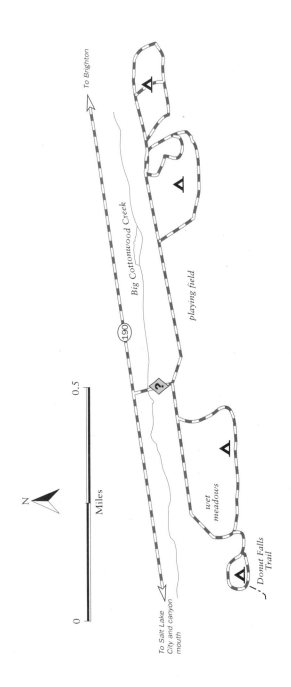

The birding: The Spruces Campground offers great birding in an easily accessed montane forest. After leaving UT 190 and passing the entrance station, you have a choice of two major loops in the campground. Each offers a different experience, and both loops are easily walked. If you're visiting only long enough to walk the loops, continue straight from the entrance station, park along the forest edge, and begin your walk. If you're staying overnight, choose a campsite and walk from there.

The right-hand, or lower canyon, loop is heavily forested in conifers, with a few aspens and open wet meadows. These little openings seem to be the focus of bird activity, and it's easier to locate birds traveling through or foraging. Look for Olive-sided Flycatchers, which call from the tops of the firs, hummingbirds, other species of flycatchers, Steller's Jays, and sparrows.

The left-hand or upper canyon loop is also heavily forested, but aspens dominate. Swainson's Thrushes seem particularly abundant. This side of the loop also seems to be better for Tree Swallows, Mountain Chickadees, Hermit Thrushes, warblers, and Black-headed Grosbeaks.

As you walk either of these loops, keep an eye toward the northern ridge, where Turkey Vultures and Golden Eagles occasionally soar. Make a few forays through unoccupied campsites to check out the creek corridor—you may see American Dippers.

Directions: To reach The Spruces Campground, head south from Salt Lake City on I-15. Take Exit 301 (7200 South) and head east on UT 48. In about 5 miles you'll reach the mouth of Big Cottonwood Canyon, where you'll pick up UT 190. The Spruces Campground is on the right side of the road, about 10 miles from the canyon mouth.

General information: Expect a day use fee of $5 or a camping fee of $11. Because of the high altitude, don't expect to find it open until June. You may have to park outside the gate and walk in if you arrive here in late May.

ADDITIONAL INFORMATION

Map grid: 5D
Elevation: 8,100 feet.
Hazards: None.
Nearest food, gas, and lodging: Midvale.
Camping: On-site.
For more information: Wasatch-Cache National Forest, Salt Lake Ranger District.

51 Silver Lake Boardwalk

Habitats: Mountain riparian, mountain meadow, spruce-fir, aspen
Specialty birds: Blue Grouse; Three-toed Woodpecker; Hammond's and Dusky Flycatchers; Western Wood-Pewee; Olive-sided Flycatcher; Townsend's Solitaire; Swainson's Thrush; Lazuli Bunting; Black Rosy-Finch; Pine Grosbeak; Red Crossbill
Other key birds: Cooper's Hawk; Black-chinned and Broad-tailed Hummingbirds; Red-naped Sapsucker; Downy and Hairy Woodpeckers; Cordilleran Flycatcher; Warbling Vireo; Steller's Jay; Tree, Violet-green, and Cliff Swallows; Mountain Chickadee; Red-breasted and White-breasted Nuthatches; Ruby-crowned Kinglet; Mountain Bluebird; Hermit Thrush; Orange-crowned, Virginia's, Yellow, Yellow-rumped, MacGillivray's, and Wilson's Warblers; Western Tanager; Chipping, Fox, Song, and Lincoln's Sparrows; Cassin's Finch; Pine Siskin; American Goldfinch
Best times to bird: June through mid-July

The birding: The Silver Lake Boardwalk is an easily hiked, level loop around an extensive high-altitude riparian complex. At the far end of the loop, the trail passes through a stand of conifers and exposes you briefly to a rocky scree slope and some small stands of aspen.

The open wet meadow is a good area for swallows, warblers, and sparrows. These species nest in the low, shrubby willow thickets that line the boardwalk. The fir stand at the far end of the lake is a good area for woodpeckers, Olive-sided and Hammond's Flycatchers, nuthatches, Pine Grosbeaks, and Red Crossbills. White-winged Crossbills also show up, but their occurrence is rare and unpredictable. As you round the far end of the trail and begin working back, you'll pass through sparse aspens and may be able to add Blue Grouse to your sightings.

Directions: Head south from Salt Lake City on I-15. Take Exit 301 (7200 South) and head east on UT 48. In about 5 miles you'll reach the mouth of Big Cottonwood Canyon, where you'll pick up UT 190. Your destination is Brighton, located at the head of the canyon about 14 miles from the canyon mouth. At the head of the canyon, the road ends in a one-way loop that winds through Brighton. Bear right, continue about 0.1 mile and turn right into the parking lot of the Solitude Nordic Center. Silver Lake lies behind the Nordic Center.

General information: The Silver Lake Boardwalk is only one of many options for hikes in this area, although the other hikes involve varying amounts of climbing. If you strike out with species like Three-toed Woodpeckers, Clark's Nutcrackers, and Black Rosy-Finches, you might consider taking one of the nearby trails up to higher elevations.

The Silver Lake Boardwalk allows viewers into the heart of a willow marsh.

51 Silver Lake Boardwalk

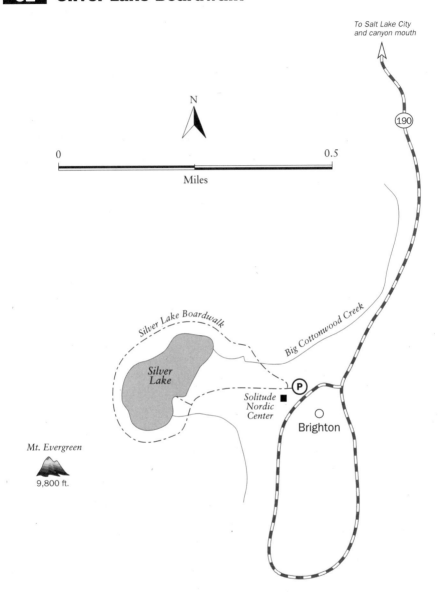

ADDITIONAL INFORMATION

Map grid: 5D
Elevation: 8,730 feet.
Hazards: Temperature extremes, biting insects.
Nearest food, gas, and lodging: Midvale.
Camping: Redman Campground (seasonal), Wasatch-Cache National Forest.
For more information: Wasatch-Cache National Forest, Salt Lake Ranger District.

52 Tanner's Flat Campground and Albion Basin, Little Cottonwood Canyon

Habitats: Mountain meadow, spruce-fir, aspen, mountain riparian
Specialty birds: Blue Grouse; Three-toed Woodpecker; Hammond's and Dusky Flycatchers; Western Wood-Pewee; Olive-sided Flycatcher; Clark's Nutcracker; American Dipper; Townsend's Solitaire; Swainson's Thrush; American Pipit; Green-tailed Towhee; Lazuli Bunting; Black Rosy-Finch; Pine Grosbeak; Red Crossbill
Other key birds: Cooper's Hawk; Black-chinned, Broad-tailed, Calliope, and Rufous (late July-August) Hummingbirds; Downy and Hairy Woodpeckers; Cordilleran Flycatcher; Warbling Vireo; Steller's Jay; Tree, Violet-green, and Cliff Swallows; Mountain Chickadee; Red-breasted and White-breasted Nuthatches; Ruby-crowned Kinglet; Mountain Bluebird; Hermit Thrush; Orange-crowned, Virginia's, Yellow, Yellow-rumped, and MacGillivray's Warblers; Western Tanager; Chipping, Vesper, Song, and White-crowned Sparrows; Cassin's Finch; Pine Siskin; American Goldfinch
Best times to bird: May through mid-July

The birding: Little Cottonwood Canyon can be quite interesting, but there are not many places to park and access the surrounding terrain. Tanner's Flat Campground, about halfway up Little Cottonwood, offers both. The campground is heavily vegetated in aspens and conifers, and Little Cottonwood Creek borders the area to the south.

Park in the picnic area (assuming you're not staying overnight) and explore the area on foot. The campground is fairly small and there is not a particular destination within it for birding, but be sure to explore along the rushing creek, where you may find American Dippers. You should also explore some of the upland slope, getting away from the creek to hear some bird calls. As you walk the campground roads, you'll encounter a few small openings in the woods, and these too are worth checking out. They hold a few wildflowers which attract a preponderance of hummingbirds.

At the head of Little Cottonwood Canyon lies Albion Basin, a magnificent, high-altitude cirque. In summer the basin is full of wildflowers that attract four species of hummingbirds, and the surrounding terrain holds breeding birds representing some of the more sought-after montane species. One of the best routes is a short, easy hike to a small lake nestled against one side of this cirque, with an option to extend your birding into some nearby trailless areas.

From the trailhead at the Albion Basin Campground, follow the trail to Cecret Lake (variously spelled Secret). The trail climbs 420 vertical feet in the course of its 0.75 mile, with numerous signed interpretive stops along the way. The trail passes mostly through meadows but also through small stands of timber. There is good birding all the way.

Cecret Lake sits against a rocky scree slope that extends around to the south and east of the basin. Both American Pipits and Black Rosy-Finches prefer these

52 Tanner's Flat Campground and Little Cottonwood Canyon

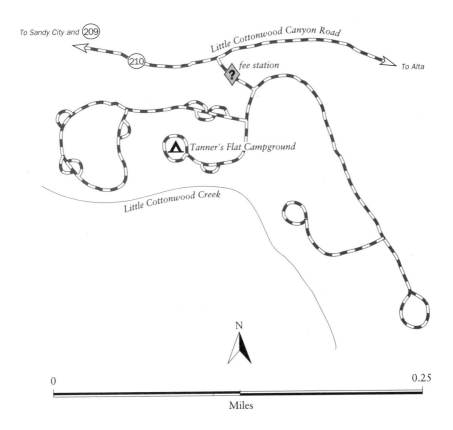

rocky slopes and nest in these areas. If you'd like to pursue these species or just extend your walk, depart from Cecret Lake and strike out cross-country, heading east and following the base of the steep mountainside. Orienteering is easy in this basin, but a good landmark is the ski lift you encounter about 0.75 mile east of Cecret Lake. Follow this lift line downhill to the Cecret Lake Trail, a distance of about 0.6 mile, turn right on the trail, and return about 0.2 mile to the parking area.

Directions: The mouth of Little Cottonwood Canyon is reached by following I-15 south of Salt Lake City to Sandy City and Exit 298 (UT 209). The route is well signed (for Snowbird and Alta Resorts). Follow UT 209 east to the mouth of the canyon, a distance of about 5 miles. Tanner's Flat Campground is on the right (south) side of the road, about 4.5 miles from the mouth of Little Cottonwood Canyon. Albion Basin lies at the end of the road (which becomes UT 210 when you enter the canyon), 10.9 miles from the canyon mouth. The road ends in a loop and a parking area for the Cecret Lake Trailhead.

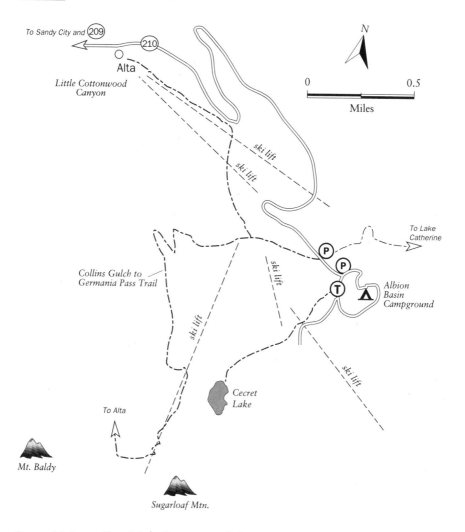

General information: Little Cottonwood Canyon is a major North American ski-ing destination, in part because the heavy snowfall can linger long into summer. If you travel here in early May, you may find more snow than leaves, and you may have to park outside the Tanner's Flat Campground gate and walk. Likewise, depending on snowfall, you may not be able to drive all the way to the road's end at Albion Basin. You may have to settle for a long hike in, or change your plans to investigate another spot around the Alta and Snowbird ski resorts.

Expect to pay a day use fee of $5, or $10 if you camp overnight at Tanner's Flat Campground. Weather in these high mountains can change rapidly, so be prepared. Water from streams or lakes must be treated before drinking.

ADDITIONAL INFORMATION

Map grid: 5D

Elevation: 7,200 to 9,500 feet.

Hazards: High altitude, temperature extremes.

Nearest food, gas, and lodging: Sandy City.

Camping: Tanner's Flat Campground or Albion Basin Campground (both seasonal).

For more information: Wasatch-Cache National Forest, Salt Lake Ranger District.

53 Mount Timpanogos Trail

Habitats: Mountain riparian, aspen, spruce-fir

Specialty birds: White-throated Swift; Olive-sided, Hammond's, and Dusky Flycatchers; American Dipper; Townsend's Solitaire; Green-tailed Towhee; Lazuli Bunting

Other key birds: Calliope (July to August), Broad-tailed, and Rufous (July to August) Hummingbirds; Cordilleran Flycatcher; Warbling Vireo; Red-naped Sapsucker; Hairy Woodpecker; Violet-green Swallow; Steller's Jay; Mountain Chickadee; House Wren; Golden-crowned and Ruby-crowned Kinglets; Hermit Thrush; Orange-crowned, Virginia's, Yellow, Yellow-rumped, and MacGillivray's Warblers; Western Tanager; Black-headed Grosbeak; Cassin's Finch

Best times to bird: Late-May through mid-July

A cool, rainy day on the Mount Timpanogos Trail.

53 Mount Timpanogos Trail

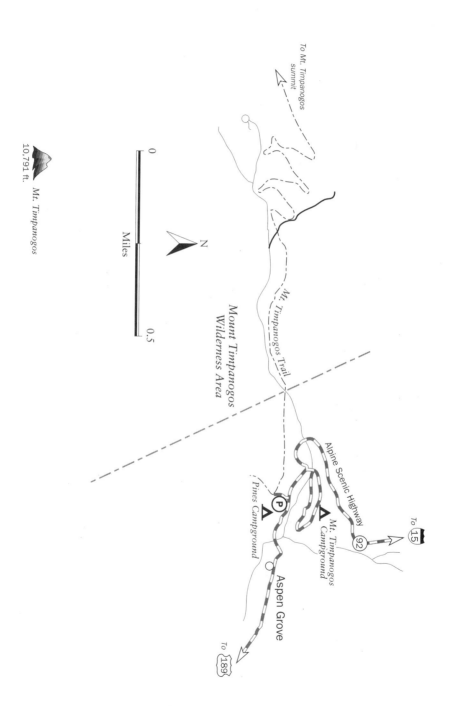

To Mt. Timpanogos summit

Mt. Timpanogos
10,791 ft.

N

Miles

0

0.5

Mount Timpanogos
Wilderness Area

Mt. Timpanogos Trail

Alpine Scenic Highway

Pines Campground

P

Mt. Timpanogos
Campground

Aspen Grove

To 15

92

To 189

The birding: Frequent avalanches maintain the habitats in this canyon, a complex of montane forests at various successional stages. Along this short 1.5-mile-long trail you'll encounter aspens, mountain maples, Gambel oak, a noisy mountain stream, and scattered spruce and fir.

The lower portion of the trail near the parking area passes through older vegetation, where you may encounter warblers, woodpeckers, flycatchers, and the Ruby-crowned Kinglet. In a short distance the trail reaches the creek draining this watershed, and you may see American Dippers, flying from rock to rock and ducking beneath the rushing stream. Higher still the vegetation is younger, and the destructive effects of avalanche activity is apparent in the bent trunks of the living trees and the scattered debris of trees ripped from the hillsides. As the path becomes more open, scan the cliff sides for swifts. It's also in this younger forest that you'll likely encounter hummingbirds, Green-tailed Towhees, and possibly warblers and flycatchers.

Directions: From I-15 in Orem, take Exit 275. Continue east on UT 52 to the mouth of Provo Canyon, where you'll turn left onto US 189 and continue into the canyon. About 6 miles from the canyon mouth, turn north on UT 92—this is the access road to the Sundance Resort, and the turn is well signed. Continue on this road for about 5 miles. The parking area for the Mount Timpanogos Trailhead is well signed, visible on the left just after you cross a creek at the boundary of Aspen Grove.

General information: The breeding season in this high and rugged mountain valley starts late in the year, and therefore tends to run a bit later than in other areas.

This section of the Mount Timpanogos Trail is heavily used; the lower section is cobbled with coarse gravel, while a short section before the Lower and Upper Falls is paved. Avalanches and freeze-thaw cycles keep the trail in constant need of repair. It is possible to continue beyond the Upper Falls, the end of the proposed birding hike, but this is a more serious undertaking. Timpanogos is one of the highest mountains in Utah (11,957 feet), and you can expect winter weather every month of the year.

ADDITIONAL INFORMATION

Map grid: 5E
Elevation: 6,900 feet.
Hazards: None.
Nearest food, gas, and lodging: Orem.
Camping: Mount Timpanogos Campground, Uinta National Forest.
For more information: Uinta National Forest, Pleasant Grove Ranger District.

54 Squaw Peak Trail

Habitats: Pinyon-juniper, spruce-fir
Specialty birds: Black Swift
Other key birds: Ruffed and Blue Grouse; Western Scrub-Jay; White-throated Swift; Yellow-rumped and Virginia's Warblers
Best times to bird: Early mornings before 9 A.M. and late afternoons for Black Swifts

The birding: In this vegetation zone, the "pinyon-juniper" belt has actually been replaced by Gambel oak. The replacement is so extensive that the oak is almost a monoculture. From the turnoff from US 189 and the start of the climb up Squaw Peak Trail Road, you'll see a scattering of spruce trees among the oaks—the only diversity other than sheer cliff faces in this landscape.

54 Squaw Peak Trail

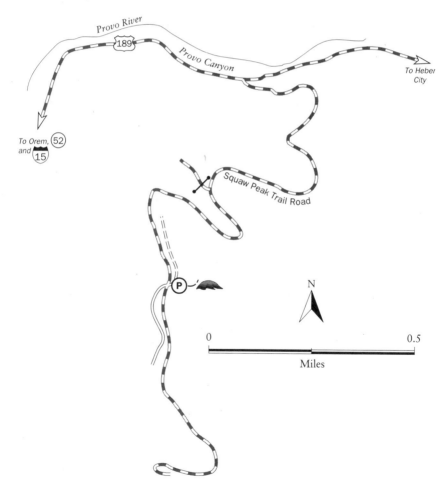

This is one of the few reliable spots in the state for Black Swifts. They make daily movements both up and down the canyon, so the best times to find them are in the mornings before about 9 a.m., and then again in late afternoon, generally an hour or two before sunset.

From the parking area, walk the short distance to the top of the knoll on the east side of the road—this is the viewpoint. The swifts fly overhead, and it is often easiest to spot them if you scan for movement against the towering cliffs to the east.

Directions: From I-15 in Orem, take Exit 275. Drive east on UT 52 to the mouth of Provo Canyon, where you'll turn left onto US 189 and continue into the canyon. The road to Squaw Peak Trail is 1.9 miles up the canyon on the right; look for a sign 0.5 mile before the turn. The road itself is unmarked; if you see a sign for Springdell, you've passed your turn.

From the intersection of Squaw Peak Trail Road and US 189, proceed another 1.4 miles to where a rough, single-lane dirt track crosses the road—park on this dirt road, which is gated and otherwise unused. Again, look carefully or you'll miss it. If you see the Uinta National Forest sign on the right side of the road, you've gone a couple of hundred yards too far.

General information: As you continue up Squaw Peak Trail Road, a number of side trails and four-wheel-drive tracks depart from the road. To explore further, look for one of these other tracks and try your luck with a short hike.

ADDITIONAL INFORMATION

Map grid: 5E
Elevation: 5,522 feet.
Hazards: none.
Nearest food, gas, and lodging: Orem.
Camping: Hope Campground, Uinta National Forest.
For more information: Uinta National Forest, Pleasant Grove Ranger District.

55 Botany Pond—BYU Campus

Habitat: Spruce-fir

Specialty birds: Western Screech-Owl; Western Wood-Pewee; Clark's Nutcracker (winter)

Other key birds: Sharp-shinned and Cooper's Hawks; Black-chinned, Calliope, Broad-tailed, and Rufous (fall) Hummingbirds; Plumbeous and Warbling Vireos; Red-naped Sapsucker; Cordilleran Flycatcher; Western Scrub-Jay; Mountain Chickadee (winter); Red-breasted and White-breasted Nuthatches; Brown Creeper; Bewick's and House Wrens; Ruby-crowned Kinglet; Hermit Thrush; Bohemian (winter), and Cedar Waxwings; Yellow, Yellow-rumped, MacGillivray's, and Wilson's (spring) Warblers; Western Tanager; Song Sparrow; Black-headed Grosbeak; Cassin's Finch (winter)

Best times to bird: Early mornings during breeding season, or throughout the day during spring (April through May) and fall (September through mid-October)

The birding: This site is a forested greenspace on the campus of Brigham Young University. BYU planted this three-block hillside, and the result is a mixed conifer-deciduous forest that more closely resembles an eastern forest than anything in Utah.

The conifers are more or less evenly dispersed with deciduous species, so there is no one place to seek out a particular species. At mid-elevation on the hillside grove, a paved trail runs along a canal, with numerous side trails departing to the street below or uphill to the campus.

Take a leisurely stroll along any or all of the paths in the grove, exploring the undergrowth and the trees for bird activity. The lower area of the forest along 800 North is planted in lawn grass, so the more natural upslope area is more appealing to birds. Still, the area is small enough that it is easy to bird the entire area in a short period of time.

Directions: From I-15 in Provo, take Exit 266 (University Avenue) and head north. At the intersection with 800 North, turn right (east). There are several access points, all located between 200 East and 500 East. Park on the roadside and enter at any of the paved walkways that enter the campus forest.

General information: If you have a little time to burn in the Provo area, the John Hutchings Museum of Natural History, in nearby Lehi, has an interesting collection of artifacts, including some bird specimens. The museum is located at 53 North Center Street in Lehi. Hours are variable, so it's worth calling ahead (801-768-7180) to make sure the museum is open before paying a visit.

55 Botany Pond—BYU Campus

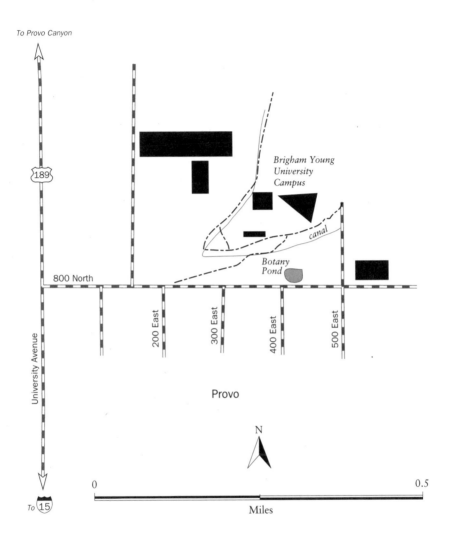

ADDITIONAL INFORMATION

Map grid: 5E
Elevation: 4,610 feet.
Hazards: None.
Nearest food, gas, and lodging: Provo.
Camping: Utah Lake State Park, Provo.
For more information: Utah Travel Council.

190

56 Midway Fish Hatchery

Habitat: Lowland riparian
Specialty birds: Sandhill Crane; Western Wood-Pewee; Willow Flycatcher
Other key birds: Black-crowned Night-Heron; White-faced Ibis; Cinnamon Teal; Virginia Rail; Sora; Spotted Sandpiper; Osprey; California Gull; Broad-tailed Hummingbird; Belted Kingfisher; Violet-green, Northern Rough-winged, and Cliff Swallows; Black-billed Magpie; House Wren; Gray Catbird; Yellow Warbler; Common Yellowthroat; Yellow-breasted Chat; Savannah, Fox, Song, and Lincoln's Sparrows; Black-headed Grosbeak; Bobolink; Brewer's Blackbird; Bullock's Oriole; American Goldfinch
Best times to bird: May through mid-July

The birding: This site begins at the springs developed by the State of Utah as a water source for the Midway Fish Hatchery and follows the watercourse as it passes along a narrow riparian corridor through wet meadows and pastureland, en route to the nearby Provo River.

Park in the signed parking lot for the hatchery, read the list of posted rules on the bulletin board by the parking lot, and then head down between the concrete raceways. Much to the dismay of fish farmers, these raceways attract a large variety of piscivorous (fish-eating) birds, and you may see Great Blue Herons, Snowy Egrets, Black-Crowned Night-Herons, or Belted Kingfishers.

Follow the raceways to their terminus. From here the stream continues southward, diverted through a series of canals and ponds in which trout are raised. Follow the road that pursues the stream bank, birding the Russian olives, cottonwoods, and shrub thickets. Various species of sparrows are usually about, as well as Marsh Wrens and Bullock's Orioles. In the surrounding fields you are likely to hear and see Sandhill Cranes, White-faced Ibis, and, if you're lucky, a Bobolink. There are Ospreys, too, nesting in platforms on the high branches of dead cottonwoods, and you may see one of these "fish hawks" over the hatchery ponds or perched near one of their nests.

The walk to the end of the property is about a mile in length.

Directions: In the town of Midway, turn south on Center Street, which is also called East Charlestown Road. Proceed 8.5 blocks to 850 South, where you'll see a left turn well signed for the Midway Fish Hatchery. Turn into this drive and proceed the short distance to the parking area at the head of the raceways.

General information: The hatchery is open from 8:00 A.M. to 4:30 P.M., so you'll have to do your birding between these hours.

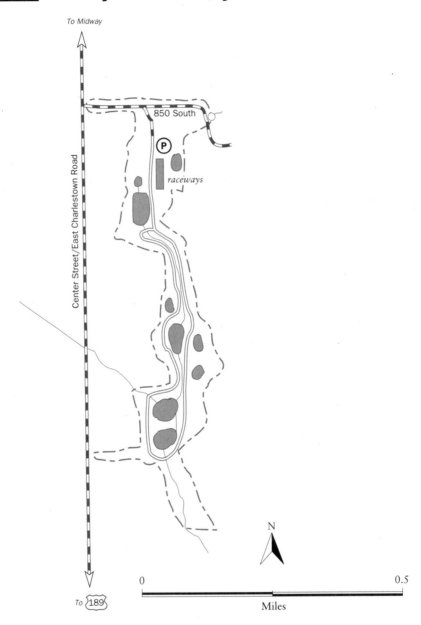

ADDITIONAL INFORMATION

Map grid: 5D
Elevation: 5,450 feet.
Hazards: None.
Nearest food, gas, and lodging: Midway.
Camping: Wasatch Mountain State Park.
For more information: Utah Division of Wildlife Resources.

57 Jordanelle HawkWatch Site

Habitat: Pinyon-juniper
Specialty birds: Bald Eagle; Northern Goshawk; Ferruginous Hawk; Peregrine and Prairie Falcons; Blue Grouse
Other key birds: Turkey Vulture; Osprey; Northern Harrier; Sharp-shinned, Cooper's, Broad-winged, Swainson's, Red-tailed, and Rough-legged Hawks; Golden Eagle; American Kestrel; Merlin
Best times to bird: March through April

The birding: The pinyon-juniper forest in this zone is actually dominated by oaks, but habitat is not what this site is about. The Jordanelle HawkWatch Site, located on a knoll, offers an excellent opportunity to observe the spring migration of several species of raptors.

Between February 26 and May 6, 1997, their first season of counting at this site, HawkWatch International observers recorded 5,049 raptors representing 17 species, for an average of 10.6 hawks per hour. Peak spring migration occurs between mid-March and mid-April, at which time anywhere from 10 to 20 individuals pass the observation post each hour. The species of raptors that HawkWatch records here vary dramatically in their abundance: Turkey Vultures, Bald Eagles, and Red-tailed Hawks comprise 65 percent of the birds seen. At the opposite extreme, only one Broad-winged Hawk was recorded at this site. The best times to bird at this site are between the hours of 9 a.m. and 2 p.m. Peak daily migration occurs during the 11 a.m. hour, with an average of about 16 birds passing the lookout.

Getting to this site requires a little forethought, because weather conditions in March and April are variable, and snow may dictate where you can park and hike. However, it's likely that HawkWatch volunteers will be using the area and will establish an informal but visible parking spot and hiking route to the top of the knoll. If the ground is clear of snow and you are able to pull to the parking area below US 40 (described in **Directions**), then the route you will take to the top of the knoll will involve following the ridge that heads north and slightly west to the knoll. Look first for evidence of a trail packed down by HawkWatch observers; otherwise, you're on your own. The route is short, about 1.2 miles. Remember, you're *not* aiming for those towering peaks looming on the horizon; rather, you're headed for the mid-elevation knoll in the foreground. Pick your way through the scrub oak, careful of ice or mud, and position yourself on the knoll for viewing.

57 Jordanelle HawkWatch Site

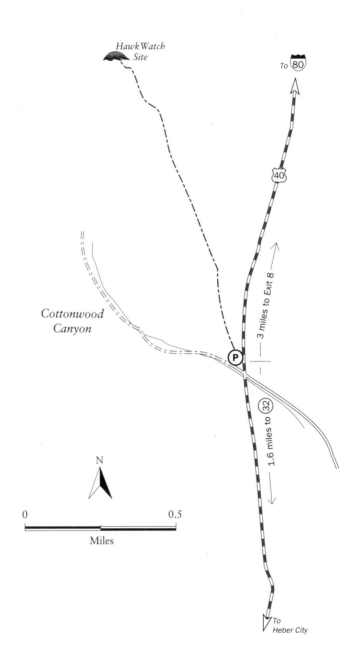

Raptors move from the Heber Valley to the south, over this knoll and ridge line beside the Provo River, and then northward toward their summer range.

Directions: To reach the current access point, you must be traveling southbound on US 40 from the direction of the intersection of US 40 and I-80. If you're northbound from Heber City on US 40, take the Mayflower exit (Exit 8) by Jordanelle Reservoir and reverse direction. Mark your mileage from the Mayflower exit; it's 3.0 miles to the access point, which lies on the right side of the road. Another landmark is the large and prominent road cut on the right side of the road as you head south—just beyond this road cut a creek drainage descends to the interstate. There is a dirt road that descends about 100 yards from the interstate to the bottom of this creek. This is a good place to park, but if there is snow cover and you're not equipped to drive in snow, park well off the shoulder of the road by the interstate and walk into the creek bottom. From this parking area, face north. The knoll that you are to hike to rises just slightly to your left. Look for a trail or path left by the HawkWatch observers as they entered.

General information: Be prepared for intemperate weather. HawkWatch observers suggest the use of snowshoes to reach the site in the latter part of the observation period, when the snow softens and thaws. Winds here are frequent and temperatures range from 0 to 70 degrees F; a sunny day makes for the most comfortable visit.

As this book heads to press, HawkWatch International is in the midst of working with the landowning agency—the Bureau of Reclamation—to develop this area as a Watchable Wildlife site. If the BuRec has the resources, they will install a parking area along Cottonwood Creek, probably improve the access road, and develop a trail to the top of the observation knoll. I have provided directions for reaching the observation site via the current undeveloped access route. You may wish to contact the BuRec to learn about current conditions at this site.

ADDITIONAL INFORMATION

Map grid: 5D
Elevation: 6,740 feet.
Hazards: Snow, cold temperatures.
Nearest food, gas, and lodging: Heber City.
Camping: Jordanelle Reservoir State Park.
For more information: Bureau of Reclamation, Salt Lake Field Office.

58 Rock Cliff Recreation Area

Habitats: Mountain riparian, upland desert shrub, aspen, mountain meadow

Specialty birds: Bald Eagle (spring and fall); Lewis's Woodpecker; Willow Flycatcher; Northern Shrike (winter); American Dipper; Green-tailed and Spotted Towhees

Other key birds: Common Loon (spring and fall); Western (spring and fall) and Eared (spring and fall) Grebes; Northern Pintail (spring and fall); Gadwall (spring and fall); Green-winged Teal (spring and fall); Common Merganser; Osprey; Northern Harrier; Sharp-shinned and Swainson's Hawks; Snowy Egret (spring and fall); Least Sandpiper (spring and fall); Common Snipe; California Gull; Forster's Tern; Short-eared Owl; Common Nighthawk; Black-chinned and Broad-tailed Hummingbirds; Belted Kingfisher; Downy Woodpecker; Plumbeous and Warbling Vireos; Black-billed Magpie; Tree, Violet-green, Northern Rough-winged, Bank, Cliff, and Barn Swallows; Mountain Bluebird; House Wren; Gray Catbird; Cedar Waxwing (spring and fall); Yellow and Yellow-rumped Warblers; Chipping, Brewer's, Fox, Song, Lincoln's, and White-crowned Sparrows; Bullock's Oriole; Cassin's Finch; American Goldfinch

Best times to bird: Mid-April through mid-May and September through mid-October for migrant songbirds; May through July for breeding birds

The birding: The Rock Cliff Recreation Area encompasses the mouth of the Provo River and a short section of its course just before it enters Jordanelle Reservoir. The river valley is narrow and constrained on one side by a rock cliff (thus the name) and on the other by a steep mountainside in sagebrush and, higher up, a pinyon-juniper forest.

Access to this area is made easy by virtue of the Nature Center and its associated complex of boardwalks. Start at the Nature Center, where bird feeders and hummingbird feeders hang from the back deck. This may be the best opportunity for viewing Broad-tailed and Black-chinned Hummingbirds in the area. If you're lucky, something more exotic than House Finches may show up at the other bird feeders.

The walkways around the Nature Center meander through the riparian corridor, which in spring can be more river than marsh. The boardwalks and the cottonwood forest are great places to view warblers, Brewer's Blackbirds, and both Plumbeous and Warbling Vireos. When the area is flooded, ducks (usually Mallards) may be foraging in the rivulets coursing through the trees.

Be sure to continue across the Provo River (via the bridge) from the Nature Center's boardwalks. If you turn left after crossing this bridge, you'll enter a small grove of aspens, where you'll see many of the same species as in the nearby cottonwoods. From here the trail turns back into the meadow, a good spot for Mountain Bluebirds, Cliff Swallows, and various species of sparrows.

58 Rock Cliff Recreation Area

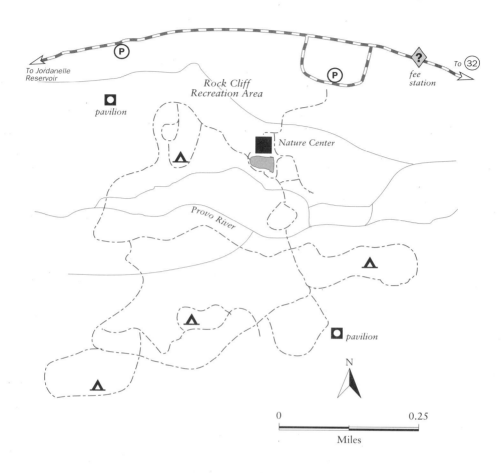

Finally, either walk or drive to the end of the entrance road, to the place where it disappears into the reservoir. To the south, at the mouth of the Provo River, you'll see a platform nest installed for Osprey, which may be on the nest or fishing over the reservoir. Scan this arm of the reservoir, too, for grebes and California Gulls, some of the more common species on the water.

Directions: From Heber City, head north on US 40 for 2 miles to the intersection with UT 32; turn right (east). Follow UT 32 east for about 6 miles, and then turn left into the entrance for Rock Cliff Recreation Area. Proceed approximately 1 mile to the fee station—the entrance to the parking area for the visitor center is on the left immediately after passing the fee station.

General information: The Rock Cliff Campground is for tents only, and it is a walk-in campground. Thoughtfully, the park provides garden carts for hauling in your gear. There are trailer sites, and more tent sites, at the nearby Jordanelle Reservoir State Park, about a 15-minute drive away.

ADDITIONAL INFORMATION

Map grid: 5D
Elevation: 6,000 feet.
Hazards: None.
Nearest food, gas, and lodging: Heber City.
Camping: Rock Cliff Campground, Jordanelle Reservoir State Park.
For more information: Utah Division of Parks and Recreation.

59 Rockport State Park

Habitats: Lowland riparian, pinyon-juniper
Specialty birds: Bald Eagle (spring and fall); Sage Grouse; Lewis's Woodpecker; Northern Shrike (winter); American Dipper; Green-tailed and Spotted Towhees
Other key birds: Common Loon (spring and fall); Western (spring and fall) and Eared (spring and fall) Grebes; Turkey Vulture; Tundra Swan (spring); Northern Pintail (spring and fall); Gadwall (spring and fall); Green-winged Teal (spring and fall); Common Merganser; Northern Harrier; Sharp-shinned and Swainson's Hawks; Snowy Egret (spring and fall); Least Sandpiper (spring and fall); Common Snipe; California Gull (spring and fall); Forster's Tern; Short-eared Owl; Common Nighthawk; Broad-tailed Hummingbird; Belted Kingfisher; Downy Woodpecker; Tree, Violet-green, Northern Rough-winged, Bank, Cliff, and Barn Swallows; Western Scrub-Jay; Black-billed Magpie; Mountain Bluebird; Gray Catbird; Cedar Waxwing (spring and fall); Yellow and Yellow-rumped Warblers; Chipping, Brewer's, Song, Lincoln's, and White-crowned Sparrows; Bullock's Oriole; Cassin's Finch; American Goldfinch
Best times to bird: March through April and September through November for migrant waterfowl; May through mid-July for breeding songbirds

The birding: Bordering Rockport Reservoir on the Weber River, Rockport State Park encompasses a sliver of an extensive pinyon-juniper forest. A slender riparian corridor, primarily along the Weber River, adds a little habitat diversity and attracts a community of birds otherwise absent from the pinyon-juniper monoculture.

Rockport Reservoir also attracts its share of migrating waterfowl, particularly in late winter and early spring. In November, Tundra Swans migrate through and can be seen on the open waters of the lake. In general, the best place to look for waterfowl is the east end of the lake, where the Weber River enters the lake and creates a low marshy area. The true open-water species, like loons, may be out toward the middle of the lake.

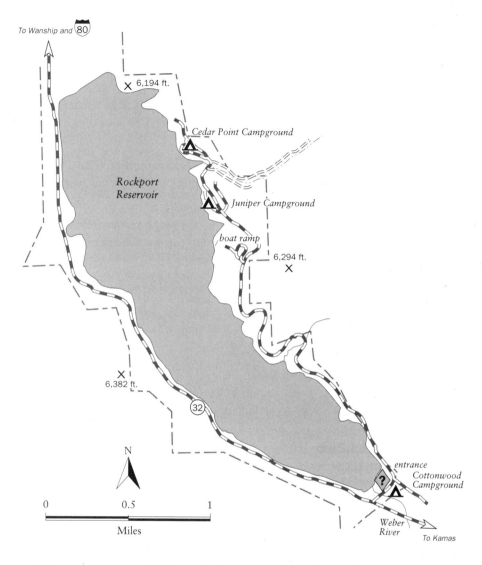

To Wanship and 80

X 6,194 ft.

Cedar Point Campground

Rockport Reservoir

Juniper Campground

boat ramp

6,294 ft. X

X
6,382 ft.

32

N

0   0.5   1

Miles

entrance
Cottonwood
Campground

?

Weber
River   To Kamas

There are two areas in the park that are worth exploring for songbirds. The first area is along the Weber River, right near the park entrance. After passing through the entrance gate, turn right and proceed into the Cottonwood Campground. The area beside the trash dumpsters as you enter the campground is a good place for day visitors to park. The campground is small and encompasses a grove of cottonwoods on the banks of the river. Take some time to walk the road through the campground, birding the cottonwood canopy as well as the shrubs in the understory. This is a good place for warblers, Gray Catbirds, Song Sparrows, and Lincoln's Sparrows.

Another good spot for a slightly different community of birds is the Juniper Campground. If you continue west from the entrance station along the only road in the park, you'll reach this campground on one of the many coves along the lake-shore. The campground has junipers and a few spruces, and it's a good area for species common to the pinyon-juniper community. Just a few yards back along the road in the direction of the entrance station, two gated dirt roads head up either side of the drainage that enters from the north. These roads pass through good stands of junipers in the vicinity of the moist canyon bottom. Either of these tracks is worth a short hike, again for pinyon-juniper species as well as the occasional warbler or Bullock's Oriole.

Directions: In the small community of Wanship, exit from I-80 (Exit 156), and proceed south on UT 32. Follow signs to Rockport State Park. The entrance lies about 6 miles from Wanship.

General information: As with all state parks, you can expect to pay an entrance fee ($3), and an additional fee ($10) if you intend to use one of the campgrounds in the park.

ADDITIONAL INFORMATION

Map grid: 5D
Elevation: 6,037 feet.
Hazards: None.
Nearest food, gas, and lodging: Kamas.
Camping: Rockport State Park campgrounds.
For more information: Rockport State Park.

60 Trial Lake

Habitat: Spruce-fir
Specialty birds: Williamson's Sapsucker; Three-toed Woodpecker; Olive-sided and Hammond's Flycatchers; Pine Grosbeak; Red Crossbill
Other key birds: Osprey; Spotted Sandpiper; California Gull; Broad-tailed Hummingbird; Downy and Hairy Woodpeckers; Gray and Steller's Jays; Mountain Chickadee; Red-breasted, White-breasted, and Pygmy Nuthatches; Brown Creeper; Ruby-crowned Kinglet; Hermit Thrush; Yellow-rumped and MacGillivray's Warblers; Lincoln's and White-crowned Sparrows; Cassin's Finch; Pine Siskin
Best times to bird: Late May through July

The birding: The habitat around Trial Lake consists of even-aged stands of conifers and as such the birding tends to be uniform. If there are any hot spots, they are transient. Still, the area is fairly good for species typical of this habitat type.

Start in the campground, working your way along the paved roads. If you're here early in the season and there is still a lot of snow on the ground, keep an eye

60 Trial Lake

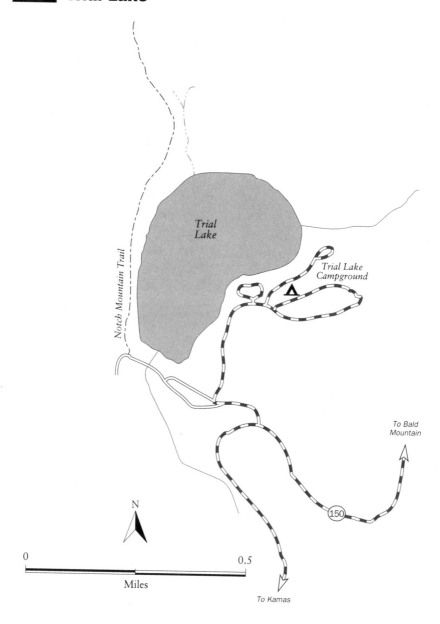

on any bare spots. The birds are often hard pressed for food at this time and tend to congregate around open ground in search of insects and arthropods.

If you reach the upper end of the campground and would like to extend your walk, you can do so by heading around the upper end of the lake. Notch Mountain Trail lies on the west side of the lake, and it's an easy hike around the north end of the lake to pick up this trail. The distance around the lake is modest, and you can keep an eye out for stray water birds. (Usually the only birds on the water are California Gulls.)

Directions: From the small community of Kamas, head east on UT 150. Trial Lake lies on the left side of the road, 25.7 miles from Kamas. The left turn is well signed and comes in a sharp, right-hand bend in UT 150. Turn left and follow the signs indicating a right turn into the campground. You can park along the road in the area of the campground turn or, if the campground is not crowded, park along the road leading into the campground.

General information: At nearly 10,000 feet in elevation, this area doesn't open until late in the season, and it closes early. Summers are fleeting, if you can identify them at all! If you're planning a visit to the area, it's definitely worth calling the Kamas Ranger District to learn whether or not the road to Trial Lake is open.

Anyone stopping, even to day hike, along UT 150 (in the national forest) must display a pass in their car window. The passes are available at entrance stations on either end of UT 150, and they are $3 per day, $10 per week, or $25 for an annual pass.

ADDITIONAL INFORMATION

Map grid: 6D
Elevation: 9,800 feet.
Hazards: Cold temperatures, rapidly changing weather.
Nearest food, gas, and lodging: Kamas.
Camping: Trial Lake Campground, Wasatch-Cache National Forest.
For more information: Wasatch-Cache National Forest, Kamas Ranger District.

61 Bald Mountain

Habitats: Alpine, mountain meadow, spruce-fir
Specialty birds: Townsend's Solitaire; American Pipit; Black Rosy-Finch
Other key birds: Rock Wren; Mountain Bluebird; Hermit Thrush; Chipping and White-crowned Sparrows; Cassin's Finch.
Best times to bird: June through mid-September

The birding: Bald Mountain may be the highest point in the Uintas easily accessed from a major road. At nearly 12,000 feet, the area is open only for a short period each year, and even this brief summer can feel more like winter.

Because this area is so accessible, it is a great place to explore in search of those high-montane species, particularly American Pipit and Black Rosy-Finch. The parking area is essentially two-tiered, with the lower area as the primary parking lot for the trailhead while the upper area is often used by road crews for loading gravel. From this upper-tier gravel pit, a rough road departs from the northwest corner and climbs to the low saddle on the east side of Bald Mountain. Follow this road

The shoulder of Bald Mountain, at left, in the High Uintas bears lingering snow in late July.

for about a hundred yards; then, as the road veers east toward a meteorological station, bear left and travel cross-country toward the cliff base of Bald Mountain. This route will take you across a low saddle and through a sparse conifer forest before the country opens into a wide meadow with an expansive view of the High Uintas. From here, walk north along the base of the cliff, birding the scree slopes and edges of retreating snowfields. These are the preferred haunts of Mountain Bluebirds, American Pipits, and Black Rosy-Finches.

The distance you hike is up to you. If this trek fails to produce the desired species, your alternative is to tackle the main trail to the summit of Bald Mountain. To do this, retrace your steps back to the parking area and trailhead, and prepare to break a sweat. The trail is steep and waterless but as summer progresses, this may be the only spot for pipits and finches.

Directions: From the small community of Kamas, head east on UT 150. Bald Mountain lies 29.5 miles from Kamas, and the trailhead is on the left side of the road. The turn is well signed and comes shortly after Bald Mountain Overlook— a good landmark. Turn into the trailhead/picnic area and park near the trailhead sign.

General information: Anyone stopping, even to day hike, along UT 150 (in the national forest) must display a pass in their car window. The passes are available

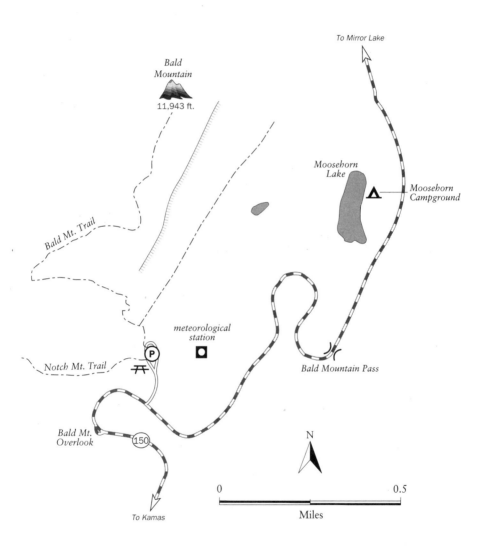

Bald
Mountain
11,943 ft.

To Mirror Lake

Moosehorn
Lake

Moosehorn
Campground

Bald Mt. Trail

meteorological
station

P

Notch Mt. Trail

Bald Mountain Pass

Bald Mt.
Overlook

150

To Kamas

N

0   0.5

Miles

at entrance stations on either end of UT 150, and they are $3 per day, $10 a week, or $25 for an annual pass.

ADDITIONAL INFORMATION

Map grid: 6D
Elevation: 10,750 to 11,943 feet.
Hazards: High altitude, temperature extremes, mosquitoes, no drinking water.
Nearest food, gas, and lodging: Kamas.
Camping: Moosehorn Campground, Wasatch-Cache National Forest.
For more information: Wasatch-Cache National Forest, Kamas Ranger District.

62 Mirror Lake

Habitats: Mountain riparian, spruce-fir, mountain meadow
Specialty birds: Northern Goshawk; Blue Grouse; Three-toed Woodpecker; Olive-sided and Hammond's Flycatchers; Clark's Nutcracker; American Dipper; American Pipit; Black Rosy-Finch; Pine Grosbeak; Red Crossbill
Other key birds: Osprey; Spotted Sandpiper; California Gull; Calliope, Broad-tailed, and Rufous (mid-July to August) Hummingbirds; Belted Kingfisher; Hairy Woodpecker; Tree and Violet-green Swallows; Gray Jay; Common Raven; Mountain Chickadee; Red-breasted and White-breasted Nuthatches; Brown Creeper; House Wren; Golden-crowned and Ruby-crowned Kinglets; Mountain Bluebird; Orange-crowned, Yellow-rumped, and MacGillivray's Warblers; Chipping, Brewer's, Vesper, Lincoln's, and White-crowned Sparrows; Cassin's Finch; Pine Siskin
Best times to bird: June through early September

The birding: This high mountain site holds numerous opportunities for exploration and bird finding. A Forest Service campground wraps around the south end of the lake, making a good place for an overnight visit and a good place to start bird finding. The campground is forested with lodgepole pine, spruce, and fir; often songbirds can be found just by walking the campground road.

Also bird the day use/picnic area, which straddles the stream draining Mirror Lake. This area is grassy and locating birds is a little easier. Walking through the picnic area is best during early mornings when birds are foraging.

Finally, two trailheads lie in or near the campground and provide access to more birding opportunities. A well-signed trailhead is on the north part of the campground loop, adjacent to the lake and small parking area that accommodates a few cars. This trail connects to the Highline Trail, a route that unites much of the Uinta Mountains and heads for Bonnie Lake (1 mile), Scudder Lake (3 miles) and Naturalist Basin.

As you drive into the campground, a road departs to the second right and drops a short distance to a parking area for a southern foray on the Highline. A

62 Mirror Lake

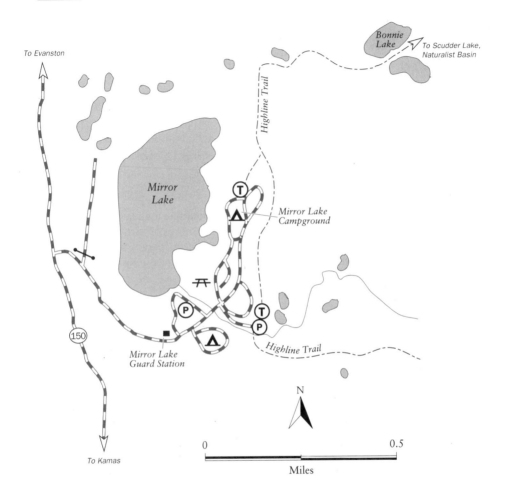

day hike through the conifer forest, meadows, and wetlands penetrated by either of these trails will expose you to more birding opportunities.

Directions: From the small community of Kamas, head east on UT 150. Mirror Lake lies on the right side of the road, about 31.5 miles from Kamas. A good landmark is the series of switchbacks and the high mountain pass at Bald Mountain, from which the road drops gradually over 2.4 miles to the turn to Mirror Lake—a Forest Service sign marks this recreation area.

General information: Mirror Lake may be the most popular destination in the Uintas, and it tends to be oversubscribed. Hiking away from the lake on either of the trails mentioned above will get you away from crowds. If the campground is full, there are a number of other Forest Service campgrounds a short drive to the north.

Anyone stopping, even to day hike, along UT 150 (in the national forest) must display a pass in their car window. The passes are available at entrance stations on either end of UT 150, and they are $3 per day, $10 a week, or $25 for an annual pass.

ADDITIONAL INFORMATION

Map grid: 6D
Elevation: 10,050 feet.
Hazards: High altitude, biting insects.
Nearest food, gas, and lodging: Kamas.
Camping: Mirror Lake Campground, Wasatch-Cache National Forest.
For more information: Wasatch-Cache National Forest, Kamas Ranger District.

63 Dahlgreen's Creek

Habitats: Mountain riparian, mountain meadow, spruce-fir, aspen
Specialty birds: Northern Goshawk; Blue Grouse; Western Wood-Pewee; Willow and Dusky Flycatchers; Townsend's Solitaire; Lazuli Bunting; Red Crossbill
Other key birds: Ring-necked Duck; Northern Harrier; Ruffed Grouse; Spotted Sandpiper; Common Snipe; Common Nighthawk; Broad-tailed Hummingbird; Belted Kingfisher; Red-naped Sapsucker; Hairy Woodpecker; Warbling Vireo; Tree, Violet-green, and Barn Swallows; Gray Jay; Mountain Chickadee; Red-breasted and White-breasted Nuthatches; House Wren; Ruby-crowned Kinglet; Mountain Bluebird; Hermit Thrush; Orange-crowned, Yellow, Yellow-rumped, and MacGillivray's Warblers; Common Yellowthroat; Wilson's Warbler; Western Tanager; Chipping, Brewer's, Fox, Song, Lincoln's, and White-crowned Sparrows; Black-headed Grosbeak; Cassin's Finch
Best times to bird: June through mid-July; early mornings are generally best, but activity is high throughout breeding season.

The birding: This is an interesting area to bird, not only for its picturesque setting, but because the habitats that occur here are in discrete units. Walking among all four habitats exposes you to the different bird communities and neatly illustrates both the commonalities and distinctions of each. The interfaces between these habitat types are zones of near-frenzied activity during nesting season, as birds zip back and forth between the habitats.

The dirt road that you drive in on divides the area in half, and Dahlgreen's Creek bisects the road. A look at the map shows four quadrants formed by these features. Although you will find four-wheel-drive tracks off the main road, there are essentially no other trails through this area, and you're on your own to wander

63 Dahlgreen's Creek

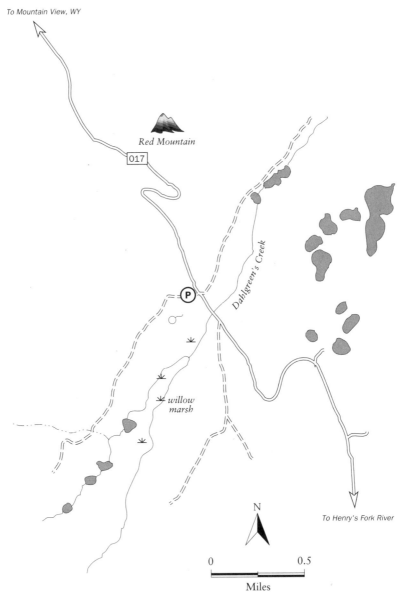

To Mountain View, WY

Red Mountain

017

Dahlgreen's Creek

willow
marsh

P

N

To Henry's Fork River

0   0.5
Miles

wherever the calling birds lead you. It's an easy area to navigate. If you lose direction, just walk downhill to the creek and reorient yourself.

Keep in mind that, in the drier part of the summer, it is possible to do the walks described below as a single, long loop through all four quadrants formed by the road and the creek. However, if Dahlgreen's Creek is running high, do these hikes as four separate routes.

A spruce-fir forest overlooks a willow marsh along Dahlgreen's Creek.

A good place to start is the north quadrant. If you drop off the road here and head down the drainage on the four-wheel-drive track, you'll wander through an expanse of meadow hemmed on the left by an aspen forest and on the right by the creek and stands of low, shrubby willows. These willow thickets are a good spot for Yellow and Wilson's Warblers and Lincoln's and Fox Sparrows. About 100 yards below the road, the hill on your left recedes farther into the woods, and the aspen grove stands on a gently sloping bench. The aspens in this area are a great spot for a variety of birds, but especially for cavity nesters. It's worth wandering into the edge of the grove and looking for House Wrens, Tree Swallows, Mountain Bluebirds, and Red-naped Sapsuckers, as well as Warbling Vireos, Dusky Flycatchers, and Yellow-rumped Warblers. This is also one of the better areas for Blue Grouse, but I have encountered most of these birds farther up the hill (still in the aspens) to the northwest. About 0.5 mile downstream from the road the willow thickets narrow to a thin line of shrubs outlining the watercourse. This is a good area to cross if the water is low; otherwise, retrace your steps.

In the eastern quadrant the creek is bordered by a drier meadow and then a lodgepole pine forest. More of the sparrows are evident in this drier meadow, which features more sagebrush and less grass. Look for Chipping and Brewer's Sparrows. As you walk through the meadow, keep an eye over the creek corridor for Northern Harrier, Red-tailed Hawk, and Belted Kingfisher. Tree and Violet-green Swallows are also likely to be in abundance, foraging above the meadow and creek. The lodgepole pine bordering this walk is interesting but largely void of bird species. Lodgepole offers little habitat diversity, a sparse understory, and little to attract most birds. If you choose to wander into the lodgepole forest, you're most likely to encounter Mountain Chickadees, Red-breasted Nuthatches, and Ruby-crowned Kinglets.

Like the aspen forest to the north, the lodgepole forest rises on a low ridge. An interesting walk is to gain the crest and hike this ridgeline, because a series of glacial-remnant lakes dot its east side. This increases the diversity of the forest, and you're likely to encounter Spotted Sandpipers, Mallards, Ring-necked Ducks, and Great Horned Owls around the ponds.

Sparrow diversity seems to be at its highest where the southern quadrant borders the road; all six sparrow species can be heard and seen in this area, although the Song Sparrows are likely to be calling from the nearby willows. An informal road penetrates this area and leads to some ad hoc campsites. In years when Red Crossbills are about, they seem to frequent the sparse stand of pines along this road—listen for their characteristic in-flight call, a *jit-jit-jit*, and scan the tops of the pines for their unmistakable silhouette. Continue to follow this road until you see the abrupt interface between the conifer forest and the marsh. A game trail, enhanced by human activity, follows this interface up the drainage and makes for interesting birding. The conifer forest here is made up of fewer lodgepole pines and more spruce and fir. This area of the forest seems to have a higher density of birds than the adjacent lodgepole forest to the east, and you're more likely to add White-breasted Nuthatches to your list in this area. If you'd like to challenge your knowledge of warbler calls, the marsh to your right (as you're heading upstream) is a good spot; I've heard Orange-crowned, Yellow, Yellow-rumped, Common Yellowthroat, and Wilson's Warblers all calling from this part of the marsh, and MacGillivray's Warbler calling from the conifers.

The upper end of the marsh is a good spot for Willow Flycatchers. You'll note a number of sizable trees in this part of the marsh, many of which have been downed by beaver activity, and these trees seem to be preferred perches for this species. If you continue up the drainage until the creek becomes a distinct, single channel, you can cross, hike over the low ridge dropping down to meet the east end of the marsh, cross the second tributary, and end up in the western quadrant.

Again starting from the main road, hike along the four-wheel-drive track that leaves the dirt road heading west and passes by a spring, marked by a post and a garden hose. (The Forest Service checks this water every season, and it was potable when I was there, but there are cows in the area and you take your chances). This track continues beside a beautiful grove of aspens. Again, the cavity nesters are numerous in this area, and White-crowned Sparrows, Western Wood-Pewees, and Hairy Woodpeckers are fairly common.

Directions: Take I-80 east from Salt Lake City and into southwestern Wyoming. Take Exit 34, continuing through Fort Bridger and into Mountain View, Wyoming.

In Mountain View, turn right onto WY 410, toward the town of Robertson. WY 410 makes two sharp right-hand bends. At the second bend, Uinta County Road 246 continues straight, due south, heading toward the Wasatch-Cache National Forest. This road crosses the national forest boundary and becomes FR 072. Twelve miles from the intersection of WY 410 and Uinta County 246 with WY 410, take the left turn onto FR 017, signed to Henry's Fork. FR 017 crosses Dahlgreen's Creek in another 4.6 miles, after dropping down two hairpin turns on the flank of Red Mountain. The track departing to the right, before crossing the creek, is a good place to park.

General information: This area can be very muddy in early spring or after heavy rain; at these times it is difficult to find a place to park without getting stuck or tearing up the road. If you're set on birding in those conditions, have a look at the turnoff on the west side of the road—on your right immediately before crossing the creek. Another option would be to drive back up the road to the last hairpin turn and pull off the road there.

This is also one of those places where you can expect snow any time of year. One year it snowed 8 inches on the Fourth of July.

ADDITIONAL INFORMATION

Map grid: 7D
Elevation: 9,067 feet.
Hazards: Extreme weather, high altitude, possibly muddy.
Nearest food, gas, and lodging: Mountain View, Wyoming.
Camping: Henry's Fork Trailhead Campground.
For more information: Wasatch-Cache National Forest, Mountain View Ranger District.

64 Henry's Fork–Upper Basin

Habitats: Alpine, mountain meadow, mountain riparian, spruce-fir
Specialty birds: Blue Grouse; White-tailed Ptarmigan; Williamson's Sapsucker; Three-toed Woodpecker; Hammond's Flycatcher; Clark's Nutcracker; American Pipit; Black Rosy-Finch; Pine Grosbeak; Red Crossbill
Other key birds: Green-winged Teal; Ring-necked Duck; Northern Harrier; Golden Eagle; Spotted Sandpiper; Gray and Steller's Jays; Mountain Chickadee; Red-breasted, White-breasted, and Pygmy Nuthatches; Brown Creeper; Rock Wren; Ruby-crowned Kinglet; Mountain Bluebird; Hermit Thrush; Yellow-rumped and Wilson's Warblers; Chipping, Fox, Song, Lincoln's, and White-crowned Sparrows; Cassin's Finch
Best times to bird: Mid-June through August

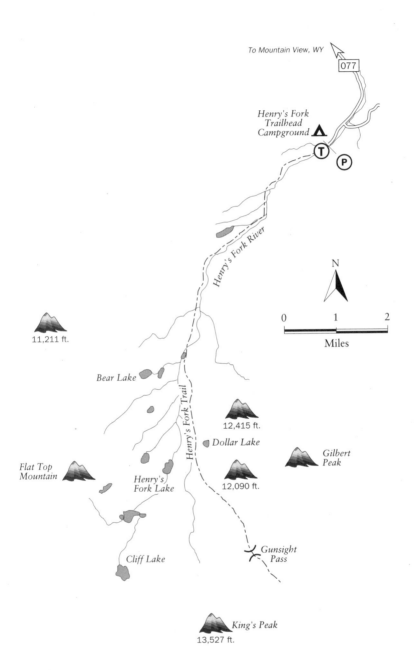

To Mountain View, WY

077

Henry's Fork
Trailhead
Campground

T P

Henry's Fork River

N

0   1   2
Miles

11,211 ft.

Bear Lake

Henry's Fork Trail

12,415 ft.

Dollar Lake

Gilbert
Peak

Flat Top
Mountain

Henry's
Fork Lake

12,090 ft.

Cliff Lake

Gunsight
Pass

King's Peak
13,527 ft.

Cross-country travel is easy around the headwaters of the Henry's Fork River.

The birding: Birding the headwaters of the Henry's Fork River is an exhilarating experience, and the scenery is unparalleled. This is one of the few places in Utah where alpine vegetation is relatively accessible, and here in this enormous glacial cirque, it is interspersed with spruce-fir forests, large expanses of meadows, and a willow-lined riparian corridor surrounding a blue-ribbon trout stream. There is, of course, a cost: you'll have to backpack in about 5 miles, set up camp, and plan to do another 4 or 5 miles of day hiking to bird this area.

Birding all along the route can be interesting, but the real destination is the portion of the watershed that lies above Dollar Lake. Feel free to deviate from these suggestions—the stunted alpine vegetation, the isolated groves of trees, and open vistas encourage cross-country exploration. The terraced slopes of the cliff face above Dollar Lake make a good landmark for making your way back.

The slopes above Dollar Lake are timbered with a virgin spruce-fir forest with an open understory that makes for easy exploration. This is a good area for Ruby-crowned Kinglets, Williamson's Sapsuckers, Three-toed Woodpeckers, Brown Creeper, nuthatches, Hermit Thrushes, Mountain Chickadees, Cassin's Finch, and Red Crossbills. The woodpeckers can be hard to find, but their territorial drumming is distinct to each species and can be heard, along with the flute-like call of the Hermit Thrush, echoing across Dollar Lake. Gray Jays are fairly common and frequently pay visits to the campsites along the shore.

If you continue following the trail and head up the watershed, the spruces and firs thin out and become more stunted. You'll encounter lots of White-Crowned Sparrows in the willows, but also keep an eye on the few copses of trees. As perches become fewer, Mountain Bluebirds, kinglets, warblers, and finches tend to concentrate. You'll also encounter American Pipits with regularity; they tend to follow hikers, scolding and darting back and forth just beyond reach. Wilson's Warblers nest among the low growing willows, and you'll discover them singing or scolding you as you continue.

As you top the rise above Dollar Lake, the view of the valley opens up. Stop and take a moment to orient yourself. Henry's Fork Lake is visible almost immediately below in the valley bottom. Above Henry's Fork Lake the river breaks into numerous tributaries that tumble down from higher elevations over short waterfalls lined with bogs and willow marshes. Following the lowest (in elevation) branch of the Henry's Fork up the valley, you'll see it climb through one of these willow marshes to its source at the base of the towering cliffs.

To find the White-Tailed Ptarmigan and the Black Rosy-Finches, set a course for those headwaters. The finches nest in the scree slopes at the base of the cliffs, and they can usually be seen flying overhead or perched in snags along the right side (looking upstream) of the river. The finches like to feed along the edges of melting snowbanks, so pay careful attention as you approach. The ptarmigan are a lot harder to find but tend to be in this headwater area. These birds are not shy and do not flush easily and, in breeding plumage, are well camouflaged. Be prepared to burn a lot of shoe leather looking for ptarmigan; you may have to wander the upper watershed. They prefer the low shrubby willow thickets. Listen for their calls.

Directions: Take I-80 east from Salt Lake City and into southwestern Wyoming. Take Exit 34, continue through Fort Bridger and into Mountain View, Wyoming. In Mountain View, turn right on WY 410, toward the town of Robertson. WY 410 makes two sharp right-hand bends. At the second bend, Uinta County Road 246 continues straight, due south, heading toward Wasatch-Cache National Forest. This road crosses the national forest boundary and becomes FR 072. Twelve miles from the intersection with WY 410, take the left turn on FR 017, signed to Henry's Fork. After another 7 miles you'll come to another fork; bear right on FR 077, continuing to follow the signs to Henry's Fork Trailhead Campground, which lies about 3.5 miles from this intersection.

From the trailhead, Dollar Lake is another 7 miles distant, and the headwaters another 2 miles farther still.

General information: I would highly recommend a detailed hiking guide for this trip (Dave Hall's *Hiking Utah*, published by Falcon, is good) as well as a detailed map. Also, it's possible to complete this trip in two days, but three or more days would allow for a more comfortable pace.

Although the entire length of this trail is in the High Uintas Wilderness Area, it is not wild in the sense of being remote. I can guarantee you'll have plenty of human company. This is a popular destination for Boy Scouts, fishermen, back-packers, horse packers, llama packers, and birders, and on some weekends the parking lot at the trailhead overflows with vehicles. Nonetheless, when you get away from the more popular campsites, and particularly if you leave the trail, it's unlikely you'll cross paths with anyone.

The hike to the upper basin is not particularly strenuous—it's a steady and gradual uphill climb all the way, and it takes about four to five hours to reach Dollar Lake. Still, weather at this altitude can fluctuate quickly, and any day of the summer can bring a combination of hot sun, wind-driven rain, and snow. Also, because of the high altitude, anyone unaccustomed to the elevation should hike slow and easy, and perhaps plan a couple of days birding at other less remote Uinta bird sites (Dahlgreen's Creek, Bald Mountain, Trial Lake, Mirror Lake) before undertaking this hike in order to acclimate to the altitude.

There is plenty of water along the route and in the basin, but it should be filtered, chemically treated, or boiled prior to consumption.

ADDITIONAL INFORMATION

Map grid: 8C

Elevation: 9,400 (trailhead) to 11,200 (headwaters) feet.

Hazards: High altitude, temperature and weather extremes, mosquitoes.

Nearest food, gas, and lodging: Mountain View, Wyoming.

Camping: Numerous dispersed sites.

For more information: Wasatch-Cache National Forest, Mountain View Ranger District.

65 Sheep Creek Loop

Habitats: Lowland riparian, pinyon-juniper, upland desert shrub, mountain riparian, spruce-fir, aspen, mountain meadow

Specialty birds: Blue Grouse; Flammulated Owl; Western Screech-Owl; Lewis's Woodpecker; Western Wood-Pewee; Hammond's and Dusky Flycatchers; American Dipper; Green-tailed and Spotted Towhees; Lazuli Bunting

Other key birds: Cooper's Hawk; Ruffed Grouse; California Quail; Broad-tailed Hummingbird; Belted Kingfisher; Red-naped Sapsucker; Say's Phoebe; Plumbeous and Warbling Vireo; Gray and Steller's Jays; Mountain Chickadee; Red-Breasted, White-breasted, and Pygmy Nuthatches; Rock, Canyon, and House Wrens; Ruby-crowned Kinglet; Mountain Bluebird; Hermit Thrush; Virginia's, Yellow, MacGillivray's, and Wilson's Warblers; Yellow-breasted Chat; Chipping, Song, and White-crowned Sparrows; Black-headed Grosbeak; Cassin's Finch; Pine Siskin; American Goldfinch

Best times to bird: May through mid-July, early mornings are generally best.

65 Sheep Creek Loop

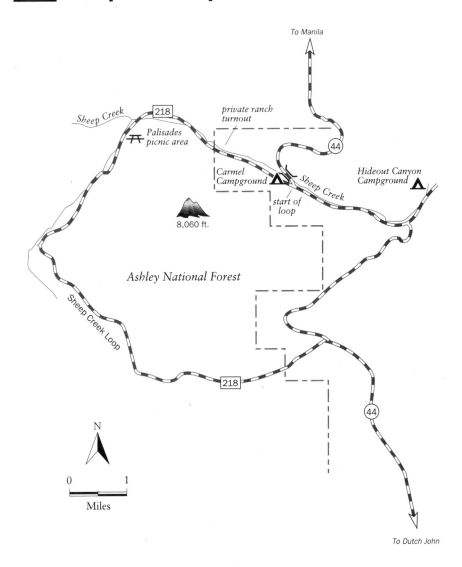

The birding: The Sheep Creek Loop is a 14-mile-long driving route through a tremendous diversity of habitats as well as dramatic geologic features sure to divert your attention from birds. The north end of the loop is arguably the best for birding, although high-elevation species may be added to your list as you drive south and climb higher into the Uinta Mountains.

There are few places to pull off the narrow road until you reach the north end of the loop. The first area worth an in-depth exploration is the Carmel Campground and picnic area, which lies at the mouth of Sheep Creek Canyon. Pull into the picnic area to park; then spend some time walking up and down the creek,

The road along Sheep Creek Road passes through dramatic scenery and numerous habitat types.

exploring the riparian area, the cottonwoods, and the sagebrush-strewn meadow surrounding the campground. Lazuli Buntings seem to be abundant in this area, and you should be able to find Western Wood-Pewees, Warbling Vireos, and various species of warblers and sparrows, including Green-tailed and Spotted Towhees.

About 2.8 miles from the start of the loop lies a private ranch. On the opposite side of the road from the ranch is another good riparian complex with a well-developed understory. A pullout here allows you to explore a bit more. Walk the road and look for birds using the thickets on the south side of the road and the orchards and arbors on the ranch property.

Continuing along the loop, the Palisades picnic area provides another good parking spot. Explore the copse of trees surrounding the picnic area and the creek across the road. Broad-tailed Hummingbirds, Violet-green Swallows, House Wrens, Warbling Vireos, Yellow and Yellow-rumped Warblers are some of the more abundant species at this stop.

There is a wide pullout 6.2 miles into the loop, and a large sign indicating the end of the Sheep Creek Geological Area. Although the terrain here is steep and generally discourages much walking, this spot is worth a quick stop to look for Green-tailed Towhees and other shrub-associated sparrows. This spot also offers an expansive view of the dramatic and rugged mountains and a chance to scan for raptors on the wing.

South of the Geological Area the turnouts disappear altogether, so if there is much traffic on the road you may not get to see much. This section of the road passes through the more montane habitat types, but because of the lack of parking, it is difficult to explore. If you happen on a section of the road with an adequate shoulder you may wish to park and explore an aspen stand, a spruce-fir forest, or some of the meadows at the south end of the loop.

Directions: From Manila, head south for 7 miles on UT 44. The right (west) turn to start the Sheep Creek Loop is well signed and comes just after crossing the bridge over Sheep Creek. Follow this paved route for 14 miles, at which point you will be returned to UT 44. Turn left (north) to return to Manila, or right to head into deeper into the Uinta Mountains.

General information: This loop is known as a great viewing area for a variety of wildlife species, not just for birds. You may also see deer, elk, moose, bighorn sheep, and in fall, a run of spawning kokanee salmon in Sheep Creek.

ADDITIONAL INFORMATION

Map grid: 8D
Elevation: 6,300 to 7,800 feet.
Hazards: None.
Nearest food, gas, and lodging: Manila.
Camping: Carmel Campground, Ashley National Forest.
For More information: Ashley National Forest, Flaming Gorge Ranger District.

66 Henry's Fork Wildlife Viewing Area

Habitats: Lowland riparian, lowland desert shrub, upland desert shrub, pinyon-juniper
Specialty birds: Lewis's Woodpecker; Western Wood-Pewee; Dusky Flycatcher; Green-tailed and Spotted Towhees; Sage Sparrow; Lazuli Bunting
Other key birds: Western Grebe; Northern Pintail; Cinnamon Teal; Northern Shoveler; Gadwall; Redhead; Osprey; Cooper's Hawk; California Quail; Black-chinned and Broad-tailed Hummingbirds; Belted Kingfisher; Hairy Woodpecker; Say's Phoebe; Tree Swallow; Plumbeous and Warbling Vireo; Western Scrub-Jay; House Wren; Virginia's and Yellow Warblers; Yellow-breasted Chat; Chipping, Brewer's, Grasshopper, Song, and White-crowned Sparrows; Black-headed and Blue Grosbeaks; Bullock's Oriole; American Goldfinch
Best times to bird: March through October; late July and August can be slow.

The birding: In its upper reaches, the Henry's Fork River is a blue-ribbon trout fishery and a noisy, clear-running mountain stream. Here at its terminus, which is in Wyoming, the stream has lost considerable volume (probably due to irrigation

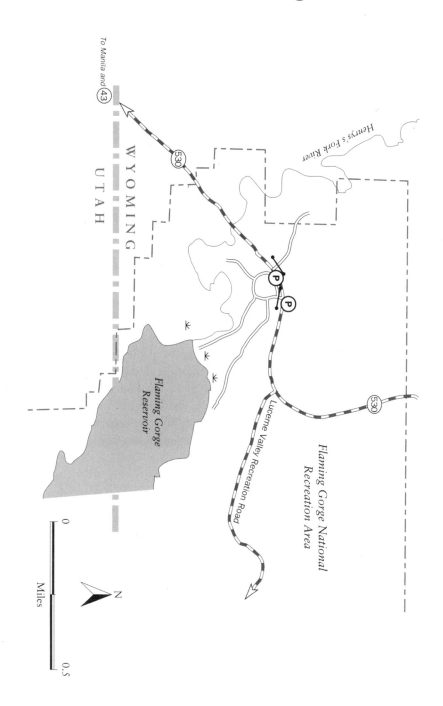

draws), and its flow is a good deal slower. Nonetheless, the riparian corridor that follows its course, along with associated desert shrub communities, make for good birding. At its meeting with Flaming Gorge Reservoir, the Henry's Fork disgorges into a sheltered cove, where a nesting platform for Osprey towers over shorebird and waterfowl habitat. It's a great mix of vegetation communities and bird species.

As of this writing, this site is under active development by the USDA Forest Service as a wildlife viewing area. During my visit it appeared as though parking areas were under construction and I understand that more ponds for waterfowl will be developed. It's likely that trails are planned as well. If you arrive to find a network of trails, by all means follow those instead of my suggested route.

The wildlife viewing area spans both sides of WY 530. On the east side lies the mouth of the Henry's Fork with the aforementioned open water and shorebird habitat. Just before entering the reservoir, the river supports a dense thicket of willows. It's worth walking the perimeter of the willows in pursuit of flycatchers, warblers, grosbeaks, and orioles. After scanning the willows and the open water, head back upstream, hiking through the scattered cottonwoods and mixed shrub habitat. Western Kingbirds, Warbling Vireos, Yellow Warblers, and Bullock's Orioles all use the trees for nesting and in summer may be seen foraging in the area.

The viewing area on the west side of the road is where you're more likely to find the desert shrub species and the few pinyon-juniper species you may encounter in the area. I heard Grasshopper Sparrows in this area and also noted a Redtailed Hawk nesting on the cliff face to the north of the dirt access road. Walk through the entrance gate and proceed up the road. It passes through the desert shrubs, and drops back to the floodplain within a few hundred yards. To take in more of the riparian corridor, depart from the road where it meets the floodplain and make your way toward the river, again walking through the mixed pasture and cottonwood groves. Then turn downstream and follow the river back toward WY 530.

Directions: From Manila, head east on UT 43. After crossing into Wyoming the route number changes to WY 530 and the road drops down into the narrow valley of the Henry's Fork River. The two entrance gates lie on either side of the road after you cross the river. There is ample room for parking near each gate or if the gates are open, proceed into the designated parking area.

General information: It's likely that this area will attract a greater diversity of birds after the wildlife viewing area is in place. In particular, you'll likely be able to find a greater diversity of waterfowl and shorebirds, particularly during spring and fall migration.

ADDITIONAL INFORMATION

Map grid: 8C
Elevation: 6,040 feet.
Hazards: None.

Nearest food, gas, and lodging: Manila.

Camping: Lucerne Peninsula, Ashley National Forest.

For more information: Ashley National Forest, Flaming Gorge Ranger District.

■67■ Lucerne Peninsula

Habitats: Desert steppe, pinyon-juniper, upland desert shrub

Specialty birds: Bald Eagle (winter); Prairie Falcon; Sage Thrasher; Sage Sparrow

Other key birds: Pied-billed, Eared (spring and fall), and Western Grebes; Snowy Egret; Turkey Vulture; Tundra Swan (spring and fall); Green-winged Teal; Northern Pintail; Blue-winged and Cinnamon Teals; Northern Shoveler; Gadwall; American Wigeon; Redhead; Ring-necked Duck (spring and fall); Lesser Scaup (spring and fall); Common (fall to spring) and Barrow's (spring and fall) Goldeneyes; Bufflehead (spring and fall); Common Merganser; Ruddy Duck; Osprey; Northern Harrier; Rough-legged Hawk (winter); Golden Eagle (winter); Spotted Sandpiper; California Gull; Common Nighthawk; Say's Phoebe; Ash-throated Flycatcher; Western Kingbird; Loggerhead Shrike; Violet-green and Northern Rough-winged Swallows; Black-billed Magpie; Common Raven; Bewick's Wren; Mountain Bluebird; Yellow and Yellow-rumped (spring and fall) Warblers; Chipping, Brewer's, Vesper, Lark, Savannah, Grasshopper, and White-crowned Sparrows; Black-headed Grosbeak; Brewer's Blackbird; Bullock's Oriole

Best times to bird: Spring and fall migration for waterfowl and shorebirds, March through April and September through October; May through June for breeding birds.

The birding: The Lucerne Peninsula extends into Flaming Gorge Reservoir. There is little or no riparian vegetation around the shore, so the appeal is the upland habitat, including one of the better examples of a desert steppe community you could hope to see. Antelope are plentiful and often graze right through the camp-grounds.

There are no developed trails in this area, so you can either do all your viewing from the car or stop whenever the mood strikes and set off across the grassland. Birds in this community tend to be sparsely distributed and difficult to identify. Look for individuals crossing the road or perched on top of the few low shrubs that dot the area.

From the turnoff at WY 530 the road passes briefly through a juniper forest and along the base of a cliff. This is a good spot for pinyon-juniper species, and if your luck is good, you might see a Prairie Falcon on the prowl. From here the road loses some elevation and enters the grassland, before eventually ending at the marina.

If you're here during migration, make the short side trip to scan the cove that lies on the north side of the peninsula. Waterfowl occasionally congregate in this area during migration; the lack of marshes probably discourages any birds from staying through the breeding season.

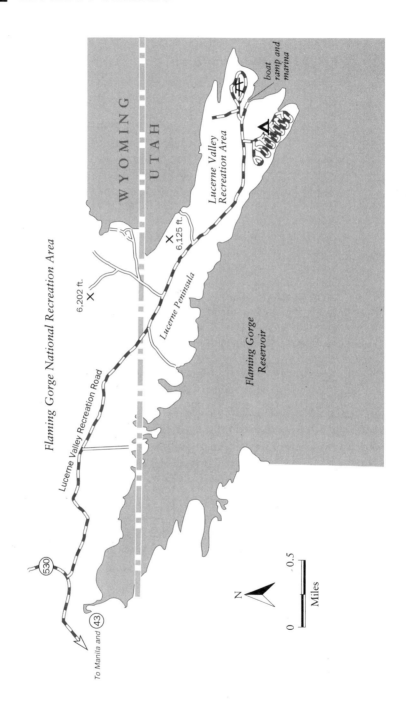

boat ramp and marina

WYOMING

UTAH

Lucerne Valley Recreation Area

6,125 ft.

Lucerne Peninsula

Flaming Gorge Reservoir

Flaming Gorge National Recreation Area

6,202 ft.

Lucerne Valley Recreation Road

530

To Manila and 43

N

Miles

0   0.5

Directions: From Manila, head east on UT 43. After crossing into Wyoming the route number changes to WY 530, and the road drops down into the narrow valley of the Henry's Fork River. As the road climbs out of the north side of the Henry's Fork River valley, you'll see a well-signed right (east) turn to the Lucerne Valley Recreation Area. Take this road and begin scanning for bird activity as soon as you leave WY 530. The road ends 4 miles away at the Lucerne Marina.

General Information: For those who have access to a motorboat, Flaming Gorge Reservoir offers plenty of additional opportunities for birding, particularly during spring and fall migration. During migration, sheltered coves on the reservoir often harbor rafts of waterfowl resting and feeding before resuming their long distance journey. There is also a visitor center for the National Recreation Area which encompasses much of the reservoir—it's located on the dam which impounds the reservoir, about 3 miles south of Dutch John on US 191. The visitor center has a small collection of field guides, a bird checklist, and often can provide visitors with up-to-date information on bird sightings in the area.

ADDITIONAL INFORMATION

Map grid: 8C
Elevation: 6,197 to 6,079 feet.
Hazards: None.
Nearest food, gas, and lodging: Manila.
Camping: Lucerne Peninsula, Ashley National Forest.
For more information: Ashley National Forest, Flaming Gorge Ranger District.

68 Swett Ranch

Habitats: Spruce-fir, mountain meadow, aspen, mountain riparian
Specialty birds: Blue Grouse; Flammulated Owl; Lewis's Woodpecker; Western Wood-Pewee; Hammond's and Dusky Flycatchers; Clark's Nutcracker
Other key birds: Cooper's Hawk; Ruffed Grouse; Broad-tailed Hummingbird; Red-naped Sapsucker; Say's Phoebe; Plumbeous and Warbling Vireos; Gray and Steller's Jays; Mountain Chickadee; Red-Breasted, White-breasted, and Pygmy Nuthatches; House Wren; Ruby-crowned Kinglet; Mountain Bluebird; Hermit Thrush; Virginia's, Yellow, MacGillivray's, and Wilson's Warblers; Chipping, Song, and White-crowned Sparrows; Cassin's Finch; Pine Siskin; American Goldfinch
Best times to bird: May through mid-July

The birding: The Swett Ranch sits in the corner of a large meadow on the northeast flank of the Uinta Mountains—surrounding the ranch is an extensive ponderosa pine forest, and passing behind the ranch site is Allen Creek. These three habitats intersect at the ranch site and provide for interesting birding.

Depending on weather conditions and the staffing demands of the USDA Forest Service, which manages this site, you may have to park along the dirt access

68 Swett Ranch

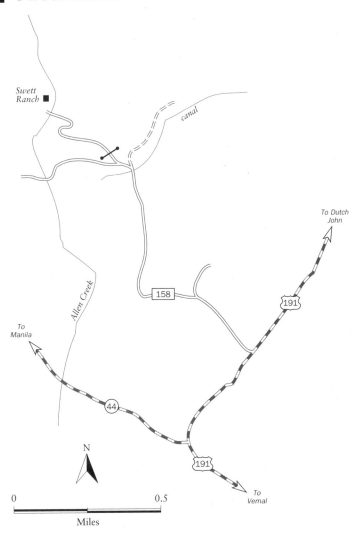

road leading to the ranch and walk in. You'll want to bird along the road anyway as it passes through a stand of mixed-age ponderosa pines. This is a good area for nuthatches, MacGillivray's Warblers and Chipping Sparrows. It's also a reasonable place to expect Flammulated Owls, but as always they are difficult to find. They're best located by their calls around dusk.

At the ranch site take some time to explore the edge of the meadow. Its north side is bounded by the pine forest you may have walked through to reach the site, while the east side is where you'll find Allen Creek. The creek is small but supports willows (good areas for warblers) and scattered aspens. The area surrounding Swett Ranch has a reputation as being one of the more reliable spots in the Uintas for finding Lewis's Woodpeckers.

Dwellings and old farm machinery linger at the Swett Ranch.

Directions: Swett Ranch is located a short distance off US 191, 6 miles south of Flaming Gorge Dam or 0.5 mile north of the intersection of US 191 and UT 44. Turn west on FR 158, and follow this route 1.5 miles to the ranch site.

General information: Oscar Swett settled this historic ranch in 1909, adding larger living quarters as his family grew and outbuildings as his ranch expanded. The Forest Service maintains the ranch as an interpretive site, and a tour provides a glimpse into life on a remote outpost at the turn of the century. The Forest Service has recently suffered from under budgeting and a subsequent staff shortage, so the ranch has only been open from Memorial Day through Labor Day, Tuesday through Saturday. Before planning a visit, call the USDAFS to check on current conditions for accessing this site.

FR 158, the last 1.5 miles of the drive to the ranch, is a narrow dirt road; the Forest Service discourages trailers and RVs on the road and warns that the route may be muddy after rain.

ADDITIONAL INFORMATION

Map grid: 8D
Elevation: 7,000 feet.
Hazards: None.
Nearest food, gas, and lodging: Dutch John.
Camping: Greendale East Campground.
For more information: Ashley National Forest, Flaming Gorge Ranger District.

69 Brown's Park Wildlife Management Area and National Wildlife Refuge

Habitats: Lowland riparian, desert steppe, lowland desert shrub, pinyon-juniper

Specialty birds: American White Pelican; Bald Eagle (winter); Sage Grouse; White-throated Swift; Western Wood-Pewee; Gray Flycatcher; Northern Shrike (winter); Pinyon Jay; Clark's Nutcracker (winter); Sage Thrasher; Green-tailed and Spotted Towhees; Sage Sparrow; Lazuli Bunting (spring and fall); Black Rosy-Finch (winter)

Other key birds: Pied-billed, Eared (spring and fall), and Western Grebes; Double-crested Cormorant; Snowy Egret; White-faced Ibis (spring and fall); Turkey Vulture; Tundra Swan (spring and fall); Green-winged Teal; Northern Pintail; Blue-winged and Cinnamon Teals; Northern Shoveler; Gadwall; American Wigeon; Redhead; Ring-necked Duck (spring and fall); Lesser Scaup (spring and fall); Common (fall to spring) and Barrow's (spring and fall) Goldeneyes; Bufflehead (spring and fall); Common Merganser; Ruddy Duck; Osprey; Northern Harrier; Cooper's (spring and fall) and Rough-legged (winter) Hawks; Golden Eagle (winter); Virginia Rail (spring and fall); Sora; Lesser Yellowlegs (spring and fall); Willet (spring and fall); Spotted Sandpiper; Long-billed Dowitcher (spring and fall); Common Snipe; Wilson's Phalarope (spring and fall); California Gull (spring and fall); Common Nighthawk; Black-chinned, Broad-tailed, and Rufous (mid-July to August) Hummingbirds; Say's Phoebe; Ash-throated Flycatcher; Western and Eastern Kingbirds; Loggerhead Shrike; Warbling Vireo; Tree, Violet-green, Northern Rough-winged, Cliff, and Barn Swallows; Black-billed Magpie; Common Raven; Red-breasted Nuthatch (spring and fall); Rock, Bewick's, House, and Marsh Wrens; Ruby-crowned Kinglet (spring and fall); Mountain Bluebird; Hermit Thrush; Western Tanager (spring and fall); Orange-crowned, Virginia's (spring and fall), Yellow, Yellow-rumped (spring and fall), Black-throated Gray, and MacGillivray's (spring and fall) Warblers; Common Yellowthroat; Wilson's Warbler (spring and fall); Yellow-breasted Chat; Chipping (spring and fall), Brewer's, Vesper, Lark, Savannah, Song, Lincoln's (spring and fall), and White-crowned (spring and fall) Sparrows; Black-headed and Blue Grosbeaks; Brewer's Blackbird; Bullock's Oriole; Pine Siskin (fall to spring); American Goldfinch

Best times to bird: Spring through fall; migration periods yield greatest diversity, April through May and September through October.

The birding: Brown's Park is an enormous bowl in the Green River Drainage. The sites described here provide good coverage of this remote area straddling the Utah–Colorado border. Starting on the Utah side, the Jarvie Historical Site offers a pleasant birding experience on the grounds of a turn-of-the-century homestead on the banks of the Green River. The home is situated in a small grove of mature cottonwoods adjacent to an extensive juniper forest. In this setting, it's possible to view

The Green River cuts through low cliffs in the Brown's Park National Wildlife Refuge.

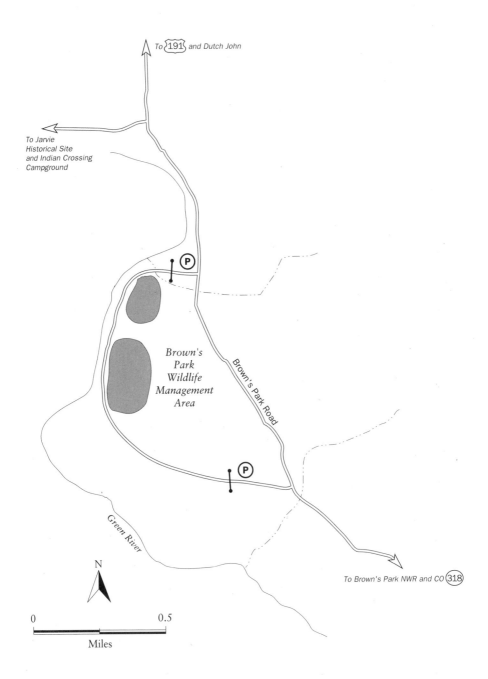

To 191 and Dutch John

To Jarvie
Historical Site
and Indian Crossing
Campground

Brown's
Park
Wildlife
Management
Area

Brown's Park Road

Green River

To Brown's Park NWR and CO 318

N

0   0.5

Miles

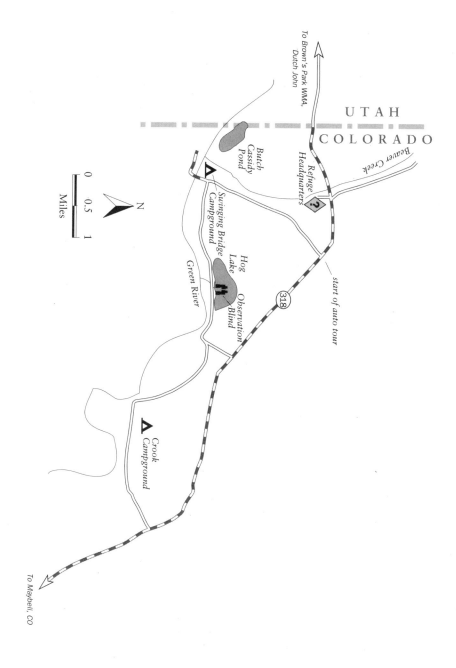

songbirds associated with both lowland riparian and pinyon-juniper habitats, as well as waterfowl using the bordering river. Start at the Jarvie Historical Site; then drive the short distance to the Brown's Park Wildlife Management Area. From there, slip across the border to the Brown's Park National Wildlife Refuge.

At the Jarvie House, walk the property, keeping an ear tuned to the branches of the sprawling cottonwoods. Bullock's Orioles, House Wrens, and Black-headed Grosbeaks are among the many species that use the trees for nesting. You're also likely to see Mountain Bluebirds and Say's Phoebes perching on fence posts and on the old farm machinery at the site, and Western Kingbirds on the electric wires overhead. Cross the road and take a short foray uphill to the cemetery, and you may encounter some of the species associated with junipers.

As you drive to nearby Brown's Park WMA you may wish to cross the bridge that lies 0.25 mile east of the Jarvie House and take a few minutes to bird Indian Crossing Campground, on the south side of the Green River. This is a cottonwood forest much like that around the Jarvie House, but there is a little more diversity in bird species. In addition to those mentioned above, you may see Blue Grosbeaks, Western Wood-Pewees, Yellow Warblers, and possibly some marsh birds.

No matter which entrance to the Brown's Park WMA you find, the strategy is basically the same. Walk the dikes that separate the two ponds, starting at the west end, where the dike and road follow the Green River for a good distance, with the ponds lying on your left. This approach allows for good viewing of warblers and Sage Thrashers, and Chipping, Brewer's, Vesper, Lark, Sage, and White-crowned Sparrows, using the brush along the river as well as a good chance to scan the ponds without flushing the waterfowl. A spotting scope would be helpful here but is not essential. Cheatgrass is king here, so high-topped boots or even gaiters will reduce the time you'll spend picking seed heads out of your socks.

The refuge bird list for Brown's Park National Wildlife Refuge contains an impressive 219 species. Most of these occur on the refuge as migrants, passing through once or twice each year, but birding on this remote refuge is interesting almost any time.

The refuge is well equipped to handle birders. Start your visit at refuge headquarters and pick up a current bird list and a brochure for the refuge's driving tour. At the information kiosk outside the headquarters, the refuge also maintains a sighting board with the latest news.

The refuge office is situated in the bottom of a drainage that supports a lush growth of riparian vegetation. This is actually one of the better places on the refuge to find songbirds because much of the driving route lacks readily accessible trees. Across CO 318 from the refuge headquarters is a dirt access road that climbs up through the drainage and passes through lands jointly managed by the refuge and the Colorado Division of Wildlife. It's worth spending some time exploring this drainage on foot, birding the riparian zone and the surrounding thickets of brush.

The auto tour route begins about a mile east of the headquarters, off of CO 318. The first 3.1 miles of the road drop through desert shrubs and a scattering of junipers before reaching the Green River. This is a good area to look for Mountain Bluebirds, Sage Thrashers, Sage Sparrows, and other species adapted to this dry upland habitat.

At 4.7 miles the road drops off the high bench and onto the floodplain. On your left you'll see a line of cottonwoods. At the eastern end of these trees lies Hog Lake. This bottomland is worth some exploration as well. The cottonwoods provide one of the two opportunities along this route to scout for flycatchers, warblers, and orioles.

The hunting/viewing blind on Hog Lake (reached via a signed side road) is well worth a stop. You can approach it without being seen by the birds and view waterfowl and common marsh species at very close range. Hog Lake is the closest you may get to waterfowl on this route, and binoculars are adequate here.

The remainder of the route alternates between lower, marshy areas adjacent to the river and upland bench areas with expansive views of the river and surrounding terrain. Although you should take the time to stop occasionally and scan, I'd recommend only one other specific place to stop: Crook Campground. This campground is in another grove of cottonwoods, so take a little time again to scan for passerines.

The auto tour takes you back onto CO 318 after 12.8 miles, and you can either return toward the headquarters (left) or continue into Colorado.

Directions: From Dutch John, head north on US 191. A few hundred yards north of the Utah–Wyoming border, turn right on an unpaved road (Brown's Park Road) opposite "The Gap" ranch. Look for the Bureau of Land Management markers pointing the way to the Jarvie Historical Site. Continue on this road, which alternates between a clay, gravel, and paved surface, for about 19 miles to the intersection marked for the Jarvie Historical Site. Turn right and drive 0.5 mile to the Jarvie House and Indian Crossing Campground.

Upon returning to Brown's Park Road, mark your mileage carefully (the WMA is poorly signed) and turn right. Proceed 0.7 mile to the first access road. Look for the single-lane gravel tracks departing downhill toward the WMA. From the main road you can see the ponds, the Green River and, if you look carefully, the gated and signed entrances to the area.

The Brown's Park NWR headquarters lies about 7 miles east of the intersection with the road to the Jarvie House. About 1.5 miles before reaching refuge headquarters, the road turns from gravel to pavement, marking the crossing into Colorado.

231

General information: This is one of those areas that combines great birding with a fascinating peek into the history of this remote corner of Utah. Brown's Park was settled in the latter part of the 1800s, and John Jarvie was one of the area's most prominent citizens. Jarvie's house is now a historical site in the care of the Bureau of Land Management and is definitely worth a stop. Brown's Park also lies on the "Outlaw Trail," and part of its colorful history is due to the historic presence of legends like Butch Cassidy and the Sundance Kid, two of many rustlers, bank robbers, and highwaymen who passed through this area and used it as a hideout.

The area is no less remote today than it was in Butch and Sundance's day, but cars have made the journey less arduous. If you approach this area from the Utah side, the last store and gas is in Dutch John, about 40 miles from the WMA. Be prepared with adequate gas and a good spare tire. The approach from the Utah/Wyoming side should not be attempted when the road is wet.

If you are traveling into Utah from Colorado, the route is paved to within about 8 miles of the WMA. This stretch of road is gravel, and certainly passable in wet or dry conditions.

It makes little sense for birders to travel to the remote Brown's Park Wildlife Management Area without venturing over the state line to the national wildlife refuge. Thus, a Colorado refuge is included in *Birding Utah*.

ADDITIONAL INFORMATION

Map grid: 9D
Elevation: 5,600 feet.
Hazards: None.
Nearest food, gas, and lodging: Dutch John.
Camping: Swinging Bridge and Crook campgrounds.
For more information: Brown's Park National Wildlife Refuge.

70 Strawberry River Valley

Habitats: Lowland riparian, upland desert shrub, pinyon-juniper, spruce-fir, aspen
Specialty birds: Northern Goshawk; Northern Pygmy-Owl; White-throated Swift; Olive-sided Flycatcher; Western Wood-Pewee; Dusky Flycatcher; Pinyon Jay; Townsend's Solitaire; Green-tailed and Spotted Towhees
Other key birds: Belted Kingfisher; Broad-tailed Hummingbird; Plumbeous and Warbling Vireos; Violet-green Swallow; Rock, Canyon, and House Wrens; Hermit Thrush; Virginia's, Yellow, MacGillivray's, and Wilson's Warblers; Yellow-breasted Chat; Western Tanager; Chipping, Fox, and Song Sparrows; Black-headed Grosbeak; Cassin's Finch
Best times to bird: Mid-May through July; mornings are best

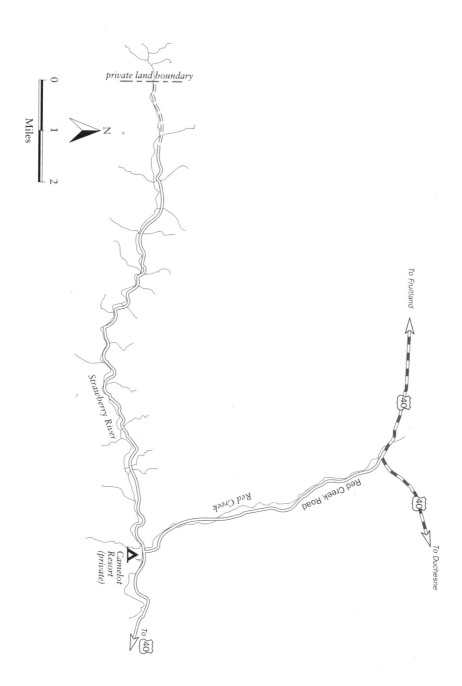

Steep cliffs flank the Strawberry River.

The birding: This is an 8-mile-long drive up the remote and extraordinarily beautiful Strawberry River Valley. For birders the draw is an excellent mix of habitat types for both desert and montane species.

After leaving the intersection at Camelot Resort, the road quickly drops down to the river, traversing cattail marshes and sloughs. From here the road climbs to a bench and passes through sagebrush meadows and cottonwood groves, as pinyon-juniper and spruce-fir forests descend to meet the valley bottom. As you climb up the valley, the vegetation becomes increasingly montane in character until you top out at a private property boundary, where you turn and retrace the route.

There is no one particular place to bird in this area—the whole route can be interesting. Stop at the various parking areas along the road and explore. My temptation is always to head for the riparian zone, but some of the more upland communities and the side canyons entering this valley are also worthwhile.

Directions: From the small community of Fruitland on US 40, head east for about 3 miles. As soon as you cross Red Creek (signed), turn right (south) onto Red Creek Road. After about 2 miles this road turns to dirt. Continue an additional 4.3 miles to a small sign pointing right (west) to Camelot Resort. Turn toward the resort; in a short distance this road forks again (it is paved here, for a very short distance); turn right, toward the Strawberry River. You're now on the road that will lead you up the Strawberry River valley.

To approach from Duchesne, head west on US 40. After crossing Starvation Reservoir, travel 3 miles and turn south onto 29520 West. Follow this road as it drops down to the Strawberry River valley. When the road turns away from the river valley and begins to climb to the north you'll see the sign indicating Camelot Resort. Turn left to the resort and follow the additional directions given above.

General information: Land ownership in this area is a real hodgepodge. There is some private land with both current dwellings and some old log cabins, but most of the land is public, managed by the Ashley National Forest, Bureau of Land Management, and the state.

There are plenty of opportunities for dispersed or primitive camping along this route, but be sure to select a spot along a side route that has already received some use. Be sure to respect any posted property.

ADDITIONAL INFORMATION

Map grid: 6E
Elevation: 6,234 to 6,726 feet.
Hazards: Remote area, no drinking water, road impassable when wet.
Nearest food, gas, and lodging: Duchesne.
Camping: Starvation Campground.
For more information: Utah Division of Wildlife Resources.

71 Desert Lake Waterfowl Management Area

Habitats: Lowland riparian, lowland desert shrub

Specialty birds: American White Pelican (spring and fall); Bald Eagle (spring and fall); Peregrine (fall) and Prairie Falcons; Snowy Plover; Long-billed Curlew; Marbled Godwit (spring and fall); Burrowing Owl; White-throated Swift; Lazuli Bunting

Other key birds: Pied-billed, Eared, and Western Grebes; Double-crested Cormorant (spring and fall); Snowy and Cattle Egrets; Black-crowned Night-Heron; White-faced Ibis; Turkey Vulture; Tundra Swan (late fall); Snow Goose (February to March); Green-winged Teal (spring and fall); Northern Pintail; Cinnamon Teal; Northern Shoveler; Gadwall; American Wigeon (spring and fall); Canvasback (spring and fall); Redhead; Ring-necked Duck (spring and fall); Lesser Scaup (spring and fall); Common Goldeneye (spring and fall); Bufflehead (spring and fall); Common (spring and fall) and Red-breasted (spring and fall) Mergansers; Ruddy Duck; Osprey; Northern Harrier; Ring-necked Pheasant; California Quail; Virginia Rail; Sora; Greater (spring and fall) and Lesser (spring and fall) Yellowlegs; Willet; Spotted, Western (spring and fall), and Least (spring and fall) Sandpipers; Long-billed Dowitcher (spring and fall); Wilson's and Red-necked (spring and fall) Phalaropes; Franklin's and California Gulls; Forster's and Black (spring and fall) Terns; Long-eared Owl; Say's Phoebe (spring and fall); Western Kingbird (spring and fall); Tree (spring and fall), Violet-green, Cliff, (spring and fall), and Barn Swallows; Black-billed Magpie; Marsh Wren; Common Yellowthroat; Indigo Bunting; Chipping (spring and fall), Brewer's (spring and fall), Vesper (spring and fall), Lark, Savannah (spring and fall), Fox (spring and fall), Song, Lincoln's (spring and fall), and White-crowned (spring and fall) Sparrows; Brewer's Blackbird; American Goldfinch (spring and fall)

Best times to bird: Diversity greatest during migration, March through April and September through mid-November

The birding: Access to the Desert Lake Waterfowl Management Area is restricted year-round but limited viewing opportunities are available, primarily from roads. Arriving from the direction of Elmo, you'll encounter a grove of cottonwoods following a dike as you reach the WMA boundary. Drive this area slowly during breeding season as it provides an opportunity to see Western Kingbirds, Black-billed Magpies, Loggerhead and Northern Shrikes, Yellow Warblers, Song Sparrows, and Indigo Buntings.

After about a mile, you'll come to the end of this tree row where the road divides—continue to the left, again following the route towards the quarry. Another 0.7 mile from this intersection the road crosses a marsh and there is an opportunity to scan one of the shallower ponds on the WMA. The best viewing is from the hillside, just before the road crosses the flat and the marsh. Although you can identify most waterfowl and some of the larger shorebirds from here with

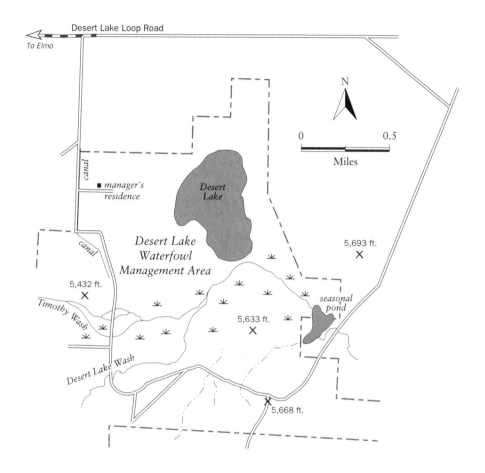

binoculars, a spotting scope would be helpful. You can expect to see any of the migrant waterfowl and shorebirds from this vantage, and during breeding season most of the common breeders are here, including Northern Shovelers, Gadwalls, Cinnamon Teals, American Avocets and Black-necked Stilts.

Another 1.2 miles beyond the hillside view of the pond, the road crosses another more extensive marsh complex. There is a pullout on the left (north) side of the road and a chance to scan the marsh for Northern Harriers, Virginia Rails, Sora, and Marsh Wrens. Ring-necked Pheasants are also in the area and can be heard calling during the breeding season.

As you drive the road around the perimeter of the WMA, you have the occasional glimpse of open water. If you have a spotting scope or strong binoculars, by all means stop and scan the area—in addition to waterfowl and shorebirds already mentioned, you'll likely see American White Pelicans, Double-crested Cormorants, and in migration, Common Loons, Ross's and Snow Geese, and Tundra Swans. At the peak of fall migration the bird population reaches 20,000 individuals.

Directions: From the small community of Elmo on UT 155, follow the signs to the Cleveland-Lloyd Dinosaur Quarry, heading east on Main Street. After 1.5 miles turn right onto a gravel road, still following the Dinosaur Quarry signs. Another 1.3 miles on this road and you'll enter the WMA, which is clearly signed and thoroughly fenced—follow the main road around the perimeter of the property, stopping to take advantage of viewing opportunities along the route.

General information: Walk-in access is available only during duck hunting season (roughly mid-October through early January). From about mid-March through the end of August all entry into the refuge is prohibited to protect bird nesting and rearing activities. In the narrow window that these two events leave, the refuge will allow supervised group tours and will accommodate some requests for walk-in access. Call the refuge manager to make arrangements. In general, expect to limit your viewing to the roadside.

ADDITIONAL INFORMATION

Map grid: 6G
Elevation: 5,600 feet.
Hazards: none.
Nearest food, gas, and lodging: Price.
Camping: Huntington State Park, Huntington.
For more information: Utah Division of Wildlife Resources, Desert Lake Waterfowl Management Area.

72 San Rafael River Recreation Site

Habitats: Lowland riparian, lowland desert shrub
Specialty birds: Peregrine Falcon; Pinyon Jay; Spotted Towhee; Lazuli Bunting
Other key birds: Cooper's Hawk; Barn Owl; Say's Phoebe; Ash-throated Flycatcher; Plumbeous Vireo; Western Scrub-Jay; Common Raven; Rock and Canyon Wrens; Mountain Bluebird (winter); Blue-gray Gnatcatcher; Yellow-rumped Warbler; Yellow-breasted Chat; Blue Grosbeak; Indigo Bunting; Scott's Oriole
Best times to bird: Early mornings during breeding season, April through June

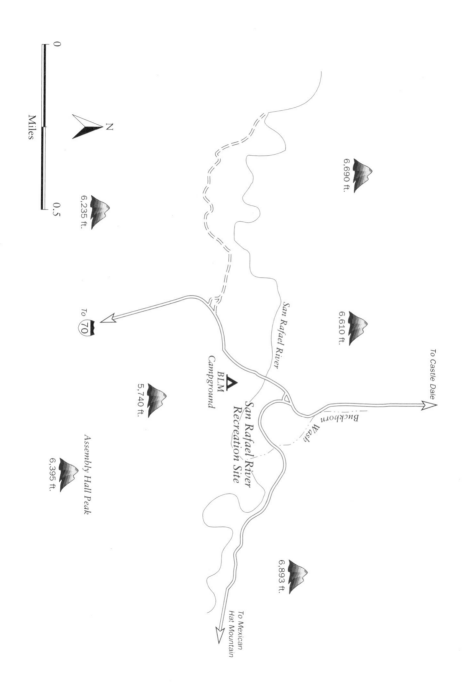

0

Miles

N

0.5

6,235 ft.

6,690 ft.

San Rafael River

6,610 ft.

To 70

BLM Campground

5,740 ft.

San Rafael River Recreation Site

Buckhorn Wash

To Castle Dale

Assembly Hall Peak
6,395 ft.

6,893 ft.

To Mexican Hat Mountain

The birding: Access to the riparian corridor along this section of the San Rafael River is possible because of a primitive camping area developed by the Bureau of Land Management and because people over the years have been making their own paths and roads into the cottonwoods and tamarisk. In spite of both official and unofficial development, there are no marked trails in the area, so you are on your own to pick your way into the river forest for birding.

You can familiarize yourself with the more abundant birds of the region in the BLM campground at the San Rafael River Recreation Site. Most of the campground is in desert shrubs, but the river borders one side, and you can walk behind the campsites, through one of the turnstiles in the fence, and stroll briefly along the banks of the river. At the least, this should uncover Ash-throated Flycatchers, Say's Phoebes, and Lazuli Buntings, all of which tend to be highly visible species.

After you've wandered this section of the river, climb to the top of the knoll situated behind the campground toilets. From here you can survey a good length of the river corridor and look for any species perched in treetops, singing to proclaim their territory. There are Peregrine Falcons in the area, probably nesting in the dramatic sandstone cliffs that frame this valley. They are a rare sight, but when they are seen it is often high over the river corridor or along the face of a cliff, so check the sky occasionally for any fast-flying raptors.

Two more nearby areas are worth checking out, and both have an informal trail or trails. From the parking area on the south side of the road, you can hike upstream along the river's edge, again keeping an eye open for flycatchers, warblers, and buntings among the trees and shrubs. Also, a road heads downriver towards the Mexican Hat area, starting on the opposite bank from the BLM campground. The first half-mile of this road follows the edge of the riparian corridor, and a number of dispersed campsites lie along side roads into the brush. Take a hike along this road, and wander periodically toward the river. The birding here is a little harder because the tamarisk limits visibility, but many species including Spotted Towhees and Yellow-breasted Chats sing from high perches.

Directions: Whether you arrive from Castle Dale to the northwest or from I-70 to the southwest, the entire route is well signed. From Castle Dale, head east on the Green River Cutoff Road, which is signed for Buckhorn Wash. Continue following the signs indicating Buckhorn Wash; the San Rafael River Recreation Site lies on the San Rafael River at the mouth of Buckhorn Wash about 23 miles from Castle Dale.

There are fewer turns from the I-70 approach. Take Exit 129 from I-70; the road to the San Rafael River first heads east, closely following along the north side of the interstate, before the route turns north to the recreation site. Total distance from the I-70 exit is about 18 miles.

General information: This is a popular recreation destination; the region is quite wild and the scenery is incomparable. The San Rafael River forms the only permanent water in the area, which is otherwise wide expanses of parched desert shrubs, a smattering of pinyon-juniper, and lots of rugged canyons with towering red sandstone cliffs.

Because this is true desert, the temperature rises rapidly during the day, and most intelligent critters retreat. Birds are most active in the early morning. Activity increases again as dusk approaches.

Finally, this area can only be reached via a long drive over gravel roads. Because this is a popular tourist destination the roads are well-maintained, but it's still a slow drive in a car from the nearest paved road.

ADDITIONAL INFORMATION

Map grid: 6G
Elevation: 5,300 feet.
Hazards: Remote location, no drinking water.
Nearest food, gas, and lodging: Castle Dale.
Camping: San Rafael Recreation Site Campground.
For more information: Bureau of Land Management, Price Field Office.

73 Ferron Reservoir and Ferron Mountain Loop

Habitats: Mountain riparian, mountain meadow, aspen, spruce-fir
Specialty birds: Northern Goshawk; Blue Grouse; Flammulated Owl; Western Screech-Owl; Northern Pygmy-Owl; Williamson's Sapsucker; Three-toed Woodpecker; Olive-sided Flycatchers; Western Wood-Pewee; Hammond's and Dusky Flycatcher; Clark's Nutcracker; Townsend's Solitaire; Green-tailed Towhee; Lazuli Bunting; Pine Grosbeak
Other key birds: Ring-necked Duck; Ruffed Grouse; Spotted Sandpiper; Broad-tailed Hummingbird; Red-naped Sapsucker; Warbling Vireo; Gray Jay; Mountain Chickadee; Red-breasted and White-breasted Nuthatches; Brown Creeper; Ruby-crowned Kinglet; Mountain Bluebird; Hermit Thrush; Western Tanager; Lincoln's and Vesper Sparrows; Cassin's Finch
Best times to bird: June through September

The birding: The Wasatch Plateau is one of the most beautiful and ecologically interesting regions in Utah. It reaches elevations of more than 10,000 feet and contains a diversity of habitats from arid pinyon-juniper stands to alpine meadows more characteristic of the Canadian Rockies. Few visit the plateau region because its diversity and appeal are well hidden from the highways and roads that bypass the area. The plateau tilts slightly eastward, so driving along its western face on I-15 travelers are confronted with steep, dry pinyon-juniper slopes. On the east side of the plateau, UT 10 passes through dry farms and along eroded sandstone cliffs that are more typical of the Colorado Plateau and slickrock desert region. The landscape gives few hints that gurgling mountain streams and flower-strewn meadows lie a short distance away. Weather permitting, the Wasatch Plateau is

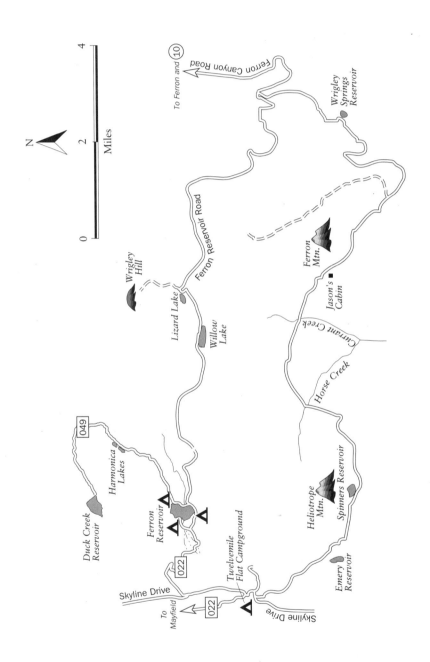

accessible by car, and a visitor with time may want to take Skyline Drive south from the small community of Tucker, on US 6, to its conclusion 90 miles south at I-70.

Whatever the length of your stay, a birding trip to Ferron Reservoir is well worthwhile. The reservoir is either a 28-mile drive west from the town of Ferron, or a 22-mile drive east from the community of Mayfield. From either approach, keep an eye open for Western Meadowlarks, Bullock's Orioles, Common Nighthawks, and Loggerhead Shrikes at lower elevations, and Pinyon Jays, White-throated Swifts and Violet-green Swallows as you pass through juniper and pinyon forests and climb along bands of cliffs on your ascent to the plateau.

The reservoir is actually a natural lake augmented with a dam in the early 1900s. The impoundment sits in a glacial cirque at 9,000 feet. Surrounding habitat includes spruce-fir, mountain meadow, aspen, riparian, and sagebrush meadow. About 90 species of birds occur in the vicinity. Look for Lazuli Buntings, Spotted Sandpipers, Ring-necked Ducks, White- and Red-breasted Nuthatches, Brown Creepers, Great Horned Owls, Mountain Bluebirds, Red-naped Sapsuckers, Hairy Woodpeckers, Mountain Chickadees, Ruby- and Golden-crowned Kinglets, Western Wood-Pewees, Olive-sided Flycatchers, Broad-tailed Hummingbirds, and Vesper Sparrows in the vicinity of the reservoir.

For a productive early-morning hike, depart from Ferron Reservoir and walk west on the Mayfield-to-Ferron Road. As you climb above the reservoir, a lush wet meadow opens to the east between the road and the campground. Many songbirds use the area for foraging, and numerous species stake out territories here and sing from prominent perches. The road becomes less steep just above the meadow and crosses a gently sloping plateau with a drier meadow area interspersed with spruce and fir stands. Higher still, the road turns south before leaving the Ferron Reservoir Watershed. At this point the road is surrounded by mature spruce and fir. This is a good spot for Three-toed Woodpeckers; they are most easily detected by the distinctive drumming males use to delineate their territories.

Another option is to take FR 049 to nearby Duck Creek Reservoir. This route crosses just below the dam face and heads north, and although it's longer than the walk described above, there is little change in elevation. You can do this either as a drive or a walk; you'll see more if you walk. This route passes through a similar mix of habitats as exists around Ferron Reservoir but is more secluded, with more aspen groves.

About 0.75 mile northeast of Ferron Reservoir dam, a large, flat, grassy meadow opens on the right. The meadow is bordered on the east and south by an aspen grove that descends to Indian Creek (which drains Ferron Reservoir). This is a good spot to park and walk the boundary between the aspens and the meadow. In addition to the expected aspen and mountain meadow species, I've seen Northern Goshawks and Olive-sided Flycatchers in this area.

Continuing along FR 049, you'll soon pass Harmonica Lakes on your left. These shallow ponds sit against the base of a sheer cliff, and I have seen Ring-necked Ducks here, as well as Spotted Sandpipers and Red-breasted Nuthatches in the small stand of conifers at the south end of the lakes. Explore the sagebrush expanse on the side of the road opposite the lakes; this may turn up sparrows. FR 049 re-enters a mixed forest just beyond Harmonica Lakes, and from here it is a short drive to the end of the passable road at Duck Creek Reservoir.

The Ferron Mountain Loop is a lengthier foray away from the reservoir that will take you into slightly drier terrain and expose you to a slightly different assemblage of birds. From Ferron Reservoir, one of your first stops should be in the saddle above the reservoir, which is a good spot for Three-toed Woodpeckers. The next major landmark along the route is Spinners Reservoir, which is worth a quick scan for Spotted Sandpipers and possibly a duck or two.

About 2 miles beyond Spinners, the road does a dogleg around the point of Heliotrope Mountain. The terrain rises slightly on one side of the road, but to the southeast a large meadow stretches toward a distant hill, passing near a sparse grove of aspens. This is an interesting area for birding, with sparrows in the meadow and Warbling Vireos and Yellow-rumped Warblers in the aspens. If you walk to the crest of the hill, you may encounter Clark's Nutcrackers, Steller's Jays, or Gray Jays in the conifers on the far side of the hill. There is also a steep, four-wheel-drive road that heads south from the point of Heliotrope Mountain. I have encountered Ruffed Grouse, Williamson's Sapsuckers, Scrub-Jays, and Pinyon Jays down this road. Walk it, don't drive.

About a mile beyond the point of Heliotrope Mountain the road crosses Horse Creek. This is a beautiful, noisy mountain creek that supports a lush forest along much of its banks. Although there is no trail, the walk along the banks of the stream is pleasant, with opportunities for seeing grouse, Western Tanagers, warblers, nuthatches, and Cassin's Finches.

Another 4 miles beyond Horse Creek you will pass Jason's Cabin, just off the right side of the road. This is also a good birding area, with more open terrain that provides a good chance to see raptors, including the Golden Eagle, which thrive on the hunting opportunities in the meadows and fields of sage brush. There are usually Red-naped Sapsuckers in the aspens around the cabin, and a short walk east along the road should turn up Green-tailed Towhees.

On the northern route back to Ferron Reservoir, be sure to stop at both Lizard and Willow lakes. Both are by the road and support a few more waterfowl than other lakes in the area. A four-wheel-drive road passes by Lizard Lake and traverses a ridgeline across open fields before fizzling out at Wrigley Hill. The views here are spectacular, and birding for finches and sparrows, among other species, can be good.

This is about a 30-mile route with more than one confusing intersection, but you can prevail with competent map skills and a good map—either USGS topographic series or the travel route map available at the Forest Service office in Ferron.

Directions: To reach Ferron Reservoir from the Forest Service office in downtown Ferron, turn west onto Ferron Canyon Road (FR 022) from UT 10. The reservoir is 28 miles from this point. From the west, drive 22 miles from the community of Mayfield, where you turn onto the Mayfield-to-Ferron Road (FR 022) from UT 137.

To complete the loop drive, head west from Ferron Reservoir on the Mayfield-to-Ferron Road, you encounter a short, steep climb to Skyline Drive. Turn south, and in about 2 more miles you'll reach Twelvemile Flat Campground. This is also the somewhat confusing intersection of four roads. Fortunately, the intersection is well signed. Head southeast toward Spinners Reservoir. This route winds past Heliotrope Point and Ferron Mountain, reuniting you with Ferron Reservoir Road just after passing Wrigley Springs Reservoir. At the intersection with Ferron Reservoir Road, turn left to return to the reservoir or right to travel to Ferron.

General information: The Wasatch Plateau was drastically overgrazed at the turn of the century, and without grasses and forbs to anchor the soil, erosion became a serious problem. The concentric rings scarring many mountains in the area are actually terraces cut by bulldozers in an effort to slow runoff and encourage the return of vegetation. The area is still actively grazed by both cattle and sheep, which you may encounter, but with the Forest Service's greater regulatory oversight the impact is less than it used to be.

Except over long holiday weekends and during hunting season, this area receives little use, and it's fairly easy to find seclusion. Also, in addition to the campground at Ferron Reservoir, there are a number of other campground facilities in the area as well as numerous opportunities for dispersed camping. Along the loop, a number of short side roads lead to secluded spots, often near water. Be sure to treat any water before drinking.

Skyline Drive is an interesting area in September and October for both migrating passerines and raptors.

ADDITIONAL INFORMATION

Map grid: 5G
Elevation: 8,226 to 10,500 feet.
Hazards: High altitude, flat tires, unpredictable weather, cold temperatures. Snow drifts may block routes even in early August. Check with the Forest Service office in Ferron before attempting travel.
Nearest food, gas, and lodging: Ferron Reservoir.
Camping: Ferron Reservoir, Twelvemile Flat Campground, Ferron Canyon
For more information: Ferron Ranger District, Manti National Forest.

74 Fruita

Habitats: Lowland riparian, upland desert shrub
Specialty birds: Peregrine and Prairie Falcons; Chukar; White-throated Swift; Western Wood-Pewee; Pinyon Jay; American Dipper; Townsend's Solitaire; Spotted Towhee; Lazuli Bunting
Other key birds: Turkey Vulture; Common Poorwill; Black-chinned, Broad-tailed, and Rufous (July to August) Hummingbirds; Red-naped Sapsucker; Downy and Hairy Woodpeckers; Say's Phoebe; Ash-throated Flycatcher; Western Kingbird; Plumbeous and Warbling Vireos; Western Scrub-Jay; Black-billed Magpie; Common Raven; Tree, Violet-green, Northern Rough-winged, Cliff, and Barn Swallows; Mountain Chickadee; White-breasted Nuthatch; Brown Creeper; Rock and Canyon Wrens; Ruby-crowned Kinglet; Mountain Bluebird; Hermit Thrush; Virginia's, Yellow, Yellow-rumped, MacGillivray's, and Wilson's Warblers; Yellow-breasted Chat; Western Tanager; Chipping, Vesper, Lark, Song, and White-crowned Sparrows; Black-headed and Blue Grosbeaks; Brewer's Blackbird; Bullock's Oriole; Pine Siskin; Lesser and American Goldfinches
Best times to bird: Late April through June

The birding: Capitol Reef National Park supports a surprising diversity of habitats in the midst of arid, slickrock desert. The historic settlement of Fruita, which is adjacent to the visitor center and the Fruita Campground, is one of the more accessible parts of the park and a great place to bird. The park maintains Fruita as a historic district, and the area retains the ambiance it must have had when it was first settled in 1881. Fruita is situated on the floodplain of the Fremont River at its confluence with Sulphur Creek, both permanent water sources that support lush riparian zones. There are also irrigated orchards to explore, an open parklike area with mown grass and large cottonwood trees, and some adjacent desert shrubs.

Start in the orchard at Fruita. Park by the orchard or in the parking area for the adjacent picnic area. There is a tall fence to keep deer at bay, but the gate is not locked. The orchard is small but it is a great place for warblers, particularly during spring migration, at which time it is not unusual to see five or more species in a short stroll.

From the orchard, walk toward the picnic area and down to Sulphur Creek. You can hike the creek on either side, but walking on the picnic ground side (i.e., south side) is easier. You can easily walk to the confluence with the Fremont River, then up the Fremont River to the Fruita Campground. This will expose you to a good stretch of riparian habitat and a chance to see American Dippers (in the creek or river), vireos, warblers, grosbeaks, and goldfinches.

Many birders at Fruita are interested in seeing Chukars, and there are about a dozen coveys in the valley bottom. The birds prefer the rocky, shrub-strewn slopes just above the valley floor. Chukars are common here, but they blend in so well with the desert rock that they can be hard to see. A good way to find them is to stroll the road between the campground and the visitor center, listening for their

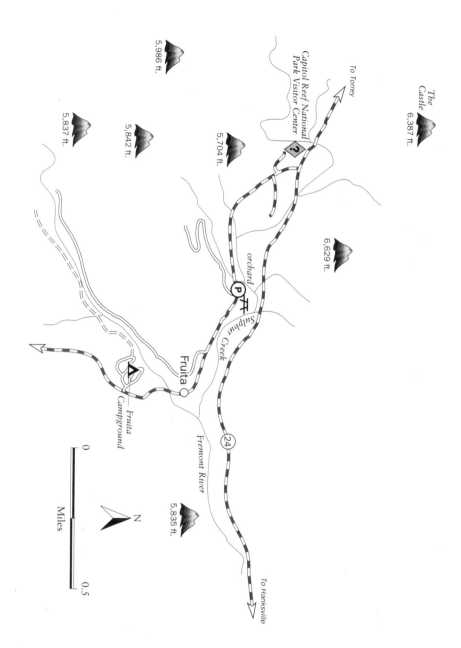

5,986 ft.

5,837 ft.

5,842 ft.

5,704 ft.

Capitol Reef National
Park Visitor Center

To Torrey

The
Castle
6,387 ft.

6,629 ft.

orchard

Sulphur Creek

P

Fruita

Fruita Campground

Fremont River

24

5,835 ft.

To Hanksville

0

Miles

0.5

N

247

calls emanating from the rocky slope. Then track them down by working your way toward their calls. Chukars are active in the early morning and again at dusk.

Directions: Fruita is about 35 miles west of Hanksville, or about 12 miles east of Torrey, on UT 24. Look for the entrance to Capitol Reef National Park Visitor Center, which is well signed. From the visitor center, continue south and east toward Fruita Campground—you'll see the orchard on your left about 0.5 mile from the visitor center, and the picnic area on your left 100 yards or so farther along the road.

General information: I have listed some of the more common species that you can expect to see at Fruita, but you can certainly expand on this list. The park bird list has about 217 species, and some of these you can find by exploring other habitats in the park. Many of the additional species seen at Fruita are migrants that appear on a somewhat unpredictable basis but make for interesting birding. There are, for example, an additional eight species of warblers seen in Fruita on a rare or occasional basis. Keep your eyes open and you may be rewarded with an interesting find.

Expect an entrance fee of about $10, and an additional fee of about $10 per night to use the campground.

ADDITIONAL INFORMATION

Map grid: 5I
Elevation: 5,450 feet.
Hazards: None.
Nearest food, gas, and lodging: Torrey.
Camping: Fruita Campground, Capitol Reef National Park.
For more information: Capitol Reef National Park.

75 Brian Head Peak

Habitats: Alpine, mountain meadow, spruce-fir
Specialty birds: Bald Eagle (fall); Northern Goshawk (fall); Ferruginous Hawk (fall); Peregrine (fall) and Prairie (fall) Falcons; White-throated Swift; Three-toed Woodpecker; Clark's Nutcracker; Townsend's Solitaire; American Pipit; Black Rosy-Finch; Pine Grosbeak (late summer); Red Crossbill
Other key birds: Osprey (fall); Northern Harrier; Sharp-shinned (fall), Cooper's (fall), Swainson's, Red-tailed, and Rough-legged (fall) Hawks; Golden Eagle; American Kestrel; Merlin (fall); Violet-green Swallow; Gray and Steller's Jays; Mountain Chickadee; Mountain Bluebird; Vesper and White-crowned Sparrows; Cassin's Finch; Pine Siskin
Best times to bird: Late May through mid-July for songbirds; mid-September through mid-October for migrating raptors, with best viewing at mid-day

75 Brian Head Peak

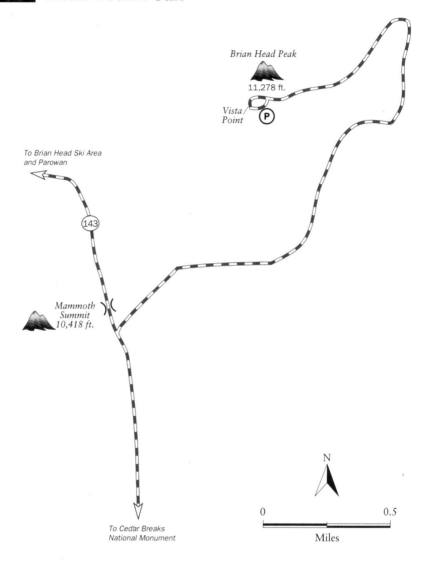

The birding: Brian Head Peak is known among birders as a reliable place to find some of Utah's more sought-after high-altitude species. It's also a place where you can expect to see migrating raptors in fall.

After leaving UT 143, begin scanning for bird activity in the sagebrush meadow on either side of the 3-mile drive to the summit. This open area is a good spot for Mountain Bluebirds, sparrows, and occasionally Townsend's Solitaires. Most of the remaining species, including fall raptors, White-throated Swifts, swallows, and Black Rosy-Finches, can be seen near the parking area at the summit.

Directions: From Parowan, head south on UT 143 for about 12 miles. Shortly after crossing into the Dixie National Forest, look for a Forest Service sign indicating a left turn to Vista Point and Brian Head Peak. Take this turn and proceed 3 miles to the parking area at Vista Point, watching the roadsides for birds as you approach the summit.

General information: This high-altitude site may not be accessible until well into summer. If you visit early in the season when snow still remains, check the open areas. Many species, particularly sparrows and finches, forage at the edge of the retreating snow.

ADDITIONAL INFORMATION

Map grid: 3J
Elevation: 11,278 feet.
Hazards: High altitude, cold temperatures.
Nearest food, gas, and lodging: Brian Head Resort (seasonal).
Camping: Cedar Breaks National Monument (seasonal).
For more information: Dixie National Forest, Cedar City Ranger District.

76 Panguitch Lake

Habitats: Upland desert shrub, pinyon-juniper, spruce-fir, aspen, mountain riparian
Specialty birds: Clark's Grebe; Bald Eagle (fall and early spring); Clark's Nutcracker; American Dipper; Green-tailed and Spotted Towhees
Other key birds: Common Loon (spring); Eared (spring and fall) and Western Grebes; Green-winged Teal; Northern Pintail; Cinnamon Teal; Northern Shoveler; Gadwall; American Wigeon (spring and fall); Canvasback (spring and summer); Lesser Scaup (spring and fall); Common Goldeneye (spring and fall); Osprey; Northern Harrier; Golden Eagle; Greater (spring and fall) and Lesser (spring and fall) Yellowlegs; Spotted Sandpiper; Long-billed Dowitcher (spring and fall); Red-necked Phalarope (spring and fall); Franklin's and California Gulls; Black-chinned, Broad-tailed, and Rufous (mid-July and August) Hummingbirds; Belted Kingfisher; Downy and Hairy Woodpeckers; Say's Phoebe; Violet-green Swallow; Gray and Steller's Jays; Black-billed Magpie; Common Raven; Mountain Chickadee; House Wren; Mountain Bluebird; Orange-crowned, Yellow, Yellow-rumped, and MacGillivray's Warblers; Common Yellowthroat; Western Tanager; Chipping, Brewer's, Vesper, Savannah, Lincoln's, and White-crowned Sparrows; Cassin's Finch
Best times to bird: May and September for migrant waterfowl and shorebirds; May through mid-July for breeding songbirds

The birding: Panguitch Lake is an important stopover area for migrating waterfowl and shorebirds; if you visit during spring or fall migration, you'll be surprised

Panguitch Lake

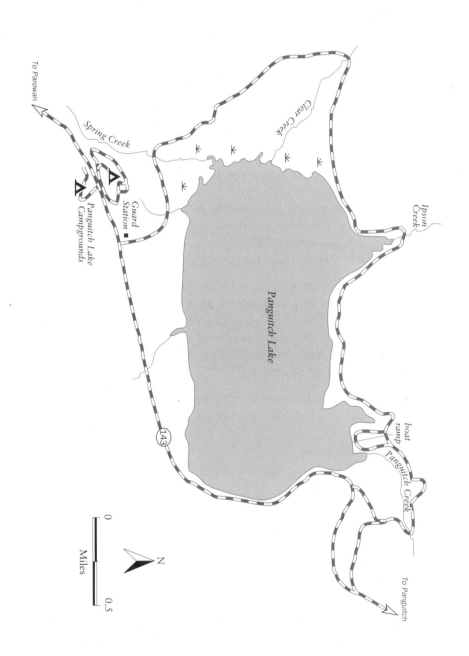

To Parowan

Spring Creek

Clear Creek

Ipson Creek

Guard
Station

Panguitch Lake
Campgrounds

Panguitch Lake

143

boat
ramp

Panguitch Creek

To Panguitch

0

Miles

0.5

N

at the diversity of birds using this high-altitude and distinctly montane area. The drive around the lake provides numerous opportunities for pulling off and scanning; a spotting scope is essential for distinguishing the shorebirds, but most waterfowl and songbirds can be identified with binoculars.

After passing the Panguitch Lake Guard Station, the road descends to the lake. There is much posted property, so please respect those landowners' wishes. The first opportunity for scanning the lake is in a gravel drive beside a small red barn, just as you turn west to follow the lakeshore. This upper end of the lake is the best for waterfowl and shorebirds, most of which congregate in this shallow and marshy area.

As you continue driving around the lake, you'll pass a willow thicket and marsh on either side of the road. Find a pulloff and spend time walking the road, scanning for warblers and sparrows. Much of the rest of the drive is through sagebrush meadows with more opportunities for pulling off the road and examining the lake for waterfowl. Open water birds like Common Loons, grebes, and gulls are more likely to be scattered across the center of the lake.

If this route fails to turn up as many songbirds as you'd like, head into one of the nearby campgrounds at the southwest corner of the lake, which are heavily timbered with conifers, and try walking the roads looping through the campsites.

Directions: From Parowan, head south on UT 143 for about 26 miles. As Panguitch Lake comes into view on your left, look for a left turn signed for the Panguitch Lake Guard Station. This road constitutes the birding route along the west, north, and east sides of the lake, with a number of turnouts from which you can scan for birds. This route takes you back onto UT 143 at the east end of the lake, in about 5 miles.

General information: Another nearby area purported to be good for birding is White Bridge Campground, about 3 miles below the dam outlet on UT 143.

ADDITIONAL INFORMATION

Map grid: 3J
Elevation: 8,120 feet.
Hazards: None.
Nearest food, gas, and lodging: Panguitch.
Camping: Panguitch Lake North.
For more information: Dixie National Forest, Cedar City Ranger District.

77 Duck Creek Reservoir and Stream

Habitats: Mountain riparian, aspen, spruce-fir
Specialty birds: Northern Goshawk; Blue Grouse; Northern Pygmy-Owl; Western Wood-Pewee; Hammond's and Dusky Flycatchers; Clark's Nutcracker; American Dipper; Townsend's Solitaire; Red Crossbill
Other key birds: Pied-billed Grebe; Green-winged Teal (winter); Gadwall; American Wigeon (spring and fall); Canvasback (spring and fall); Lesser Scaup (spring and fall); Common Goldeneye (spring and fall); Bufflehead (spring and fall); Cooper's and Rough-legged (winter) Hawks; Spotted Sandpiper; Wilson's (spring and fall) and Red-necked (spring and fall) Phalaropes; Northern Saw-whet Owl; Broad-tailed and Rufous (August to September) Hummingbirds; Red-naped Sapsucker; Downy and Hairy Woodpeckers; Cordilleran Flycatcher; Warbling Vireo; Steller's Jay; Tree and Violet-green Swallows; Mountain Chickadee; Red-breasted and White-breasted Nuthatches; Brown Creeper; House Wren; Ruby-crowned Kinglet; Hermit Thrush; Yellow, Yellow-rumped, and MacGillivray's Warblers; Common Yellowthroat; Chipping, Fox, and Lincoln's Sparrows; Cassin's Finch
Best times to bird: Year-round, although site access and bird diversity is optimal spring through fall, roughly May through October

The birding: This small riparian zone high on the Markagunt Plateau boasts a lake that attracts waterfowl and a pleasant, rushing mountain stream that supports a diverse community of montane birds. Waterfowl diversity is generally highest during migration, typically from April through May and September through October. In summer you can expect to see some of the common breeding waterfowl (Gadwall, Mallard, American Coot) as well as Spotted Sandpipers scurrying around the perimeter of the pond. Viewing is easy for birds on the pond: you can scan from pullouts along the road, park below the spillway and walk to the top of the dam, or walk through the forest bordering the north side of the lake.

Although there are no formal trails along the creek exiting the reservoir, the riparian area is well traveled, particularly by anglers who have beaten a network of paths through the willows. A good approach to birding the creek is to park below the dam and follow the stream east, walking among the trees and along the paths. Be sure to make the occasional foray into the willows; this is where you'll encounter most of the warblers and sparrows. If you hike in this direction for about 0.6 mile, you'll encounter a dirt road that cuts across your path. This is a good landmark, and you can follow this road (to the right) back to UT 14, or cross the creek and head back upstream to make a loop.

In winter Duck Creek Reservoir often contains the only open water around. Diversity is at its lowest at that time of year, but if you're traveling southeast from Cedar City in winter this can be an interesting place to stop.

Directions: Duck Creek Reservoir is 25 miles east of Cedar City on UT 14. Watch for the small body of open water just beyond the sign for Duck Creek Campground,

77 · Duck Creek Reservoir and Stream

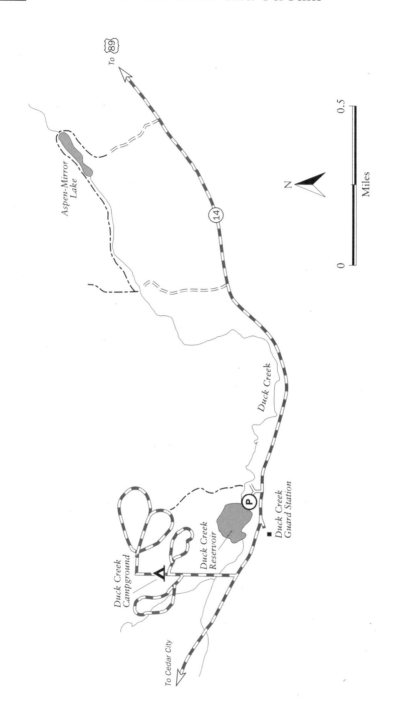

about 8 miles east of the intersection of UT 14 and UT 148. A good parking spot can be found at the pullout below the dam, or if there is snow on the ground, you can usually pull off the road on the side overlooking the lake.

General information: This high-altitude site often has snow well into summer; in general, the associated campground does not open until Memorial Day. Another area within an easy drive of the lake that offers good birding is Navajo Lake (which is frozen much of the year), about 3 miles to the west of Duck Creek Reservoir.

ADDITIONAL INFORMATION

Map grid: 3J
Elevation: 8,534 feet.
Hazards: Cold temperatures.
Nearest food, gas, and lodging: Cedar City.
Camping: Duck Creek Campground (seasonal), Dixie National Forest.
For more information: Dixie National Forest, Cedar City Ranger District.

78 Tropic Reservoir

Habitats: Mountain riparian, mountain meadow, spruce-fir, pinyon-juniper
Specialty birds: Clark's Grebe; Bald Eagle (winter); Prairie Falcon; Blue Grouse; Flammulated Owl; White-throated Swift; Olive-sided and Gray Flycatchers; Western Wood-Pewee; Hammond's and Dusky Flycatchers; Clark's Nutcracker; Pygmy Nuthatch; Townsend's Solitaire; Red Crossbill
Other key birds: Common Loon (spring); Pied-billed, Eared, and Western Grebe; Green-winged Teal; Northern Pintail; Blue-winged and Cinnamon Teals; American Wigeon (winter); Redhead; Ring-necked and Ruddy Ducks; Sharp-shinned, Cooper's, and Rough-legged (winter) Hawks; Golden Eagle; Spotted Sandpiper; Wilson's Phalarope (spring and fall); Common Nighthawk; Black-chinned and Broad-tailed Hummingbirds; Hairy Woodpecker; Cordilleran Flycatcher; Say's Phoebe; Plumbeous Vireo; Steller's Jay; Black-billed Magpie; Common Raven; Violet-green Swallow; Mountain Chickadee; Red-breasted and White-breasted Nuthatches; Brown Creeper; Western and Mountain Bluebirds; Hermit Thrush; Virginia's and Yellow-rumped Warblers; Western Tanager; Chipping and Vesper Sparrows; Pine Siskin
Best times to bird: Early mornings, May through June and September through October

The birding: The entire upper drainage of the East Fork of the Sevier River is an intriguing area that promises lots of good birding for passerines; the reservoir combines opportunities for both waterfowl and songbirds.

Waterfowl are most diverse here during spring and fall migration, and viewing these species is as simple as driving the main road as it passes above the east side of

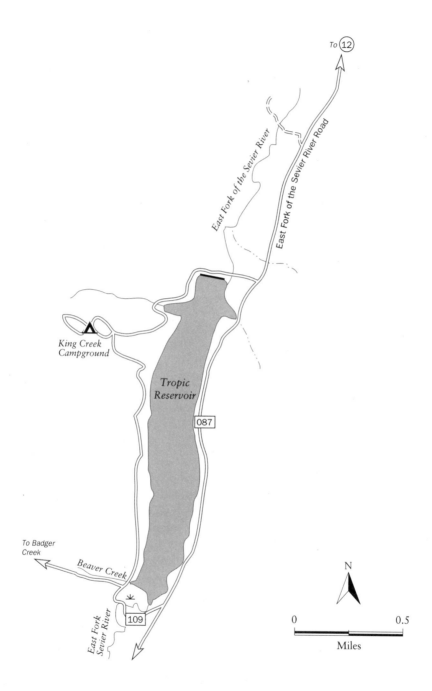

To (12)

East Fork of the Sevier River

East Fork of the Sevier River Road

King Creek
Campground

*Tropic
Reservoir*

087

To Badger
Creek

Beaver Creek

East Fork
Sevier River

109

N

0   0.5

Miles

A White-crowned Sparrow perches on a snowy fir tree.

the lake. Although you can stop at any point along the road, you'll likely discover that most of the waterfowl is concentrated along the upper (south) end of the lake, where the water is shallow and a modest amount of marsh vegetation is available. Scan the lake surface from whatever vantage you find convenient; binoculars are adequate for the task. If species more characteristic of open waters—loons, grebes, or gulls—are about, you'll likely to find them in the middle of the lake.

Opportunities for songbirds are somewhat less predictable. The riparian zone below the lake is difficult to access, so the best place to bird is upstream, above the lake. Drive south on the main access road until you reach the south end of the lake, turn right onto FR 109 (toward Badger Creek), proceed to the opposite side of the lake, and park near the dispersed campsites by the lake's edge. The East Fork of the Sevier at this point is stream sized, and it meanders in lazy oxbows through sagebrush and grass meadows before entering Tropic Reservoir. There are no trails, other than those made by anglers, so pick your way up the meadow, looking for birds using the stream corridor and flying back and forth between the meadow and adjacent forest.

Directions: From Tropic, head west on UT 12 for about 8 miles. After passing the intersection with UT 63, begin looking for a left turn, 2 miles away, signed for King Creek Campground. Take this turn onto a gravel road (East Fork of the Sevier River Road), and proceed 7 miles to Tropic Reservoir, which lies on the right side of the road. To reach the campground follow the signs and cross the dam to the campground.

257

General information: Expect to pay a $10 fee if you plan to camp overnight in King Creek Campground.

A road also follows the west side of the lake, connecting the campground with the upper end of the lake and the Badger Creek road. Although passable to passenger cars when dry, the road becomes slick when wet and should not be driven under these conditions.

ADDITIONAL INFORMATION

Map grid: 4J
Elevation: 7,835 feet.
Hazards: None.
Nearest food, gas, and lodging: Intersection of UT 12 and UT 63.
Camping: King Creek Campground, Dixie National Forest.
For more information: Dixie National Forest, Cedar City Ranger District.

79 Bryce Canyon National Park

Habitats: Spruce-fir, pinyon-juniper, mountain meadow
Specialty birds: Bald Eagle (winter); Prairie Falcon; Blue Grouse; Flammulated Owl; White-throated Swift; Olive-sided and Gray Flycatchers; Western Wood-Pewee; Hammond's and Dusky Flycatchers; Clark's Nutcracker; Pygmy Nuthatch; Townsend's Solitaire; Red Crossbill
Other key birds: Eared Grebe; Green-winged, Blue-winged, and Cinnamon Teals; American Wigeon (winter); Ruddy Duck; Sharp-shinned, Cooper's, and Rough-legged (winter) Hawks; Golden Eagle; Spotted Sandpiper; Wilson's Phalarope (spring and fall); Common Nighthawk; Black-chinned and Broad-tailed Hummingbirds; Hairy Woodpecker; Cordilleran Flycatcher; Say's Phoebe; Plumbeous Vireo; Steller's Jay; Black-billed Magpie; Common Raven; Violet-green Swallow; Mountain Chickadee; Red-breasted and White-breasted Nuthatches; Brown Creeper; Western and Mountain Bluebirds; Hermit Thrush; Virginia's, Yellow-rumped, and Grace's Warblers; Western Tanager; Chipping and Vesper Sparrows; Pine Siskin
Best times to bird: Early mornings, May through June and September through October

The birding: Much of Bryce Canyon National Park is a conifer-dominated monoculture, and bird diversity is not one of its selling points. Nonetheless, an attentive birder can see some very interesting species, particularly during migration. The walk described here is one of many possibilities and provides the greatest habitat diversity within an easy walk.

The North Campground is an easy area to walk, and it provides an opportunity to bird in a mature ponderosa pine forest with an open understory. I'd recommend starting in loops C and D, although you can start anywhere in the campground or

79 Bryce Canyon National Park

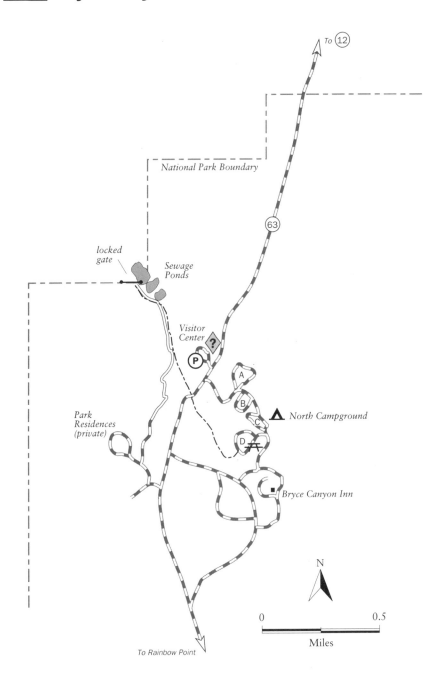

To ⑫

National Park Boundary

locked
gate

Sewage
Ponds

㉓

Visitor
Center

P

A

B

C

D

North Campground

Park
Residences
(private)

Bryce Canyon Inn

N

0   0.5

Miles

To Rainbow Point

on the nearby Rim Trail. Most of the activity in this area takes place on the tree trunks or fairly high in the branches, but keep an eye open for Steller's Jays, nuthatches, Brown Creepers, and warblers. An evening walk is the most likely time to detect Flammulated Owls by listening for their call, which sounds like a single "bark."

A large, open field of grasses and sagebrush lies at the bottom of the hill below the campground and is bisected by the park's main road. From the campground, descend to the meadow and continue birding toward the road, walking toward the conifer forest on the far side of the field and on the east side of the park road. This field area is good for Prairie Falcons (though rare), Western and Mountain Bluebirds, Townsend's Solitaire, and sparrows.

A dirt road follows the far edge of the field, tracing the edge of the young forest bounding the western edge of the field. Continue birding the field area and the adjacent forest as you walk along this road. You will be able to see the terminus of this route, where a locked gate blocks the road. As you approach this gate you'll notice a series of three ponds on your right. These are the park's sewage ponds, a great place for waterfowl, particularly during migration. The ponds are small and there is no riparian vegetation, so you can easily scan them. Return via the route you followed down to the ponds or follow the opposite side of the meadow to the visitor center and walk back through the campground along park roads.

Directions: From the community of Tropic, head west on UT 12 for about 8 miles to the intersection with UT 63. This intersection is well signed for Bryce Canyon National Park, so turn left (south) on UT 63 and proceed about 2 miles, past the entrance station and visitor center. Just a few yards beyond the visitor center, turn left into North Campground, follow the main road through the campground to Loop D, and park in the picnic area.

General information: An entrance fee of $10 per vehicle is required to enter the park, and an additional fee (about $10 per night) is charged for camping. A stop at the visitor center is worthwhile. Ask for birding tips and a current bird checklist from the ranger on duty.

ADDITIONAL INFORMATION

Map grid: 4J
Elevation: 8,000 feet.
Hazards: None.
Nearest food, gas, and lodging: Bryce Canyon Lodge.
Camping: North Campground, Bryce Canyon National Park.
For more information: Bryce Canyon National Park.

80 Pine Valley Campgrounds

Habitats: Spruce-fir, mountain riparian

Specialty birds: Northern Goshawk; Flammulated Owl; Northern Pygmy-Owl; Williamson's Sapsucker; Olive-sided, Hammond's, and Dusky Flycatchers; Gray Vireo; Clark's Nutcracker; Pygmy Nuthatch; American Dipper; Townsend's Solitaire; Spotted Towhee

Other key birds: Green-winged Teal; Sharp-shinned and Cooper's Hawks; Black-chinned Hummingbird; Belted Kingfisher; Hairy Woodpecker; Cordilleran Flycatcher; Plumbeous Vireo; Gray and Steller's Jays; Tree, Violet-green, Cliff, and Barn Swallows; Mountain Chickadee; Red-breasted and White-breasted Nuthatches; Brown Creeper; Western and Mountain Bluebirds; Hermit Thrush; Virginia's, Yellow-rumped, Black-throated Gray, Grace's, and MacGillivray's Warblers; White-crowned Sparrow

Best times to bird: Mid-May through September

The birding: This exquisite high-elevation valley lies at the headwaters of the Santa Clara River, a tributary of the Virgin River. It's one of the more beautiful settings in the state for birding with a mix of montane and southwestern desert bird species. A mature stand of ponderosa pines and subalpine fir interspersed with an understory of mountain mahogany fills the upper valley, while the headwaters of the Santa Clara meander through the center of the watershed. The approach to the area also includes an ascent through pinyon-juniper and open pastureland.

An impounded lake on Pine Valley Creek, next to the campgrounds.

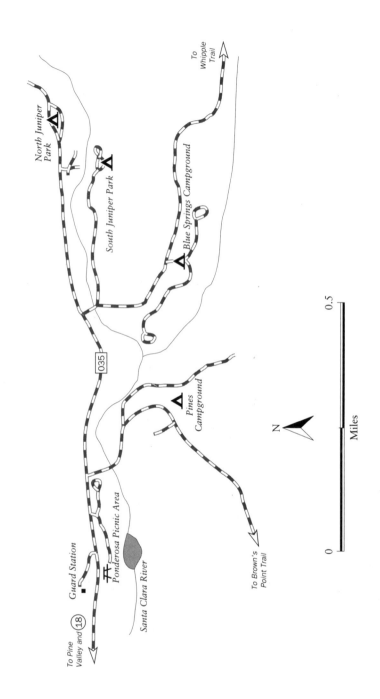

Although numerous trails in the area depart for the surrounding mountains, the birding in the campground area is representative of the area as a whole, and you don't have to put in miles of strenuous hiking. Simply walk the main access road and through the campgrounds. The road passes along a stream where bird diversity seems greatest, but be sure to explore some of the higher and drier slopes rising above the creek—for this, the Pines Campground is particularly good.

Directions: The turnoff to Pine Valley is located about 23 miles north of St. George on UT 18. The well-signed turn onto FR 035 is in the small community of Central, and the road soon enters the Dixie National Forest. Stay on this route through the community of Pine Valley; it leads directly into the network of campgrounds about 10 miles from the intersection with UT 18.

General information: Vehicle access to the upper end of this high valley and to the campgrounds is restricted to a few months of the year; you can reasonably expect to get in here from Memorial Day through the end of September. The remainder of the year a gate prevents vehicle access beyond a small impoundment on the creek. If you arrive before tourist season and the opening of the road, there is a parking area at the gate, and the walk to the campgrounds and birding areas is short. Cross-country skiing is also popular here, but there is little bird activity in the depths of winter.

ADDITIONAL INFORMATION

Map grid: 2J
Elevation: 6,600 feet.
Hazards: Cold temperatures.
Nearest Food, gas, and lodging: Pine Valley.
Camping: Pine Valley campgrounds (several), Dixie National Forest.
For more information: Dixie National Forest, Pine Valley District.

81 Silver Reef to Oak Grove Campground

Habitats: Lowland riparian, mountain riparian, upland desert shrub, pinyon-juniper, spruce-fir, aspen
Specialty birds: Flammulated Owl; Western Screech-Owl; Lewis's Woodpecker; Gray Flycatcher; Gray Vireo; Pygmy Nuthatch; Green-tailed and Spotted Towhees; Lazuli Bunting
Other key birds: Black-chinned Hummingbird; Hairy Woodpecker; Black Phoebe; Western Scrub-Jay; Red-breasted and White-breasted Nuthatches; Brown Creeper; Ruby-crowned Kinglet; Western Bluebird; Hermit Thrush; Plumbeous Vireo; Yellow-rumped and Grace's Warblers; Black-chinned Sparrow
Best times to bird: May through mid-July, and September for fall migrants

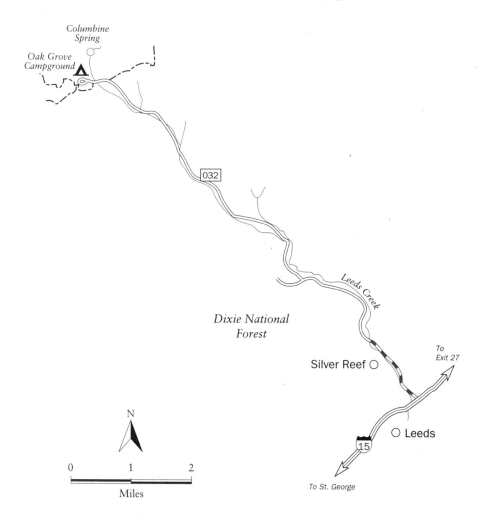

The birding: Leeds Creek is a rushing mountain stream that descends through a number of vegetation zones before flowing into nearby Quail Creek Reservoir. The perennial stream and its narrow riparian corridor attract a variety of birds, and it can be particularly interesting during spring and fall migration when passerines stop for resting and feeding. Much of this route is characterized by dense, shrubby vegetation, but there are some open stretches of pinyon-juniper, scrub oaks, aspens, and cottonwoods.

The narrowness of the road limits your birding to two strategies. You can drive the road and stop, assuming no one is behind you, whenever you spot a bird, or you can take advantage of the sporadic pullouts and dispersed campsites along the route to pull off and walk around. Time permitting, I'd recommend the latter approach. Try to stop at least once in each of the distinct vegetation types the road passes through. The species tolerant of dry conditions will be along the lower portion of the route; look for Gray Flycatchers, Western Scrub-Jays, Black-chinned Hummingbirds, towhees, Lazuli Buntings, and Black-chinned Sparrows in the pinyon-juniper forests, in the scrub oaks, and on dry slopes above the creek. In the aspens and cottonwoods you'll more likely see warblers and vireos.

The road ends in a magnificent grove of ponderosa pines nestled in a cove beneath towering cliffs. Two trails depart from here and climb higher into the adjacent Pine Valley Mountain Wilderness, but Oak Grove Campground, which lies in the pines and touches on thickets of Gambel oak, is a great destination for owls, woodpeckers, nuthatches, Brown Creepers, and Western Bluebirds.

Directions: Take I-15 north from St. George for 15 miles to Exit 23, just north of Leeds. It's only possible to go in one direction from this exit—west toward Silver Reef. This access road takes you along the edge of Silver Reef and into the Dixie National Forest. The birding starts where the road crosses Leeds Creek and enters the national forest (the road becomes FR 032) and essentially ends at Oak Grove Campground 8 miles away.

General information: The narrow gravel road accessing this site seems like the last place I'd want to take a travel trailer, but I'm sure people do. I'd advise against it. Once at the top of the road in the campground there isn't much room for maneuvering. The road is certainly passable to passenger vehicles.

If you'd like a wilder, but otherwise similar, birding experience and have a four-wheel-drive vehicle, the next watershed north is also an interesting birding route. This area can be reached by heading northwest from Exit 27, at Anderson Junction, onto FR 029.

ADDITIONAL INFORMATION

Map grid: 2K
Elevation: 3,560 feet.
Hazards: None.
Nearest food, gas, and lodging: Hurricane.
Camping: Oak Grove Campground, Dixie National Forest.
For more information: Dixie National Forest, Pine Valley District.

82 Kolob Reservoir Road

Habitats: Pinyon-juniper, upland desert shrub, spruce-fir, aspen, mountain meadow, mountain riparian, lowland riparian

Specialty birds: Bald Eagle (spring and fall); Prairie Falcon; Blue Grouse; Flammulated Owl; Northern Pygmy-Owl; Lewis's Woodpecker; Olive-sided Flycatcher; Western Wood-Pewee; Dusky and Gray Flycatchers; Gray Vireo; Pinyon Jay; Pygmy Nuthatch; Townsend's Solitaire; Green-tailed and Spotted Towhees; Red Crossbill

Other key birds: Eared Grebe (spring); Green-winged and Cinnamon Teals; American Wigeon (spring); Ring-necked Duck (spring); Turkey Vulture; Sharp-shinned, Cooper's, and Swainson's Hawks; Golden Eagle; Spotted Sandpiper; Band-tailed Pigeon; Common Nighthawk; Common Poorwill; Black-chinned, Costa's, Broad-tailed, and Rufous (July to August) Hummingbirds; Red-naped Sapsucker; Downy and Hairy Woodpeckers; Cordilleran Flycatcher; Say's Phoebe; Ash-throated Flycatcher; Loggerhead Shrike; Plumbeous and Warbling Vireo; Tree and Violet-green Swallows; Steller's Jay; Western Scrub-Jay; Red-breasted and White-breasted Nuthatches; Brown Creeper; Bewick's and House Wrens; Ruby-crowned Kinglet; Western and Mountain Bluebirds; Virginia's, Yellow, Yellow-rumped, Black-throated Gray, and Grace's Warblers; Western Tanager; Rufous-crowned, Chipping, Brewer's, Vesper, and Lark Sparrows; Black-headed Grosbeak

Best times to bird: May through July and mid-September through October

The birding: The road to Kolob Reservoir passes through a sample of diverse habit types, essentially rising through several vegetation–life zones from the low desert to the conifer-aspen–dominated environment. Scan either side of the road on your way to the reservoir. Try to pay a visit to each of the habitats that the road passes through, because the bird community changes dramatically as elevation increases.

There are a few spots in particular that are worth further exploration. Unfortunately, because of private lands and limited access, the lower communities are under represented on this list. In the lower section of the route you'll pass through an expanse of desert shrubs. Look for desert-adapted birds here, including Gambel's Quails, Costa's Hummingbirds, Western Kingbirds, and Rufous-crowned, Lark, and Black-Throated Sparrows.

Your best exposure to a lowland riparian community comes 3.4 miles from the intersection of Kolob Reservoir Road and UT 9 where you'll cross North Creek. Pull off and scan the cottonwoods and narrow riparian corridor. The land on either side is private so you're limited to viewing from the road, but you may see Western Wood-Pewees, Black Phoebes, Warbling Vireos, or warblers.

After crossing the creek, the road begins to climb through a pinyon-juniper forest. Two side roads, one at about 5 miles (at the Zion National Park boundary) and one about a mile farther north, depart to the left. Both provide places to pull off and hike the pinyon-juniper zone. Activity here tends to be sporadic; hot spots

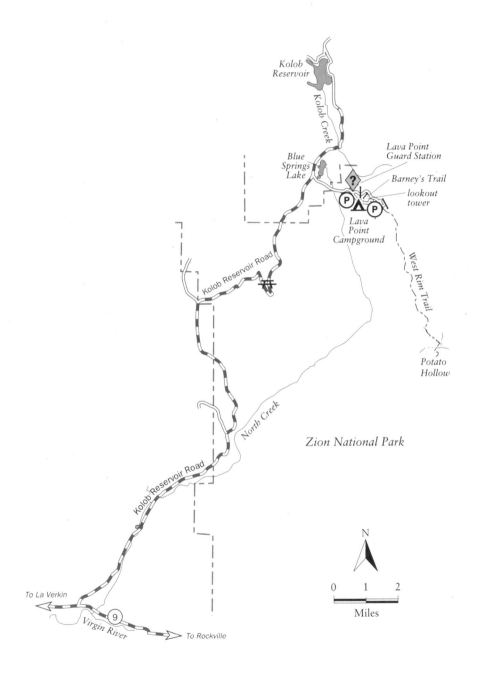

Kolob
Reservoir

Kolob Creek

Lava Point
Guard Station

Blue
Springs
Lake

Barney's Trail

lookout
tower

Lava
Point
Campground

Kolob Reservoir Road

West Rim Trail

Potato
Hollow

North Creek

Zion National Park

Kolob Reservoir Road

N

0   1   2
Miles

To La Verkin

9

Virgin River → To Rockville

erupt, die out, and then erupt somewhere else. You just have to be in the right place at the right time. With luck you may find a flock of Pinyon Jays, Western Scrub-Jays, Gray Flyctachers, Townsend's Solitaires, or Gray Vireos.

Climbing higher still, there is a pullout and picnic area on the left side of the road at 15.5 miles in a grove of towering ponderosa pines. Stop here and cross the road into the adjacent grassy meadow, and wander among the ponderosas. There should be nuthatches of all species and possibly some Brown Creepers in this area. This is also good habitat for Flammulated Owls, but they are hard to find; listen for their calls around twilight, which sound like a dog emitting a single "bark."

The two reservoirs at the top of the route are both interesting. The first, Blue Springs Lake, is on the right side of the road at 19.9 miles. This reservoir is surrounded by private lands, so access (and visibility) is limited. If you stay on the Kolob Reservoir Road, you will get a brief view another 0.2 mile or so up the road. If you take the right turn to Lava Point (at 19.9 miles), you'll cross a dike and find most of the reservoir within sight. Kolob Reservoir, another 3.3 miles up the reservoir road, is surrounded by Forest Service lands and is more accessible. Both lakes host migrating waterfowl, Bald Eagles (migrating), Ospreys, and Spotted Sandpipers. The aspen forest around Kolob Reservoir is good for owls, songbirds, and occasionally Lewis's Woodpeckers.

Directions: From the small community of La Verkin (just north of Hurricane), head east on UT 9. After traveling about 5 miles, you'll reach Kolob Reservoir Road, a left turn signed to Kolob Reservoir. Take this left turn and begin the birdwatching route. The tour route ends 23.5 miles northeast at Kolob Reservoir.

General information: The high country of Zion can be a welcome refuge from the oppressive heat of summer in the main canyon. This temperature differential affects the bird community: in areas around Blue Springs Lake and Kolob Reservoir, early season activity lags behind the main canyon of Zion, and the breeding season for some species extends well into July, long after the main canyon has fallen silent. If you bird this route in the later summer, expect to see little activity in the lower pinyon-juniper and shrub communities. You may want to focus on the high plateau around the two lakes and at nearby Potato Hollow (site 83, which follows).

ADDITIONAL INFORMATION

Map grid: 2J and 2K
Elevation: 3,550 to 8,094 feet.
Hazards: None.
Nearest food, gas, and lodging: La Verkin.
Camping: Lava Point Campground, Zion National Park.
For more information: Zion National Park and Dixie National Forest, Cedar City Ranger District.

83 Potato Hollow

Habitats: Spruce-fir, aspen, mountain meadow, mountain riparian, pinyon-juniper, upland desert shrub, lowland riparian

See Map on Page 267.

Specialty birds: Western Wood-Pewee; Dusky Flycatcher; Clark's Nutcracker; Pygmy Nuthatch; Townsend's Solitaire; Green-tailed Towhee; Red Crossbill

Other key birds: Turkey Vulture; Sharp-shinned and Cooper's Hawks; Golden Eagle; Spotted Sandpiper; Band-tailed Pigeon; Common Poorwill; Black-chinned, Broad-tailed, and Rufous (July to August) Hummingbirds; Red-naped Sapsucker; Downy and Hairy Woodpeckers; Ash-throated Flycatcher; Violet-green Swallow; Plumbeous and Warbling Vireos; Steller's Jay; Western Scrub-Jay; Mountain Chickadee; Red-breasted and White-breasted Nuthatches; Brown Creeper; Ruby-crowned Kinglet; Western and Mountain Bluebirds; Hermit Thrush; Orange-crowned, Virginia's, Yellow, Yellow-rumped, Black-throated Gray, Grace's, and MacGillivray's Warblers; Western Tanager; Chipping, Lark, Black-throated, and Lincoln's Sparrows; Cassin's Finch; Pine Siskin

Best times to bird: May through July and mid-September through October; early morning is best

The birding: The route to Potato Hollow is either a long day hike or, better yet, a leisurely overnight backpacking trip. Either way, once you reach the trailhead there is little change in elevation, and the route is not strenuous.

This pond at Potato Hollow is fed by a spring.

At the upper end of this hike, the trail passes through an open ponderosa pine forest with an understory of shrubs and oaks. This is a great area for woodpeckers, Clark's Nutcrackers, nuthatches, and creepers, as well as Western Scrub-Jays. I was lucky enough to see two Acorn Woodpeckers here in 1997, a relatively rare sighting. Time will tell whether a breeding colony will become established.

Most of the hike is through dry habitats, but in addition to the species just mentioned, the route is good for Ruby-crowned Kinglets, Black-chinned Hummingbirds, Western and Mountain Bluebirds, Hermit Thrushes, Plumbeous Vireos, MacGillivray's Warblers, Green-tailed Towhees, and Chipping, Lark, and Black-throated Sparrows.

The trail eventually drops off the long ridge and enters a narrow valley, which is green and well watered in spring. From here it's a short distance to Potato Hollow, a small impounded spring at the head of a dramatic sandstone canyon. The pond and the ponderosa-aspen forest around it attract Dusky Flycatchers, vireos, warblers, the occasional duck, and Spotted Sandpipers.

Directions: From the small community of La Verkin (just north of Hurricane), head east on UT 9. After traveling about 5 miles, you'll reach Kolob Reservoir Road, a left turn signed to Kolob Reservoir. Turn right at the southern end of Blue Springs Lake, where a sign indicates the route to Lava Point. Although your destination is Potato Hollow, it is the West Rim Trail that you will hike to get there. Proceed about 1 mile to the guard station. The road to the trailhead, which is still 4 miles away, descends steeply to the right from the guard station parking area. If the road is wet, it will be gated and closed; you can park here and walk in, but in this situation a better alternative is to continue out the access road to the Lava Point Campground, another mile down the road.

If you leave from the Lava Point Campground, take Barney's Trail, which starts between campsites 2 and 3. This trail drops off the plateau and reaches the trailhead access road in 0.3 mile. Turn right on the access road and proceed to the West Rim Trailhead, about a mile to the southwest.

General information: Many areas around Potato Hollow and the West Rim Trail burned in a forest fire in 1996. Although it remains to be seen exactly how the bird community will respond, this is a fire-adapted environment and should rebound quickly. The immediate implication for hikers is that much of the route that was shaded will be open to the sun for years to come, which makes for hot hiking even at this altitude. Be sure to carry plenty of water. Water is available near the trailhead (requires a 0.3 mile hike off the West Rim Trail, but the route is signed) and not again until Potato Hollow. Be sure to carry plenty of water, and treat any water you collect at either of the aforementioned sources.

Finally, if you plan to stay at Lava Point Campground, there are only six sites and no water available. Plan to get there early in the day to claim a site, and carry in all of your water.

ADDITIONAL INFORMATION

Map grid: 2K and 2J
Elevation: 3,550 to 8,094 feet.
Hazards: Biting insects, remote location.
Nearest food, gas, and lodging: La Verkin.
Camping: Lava Point Campground, Zion National Park.
For more information: Zion National Park.

84 Pa'rus and Emerald Pools Trails, Zion National Park

Habitats: Lowland riparian, upland desert shrub, pinyon-juniper
Specialty birds: Peregrine Falcon; Flammulated Owl; Western Screech-Owl; Northern Pygmy-Owl; White-throated Swift; Western Wood-Pewee; Willow Flycatcher; Cassin's Kingbird; Gray Vireo; Pinyon Jay; American Dipper; Spotted Towhee; Lazuli Bunting
Other key birds: Turkey Vulture; Northern Harrier; Sharp-shinned Hawk; Cooper's Hawk; Merlin; Gambel's Quail; Barn Owl; Common Poorwill; Black-chinned, Broad-tailed, and Rufous (July to August) Hummingbirds; Belted Kingfisher; Violet-green Swallow; Red-naped Sapsucker; Downy and Hairy Woodpeckers; Cordilleran Flycatcher; Say's Phoebe; Ash-throated Flycatcher; Western Kingbird; Loggerhead Shrike; Plumbeous and Warbling Vireos; Steller's Jay; Western Scrub-Jay; Common Raven; Violet-green and Cliff Swallows; Mountain Chickadee; White-breasted Nuthatch; Brown Creeper; Rock, Canyon, and House Wrens; Hermit Thrush; Virginia's, Lucy's, Yellow, Yellow-rumped, and Black-throated Gray Warblers; Yellow-breasted Chat; Western Tanager; Chipping, Song, Lincoln's, White-crowned (winter), and Harris's (winter) Sparrows; Black-headed and Blue Grosbeaks; Bullock's Oriole; Lesser Goldfinch
Best times to bird: May, June, and October

The birding: Pa'rus Trail is probably the single best all-round birding destination in the Virgin River Canyon. The trail is an easy walk and although it passes primarily through riparian vegetation, its proximity to other habitats creates greater diversity. The Virgin River is also a migration corridor, which acts to increase diversity and your chances of seeing something interesting.

Early mornings are probably best, if for no other reason than you'll encounter fewer people. Birding by ear is difficult because the river is a constant and noisy companion, so keep a sharp eye out for movement. This can also be a good area for an evening owl walk. Follow the path listening for calls; if you bring a strong flashlight you may find their source.

The nearby Emerald Pools Trail leads to a series of natural ponds along a shallow stream descending into Zion Canyon. The trail is paved to the first pool, and above this point it turns to dirt and gravel. The distance to the uppermost pool is not great, about 3 miles round-trip, and the climb is moderate. Much of the

84 Pa'rus and Emerald Pools Trails, Zion National Park

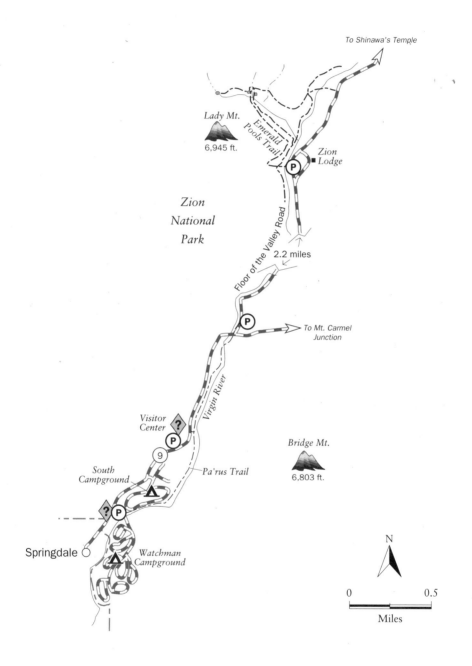

To Shinawa's Temple

Lady Mt.
6,945 ft.

Emerald Pools Trail

Zion Lodge

P

Zion National Park

Floor of the Valley Road

2.2 miles

P

To Mt. Carmel Junction

Virgin River

Visitor Center

P

?

9

Bridge Mt.
6,803 ft.

South Campground

Pa'rus Trail

P

?

Springdale

Watchman Campground

N

0   0.5
Miles

Two hikers are dwarfed by canyon walls at Upper Emerald Pool.

vegetation along the route is dense and low-growing; juniper and oaks dominate.

Starting from the trailhead you'll pass along a short section of the Virgin River through mature cottonwoods. This is the best area on this trail for most riparian species, including Warbling Vireo, Yellow and Yellow-rumped Warblers, Yellow-breasted Chat, Black-headed and Blue Grosbeaks, Song Sparrow, Bullock's Oriole, and Lesser Goldfinch.

From the river the trail climbs into drier terrain. Look overhead for swifts and swallows, which forage in the air rising from the canyon floor. Patience is required for finding the birds that inhabit this dense vegetation. The earlier part of the year—when most birds will be singing conspicuously—is often the best time to bird here. Spring is also a good time of year for evening owl walks along the paved section of the trail.

Birding in this side canyon is usually uniform along the entire route. The trail climbs behind a waterfall plunging between the middle and lower pools, and from there the trail becomes steeper and somewhat less traveled. Return via the same route, or by the middle pool, take the return trail that follows the cliff face above the canyon.

Directions: The Pa'rus Trail follows the Virgin River from the South Campground to the Main Canyon Junction. After passing through the South Entrance (near Springdale), drive less than 0.2 mile, then turn right as if you were driving into the Watchman Campground. Do not cross the Virgin River. Instead, park on the side of the road before crossing the bridge. The Pa'rus Trailhead is on the north side of the road just before the bridge. Most people simply return via the same route, but a car or bike shuttle is another option.

The trailhead for Emerald Pools is located opposite Zion Lodge, in Zion National Park, about 5 miles north of Springdale on Zion Canyon Scenic Drive. Park either in the trailhead parking lot or, if this lot is full, park across the road in Zion Lodge's parking area. The trailhead is well signed with an information kiosk.

General information: Some very interesting birds show up unpredictably in Zion National Park. Stop first at the visitor center, where you can get current information on what has been sighted in the park. The options detailed here are only a few of many possibilities for birding in Zion. Other suggestions include the Riverside Trail (where Spotted Owls are sometimes heard or seen), Hidden Canyon (a better location for Spotted Owls), and the Watchman Trail.

ADDITIONAL INFORMATION

Map grid: 3K
Elevation: 4,000 feet (Pa'rus) and 4,400 feet (Emerald Pools).
Hazards: None.
Nearest food, gas, and lodging: Springdale.
Camping: South or Watchman campgrounds, Zion National Park.
For more information: Zion National Park.

Uinta Basin Region

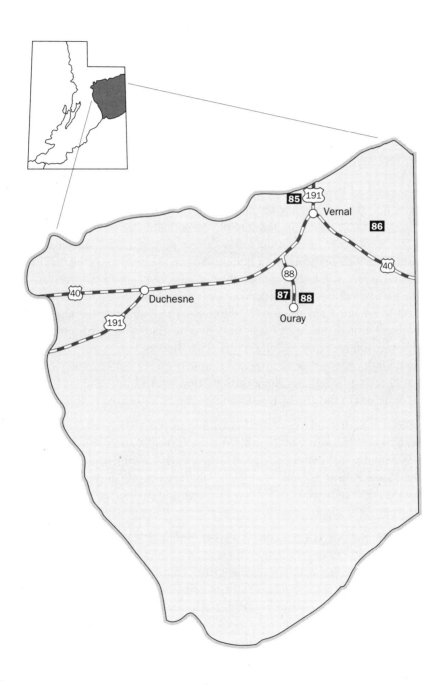

85 Remember The Maine Park

Habitat: Lowland riparian
Specialty birds: American Dipper; Western Screech-Owl; Spotted Towhee
Other key birds: Sharp-shinned and Cooper's Hawks; California Quail; Sora; Common Nighthawk; Common Poorwill; Black-chinned and Broad-tailed Hummingbirds; Belted Kingfisher; Plumbeous and Warbling Vireo; Western Scrub-Jay; Violet-green, Cliff, and Barn Swallows; House Wren; Mountain Bluebird; Gray Catbird; Virginia's and MacGillivray's Warblers; American Redstart (spring); Song Sparrow
Best times to bird: May through June, early mornings are best

The birding: This small county park encompasses a swath of the riparian zone along Ashley Creek, a permanent water source draining the south slope of the Uinta Mountains. Park in the small lot adjoining the picnic area and choose any of the paths into the surrounding forest. The area is quite small and easily covered, but you should take your time and carefully inspect all of the habitat available for birds. The understory beneath the forest canopy needed a good mowing on my last visit. Nonetheless, the network of informal trails through the grove of cottonwoods and aspens will lead you through good nesting habitat for songbirds.

The backside of the park borders on Ashley Creek so be sure to follow one of the trails to the hurricane fence along the creek. There were several breaks in the fence when I visited, making it easier to step to the edge of the creek and scan up and downstream for birds, including American Dippers.

Finally, take a little time to inspect the more open area surrounding the parking lot. There are hedgerows along the road that attract birds, and many species make forays out of the nearby forest and into this fieldlike area to forage.

Directions: In Vernal, turn north on Vernal Avenue (US 191). After 5 blocks, turn left on Maeser Highway (500 North). Your next turn is about 4 miles away, on 3500 West and at an intersection signed for Dry Fork Canyon; turn right. Remember the Maine Park is 3.7 miles away, and on the right side of the road. A small sign marks this county park, and the parking area and pavilion facilities are clearly visible from 3500 West.

General information: Ashley Creek is a good birding destination along nearly its entire length, from its genesis in the Uintas to its termination in the Green River at the Stewart Lake Waterfowl Management Area. Unfortunately, the creek is almost entirely inaccessible since it passes through private property almost anywhere a road crosses the creek. This site, although small, does provide the only good access for birding Ashley Creek.

85 Remember The Maine Park

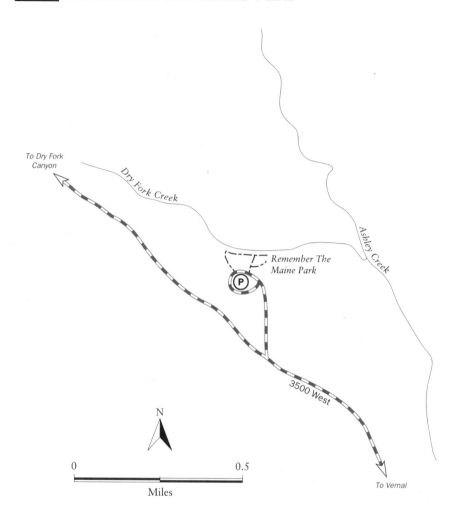

ADDITIONAL INFORMATION

Map grid: 8D
Elevation: 5,877 feet.
Hazards: None.
Nearest food, gas, and lodging: Vernal.
Camping: Steinaker State Park.
For more information: Utah Travel Council.

86 Green River and Split Mountain Campgrounds

Habitats: Lowland riparian, lowland desert shrub
Specialty birds: Bald Eagle (winter), Peregrine Falcon, Pinyon Jay, White-throated Swift, Western Wood-Pewee, Spotted Towhee, Lazuli Bunting
Other key birds: Common Goldeneye (winter); Spotted Sandpiper; Golden Eagle; Black-chinned and Broad-tailed Hummingbirds; Eastern and Western Kingbirds; Ash-throated Flycatcher; Say's Phoebe; Plumbeous Vireo; Western Scrub-Jay; Black-billed Magpie; Violet-green, Cliff, and Barn Swallows; House and Rock Wrens; Mountain Bluebird; Yellow Warbler; Yellow-breasted Chat; Lark, Black-throated, and White-crowned Sparrows; Brewer's Blackbird; Bullock's Oriole; American Goldfinch
Best times to bird: May through mid-July

The birding: These two campgrounds, separated by a 1.8-mile walk, feature some of the best riparian habitat in Dinosaur National Monument, at least for those without a boat and several days to float the Green or Yampa rivers. Both campgrounds have groves of tall cottonwoods, although the Green River Campground has a more well-developed understory of shrubs and emergent marsh vegetation. The trail connecting the two areas passes along a narrow bench beside the river covered with a short "forest" of sagebrush.

Start at the Green River Campground; Split Mountain Campground is reserved for group use, although you can certainly drive in and picnic and hike from the parking area. Take time to wander the roads in the campground. Western Kingbirds are abundant, and you're also likely to see or hear Western Wood-Pewees, Ash-throated Flycatchers, Black-headed Grosbeaks, Northern Flickers, and Yellow Warblers.

The trail to Split Mountain Campground is signed, and it departs from the upper end of the Green River Campground. The birding here is a bit more challenging because the vegetation is thicker and the birds more reclusive. Take time to stop and listen as you hike, and with luck some of those birds calling from the undergrowth will make their way to the tops of the sagebrush where they can be seen. In this area you'll likely encounter Say's Phoebe, Eastern Kingbirds, Blue-gray Gnatcatchers, Lazuli Buntings, Black-chinned Hummingbirds, and a confusing assortment of sparrows, including Sage Sparrows.

As you reach the Split Mountain Campground, keep an eye on the sky. There are Cliff and Violet-green Swallows and White-throated Swifts riding the air currents. If you're lucky, you may see a Peregrine Falcon in hot pursuit.

Directions: The west entrance to Dinosaur National Monument is on UT 149, 7 miles north of Jensen on US 40. From the entrance station and visitor center, the entrance to the Split Mountain Campground is about 2.5 miles away; Green River

Rough-textured cryptobiotic soil in the foreground is a delicate community of micro-organisms that helps hold desert soils in place. Don't walk on it.

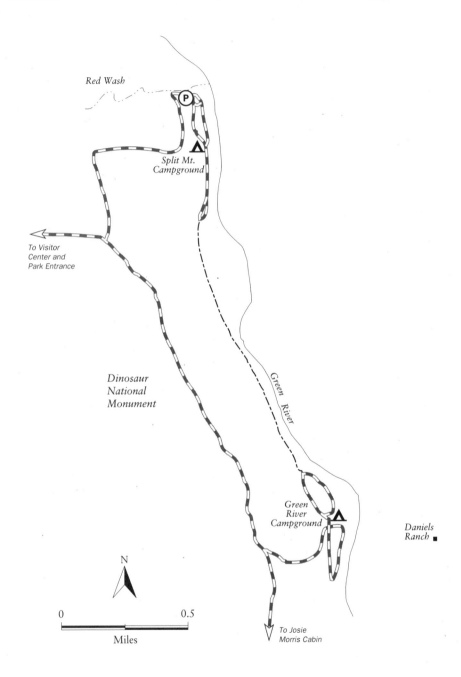

Red Wash

P

Split Mt.
Campground

To Visitor
Center and
Park Entrance

Dinosaur
National
Monument

Green River

Green
River
Campground

Daniels
Ranch

N

0   0.5

Miles

To Josie
Morris Cabin

Campground is about 4 miles from the entrance station. Proceed to either campground and park, then walk the described trail either south from Split Mountain or north from Green River.

General information: There are many places to explore Dinosaur National Monument for birds. If, after this jaunt, you still have a hankering for birds, try the walk to Josie Morris' cabin, which begins about 5 miles south of Green River Campground; this trail passes through an expanse of pinyon-juniper forest interspersed with sagebrush. Further east still, but out of the Utah portion of the monument, you might try the Harper's Corner Scenic Drive and Harper's Corner Trail, both accessible from the Dinosaur, Colorado, entrance to the monument. This latter area is the best place in the park to see Sage Grouse.

ADDITIONAL INFORMATION

Map grid: 9E
Elevation: 4,800 feet.
Hazards: None.
Nearest food, gas, and lodging: Vernal.
Camping: Green River Campground, Dinosaur National Monument.
For more information: Dinosaur National Monument.

87 Pelican Lake

Habitats: Lowland riparian, lowland desert shrub
Specialty birds: American White Pelican (fall); Bald Eagle (winter); Sandhill Crane (spring and fall); Lewis's Woodpecker; Lazuli Bunting
Other key birds: Pied-billed, Horned, Eared, and Western Grebes; Double-crested Cormorant; American Bittern; Snowy Egret; Black-crowned Night-Heron; White-faced Ibis; Turkey Vulture; Green-winged Teal; Northern Pintail; Blue-winged and Cinnamon Teals; Northern Shoveler; Gadwall; American Wigeon; Redhead; Ring-necked Duck (fall); Lesser Scaup (fall); Bufflehead (spring and fall); Common Merganser; Ruddy Duck; Northern Harrier; Golden Eagle; Ring-necked Pheasant; Sora; Lesser Yellowlegs (spring); Willet; Spotted Sandpiper; Wilson's Phalarope; Ring-billed and California Gulls; Forster's and Black Terns; Common Nighthawk; Black-chinned and Broad-tailed Hummingbirds; Say's Phoebe; Western Kingbird; Tree, Violet-green, Northern Rough-winged, and Barn Swallows; Black-billed Magpie; House and Marsh Wrens; Orange-crowned, Virginia's, Yellow, and Yellow-rumped Warblers; Vesper, Lark, and Song Sparrows; American Goldfinch; Brewer's Blackbird
Best times to bird: Spring migration for most waterfowl and shorebirds begins in March and peaks in April; fall migration begins in August and peaks in October. Breeding birds are best viewed May through June.

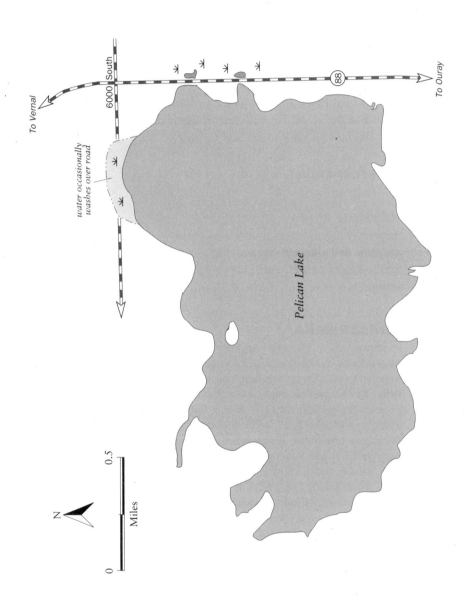

A breeding male American White Pelican sports a bony plate rising like a fin on its top beak.

The birding: Pelican Lake can be excellent for shorebirds, particularly in spring, as well as for transient passerines during both spring and fall migration.

Access to Pelican lake is simple—all the birding is from the road, either UT 88 or 6000 South in Leota. Birding along 6000 South is the quieter of the two options; the road disappears into the north end of the lake at times of high water. This route passes through a short section of lowland desert shrub, where it's possible to see Sage Thrashers, and Lark, Brewer's, and Vesper Sparrows. Western Tanagers, Bullock's Orioles, and the occasional Lazuli Bunting can be seen flying from nearby trees to the shrub community. Where this route disappears into the marsh, stop and scan the area for ducks.

UT 88 cuts across the east side of Pelican Lake, and in wet years there is standing water and marshes on both sides of the road. There generally isn't much traffic on this road, but be careful while driving and scanning both sides of the road for waterfowl, and pull clear onto the shoulder when you stop. In breeding season you'll see Willets, Ruddy Ducks, and American Coots nesting by the road, and Cinnamon Teals, Redheads, and possibly a few other species of ducks using the small marsh complex along the shore.

Directions: From Vernal, head west on US 40/191—this is the main street through town. About 11 miles out of Vernal, turn south on UT 88, which is signed for Ouray. You'll encounter Pelican Lake about 8 miles south on UT 88; 6000 South is a signed street on the north end of the lake.

General information: The lake holds many of the same species of waterfowl, particularly during migration, as Ouray National Wildlife Refuge, which lies a short distance to the west. It's a good place to whet your appetite on your way to Ouray NWR.

ADDITIONAL INFORMATION

Map grid: 8E
Elevation: 4,797 feet.
Hazards: None.
Nearest food, gas, and lodging: Vernal.
Camping: Vernal KOA, Vernal.
For more information: Bureau of Land Management, Vernal Field Office.

88 Ouray National Wildlife Refuge

Habitats: Lowland riparian, lowland desert shrub, desert steppe, upland desert shrub
Specialty birds: American White Pelican (fall); Bald Eagle (winter); Prairie Falcon; Sandhill Crane (spring and fall); Burrowing Owl; White-throated Swift; Lewis's Woodpecker; Sage Thrasher; Sage Sparrow; Lazuli Bunting
Other key birds: Pied-billed, Eared, and Western Grebes; Double-crested Cormorant; American Bittern; Snowy Egret; Black-crowned Night-Heron; White-faced Ibis; Turkey Vulture; Green-winged Teal; Northern Pintail; Blue-winged and Cinnamon Teals; Northern Shoveler; Gadwall; American Wigeon; Redhead; Ring-necked Duck (fall); Lesser Scaup (fall); Bufflehead (spring and fall); Common Merganser; Ruddy Duck; Northern Harrier; Rough-legged Hawk (winter); Golden Eagle; Ring-necked Pheasant; Virginia Rail; Sora; Lesser Yellowlegs (spring); Willet; Spotted Sandpiper; Wilson's Phalarope; Ring-billed and California Gulls; Forster's and Black Terns; Short-eared Owl; Common Nighthawk; Black-chinned and Broad-tailed Hummingbirds; Say's Phoebe; Western and Eastern Kingbirds; Tree, Violet-green, Northern Rough-winged, Cliff, and Barn Swallows; Black-billed Magpie; Rock, House, and Marsh Wrens; Orange-crowned, Virginia's, Yellow, and Yellow-rumped Warblers; Yellow-breasted Chat; Vesper, Lark, and Song Sparrows; American Goldfinch; Brewer's Blackbird
Best times to bird: Spring migration for most waterfowl and shorebirds begins in March and peaks in April; fall migration begins in August and peaks in October. Breeding birds are best viewed May through June.

The birding: Ouray National Wildlife Refuge is well designed for a quality birding experience. Begin with a stop at the information kiosk on the entrance road, where you can pick up a refuge map, a bird list, and an auto tour route guide.

From the kiosk, the auto tour route departs to the right and passes through fields cultivated to feed wildlife. This can be a good area for wading birds, particularly in

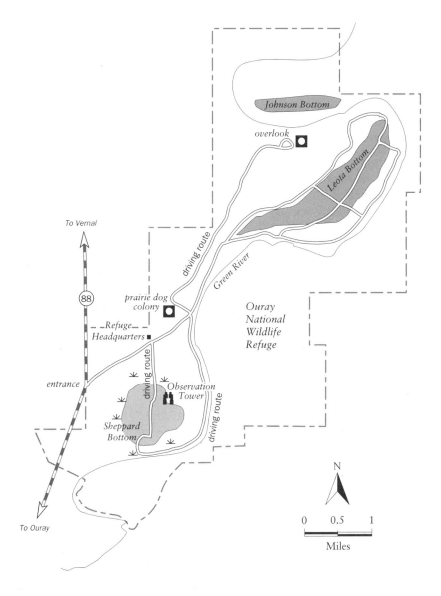

spring when you're likely to see American Avocets, Black-necked Stilts, Snowy Egrets, White-faced Ibis, Lesser Yellowlegs, Willet, Spotted Sandpiper, and Wilson's Phalarope. The refuge also receives less frequent visits from some interesting migrant shorebirds like Marbled Godwit, Western, Least and Baird's Sandpipers, Dunlin, and Short- and Long-Billed Dowitchers.

The road soon enters Sheppard Bottom, an extensive marsh complex, where you'll find a viewing tower that overlooks the area. Farther along, the road follows the Green

River, a corridor which many species of migrants follow on their biennial north-south movements. The marsh, ponds and river hold such waterfowl as Green-winged Teals, Northern Pintails, Blue-winged and Cinnamon Teals, Northern Shovelers, Gadwalls, American Wigeons, Redheads, Ring-Necked Ducks, Lesser Scaups, Buffleheads, Common Mergansers, and Ruddy Ducks. This is also a good area for raptors, including Ospreys and Northern Harriers. Eastern Kingbirds breed in the marsh area, with Black-headed Grosbeaks, Bullock's Orioles, and warblers nesting in cottonwoods along the river.

As you exit this lowland marsh area, the road climbs slightly and passes through the first area of lowland desert shrub you'll encounter on the auto route. This area can be hot for songbirds, so take a few minutes to scan the area for Sage Thrashers, Lazuli Buntings, American Goldfinches, and Lark Sparrows. Continue on the auto route, climbing a low line of bluffs beside the river. As you enter this area you'll encounter stop number nine on the route, a prairie dog colony; look for Burrowing Owls standing on mounds among the prairie dogs.

The auto route passes the prairie dog colony and continues to the top of the bluff above the Green River. Here the route passes through mixed desert shrub and desert steppe communities, both in excellent condition, and it's a likely spot to locate Sage Sparrows. These are the dullest of birds among a group already noteworthy for its lack of distinguishing characteristics; they are therefore best identified by their song. Few birds occupy this habitat type, and in addition to a Brewer's, Sage, and a few other species of sparrows, you're most likely to see Horned Larks. Raptors may be about; in addition to Golden Eagles and Red-tailed Hawks you may be privileged to see Swainson's and Ferruginous Hawks or Prairie Falcons.

Directions: From Vernal, head west on US 40/191—this is the main street through town. About 11 miles out of Vernal, turn south on UT 88, which is signed for Ouray. The entrance to the refuge is a well-signed left turn, about 12 miles south on UT 88. Enter the gravel access road and proceed to the information kiosk, bathrooms, and start of the auto tour route, about 1 mile into the refuge.

General information: Part of the auto route, the portion that climbs the bluff above the Green River, is a fair weather road and should not be attempted when the ground is saturated or after a heavy rain.

ADDITIONAL INFORMATION

Map grid: 8E
Elevation: 4,800 feet.
Hazards: None.
Nearest food, gas, and lodging: Vernal.
Camping: Vernal KOA, Vernal.
For more information: Ouray National Wildlife Refuge.

Colorado Plateau Region

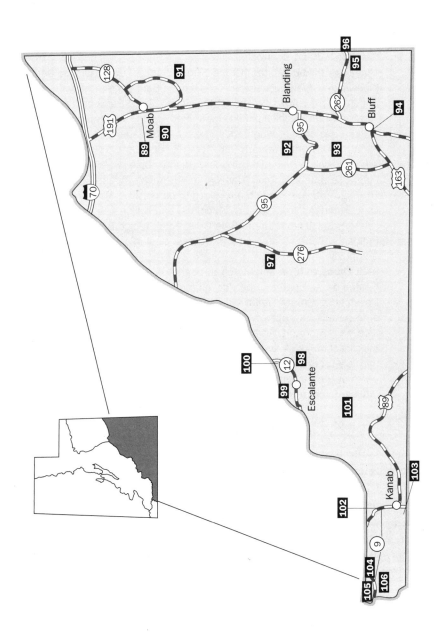

89 Scott M. Matheson Preserve and Courthouse Wash

Habitats: Lowland riparian, upland desert shrub, pinyon-juniper
Specialty birds: Peregrine and Prairie Falcons; Lewis's Woodpecker;
White-throated Swift (April); Olive-sided Flycatcher; Gray Flycatcher;
Northern Shrike (winter); Gray Vireo; Pinyon Jay; Townsend's Solitaire
(winter); Sage Thrasher; American Pipit (winter); Lazuli Bunting;
Green-tailed and Spotted Towhees
Other key birds: Western Grebe; Turkey Vulture; Green-winged and
Blue-winged Teals; Lesser Scaup; Osprey; Bald Eagle; Cooper's and
Rough-legged Hawks; Virginia Rail (winter); Sora; Black-necked Stilt;
Forster's Tern; Black-chinned Hummingbird; Say's Phoebe;
Loggerhead Shrike; Plumbeous Vireo; Ash-throated Flycatcher;
Western Kingbird; Western Scrub-Jay; Horned Lark; Northern Rough-
winged Swallow; Juniper Titmouse; Bushtit; Blue-gray Gnatcatcher;
Mountain Bluebird; Rock, Canyon, and Bewick's Wrens; Hermit
Thrush (winter); Virginia's and Black-throated Gray Warblers; Vesper,
Lark, American Tree (winter), Lincoln's, and Harris's Sparrows
(winter); Black-headed and Blue Grosbeaks; Indigo Bunting;
Bullock's, Scott's and Northern Orioles; Cassin's Finch; Lesser
Goldfinch
Best times to bird: Mid-March through April for spring migrants and
September through October for fall migrants. Migrating Long-billed
Dowitchers, Greater Yellowlegs, and Solitary Sandpipers arrive as
early as mid-July. April brings the peak in migrating ducks; Double-
crested Cormorant, American Bittern, Osprey, and shorebirds also
migrate through in April. Early mornings are productive April through
mid-July for resident breeding birds. July through August the coolest
parts of the day (morning and evening) are most productive, as all
intelligent creatures seek refuge from the heat of the desert.

The birding: Approximately 175 species of birds have been recorded on the
Matheson Preserve, although no single species is particularly common. You are
almost guaranteed some of the more common riparian species, like American Coot,
Great Blue Heron, Mallard, Mourning Dove, Black-chinned Hummingbird, Belted
Kingfisher, Tree Swallow, Marsh Wren, Yellow Warbler, Yellow-rumped Warbler,
Chipping Sparrow, White-crowned Sparrow, Red-winged Blackbird, and Yellow-
headed Blackbird. Beyond this list and a few other common species, what you
encounter depends on the time of year and just plain luck.

The preserve plays a valuable role as a stopover for both spring and fall migrants;
during these times the diversity of bird life is at its greatest. To give you an idea of
the potential here: 12 species of sparrows, 11 species of warblers, 3 hummingbird
species, 14 shorebird species, 18 duck species, and 4 species of goose have been
recorded, but many of these are migrants, not winter or summer residents.

Nestled among towering red cliffs and bounded on one side by the Colorado
River, the preserve is not only beautiful, it's designed to accommodate the needs of

89 Scott M. Matheson Preserve and Courthouse Wash

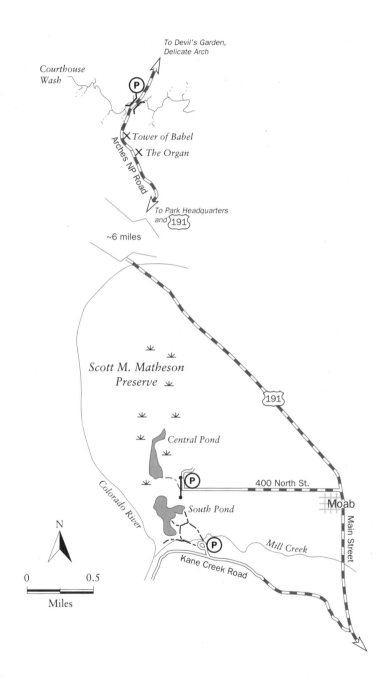

To Devil's Garden, Delicate Arch

Courthouse Wash

Tower of Babel

The Organ

Arches NP Road

To Park Headquarters and 191

~6 miles

Scott M. Matheson Preserve

Central Pond

South Pond

400 North St.

Moab

Colorado River

Mill Creek

Main Street

Kane Creek Road

N

0   0.5

Miles

191

The south entrance to Scott M. Matheson Preserve.

bird watchers. At the southern (main) entrance to the preserve, a boardwalk, made from a weathered railroad trestle which once spanned the Great Salt Lake, winds through cottonwood groves and thickets of marsh plants. The walk descends from the parking area in a horseshoe-shaped trail, with one end of the path ending at a wildlife viewing blind and the second path ending at a platform with benches. The hike is short (less than half a mile).

The trail at the middle entrance of the preserve is really just an informal path that leads to another part of the marsh complex. The trail is short, only about 50 yards from the gate to the water's edge, and you may get a glimpse of some water-fowl and songbirds not seen along the southern boardwalk, but it will be a quick stroll—the area is densely vegetated and the trail quickly disappears into the marsh.

A better strategy for birding this middle entrance is to bring a canoe. The preserve is closed to boating during nesting season (March through July), but other times of year, particularly October, canoeing can be very rewarding. Your route will be dictated by the depth of the water which varies from year to year according to rainfall, irrigation needs, power-generating needs, and other parameters.

Courthouse Wash has one of the few riparian zones in Arches National Park. Even so, you're likely to find little or no water in the upper wash unless you happen to be there in late winter or after a rain storm. The wash changes abruptly from an open drainage to a narrow canyon a few yards below the bridge on

Arches Road with a highly restricted riparian zone. There are no developed trails, but if you like exploring canyons, follow the wash downstream from the road crossing in Arches National Park to where it enters the Colorado River along US 191, about 5 miles away Although this area may be worth a brief exploration for birders, the best opportunities lie upstream from the bridge.

From the pullout you'll see the paths created by other hikers heading up the northwest side of the wash. Work your way along these trails, choosing paths that lead along the boundary between the riparian zone and the surrounding desert— this will give you the best of both worlds. There is cryptobiotic soil in the area so watch where you step and stick to the already traveled paths.

You can wander as far up the wash as your interest and water supply will take you. Scan the cottonwoods for Scott's and Bullocks Orioles, Blue Grosbeaks, and Lazuli Buntings. The willow thickets along the stream should hold some interesting warblers, particularly during migration, including Orange-crowned, Virginia's, Yellow, Yellow-rumped, and Wilson's Warblers. Yellow-breasted Chats are also fairly common in summer and may be seen foraging along the riparian-desert interface.

Be sure to scan the surrounding cliff faces. Those white stains beneath ledges and fissures in the sandstone mark favored perches and nesting sites for Red-tailed Hawks, Golden Eagles, American Kestrels, and Prairie Falcons. You'll also see White-throated Swifts, Violet-green Swallows, and Cliff Swallows.

Directions: To reach the middle entrance to the Scott M. Matheson Preserve, head west on 400 North in Moab and follow the road until it dead-ends in a turnaround just beyond the sewage disposal plant. There are two gates in this turnaround—the south gate leads to South Pond.

To reach the south entrance, turn west off Main St. onto Kane Creek Boulevard. After 0.7 mile the road forks; continue to the left on Kane Creek Road for another 0.7 mile to the preserve entrance, marked by a green metal gate and a very small, tan Nature Conservancy sign. Proceed through the gate and into the parking area below the high-tension power lines.

The entrance to Arches National Park is 8 miles north of Moab on US 191. The only road in the park crosses Courthouse Wash 4 miles beyond the park entrance station. The wash is clearly signed, and there is a pullout on the north side of the bridge. Informal trails leave from here, heading both up- and downstream.

General information: The 875-acre Matheson Preserve is situated on a low floodplain of the Colorado River, literally a desert oasis. Surrounded by imposing cliffs of red Wingate sandstone on three sides and with views of the towering La Sal Mountains on the fourth, it's hard to imagine a more dramatic setting.

The preserve is cooperatively owned and managed by The Nature Conservancy, which oversees the south end, and the Utah Division of Wildlife Resources, which governs the north. The different land uses assigned these two halves of the preserve reflect the somewhat differing missions of these two agencies. DWR encourages hunting, particularly for waterfowl, on the north end of the preserve, while the south end is clearly signed as a "wildlife resting area" and a sanctuary from hunting pressure. It's no fault of the DWR but the habitat is probably in better shape on the south end, at least to the extent that tamarisk has not yet displaced native plants.

The Conservancy continues to add interpretive signs and maintain its end of the preserve with an eye toward accommodating the casual visitor. If you're interested in using the aforementioned blind for photography, it is thoughtfully situated to take advantage of early morning light.

The preserve is on the west edge of the town of Moab, so amenities are close at hand. Camping options abound, particularly if you appreciate primitive conditions. Dispersed camping is allowed along Kane Springs Road if you continue west and then south along the Colorado River (some land here is posted, so be sure to respect landowner's wishes). Additional information about camping on the extensive Bureau of Land Management lands in the area can be obtained from the Moab Information Center on the corner of Main and Center Streets in Moab. Arches National Park is a 15-minute drive north of the Matheson Preserve, but it's a heavily visited park with limited camping facilities.

Arches was set aside for its outstanding scenery and not its birding. The majority of the park is a monotype of sparse pinyon-juniper forest merging into upland shrubs. Although there are certainly some interesting species, overall diversity is low.

Nonetheless, 189 species have been recorded in the park. Many of these are transient migrating birds or are simply present in low numbers; only 44 species have been recorded as breeding in the park.

As long as you're in the park, you may want to try two other places. The area around the parking lot for the Delicate Arch Trailhead (Wolfe Ranch) and the first half of a mile of the Delicate Arch Trail lie along the boundary of a riparian area and the surrounding desert. You may encounter a few warblers, sparrows, Western Scrub-Jays, Pinyon Jays and Juniper Titmice in this area. The trail to the Devil's Garden has the common pinyon-juniper species, and you may encounter a Sharp-shinned or Cooper's Hawk hunting between the fins of sandstone. Both of these trails are clearly identified and described in the literature you receive at the park entrance.

As with all national parks in Utah, an entrance fee is required to use the park and its facilities. Arches charges $10 per vehicle for a seven-day pass; if you anticipate visiting more parks or returning a few times after your initial visit, you might consider the Golden Eagle pass, which for $50 covers your entrance fee at all national parks for the subsequent year.

ADDITIONAL INFORMATION

Map grid: 8H

Elevation: 3,960 to 4,125 feet.

Hazards: Mosquitoes, heat, lack of water.

Nearest food, gas, and lodging: Moab.

Camping: Various commercial campgrounds in Moab or camp on BLM lands; Devil's Garden Campground, Arches National Park.

For more information: The Nature Conservancy, Scott M. Matheson Preserve, and Devil's Garden Campground, Arches National Park.

90 Dead Horse Point State Park

Habitats: Pinyon-juniper
Specialty birds: Bald Eagle; Peregrine and Prairie Falcons; Chukar; White-throated Swift; Gray Flycatcher; Gray Vireo; Pinyon Jay
Other key birds: Turkey Vulture; Northern Harrier (year-round); Red-tailed Hawk (year-round); Golden Eagle; Black-chinned and Broad-tailed Hummingbirds; Say's Phoebe; Western Scrub-Jay; Horned Lark; Juniper Titmouse; Canyon Wren
Best times to bird: Early afternoons mid-September through October for raptors; early mornings April through May and September through October for migrating songbirds

The birding: Dead Horse Point State Park lies on a high plateau 2,000 feet above the Colorado River. Several walking trails wander through the 5,000-acre park, with little change in elevation, and make for a leisurely birding experience. Overall diversity is highest during spring and fall migrations, probably due to the park's proximity to the Colorado River.

For viewing raptors during fall migration, any of the trails which skirt the perimeter of the park and pass along the cliff line, will offer unhindered views of raptors soaring in search of thermals. The viewing platform at the end of the park road is also a great place to just sit and watch for whatever comes along.

Species commonly associated with pinyon-juniper can be found by walking any of the trails through the park. The area is not particularly large and, coupled with a lack of habitat diversity, this means that there is not a tremendous number of birds for viewing. The park's checklist does contain 63 species, many of them among the more unusual birds in the state.

Directions: From Moab, head north on US 191 for 9 miles. The turnoff to Dead Horse Point State Park is clearly signed, and you'll turn west on UT 313, which will lead you to the park entrance and visitor center 23 miles away.

General information: The views at this state park are stunning, perhaps second only to the south rim of Grand Canyon National Park. Dead Horse Point presents a unique vantage point for seeing raptors, many of which pass below you along

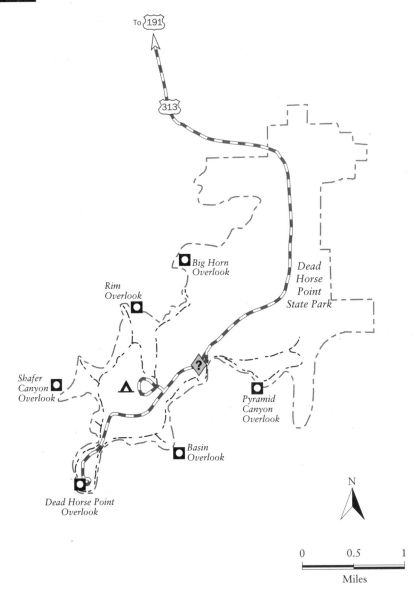

the cliff face. Some of the park's appeal lies in its convenience. You can walk anywhere in the park, and if you camp here, many birds of the pinyon-juniper habitat will be flying through your campsite.

As with other state parks in Utah, there is an entrance fee of $4 per vehicle, or $1.50 per person for walk-ins. Additional fees apply for those using the camping facilities, and·advance reservations will assure you a place in the small campground.

You'll notice as you approach the park that the road passes through an extensive desert steppe/grassland community. If you need a little variety, drive back to this area and wander through some of these high meadow expanses.

ADDITIONAL INFORMATION

Map grid: 8H
Elevation: 5,900 feet.
Hazards: Heat, shear cliffs.
Nearest food, gas, and lodging: Moab.
Camping: Dead Horse Point State Park.
For more information: Utah Division of Parks and Recreation.

91 Warner Lake

Habitats: Aspen, mountain meadow, spruce-fir
Specialty birds: Northern Goshawk; Blue Grouse; Western Wood-Pewee; Dusky Flycatcher; Clark's Nutcracker; Townsend's Solitaire; Swainson's Thrush; American Pipit; Green-tailed and Spotted Towhees; Black Rosy-Finch
Other key birds: Turkey Vulture; Cooper's Hawk; Golden Eagle; Ruffed Grouse; Black-chinned, Broad-tailed, Rufous, and Calliope Hummingbirds; Hairy and Downy Woodpeckers; Cordilleran Flycatcher; Warbling Vireo; Steller's Jay; Western Scrub-Jay; Violet-green and Tree Swallows; Mountain Chickadee; White-breasted and Red-breasted Nuthatches; Brown Creeper; House and Rock Wrens; Hermit Thrush; Ruby-crowned Kinglet; Orange-crowned, Yellow, Yellow-rumped, and MacGillivray's Warblers; Western Tanager; Chipping and Brewer's Sparrows; Cassin's Finch; Pine Siskin; American Goldfinch
Best times to bird: Summer through fall; late May through mid-July is best

The birding: Warner Lake is a tiny impoundment nestled at the 9,000-foot level on the shoulder of 12,334-foot Mount Waas in the La Sal Mountain Range. The reservoir itself is not the birding destination, but you'll find a variety of montane habitats in the immediate vicinity that offer great opportunities for bird finding. One of the appealing qualities of this site is that it offers a cool retreat from the heat of the nearby Colorado Plateau desert. Although this area is a short drive from Moab and other nearby birding sites, the best approach for birding the area is to plan for a night in the campground and at least a day exploring the environs.

The road from Moab passes through the whole gamut of desert-to-montane vegetation communities on the way to Warner Lake, but there are few pullouts along the way and not many opportunities for exploring those habitats and bird communities. Depending on your schedule and time of arrival, the first place to explore may be the side road on your left just before you enter the aspen forest surrounding Warner Lake; this is off the entrance road so keep an eye on the

91 Warner Lake

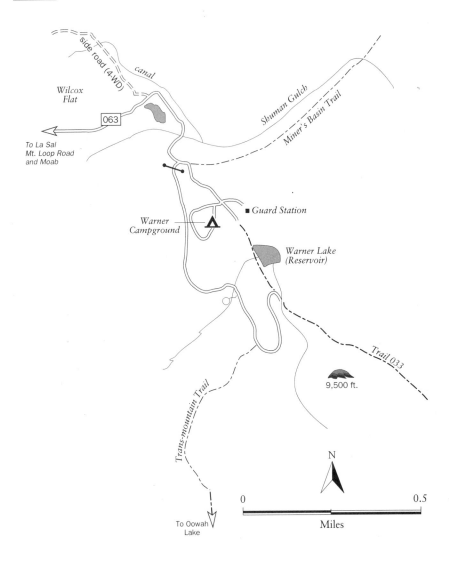

accompanying map, or backtrack after you've discovered the campground. Either way, this side road is rough, so you should pull off the main road and walk in. This road follows a canal while tracing the interface between the aspen forest and the mountain meadow. The side road continues for quite a distance, but a half mile stroll should expose you to most of the birds here, including Black-chinned Hummingbirds, Western Scrub-Jays (in the nearby oak groves), Tree Swallows, Mountain Bluebirds, House Wrens, Warbling Vireos, Green-tailed Towhees, and Lincoln's Sparrows. Occasionally a Golden Eagle may be seen soaring in the thermals, but be sure you're not looking at a Turkey Vulture; they're in the area as well.

The campground is in a thick forest of aspen with some quite large and impressive trees and an open, parklike understory. It seems to have plenty of breeding birds common to this habitat type, including Broad-tailed Hummingbirds, Red-naped Sapsuckers, Downy and Hairy Woodpeckers, Western Wood-Pewees, Dusky Flycatchers, Warbling Vireos, House Wrens, and Yellow and MacGillivray's Warblers. Stroll the loop of campsites; if you feel lazy, sit and wait for the birds to come to you.

The area between the small lake and the mountain to the east can be worthwhile though it can also be too wet for walking in heavy snow years. This small zone is trailless so you'll have to pick your way through spruce-fir and thickets of willows in the marshy area behind the lake. You should find, among other species, Calliope and Rufous Hummingbirds (late summer or early fall), more warblers (Common Yellowthroat and Orange-Crowned in addition to those already mentioned), and Mountain Chickadees.

Several hiking trails depart from the Warner Lake area and each crosses a mix of montane habitats with more opportunities for birding. Short hikes on the Miner's Basin Trail or the Trans-mountain Trail, in the direction of Oowah Lake, are recommended. Hiking these trails will improve your chances for seeing Northern Goshawks, Cooper's Hawks, grouse, Steller's Jays, Clark's Nutcrackers, White-Breasted and Red-Breasted Nuthatches, Brown Creepers, Hermit and Swainson's Thrushes, Cordilleran Flycatchers, Townsend's Solitaires, Western Tanagers, Spotted Towhees, and Cassin's Finches. In places these trails reach high enough to meet the scree slopes where you may encounter Black Rosy-Finches.

Directions: From Moab, head south on US 191 for 8 miles; then turn east where a Forest Service sign indicates Ken's Lake and the La Sal Mountain Loop Road. Follow the loop road for about 15 miles (it's mostly paved, with a couple of short sections of gravel) to the right turn (east) signed for Warner Lake. This road is gravel (fair-weather only) and climbs steeply for 5 miles to the campground and reservoir area.

General information: Two weather-related warnings regarding this site: the campground does not open until quite late, typically June, because of snow; and the 5 miles of road from the La Sal Mountain Loop Road into the campground should be driven only after it's dried out. It's worth calling the Moab Ranger District for current conditions before making a long trip. Also, don't let the proximity to the desert fool you—a jacket and sleeping bag serve you well here, even in summer.

As an aside, this area is popular for viewing a variety of wildlife, including pikas, a member of the rabbit family that looks and acts nothing like a rabbit. Pikas inhabit the scree slopes where they spend their brief summers making preparations for the long winters that dominate their existence. The first and easiest place to encounter these endearing critters is the small scree slope that descends almost to the rough side road described above as the first birding destination.

If you're up for more birding in the La Sals, visit nearby Oowah Lake. The lake can be accessed over a rough road passable to any passenger car, but it's slow going and like the Warner Lake approach, it's for fair-weather use only. The turn to Oowah Lake is about 2 miles south of the Warner Lake turn on FR 062. Oowah Lake is cradled in a tiny bowl surrounded by spruce-fir, and its advantage over the Warner Lake area is that it provides ready access to an extensive stand of conifers and the bird species typical of the spruce-fir habitat type.

ADDITIONAL INFORMATION

Map grid: 8H
Elevation: 9,400 feet.
Hazards: None.
Nearest food, gas, and lodging: Moab.
Camping: Warner Lake Campground.
For more information: Manti-La Sal National Forest, Moab Ranger District.

92 Elk Ridge

Habitats: Spruce-fir, aspen, mountain meadow, upland desert shrub
Specialty birds: Northern Goshawk; Blue Grouse; Flammulated Owl; Western Screech-Owl; Northern Pygmy-Owl; White-throated Swift; Williamson's Sapsucker; Olive-sided and Gray Flycatchers; Western Wood-Pewee; Hammond's and Dusky Flycatchers; Clark's Nutcracker; Pygmy Nuthatch; Townsend's Solitaire; Green-tailed and Spotted Towhees; Red Crossbill
Other key birds: Sharp-shinned and Cooper's Hawks; Ruffed Grouse; California Quail; Spotted Sandpiper; Band-tailed Pigeon; Long-eared Owl; Common Poorwill; Black-chinned, Broad-tailed, and Rufous (August) Hummingbirds; Red-naped Sapsucker; Downy and Hairy Woodpeckers; Cordilleran Flycatcher; Warbling Vireo; Steller's Jay; Western Scrub-Jay; Common Raven; Tree, Violet-green, Northern Rough-winged, and Cliff Swallows; Mountain Chickadee; Red-breasted and White-breasted Nuthatches; Brown Creeper; Rock and House Wrens; Ruby-crowned Kinglet; Hermit Thrush; Virginia's, Yellow, and Yellow-rumped Warblers; Western Tanager; Chipping and White-crowned Sparrows; Cassin's Finch
Best times to bird: May through June

The birding: This long scenic drive through a corner of the Manti-La Sal National Forest traverses a variety of habitat types, but most of the higher-altitude country supports mature aspen and ponderosa pine stands; the open understory there makes for easy walking. It is possible to experience the area and its birds without having to cover the entire length of the rather long loop.

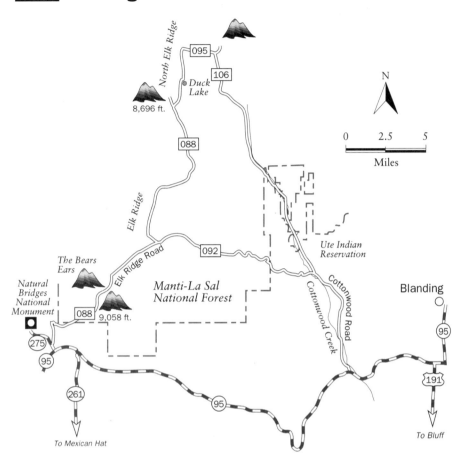

The habitat is fairly uniform throughout this plateau region, and there are few trailheads for hiking. You're essentially on your own to walk and explore. It is certainly possible to see some species from the road, but the best strategy is to periodically park the car on the roadside and walk, either along the road or off into the surrounding forest. At the least you should bird a representative sample of each habitat type.

The northeast portion of this route along FR 106 follows and frequently crosses Cottonwood Creek. These crossings may be impassable at high water, particularly in the early part of the season. It is possible to avoid this section of the loop by restricting your birding to FR 092 and FR 088; this will provide plenty of opportunities to see the species indicated above.

Directions: From Blanding, travel south on US 191 for 4 miles, and then continue west on UT 95 for an additional 5.5 miles. Turn right (north) on Cottonwood Road (FR 106). Follow this road north for about 25 miles to the intersection with

FR 095; turn left and travel 2.5 miles to FR 088. At the junction with FR 088, turn left and follow this route for about 11 miles to the intersection with FR 092. From here you can either turn right and drive to Natural Bridges National Monument and UT 95 (11 miles), or turn left and return to Cottonwood Road and UT 95 (about 18 miles) where you started the loop.

It's possible to approach this route from the west by departing from UT 95 on UT 275 towards Natural Bridges National Monument. Drive about 0.3 mile toward the monument, then turn right on Elk Ridge Road (FR 088), and proceed along the route described above.

General information: The roads throughout the forest are dirt or gravel and generally well maintained. Travel by passenger car is certainly possible, but traveling when roads are wet is not recommended for any vehicle.

To fully appreciate the possibilities of this site, you must spend a little time traveling at lower elevations—the majority of the terrain—in southern Utah. When the surrounding desert feels like a campfire and your car a Dutch oven, Elk Ridge at 9,000 feet is a welcome and cool oasis of forest and wildflowers.

ADDITIONAL INFORMATION

Map grid: 8J
Elevation: Approximately 8,500 feet.
Hazards: Stream crossings on FR 106.
Nearest food, gas, and lodging: Blanding.
Camping: Natural Bridges National Monument or Kampark, Blanding.
For more information: Manti-LaSal National Forest.

93 Fish Creek and Owl Creek Canyons

Habitats: Lowland riparian, pinyon-juniper
Specialty birds: Chukar; Flammulated Owl; Northern Pygmy-Owl; White-throated Swift; Gray Flycatcher; Spotted Towhee
Other key birds: Turkey Vulture; Cooper's Hawk; Common Nighthawk; Common Poorwill; Black-chinned Hummingbird; Ash-throated Flycatcher; Western Kingbird; Plumbeous and Warbling Vireo; Western Scrub-Jay; Common Raven; Violet-green and Cliff Swallows; Juniper Titmouse; Rock, Canyon, and Bewick's Wrens; Blue-gray Gnatcatcher; Hermit Thrush; Yellow-rumped and Black-throated Gray Warblers; Lark and Black-throated Sparrows; Blue Grosbeak; Lesser Goldfinch
Best times to bird: Early mornings, April through mid-June

The birding: These trails begin at the same trailhead. They can be combined into an extended day hike (not recommended), or as a two-to-three-day backpacking trip.

93 Fish Creek and Owl Creek Canyons

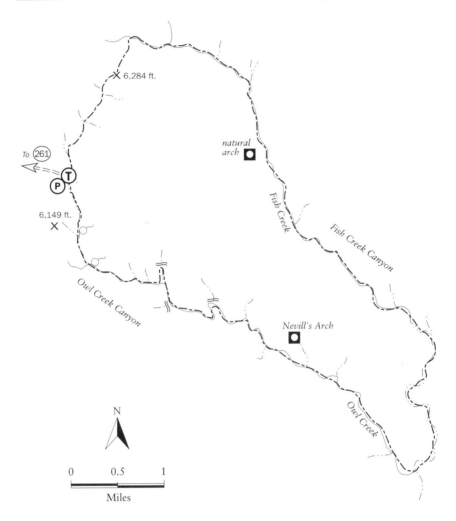

To 261

6,284 ft.

natural arch

6,149 ft.

Fish Creek

Fish Creek Canyon

Owl Creek Canyon

Nevill's Arch

Owl Creek

N

0   0.5   1

Miles

   The first 1.5 miles of the Fish Creek Trail traverse a mesa top covered with a dense pinyon-juniper forest. This is a good area for Flammulated Owls, and if you camp at the trailhead the night before tackling this hike, this mesa can be a productive site for owling. Take a good flashlight and start hiking the trail after sunset, listening for the call of owls, then searching for the birds with the aid of the flashlight. Straying from the path is discouraged for two reasons: the area supports an expanse of fragile, cryptobiotic soils that are impossible to avoid if you leave the trail; and it's very easy to get turned around in this forest, because all the even-aged trees look identical. During daylight hours, you can expect to encounter most of the usual denizens of the pinyon-juniper, especially Juniper Titmice, Blue-gray Gnatcatchers, and Common Ravens.

From the mesa top, the trail plummets 600 feet to a narrow riparian corridor in the canyon bottom. Before scooting over the lip of the canyon, take a few minutes to look for Violet-green Swallows and White-throated Swifts, both of which hunt in the air currents rising out of the canyon. Although there are no dangerous exposures on this route, it is steep enough that most backpackers completing the Owl-Fish Creek loop choose to come *up* this way and *descend* via Owl Creek. Either way, the most unnerving part of the trail is right at the canyon rim, a 15-foot crevice in the cliff wall that requires some coordinated hand- and foot-work.

The family of beavers in Fish Creek is doing a thorough job of discouraging cottonwood growth in the canyon bottom, and only a few of the larger cotton-woods were still standing when I hiked the canyon in 1997. Consequently, the riparian corridor is composed mostly of shrubby willows, cattails, and some young cottonwoods. The bird community has certainly been affected by the beaver activity, and the chance of seeing Blue Grosbeaks, Yellow-Rumped Warblers, Lesser Goldfinches, and Lazuli Buntings is somewhat diminished.

A pinyon-juniper forest rises above the riparian zone to meet the sheer cliff walls of the canyon, and about 5 miles down the canyon this becomes the dominant habitat type. Hot spots of bird activity pop up in unpredictable places. Watch for small flocks of birds foraging among the pinyon-junipers or making their way between the riparian zone and this upland forest.

Owl Creek is a narrow slickrock canyon that features towering, sheer sandstone cliffs, Anasazi ruins, and pleasant birding in a well-developed cottonwood riparian corridor.

A one-way excursion along the length of Owl Creek to its confluence with Fish Creek requires a hike of 6.5 miles. However, one of your many options would be to hike only to the end of the riparian corridor and perhaps a short distance into the pinyon-juniper to investigate that bird community, a one-way trip of about 4 miles. Still two more options arise: plan to do the entire Owl Creek–Fish Creek loop, in which case an overnight stay is recommended; or camp overnight in the bottom of Owl Creek, bird the next morning, and hike back out the way you came in. Your choice depends on how much time you'd like to spend in this area.

From the parking area, the trail descends to the right as you face the trail register and information board. The first quarter of a mile is through pinyon-juniper, and you can expect to see a few of the representative species before making your way into the head of the canyon. Just before dropping into the canyon, take a moment to scan overhead for Violet-green Swifts and White-throated Swallows—they're often careening about in the updrafts.

Pick your way down into the canyon, following the cairns and the tracks of hikers before you. This upper region is a good one for Canyon and Rock Wrens, but if you don't hear or see any here, there will be plenty of opportunities below. Your first encounter with the riparian zone comes with the first falls you'll have to negotiate—make your way to the right of the pour-off, and scramble down to the bottom of the canyon. You'll have to pick your way through the dense vegetation along the creek bottom for a short distance before emerging into more open terrain. The hike below this point is through cottonwood groves, occasional stretches of slickrock, and some oak and pinyon-juniper groves. In places the canopy of cottonwoods becomes quite dense, with an almost impenetrable undergrowth of horsetail ferns. You'll also encounter two more waterfalls, substantially larger than the first, but the trail leading around the left side of each is far more obvious and easily negotiated than the path through the first.

You should encounter your first songbirds (other than wrens) after negotiating the first pour-off and reaching the canyon floor. It's worth lingering in each of the cottonwood groves that you encounter and waiting for the bird activity to unfold. In general, the riparian zone is the area of greatest activity, as both riparian-dependent birds as well as species of the pinyon-juniper forest use the area for foraging opportunities. One of the benefits, too, of these narrow, densely vegetated canyons is that all of the bird activity is focused. It is possible to sit on a rock overlooking the cottonwoods and the willow scrub of the canyon bottom, while enjoying a view of the talus slopes only slightly higher up, where Chukars lurk among the boulders and Rock Wrens bob and flit from rock to rock.

About 4 miles down canyon, the terrain begins to open up and become drier. Pinyon-juniper becomes dominant, with an occasional line of cottonwoods on the creek; sagebrush and grasses dominate, the openings. The bird community changes accordingly, although a few riparian species may still be encountered.

Directions: About 2 miles east of the intersection of UT 275 (which leads to Natural Bridges National Monument) and UT 95, turn south on UT 261; this turn is signed to the Grand Gulch Primitive Area and to Mexican Hat. Drive about 5 miles south on UT 261; about 0.5 mile beyond the Kane Gulch Ranger Station, a graded dirt road departs to the east. Take this turn, which has a small and inconspicuous sign indicating Owl Creek. The trailhead lies at the end of this road, about 5 miles distant.

General information: The 5-mile-long access road to the trailhead has a clay base, passable only when the road is dry.

A number of Native American cultures, including the Anasazi, once inhabited this area. If you are lucky enough to find any prehistoric artifacts, whether pottery, stone tools, or buildings, leave them exactly as you found them. Ignore any overwhelming urge to climb on any structures.

There are a number of campsites throughout Fish Creek, but there is also some rather impressive evidence of flash flooding. One campsite in the upper canyon particularly struck me: as I stood in a neatly-groomed and dead-level site where someone recently had pitched a tent, I lifted my head and saw massive tree trunks deposited by a flood, lodged atop a boulder about 5 feet above my head. Keep this in mind when selecting a campsite, and look for a spot that will get you up off the canyon floor and preferably higher than the rack line from that not-too-long-ago flood event.

This is an increasingly popular area, particularly during late winter/early spring when colleges hold spring break. If you seek solitude, this may not be the place. Most other times it is not unusual to have the place to yourself. The isolation is usually a blessing, but if you get in trouble, help can be a long time coming. This trail does require a good deal of scrambling over rocks and some modest route-finding skills. The climb out requires a good deal of exertion.

A good hiking guide for these and numerous other trails across the state is David Hall's *Hiking Utah* (Falcon). I highly recommend it as a companion for these trails. Also, the nearest developed campground is at Natural Bridges National Monument, about 15 miles away. However, primitive camping is available at the trailhead. Owl Creek canyon seems less prone to flash flooding than Fish Creek, but if there is a chance of rain in the area, choose a campsite well off the canyon floor.

There is beaver activity and there are fish in Fish Creek to within a mile of its confluence with Owl Creek. This leads me to believe there is year-round water in most of Fish Creek, at least in the form of pools. Almost certainly you'll find water throughout the canyon if you hike in spring. Mr. Hall reports the last reliable water is to be found in a spring about halfway down the canyon, so it is best to be prepared to carry ample water below this point.

The lower portion of Owl Creek sometimes dries out and the last reliable water is to be found just below the second pour-off. Be prepared to carry ample water below that point.

No matter what time of year you hike, be sure to either purify the water through boiling, chemicals, or with a pump.

ADDITIONAL INFORMATION

Map grid: 8J
Elevation: 6,000 to 4,900 feet.
Hazards: Remote location, heat, biting insects.
Nearest food, gas, and lodging: Mexican Hat.
Camping: Natural Bridges National Monument.
For more information: Bureau of Land Management, San Juan Field Office.

94 Sand Wash

Habitat: Lowland riparian
Specialty birds: White-throated Swift; Lewis's Woodpecker; Western Wood-Pewee; Willow Flycatcher; Cassin's Kingbird; Green-tailed and Spotted Towhees; Lazuli Bunting
Other key birds: California Quail; Black-chinned and Broad-tailed Hummingbirds; Belted Kingfisher; Hairy Woodpecker; Say's Phoebe; Ash-throated Flycatcher; Western Kingbird; Plumbeous and Warbling Vireo; Western Scrub-Jay; Violet-green and Cliff Swallows; Rock, Canyon, and Bewick's Wrens; Virginia's, Lucy's, Yellow, and Yellow-rumped Warblers; Common Yellowthroat; Yellow-breasted Chat; Chipping and Song Sparrows; Black-headed and Blue Grosbeaks; Scott's Oriole; Lesser and American Goldfinches
Best times to bird: Spring (April) and fall (September through October) migration; mornings May through June for breeding birds

The birding: Sand Wash is a wide floodplain on the San Juan River with a Bureau of Land Management campground at the east end, a boat ramp in the center, and an undeveloped stretch of river forest and desert grassland stretching away to the west. It's also a popular launch point for river runners heading down the San Juan River and a great spot for access to a strip of riparian vegetation that supports migrating and nesting passerines.

Towering cottonwoods along the river and in the campground support a large population of birds, including breeding Willow Flycatchers and Scott's Orioles. The campground is small. Walk through the area, keeping an eye out for bird activity.

From the campground, make your way downstream along the San Juan. Walking the line between the cottonwoods on the river shore and the more open grassland behind the cottonwoods tends to be productive. Keep an eye out for birds flying up or down the river corridor.

West of the boat ramp things get a little wilder. There are informal trails in this area, primarily from the passage of anglers and other ad hoc explorers, so you can follow these paths or wander at will. This western area also contains more of an understory in the form of young cottonwoods and shrubs, so it can be quite productive for songbirds. At any rate, all of Sand Wash is bounded by a cliff wall so you can't get lost. Just be sure to carry adequate water—it does get hot.

Directions: From Bluff, travel west for about 3 miles on UT 163, where you'll see a well-signed turn left into the Sand Wash Recreation Area. Take this turn and follow the road down to the floodplain of the San Juan. Bear left toward the campground and park by the restrooms.

General information: There is a truly spectacular petroglyph panel at Sand Wash, which should not be missed. Be sure to take time to explore the western road on the floodplain, which passes beneath the cliff face bearing several hundred yards of these ancient and largely undecipherable images.

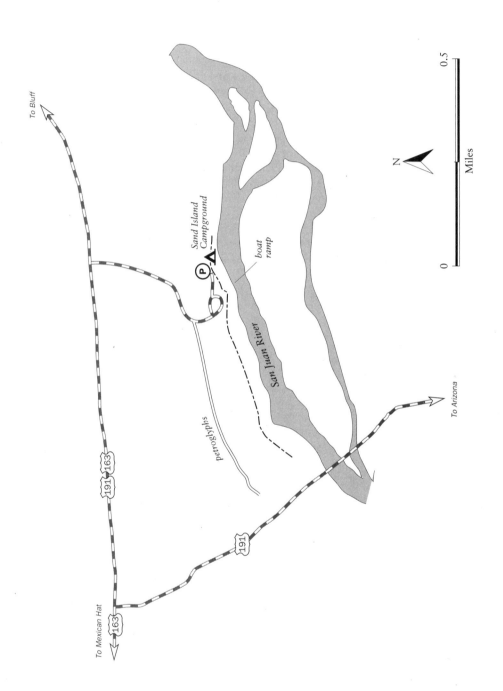

ADDITIONAL INFORMATION

Map grid: 8K
Elevation: 4,300 feet.
Hazards: No drinking water, biting insects, high temperatures.
Nearest food, gas, and lodging: Bluff.
Camping: Sand Wash Campground.
For more information: Bureau of Land Management, San Juan Field Office.

95 Square Tower Loop, Hovenweep National Monument

Habitats: Pinyon-juniper, upland desert shrub
Specialty birds: Western Screech-Owl; Cassin's Kingbird; Gray Flycatcher; Northern Shrike (winter); Gray Vireo; Pinyon Jay; Clark's Nutcracker (winter); Townsend's Solitaire; Sage Thrasher; Green-tailed and Spotted Towhees; Sage Sparrow; Lazuli Bunting
Other key birds: Turkey Vulture; Sharp-shinned, Cooper's, and Swainson's Hawks; Golden Eagle; Long-eared and Short-eared Owls; Common Nighthawk; Common Poorwill; Black-chinned and Broad-tailed Hummingbirds; Hairy Woodpecker; Cordilleran and Ash-throated Flycatchers; Western Kingbird; Loggerhead Shrike; Violet-green and Barn Swallows; Steller's Jay; Western Scrub-Jay; Black-billed Magpie; Mountain Chickadee (fall to early spring); White-breasted Nuthatch; Rock, Canyon, and Bewick's Wrens; Mountain Bluebird; Hermit Thrush; Northern Mockingbird; Orange-crowned, Nashville, Virginia's, Yellow-rumped, Black-throated Gray, MacGillivray's, and Wilson's (spring) Warblers; Western Tanager; Brewer's, Lark, Black-throated, and White-crowned Sparrows; Black-headed Grosbeak; Brewer's Blackbird; Bullock's and Scott's (May to June) Orioles; Cassin's Finch; American Goldfinch
Best times to bird: Diversity is highest in spring and fall, April through early May and September through early October. Still interesting in breeding season, May through mid-June

The birding: This fascinating site combines some of the better birding in the area with some of the most fascinating archaeology in North America. The habitat is primarily pinyon-juniper, but the pueblo sites in the monument are located at springs situated at the head of finger canyons. These sites feature a modest amount of riparian vegetation and a concentration of birds, particularly during migration, when the canyon heads act as migrant traps.

The Square Tower Loop Trail is in the heart of this national monument, which is actually composed of a series of disjunct units scattered across this corner of Utah and the adjacent state of Colorado. The place to start is the ranger station, which is at the trailhead, where you should pay your entrance fee and pick up a trail guide. The trail is about 1.5 miles long, and it follows along the rim of the canyon. Bird activity here peaks in the cool morning hours and drops off quickly as the day heats.

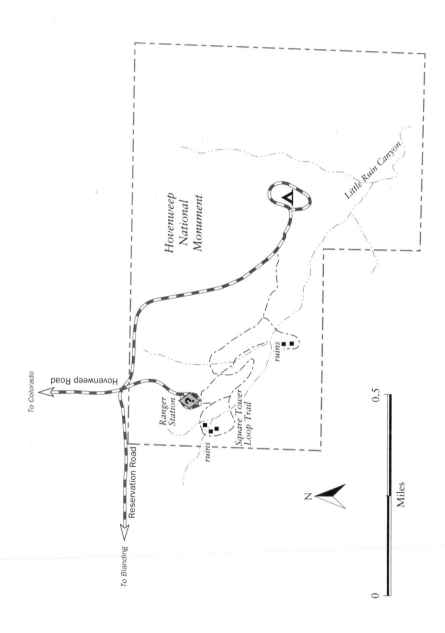

As you hike this loop, keep an eye out for birds flying between the bottom of the canyon and the rim and surrounding vegetation. Violet-green Swallows are common, as are Ash-throated Flycatchers and Black-throated Sparrows. There are Sage Sparrows, too, and they are easiest to detect early in the spring when they perch and sing on top of the sagebrush; otherwise, they tend to taunt you by flitting around the bottoms of the shrubs.

Directions: From Blanding, head south on US 191 for about 14 miles to the intersection with UT 262 (Hovenweep Road), and turn left (east). Continue following this route for about 15 miles, at which point you will need to bear right to stay on Hovenweep Road. The intersection (and the entire route) is well signed to get visitors to the monument. The monument headquarters and the trailhead lie about 8 miles farther down Hovenweep Road.

General information: The monument campground is within an easy walk of the loop described above. This spot is remote enough that I'd advise an overnight stay, in which case you can also bird the campground, where many of the same species can be seen.

Of the many sites in the monument, the nearby Hackberry Ruins, also described in this guide, is another good spot for birding.

ADDITIONAL INFORMATION

Map grid: 9J
Elevation: 5,220 feet.
Hazards: Remote site, high temperatures, biting insects.
Nearest food, gas, and lodging: Montezuma Creek.
Camping: Hovenweep National Monument Campground.
For more information: Hovenweep National Monument.

96 Hackberry Ruins, Hovenweep National Monument

Habitats: Pinyon-juniper, upland desert shrub, lowland riparian
Specialty birds: Prairie Falcon; Western Screech-Owl; Northern
Pygmy-Owl; Cassin's Kingbird; Gray Flycatcher; Northern Shrike
(winter); Gray Vireo; Pinyon Jay; Clark's Nutcracker (winter);
Townsend's Solitaire; Sage Thrasher; Green-tailed and Spotted
Towhees; Sage Sparrow; Lazuli Bunting
Other key birds: Mallard; Turkey Vulture; Northern Harrier; Sharp-
shinned, Cooper's, and Swainson's Hawks; Golden Eagle; Killdeer;
Long-eared and Short-eared Owls; Common Nighthawk; Common
Poorwill; Black-chinned and Broad-tailed Hummingbirds; Hairy
Woodpecker; Cordilleran, and Ash-throated Flycatchers; Western
Kingbird; Loggerhead Shrike; Violet-green and Barn Swallows;
Steller's Jay; Western Scrub-Jay; Black-billed Magpie; Mountain
Chickadee (fall to early spring); White-breasted Nuthatch; Rock,
Canyon, and Bewick's Wrens; Mountain Bluebird; Hermit Thrush;
Northern Mockingbird; Orange-crowned, Nashville, Virginia's, Yellow-
rumped, Black-throated Gray, MacGillivray's, and Wilson's (spring)
Warblers; Western Tanager; Indigo Bunting; Brewer's and Lark
Sparrows; Lark Bunting; Black-throated and White-crowned Sparrows;
Black-headed Grosbeak; Red-winged and Brewer's Blackbirds;
Bullock's and Scott's (May to June) Orioles; Cassin's Finch; Lesser
and American Goldfinches
Best times to bird: Spring (April through early May) and fall
(September through early October) yield the most diversity; birding
still interesting in breeding season (May through mid-June)

The birding: The first stop on this tour is Cahone Lake, a small impoundment
created more than 800 years ago by the Anasazi to trap water. The pond has been
maintained and improved more recently by the Utah Division of Wildlife Resources.
The reservoir is tiny and in some years it's more marsh vegetation than standing
water. In dry years the pond disappears completely. The standing water attracts a
wide variety of migrating passerines, including warblers and orioles. Breeding birds
tend to represent the more common species—Killdeer, Mallard, and Red-winged
Blackbird. In wet years, you may also find Lark Bunting here as well. As you
approach the area, either by foot or by car, you'll recognize the cottonwoods and
other riparian vegetation before you see the water. It's best to park at a discrete
distance and approach quietly on foot to see what species are here.

Continue birding on the half-mile walk to Hackberry Ruins. The trail passes
through a pinyon-juniper forest along the canyon rim, and you can expect to see
Common Ravens, Western Scrub-Jays, Ash-throated Flycatchers, Bewick's Wrens,
and Chipping Sparrows. This site, like the others in the monument, is situated at
the head of a canyon and around a running spring. The riparian vegetation here is
particularly evident. A dense stand of hackberry trees surround the spring and give

96 Hackberry Ruins, Hovenweep National Monument

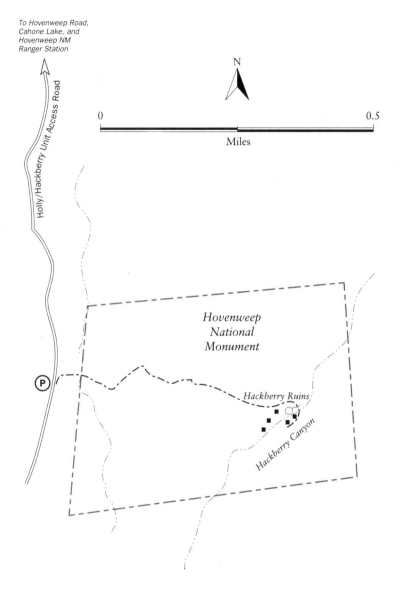

the site its name. The trees and the canyon below are great places for birds, although the park service discourages walking in the canyon bottom.

Position yourself for the best views of the area on the canyon rim at either end of the line of ruins. Keep an eye on the bird traffic in the canyon bottom. You'll be right on the edge of a cliff, so watch your footing; and away from the cliff, the ground is often covered with fragile cryptobiotic soil, so again, watch where you step.

Directions: To reach Cahone Lake, exit the ranger station at the Square Tower unit of Hovenweep National Monument and drive northeast (a right turn) on Hovenweep Road toward Colorado. From the intersection with Hovenweep Road, it is 2.8 miles to the right turn to Cahone Lake. The road is signed for Cahone Lake, but the sign is small and easily missed. The lake is 0.2 mile down this dirt road—it's an easy walk if the road seems too rough to drive.

Entrance to the various units of Hovenweep is carefully controlled by national monument staff; check in at the ranger station (open 8 a.m. to sunset) for specific directions. The Hackberry ruins lies 5 miles northeast of the ranger station, a short distance from Cahone Lake, and down a fair-weather road. Remember: check with the ranger on duty.

General information: This spot is remote enough that I'd advise an overnight stay in the nearby monument campground at Square Tower Ruin, in which case you can also bird that area.

ADDITIONAL INFORMATION

Map grid: 9J
Elevation: 5,497 feet.
Hazards: No drinking water, high temperatures.
Nearest food, gas, and lodging: Montezuma Creek.
Camping: Hovenweep National Monument Campground (Square Tower Unit).
For more information: Hovenweep National Monument.

97 Starr Springs

Habitats: Pinyon-juniper, lowland riparian
Specialty birds: Green-tailed and Spotted Towhees
Other key birds: Black-chinned Hummingbird; Ash-throated Flycatcher; Plumbeous and Warbling Vireos; Western Scrub-Jay; Western and Mountain Bluebirds; Yellow-rumped and Black-throated Gray Warblers; Western Tanager; Lark Sparrow; Lesser Goldfinch
Best times to bird: Early mornings, May through early July

The birding: This is a beautiful and remote spot in a Gambel oak forest, interspersed with modest wetlands that support sedges and grasses, willows, and a few cottonwoods. The area is surrounded, too, by extensive pinyon-juniper forests.

There are several spots to investigate in this relatively small area. The campground is nestled under an unusually tall canopy of oaks. Stroll the loop and look for both species of towhee, Western Tanagers, Ash-throated Flycatchers, and Yellow-rumped and Black-throated Gray Warblers, or occupy a campsite and wait for the birds to come to you.

The short Panorama Knoll Nature Trail forms a loop between the campground and the picnic area, which is behind the campground registration board. The trail

97 Starr Springs

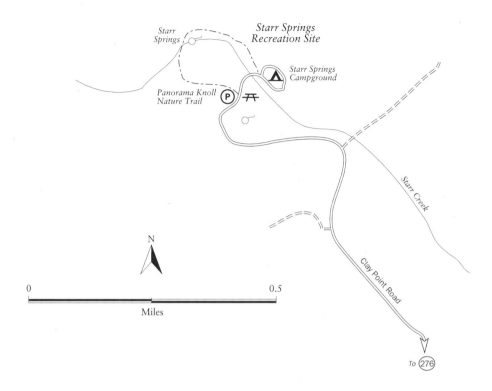

is worth a hike, and one area in particular is worth lingering in. The upper end of the loop crosses the drainage occupied by Starr Springs—the water exits under the trail via a pipe installed by the Bureau of Land Management. Take time to walk up this drainage. You'll notice a trail, created by the passage of other hikers, leading through a turnstile in the fence. In another 50 yards you'll reach a grass- and sedge-carpeted opening—the spring—and possibly a little water running from this tiny meadow. Approach this area quietly as you may encounter a variety of wildlife in addition to birds drinking here. The oak grove that lies in the bottom of the wash—back by the fence—is also worth visiting. Choose a seat on the hillside opposite the grove and observe bird activity.

Back toward the road, be sure to walk the short distance into the picnic area, and explore the willow marsh and small cottonwood grove. There is also a small wetland complex visible from the side of the picnic area trail, although there was little bird activity around it on my last visit.

Directions: From Hanksville, follow UT 95 south and turn onto UT 276 toward Bullfrog Marina. From the intersection of UT 95 and 276, the turnoff to Starr Springs lies 16.8 miles away. The turn is well signed for Starr Springs Recreation Site. Follow Clay Point Road for 4 miles, where it deadends in the campground.

General information: Starr Springs is the site of the Starr Ranch, whose stone house and cellar sit in ruins near the entrance to the site, adding to the sense of isolation. The ranch was occupied for only a few years in the late 1800s—Al Starr's mining interests failed and locoweed killed most of his horses.

ADDITIONAL INFORMATION

Map grid: 6J
Elevation: 6,171 feet.
Hazards: Remote location.
Nearest food, gas, and lodging: Hanksville.
Camping: Starr Springs Campground.
For more information: Bureau of Land Management, Henry Mountains Field Office.

98 Harris Wash

Habitats: Lowland riparian, upland desert shrub
Specialty birds: Gray and Willow Flycatchers; Green-tailed and Spotted Towhees
Other key birds: Common Nighthawk; Common Poorwill; Black-chinned Hummingbird; Hairy Woodpecker; Ash-throated Flycatcher; Plumbeous Vireo; Common Raven; Violet-green Swallow; Rock, Canyon, and Bewick's Wrens; Cedar Waxwing; Orange-crowned, Virginia's, and Yellow Warblers; Yellow-breasted Chat; Black-headed Grosbeak; Bullock's Oriole; Lesser Goldfinch
Best times to bird: Early mornings May through June are best. Some interesting migrants may be encountered in September and October.

The birding: Harris Wash is a tributary of the Escalante River and offers an interesting birding experience in a remote, cottonwood-lined sandstone canyon. Birding can be good even in the parking area, which sits on the edge of the wash in a thicket of tamarisk, Russian olive, and cottonwoods, but the warblers and towhees that frequent this area mostly remain well hidden in the brush.

There is no signed trail here. Just head down the bed of the wash. From the parking area, follow the road and turn right, walking down the stream corridor. Where you'll find birds along this route is somewhat dependent on where you find water, which in turn varies with the seasons. An island of cottonwoods sits in the middle of the channel about a quarter of a mile downstream, and in years when the stream surfaces beside these trees, there is often a good deal of activity; if so, take a seat on the bank and watch.

Following this section is a half of a mile or so with little vegetation before the canyon bottom opens up to support a lush cottonwood forest. Again, this can be an active area, and whenever you detect signs of activity, sit for a few minutes. This is also the section of the wash where sheer sandstone walls begin to rise

98 Harris Wash

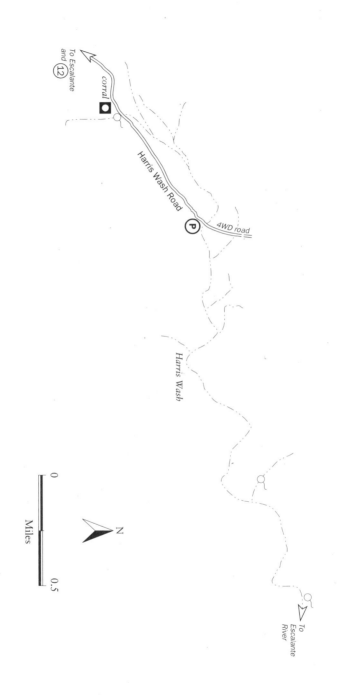

315

prominently on either side. These can harbor Common Ravens, swallows, and Great Horned Owls.

Expect to hike about 2 miles to have a good birding experience at Harris Wash. You can extend the walk as far as you wish, even making an overnight backpacking trip. Harris Wash intersects the Escalante River about 8 miles from the parking area, and most of this route passes through good riparian habitat with interesting birding.

Directions: From Escalante, head east on UT 12 for 5 miles. Turn right at the sign for Hole-in-the-Rock. This is Hole-in-the-Rock Road. Turn left after 10.4 miles at a well-signed intersection indicating the route to Harris Wash. The small parking area and trailhead are 5.9 miles down this road.

General information: Hole-in-the-Rock Road is a well traveled, all-weather road, suitable for passenger cars, but it is also notorious for generating flat tires; take it slow. Harris Wash Road is rough but passable, except in wet weather.

ADDITIONAL INFORMATION

Map grid: 5J
Elevation: 5,200 feet.
Hazards: Remote location, no drinking water, biting insects.
Nearest food, gas, and lodging: Escalante.
Camping: Escalante State Park Campground.
For more information: Bureau of Land Management, Escalante Field Office.

99 Wide Hollow Reservoir, Escalante State Park

Habitats: Lowland riparian, upland desert shrub, pinyon-juniper
Specialty birds: Clark's Grebe; American White Pelican (spring and fall); Bald Eagle (winter); Chukar; Marbled Godwit (spring and fall); Gray Vireo; Pinyon Jay; Green-tailed and Spotted Towhees; Sage Sparrow
Other key birds: Common Loon; Pied-billed and Western Grebes; Double-crested Cormorant; Tundra Swan (November); Snow Goose (February to March); Green-winged Teal; Northern Pintail; Blue-winged and Cinnamon Teals; Northern Shoveler; Gadwall; American Wigeon; Redhead; Ring-necked Duck (spring and fall); Lesser Scaup (spring and fall); Common (spring and fall) and Red-breasted (spring and fall) Mergansers; Ruddy Duck; Osprey; Cooper's Hawk; Willet; Spotted Sandpiper; Wilson's Phalarope; Franklin's and California Gulls; Forster's and Black Terns; Black-chinned and Broad-tailed Hummingbirds; Belted Kingfisher; Downy Woodpecker; Say's Phoebe; Ash-throated Flycatcher; Western Kingbird; Violet-green and Barn Swallows; Western Scrub-Jay; Black-billed Magpie; Common Raven; Canyon Wren; Mountain Bluebird; Yellow, Black-throated Gray, and Wilson's Warblers; Western Tanager; Lark and White-crowned Sparrows
Best times to bird: Early mornings, May through early July, and September through October for migrants

The birding: A small but well-developed riparian zone on the north side of this reservoir and a flooded marsh on the west side attract both songbirds and waterfowl; the latter are best represented during spring and fall migration. The reservoir is bounded by a state park, making access particularly convenient.

From the visitor center and picnic area, walk west on the gravel road that lies between the lakeshore and the campground. The road is bounded on one side by willows and cottonwoods, and on the other by sagebrush and scattered junipers. In the latter habitat, look for White-crowned, Sage, and Lark Sparrows, as well as Green-tailed and Spotted Towhees. This short walk is good for songbirds and the Cooper's Hawks that hunt them. Flycatchers and warblers are usually some of the more conspicuous birds in the riparian vegetation.

The two best areas for scanning the lake for waterfowl are the entrance road just before the visitor center and the end of the gravel road described above. The latter spot will get you to a vantage point from which binoculars are adequate. At the former site you'll do best with a spotting scope. The waterfowl tend to congregate at the west end of the lake, adjacent to the emergent marsh vegetation. The gravel road, by the way, terminates at a locked gate signed against trespassing.

Finally, Chukars can usually be found in the campground and at the visitor center, where they are fed cracked corn.

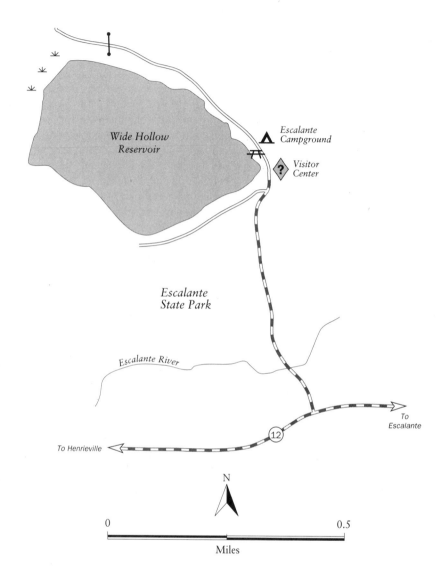

Directions: From Escalante, head west on UT 12 for about 1.5 miles. The well-signed turn to Escalante State Park points you north (right), and the visitor center lies less than a half of a mile from this turn.

General information: Expect a user fee—$3 for day use and another $10 if you plan to camp. Hikes in the state park lead to interesting "forests" of petrified wood and provide a good alternative for traveling companions uninterested in birding.

ADDITIONAL INFORMATION

Map grid: 5J
Elevation: 6,000 feet.
Hazards: None.
Nearest food, gas, and lodging: Escalante.
Camping: Escalante State Park Campground.
For more information: Escalante State Park.

100 Calf Creek Recreation Area

Habitats: Lowland riparian, upland desert shrub, pinyon-juniper
Specialty birds: Peregrine Falcon; Gray and Willow Flycatchers;
Green-tailed and Spotted Towhees
Other key birds: Common Nighthawk; Common Poorwill; Black-
chinned Hummingbird; Downy and Hairy Woodpeckers; Western
Bluebird; Ash-throated Flycatcher; Plumbeous Vireo; Common Raven;
Violet-green Swallow; Rock, Canyon, and Bewick's Wrens; Cedar
Waxwing; Orange-crowned, Virginia's, and Yellow Warblers; Yellow-
breasted Chat; White-crowned Sparrow; Black-headed Grosbeak;
Bullock's Oriole; Lesser Goldfinch
Best times to bird: Early mornings, May through June

The birding: A note in my field book says, "Only one word is necessary to describe this canyon: *enchanting.*" Nonetheless, I'll try to expound. Calf Creek Canyon is a narrow gorge bounded by sandstone cliffs. Calf Creek is a perennial stream with a strong flow, healthy beaver population, and lush marshes and cottonwood groves. A number of side canyons descend into Calf Creek and support oaks and junipers. In addition to good birding, the area is historically fascinating, with evidence of Anasazi petroglyphs and cliff dwellings.

The area around the campground, located more or less at the mouth of the canyon, can be quite productive. Walk through the campground, keeping an eye on the dense understory as well as the cottonwood overstory.

The second area for birding requires a good hike, but it takes you to the area for which most people come to Calf Creek. A trail departs from the upper end of the parking area and follows the west side of the creek up the watershed to Lower Calf Creek Falls. Be sure to pick up a trail guide at the trailhead. The trail offers great views of the riparian zone, where typical wetland species can be seen, and also exposes you to some of the drier, upland vegetation. The best birding along the trail, however, is in the upper third of the canyon, above Trail Marker 22, where the canyon floor is shaded and cool and beaver ponds slow the water. Even in the heat of the afternoon this area still fosters bird activity. The round-trip hiking distance is 5.5 miles.

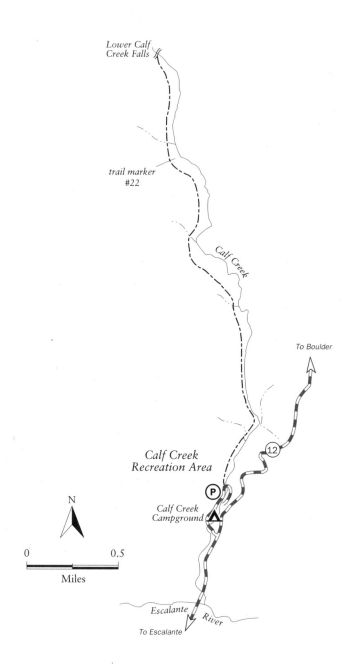

Lower Calf
Creek Falls

trail marker
#22

Calf Creek

To Boulder

12

Calf Creek
Recreation Area

P

Calf Creek
Campground

N

0   0.5

Miles

Escalante River

To Escalante

Beaver dams pool and slow this stretch of Calf Creek.

Directions: Calf Creek Recreation Area is about 12 miles east of Escalante on UT 12 or 10 miles south of Boulder, also on UT 12. The turn into the parking area is well signed and lies about a quarter of a mile north of the Escalante River crossing.

General information: A day use fee of $4 is required, with an additional $10 camp fee if you plan to stay overnight.

ADDITIONAL INFORMATION

Map grid: 5J
Elevation: 5,700 feet.
Hazards: High temperatures, no drinking water along trail.
Nearest food, gas, and lodging: Boulder.
Camping: Calf Creek Campground.
For more information: Bureau of Land Management, Escalante Field Office.

101 Cottonwood Canyon

Habitats: Lowland riparian, upland desert shrub
Specialty birds: Western Screech-Owl; White-throated Swift; Gray and Willow Flycatchers; Cassin's Kingbird; Pinyon Jay; Sage Thrasher; Green-tailed and Spotted Towhees; Sage Sparrow; Lazuli Bunting
Other key birds: Turkey Vulture; Common Nighthawk; Common Poorwill; Black-chinned and Broad-tailed Hummingbirds; Hairy Woodpecker; Western Wood-Pewee; Say's Phoebe; Ash-throated Flycatcher; Western Kingbird; Plumbeous and Warbling Vireos; Western Scrub-Jay; Common Raven; Tree, Violet-green, and Cliff Swallows; Rock, Canyon, and Bewick's Wrens; Northern Mockingbird; Lucy's, Yellow, Yellow-rumped, and Black-throated Gray Warblers; Black-throated Sparrow; Black-headed Grosbeak; Bullock's Oriole; Lesser and American Goldfinches
Best times to bird: Early mornings, May through June and September through early October

The birding: From the south end, the first 12.8 miles of this route pass through sparse desert shrub and along the Paria River, which at this point supports little riparian vegetation. After passing this less-than-promising area for birds, the road enters the dramatic and narrow Cottonwood Canyon, which is bounded on either side by rugged sandstone cliffs. In the bottom of the canyon and always in view of the road is the cottonwood-riparian zone that holds the best birding.

There are numerous access points along the route in the form of side roads that depart toward the creek, most ending in primitive campsites. As of this writing, this area was included in a wilderness study area, and all of the side access roads are closed to motorized travel; plan on parking by the main road and walking the short distance to the creek.

101 Cottonwood Canyon

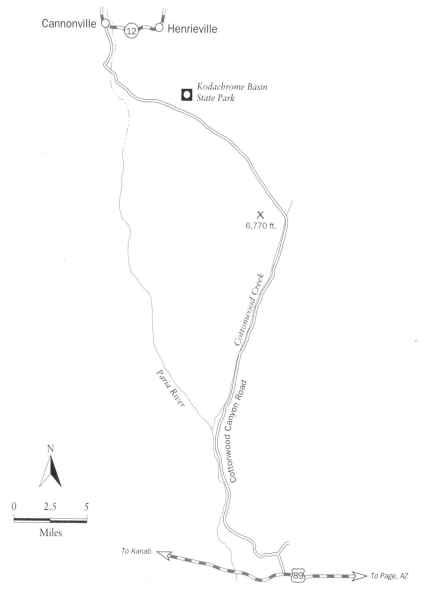

One of the best access points and birding areas is the first access road encountered, at the 12.8-mile mark. The creek here is lined with massive cottonwoods, and a hike can produce a satisfying list of species. The strategy is to bird your way up or down the stream. Walking in the streambed is easiest; there's usually little or no standing water. If you only have time for one stop in Cottonwood Canyon I'd recommend this one, and there are a couple of good primitive campsites by the creek.

The stream bed in Cottonwood Canyon is often dry enough for birders to walk in.

As you drive the Cottonwood Canyon Road you'll see many other access points, and a hike in to reconnoiter the stream corridor at any of these points can be worthwhile. In general, though, I think the best birding is in the southern portion of the canyon. As you head north it becomes even narrower, and the riparian zone becomes sparse or poorly developed. Some of those additional access points in the lower canyon include stops at 13.8, 14, 16.1, 17.6, and 18.5 miles.

Directions: This designated Scenic Drive connects the Bryce Canyon area with Lake Powell to the south. From the southern end of the route, turn off US 89 about 18 miles west of the Utah–Arizona border and about 32 miles east of Kanab. If coming east on US 89, look for the Paria Ranger Station, just east of the Paria River crossing; from the ranger station it is 3 miles to the Cottonwood Canyon Road. The road is signed for Cottonwood Canyon, Grosvenor Arch, and Cannonville, but the sign is small and hard to see until you actually turn onto the road. From US 89, the Cottonwood Canyon Road goes north 46 miles to Cannonville and UT 12—the best birding is found in Cottonwood Canyon, above the confluence of Cottonwood Creek and the Paria River.

General information: Although this road receives a lot of travelers in the summer, it does become impassable when wet. If you're traveling the route in early spring or late fall, or if you're concerned about weather, check with the Bureau of Land Management or the National Park Service for information on current road conditions. This is a long stretch of road without services; make sure your gas tank is full when you leave civilization.

ADDITIONAL INFORMATION

Map grid: 4J and 4K
Elevation: 4,500 to 6,000 feet.
Hazards: No drinking water, biting insects, high temperatures, remote location.
Nearest food, gas, and lodging: Page, Arizona (south end) or Tropic (north end).
Camping: Primitive camping along route, or Kodachrome Basin State Park at the north end.
For more information: Bureau of Land Management, Grand Staircase-Escalante National Monument.

102 Three Lakes Canyon

Habitats: Lowland riparian, pinyon-juniper
Specialty birds: White-throated Swift; Willow Flycatcher; Spotted Towhee; Lazuli Bunting
Other key birds: Common Snipe; Violet-green and Cliff Swallows; Western Scrub-Jay; Yellow Warbler; Song Sparrow
Best times to bird: May and June; some migrants possible in September through early October

The highest lake in the Three Lakes chain.

325

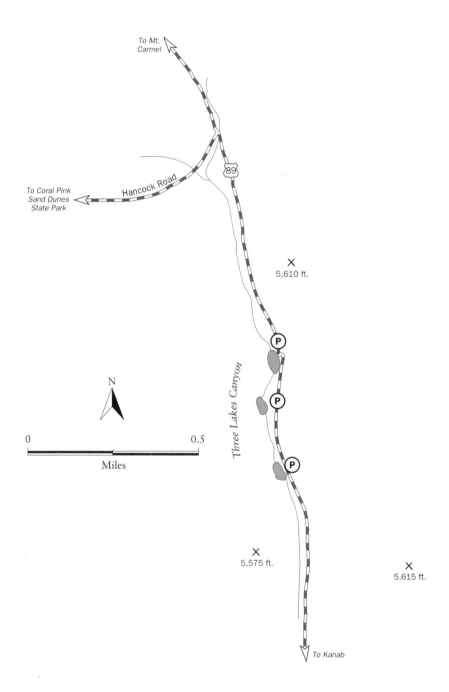

To Mt.
Carmel

89

Hancock Road

To Coral Pink
Sand Dunes
State Park

X
5,610 ft.

P

P

N

Three Lakes Canyon

P

0   0.5
Miles

X
5,575 ft.

X
5,615 ft.

To Kanab

The birding: The focus of this site is three small ponds, known as Three Lakes, that lie on the west side of US 89 about 4 miles north of Kanab. The ponds are on an intermittent tributary to the much larger Kanab Creek. Nestled among sandstone cliffs, they draw a handful of interesting bird species. All three ponds can be viewed from the road, although the middle pond requires a short scramble.

Scan the ponds and the surrounding marshes and cottonwoods for bird activity. Don't neglect the cliff faces where swifts and swallows may be found, and occasionally an interesting bird may perch in the pinyon-juniper forest visible on top of the cliffs.

Hancock Road is a good landmark for locating the lakes. Driving south on US 89 towards Kanab, the first lake is about 0.5 mile south of Hancock Road. There is a wide pullout here, a good place to sit and watch bird activity on the pond.

Continuing south, the next pond is about 0.1 miles away. The pond, however, is difficult to see because it is partially hidden by an embankment that separates the road from the creek and pond. Watch for a gated dirt road leading toward the pond (you'll catch just a glimpse), and just a few yards south of the gate you will see a low saddle, about 6 feet high, in the embankment. Pull off the highway here and scramble to the top of the saddle for a view to the second lake.

The third pond, about 0.2 mile to the south, is the most heavily impacted (by development) and contains the least amount of riparian vegetation. It's still worth a quick scan, which can be accomplished from the roadside.

Directions: From Kanab, head north on US 89. The southernmost lake lies to the west of the road about 4 miles north of town. From Mount Carmel, drive south on US 89 past Hancock Road on the right, which is signed for Coral Pink Sand Dunes State Park. The northernmost lake is about 0.5 mile past Hancock Road.

General information: All of the lakes are posted against trespassing, so plan on doing all your viewing from the road. Binoculars are adequate for the task.

ADDITIONAL INFORMATION

Map grid: 3K
Elevation: 5,800 feet.
Hazards: None.
Nearest food, gas, and lodging: Kanab.
Camping: Ponderosa Grove (BLM, on Hancock Road).
For more information: Utah Travel Council.

103 Kanab Creek

Habitats: Lowland riparian, upland desert shrub
Specialty birds: Willow Flycatcher; Green-tailed and Spotted Towhees
Other key birds: Turkey Vulture; Gambel's Quail; Spotted Sandpiper; Greater Roadrunner; Barn Owl; Black and Say's Phoebes; Ash-throated Flycatcher; Violet-green, Northern Rough-winged, and Cliff Swallows; Common Raven; Northern Mockingbird; Yellow and Yellow-rumped Warblers; Common Yellowthroat; Brewer's Sparrow; Blue Grosbeak; Brewer's Blackbird; Lesser Goldfinch
Best times to bird: Temperatures soar quickly here, so early morning before 9 A.M.; the months of May and June are best.

The birding: South of the town of Kanab, Kanab Creek carves a deep and narrow gully, perhaps 75 feet deep and varying in width up to 100 yards or so. The bottom of this gully supports a well-developed riparian zone with some marshy areas and a band of cottonwoods, Russian olives, and of course tamarisk that follows the stream course. The area seems to attract enough songbirds, some of which are more characteristic of Arizona, to make this an interesting stop.

From the parking area, head north along the west side of the creek on the dirt track that follows the narrow floodplain of the creek. This track traces the edge of the riparian zone before crossing the creek about 0.75 mile north of the access road, at which point it becomes a faint and overgrown track that is difficult to follow.

You'll hear a lot of songbirds calling from the thickets if you visit in breeding season. The birds can be hard to see, so find a comfortable spot, preferably overlooking the creek, and just sit and wait to see what flies by. Although rare, you may even see Vermilion Flycatchers or Phainopeplas during a visit to this site.

As you follow the dirt track north, keep an eye out for snags arching over the path. There is much evidence that raptors (probably Cooper's or Sharp-shinned Hawks) like to use these for perches. Also, there are holes in the banks that show evidence of roosting birds, and Barn Owls have been known to use these cavities; Common Ravens might be another possibility for residents of these little alcoves.

Directions: From Main Street in Kanab, head south on UT 11/US Alternate 89. Follow this route about 0.4 mile south of town, watching for a sign for a subdivision on the right (west) called Kanab Creek Ranchos. Turn right at this sign, onto Kanab Creek Drive, following the road for 0.6 mile to the place where it drops down into a gully and crosses Kanab Creek. As you cross the creek and begin to climb the other side of the gully, there is a small pullout on the right-hand side and a dirt road that drops into the creek's floodplain. You can park in the pullout, or if the road is dry, you can follow it and park by the creek.

General information: You may wish to explore south of the road crossing. Be forewarned that there are no trails south of the road, so you'll be bush-bashing, but you'll also increase the likelihood of seeing some interesting species.

103 Kanab Creek

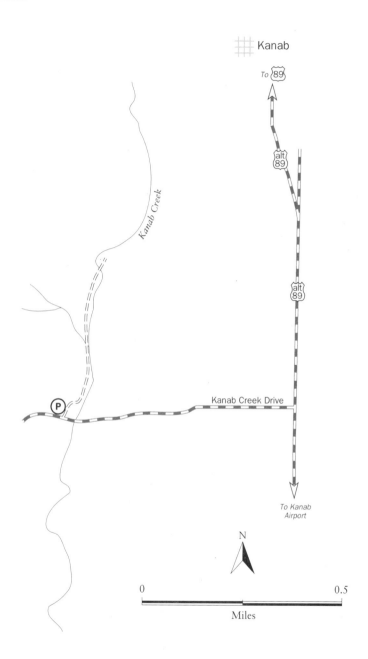

ADDITIONAL INFORMATION

Map grid: 3K
Elevation: 4,850 feet.
Hazards: None.
Nearest food, gas, and lodging: Kanab.
Camping: Ponderosa Grove (BLM, on Hancock Road).
For more information: Utah Travel Council.

104 Springdale Pond

Habitat: Lowland riparian
Specialty birds: Willow Flycatcher; Cassin's Kingbird; American Dipper; Lazuli Bunting
Other key birds: Eared Grebe (spring and fall); Green-winged Teal (spring and fall); American Wigeon (spring and fall); Ring-necked Duck (spring and fall); Virginia Rail; Sora; Spotted Sandpiper; Common Snipe (winter); Black-chinned Hummingbird; Belted Kingfisher; Black Phoebe; Ash-throated Flycatcher; Western Kingbird; Bell's and Warbling Vireos; Winter (winter) and Marsh (winter) Wrens; Phainopepla; Orange-crowned, Virginia's, Lucy's, Yellow, and Yellow-rumped Warblers; Common Yellowthroat; Yellow-breasted Chat; Summer Tanager; Song and Lincoln's Sparrows; Black-headed and Blue Grosbeaks
Best times to bird: May, June, and October. The pond is also a popular spot for birders during the Audubon Christmas Bird count.

The birding: This small pond and the adjacent stretch of the Virgin River constitute a valuable resource for birds in this area—water. Because most of the water around is fast moving, ponds or lakes are a rarity that can attract some unusual waterfowl.

This is a very small area, and the layout of the terrain is quickly apparent from a cursory scan from the road. The pond, which is the focal point of the birding experience here, is also visible from the paved road that runs behind the Zion Park Inn. Park along the road and walk in using one of the graveled trails. The strategy here is to check the pond and the surrounding brush for bird activity. Be sure to take a moment to scope out the river corridor, where American Dippers may be seen, and also walk the marsh area immediately below the inn's parking lot.

Directions: Springdale lies at the southern entrance to Zion National Park, and UT 9 is the main street (Zion Park Boulevard) through the narrow town. Look for the unsigned but paved road that turns east off Zion Park Boulevard just north of the Zion Park Inn (1215 Zion Park Boulevard). Turn onto this road, drop down the low hill, and park along the road as you reach the floodplain of the Virgin River.

104 Springdale Pond

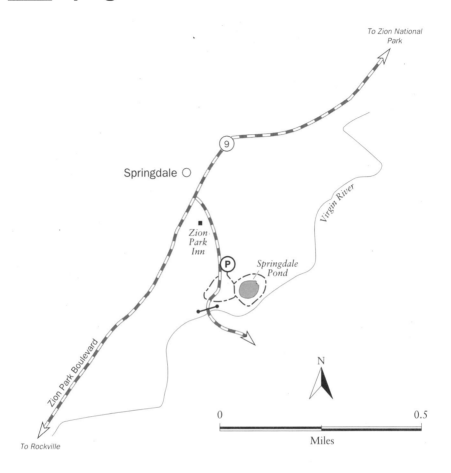

To Zion National Park

9

Springdale ○

Zion Park Inn

P

Springdale Pond

Virgin River

Zion Park Boulevard

To Rockville

N

0   0.5

Miles

General information: This property recently changed hands from a private individual, who welcomed birders, to the Zion Park Inn, which may or may not tolerate birders in the future. As of this writing, the area is being developed as a park or strolling area for guests from the inn. Stop at the inn and ask about the current status of the pond area.

ADDITIONAL INFORMATION

Map grid: 3K
Elevation: 3,900 feet.
Hazards: None.
Nearest food, gas, and lodging: Springdale.
Camping: Zion Canyon Campground.
For more information: Utah Travel Council.

105 Coalpits Wash, Zion National Park

Habitats: Upland desert shrub, lowland riparian, pinyon-juniper
Specialty birds: Prairie Falcon; Northern Shrike (winter); Gray Vireo; American Pipit (winter); Green-tailed and Spotted Towhees; Lazuli Bunting
Other key birds: Turkey Vulture; Gambel's Quail; Greater Roadrunner; Black-chinned and Costa's Hummingbirds; Ladder-backed Woodpecker; Say's Phoebe; Western Kingbird; Northern Rough-winged Swallow; Common Raven; Rock, Canyon, and Bewick's Wrens; Northern Mockingbird; Rufous-crowned, Lark, and Black-throated Sparrows; Bullock's and Scott's Orioles
Best times to bird: Late April through June, October. Early mornings are best.

The birding: This birding route involves a hike through true desert terrain to the confluence of Coalpits and Scoggins washes, a one-way distance of 1.8 miles. The trail occasionally descends to touch on short sections of Coalpits Wash but sticks mostly to the higher and drier bench areas. Hike up to the confluence via the trail, spend a half hour or so exploring the birding opportunities at the confluence, then hike back down the wash itself.

The vegetation along this route is a mix of sagebrush, manzanita, junipers, and in the wash, scattered cottonwoods. In the drier upland vegetation, expect to see Greater Roadrunner; Gambel's Quail; Rock, Canyon, and Bewick's Wrens; Gray Vireo; Lazuli Bunting; and Green-tailed and Spotted Towhees. The hummingbirds and sparrows are also active in this habitat type. Keep an eye toward the sky for Turkey Vultures, Red-tailed Hawks, and perhaps a glimpse of a Prairie Falcon.

At the confluence of the two washes, find some shade and spend half an hour or so. The confluence supports some of the lusher vegetation in the area, so bird activity between the trees and surrounding shrubs can be high.

If you decide to walk back down the wash, be prepared to rock-hop or resign yourself to wet feet. The wash is not deep—usually just enough to wet your shoes. If walking the wash gets too tiring, you can walk up onto the bench and relocate the trail. Be careful of fragile cryptobiotic soil if you hike off the trail or away from the stream. In the wash and surrounding cottonwoods, look for Ladder-backed Woodpeckers, Lazuli Buntings, and both species of oriole. Scott's Oriole was only recently reported breeding here, and it remains to be seen whether a breeding population will establish a long-term presence.

Directions: From the south entrance of Zion National Park, proceed south and east on UT 9 for 7.4 miles. Coalpits Wash passes under UT 9, but immediately before the bridge crossing, the wash is a dirt road that leads to a parking area beside the highway. Pull into this road and drive the 100 or so yards to its terminus. The trailhead begins at the turnstile and information board by the barbed wire fence along the north side of the parking area. Walk through the turnstile and proceed upriver on the trail.

105 Coalpits Wash, Zion National Park

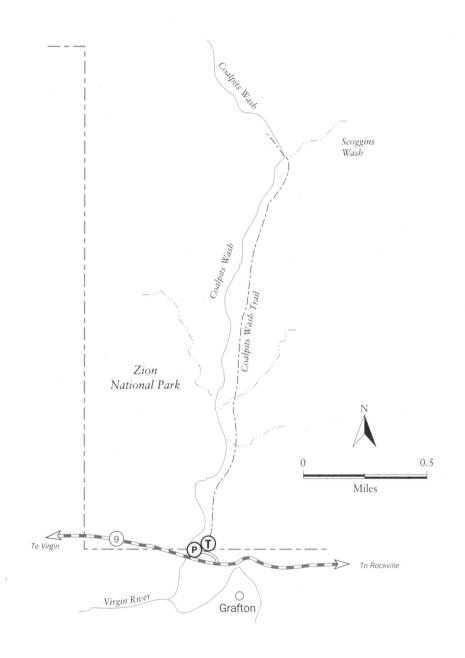

General information: It is possible to extend this hike by continuing up Coalpits Wash (the left fork at the confluence as you face upstream). This route connects with the Chinle Trail and Huber Wash, both of which lead back to UT 9, but not back to the Coalpits Wash Trailhead. Check at the national park visitor center for additional travel and route information.

ADDITIONAL INFORMATION

Map grid: 3K
Elevation: 3,660 feet.
Hazards: No drinking water, high temperatures.
Nearest food, gas, and lodging: Springdale.
Camping: Zion Canyon Campground, Springdale.
For more information: Zion National Park.

106 Grafton

Habitats: Lowland riparian, upland desert shrub
Specialty birds: Bald Eagle (winter); Western Screech-Owl; Willow Flycatcher; Cassin's Kingbird; Lazuli Bunting
Other key birds: Turkey Vulture; Gambel's Quail; Common Nighthawk; Black-chinned and Costa's Hummingbirds; Belted Kingfisher; Ladder-backed Woodpecker; Black Phoebe; Vermilion and Ash-throated Flycatchers; Western Kingbird; Bell's and Warbling Vireos; Common Raven; Northern Rough-winged and Cliff Swallows; Bewick's and House Wrens; Phainopepla; Lucy's, Yellow, and Yellow-rumped Warblers; Yellow-breasted Chat; Summer Tanager; Song Sparrow; Black-headed and Blue Grosbeaks; Bullock's Oriole; Lesser Goldfinch
Best times to bird: Early mornings in May, June, and October

The birding: The banks of the Virgin River near the ghost town of Grafton hold some of the best riparian vegetation on this stretch of the river. There are no trails here (except for cattle trails), so the object is to walk down to the floodplain and make your own way among the cottonwoods and Russian olives, and along the edge of the small section of pasture that breaks up the river forest. A productive trip will usually require about a mile hike up the river, inspecting the high branches of the trees for bird activity and in spring, listening for calling birds.

A second and very short route that is worth exploring starts back at the parking area. From here, the road continues east, following the course of the river for a short distance before terminating at a locked and posted gate. Walking this 100-yard stretch of road leads you between an old orchard and some pastureland on the left and riparian vegetation on the right. Songbird activity is sometimes concentrated in this area, and birds can be seen flying back and forth between the orchard and the cottonwoods.

Grafton is a ghost town now, but it attracts visiting birds and birders.

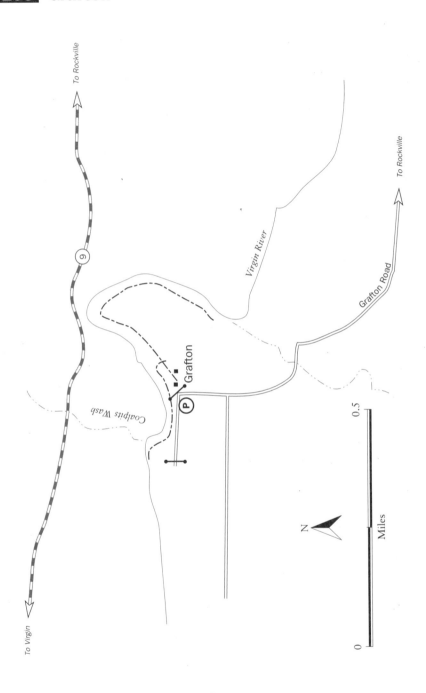

To Rockville

To Rockville

Virgin River

Grafton Road

9

Grafton

P

Coalpits Wash

To Virgin

N

Miles

0.5

0

Directions: Access to Grafton, which lies on the south side of the Virgin River, is via the small community of Rockville, about 3 miles south and west of Springdale on UT 9. In Rockville, turn south on Bridge Road—a small sign indicates the route to Grafton. From this intersection, Grafton is a 3.8-mile drive over a good gravel road. Proceed across the old trestle bridge over the Virgin River, and bear right on Grafton Road; continue to bear right at each of the next two junctions, and park near the orange gate in Grafton. Walk through the gate, between the old church and adjacent house/store, and then down to the floodplain.

General information: In July and August, when it seems too hot for anything to move, Grafton is one of the few places around where birding can still be interesting. Interesting is relative, of course, but an early morning walk here can produce 20 to 30 species.

Grafton is probably one of the more intact ghost towns in Utah, although I have seen pictures only a decade or two old that indicated many more buildings stood here until quite recently. A nearby information marker indicates that pioneers settled Grafton in 1859, but a combination of floods and Indian attacks took a heavy toll. The population of the community peaked in 1864 (164); the town was finally abandoned in the 1930s.

Most of Grafton is still privately owned—so respect those no trespassing signs.

ADDITIONAL INFORMATION

Map grid: 3K
Elevation: 3,700 feet.
Hazards: No drinking water.
Nearest food, gas, and lodging: Springdale.
Camping: Zion Canyon Campground, Springdale.
For more information: Utah Travel Council.

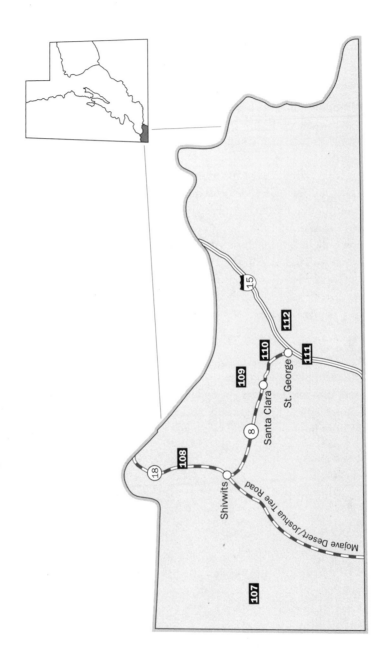

Lytle Ranch Preserve (Beaver Dam Wash)

Habitats: Lowland riparian, lowland desert shrub, upland desert shrub

Specialty birds: Western Screech-Owl; Gray Flycatcher; Gray Vireo; Green-tailed and Spotted Towhees; Black-chinned Sparrow; Lazuli Bunting

Other key birds: Black-crowned Night-Heron; Cooper's Hawk; Common Black-Hawk; Gambel's Quail; White-winged and Inca Doves; Greater Roadrunner; Lesser and Common Nighthawks; Black-chinned and Costa's Hummingbird (March to mid-June); Ladder-backed Woodpecker; Black Phoebe; Vermilion, Ash-throated, and Brown-crested Flycatchers; Western Kingbird; Loggerhead Shrike; Bell's Vireo; Verdin; Cactus and Bewick's Wrens; Black-tailed Gnatcatcher; Crissal and Le Conte's Thrashers; Cedar Waxwing (winter to spring); Phainopepla; Virginia's, Lucy's, Yellow, and Yellow-rumped Warblers; Summer Tanager; Abert's Towhee; Rufous-crowned (winter), Lark, Lincoln's, and White-crowned Sparrows; Black-headed Grosbeak; Hooded, Bullock's, and Scott's Orioles; Lesser Goldfinch

Best times to bird: Interesting year-round, activity is generally greatest in coolest part of the day. Birding in July through August is probably the *least* productive time.

The birding: Birding at the Lytle Ranch Preserve is legendary in Utah birding circles. The Lytle Ranch encompasses a section of Beaver Dam Wash, and the two names

A walk through the orchard at the Lytle Ranch leads to Beaver Dam Wash.

107 Lytle Ranch Preserve (Beaver Dam Wash)

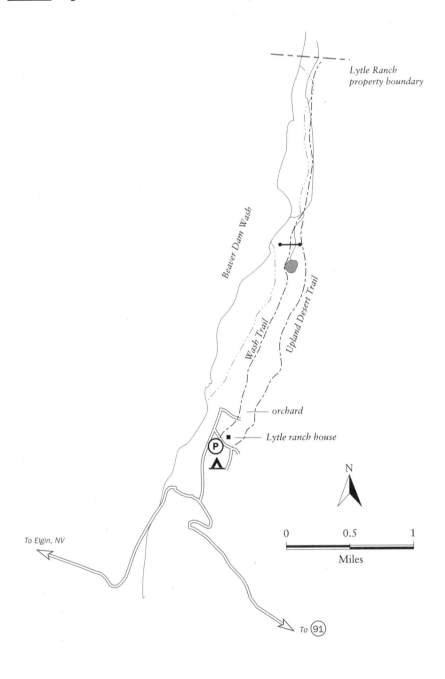

Lytle Ranch property boundary

Beaver Dam Wash

Wash Trail

Upland Desert Trail

— *orchard*

— *Lytle ranch house*

P

N

| 0 | 0.5 | 1 |

Miles

To Elgin, NV

To 91

are used interchangeably to designate the same birding destination. Part of its mystique and appeal is its remote setting in a landscape that seems foreign even by the fantastic standards of Utah. Although a permanent stream meanders through Beaver Dam Wash, the area as a whole is intensely arid and dominated by Mojave Desert vegetation, particularly mesquite, creosote bush, and Joshua trees. The wash itself, the focal point of the birding experience, supports mature cottonwood groves with an understory of willows. For birds, the wash has the important function of a migratory corridor, so a great variety of species pass through the area in spring and fall. The mix of bird species is quite appealing, too—a blend of species typically associated with Utah along with a large proportion of species more characteristic of Arizona and the Mojave Desert. It's unlikely you'll find Common Black-Hawk, White-winged Dove, Brown-crested Flycatcher, and Black-tailed Gnatcatcher anywhere else in Utah.

The best way to bird the ranch is to arrive the night before and stay in the campground. This will give you an early start, which is hard to achieve if you have to make the drive from Santa Clara or St. George or any of the other nearby birding sites. This will allow you one other luxury, which is to check in with the ranch manager at the ranch house. In exchange for signing the guest register, you'll get invaluable information about current birding conditions—what's been seen lately and where. Also, if you intend to bird all the way to the top of the ranch's property, you'll need to ask for permission to hike beyond the pond where a gate blocks the trail.

Unless the report you get sends you scurrying elsewhere, start your birding at the ranch house. Huge velvet ash trees tower over the property and, with the adjacent grove along the wash, this area can be very active. Scan the trees for flycatchers, warblers, orioles, and Summer Tanagers in search of food or, depending on the time of year, nesting materials.

Two trails depart from the vicinity of the ranch house and head up the wash. One follows the dry hillside above the ranch house and the wash, while the other goes behind the house and beside the orchard, then through the hay fields. Both of these routes can be productive, particularly in the cooler part of the day. One good option is to start by hiking up the higher and drier trail, where activity will drop off sooner as the day warms. Then return on the lower trail, which more closely follows the wash.

The orchard is worth exploring in some detail. This is a good area for sparrows, warblers, wrens, and Lazuli Buntings, and a good area to sit and wait to see what species are active.

A small pond lies along the lower wash trail about halfway to the end of the Lytle Ranch property. You can find the occasional duck or coot on the pond, or a Great Blue Heron or Black-crowned Night-Heron perched nearby. Flycatchers, including Black Phoebes, vireos, and warblers are usually in evidence here as well.

Beyond the pond, a gate blocks the path with a sign indicating the area is closed for research. If you obtained permission to pass this point from the manager, continue up the gravel road. (Otherwise, retrace your steps to the ranch house.) A fence marks the northern end of the ranch's property, and it is in this area of the wash that Common Black-Hawks have been seen. The Common Black-Hawk is a bird of riparian forests, where it hunts from perches, often over the water; with that in mind, restrict your hunt for this rare species to the cottonwoods along the wash.

Another area well worth investigating is the cottonwood forest that starts at the ranch house and follows the wash south. This is a beautiful grove of mature trees with a good understory, and bird activity can be high. Water flows in the wash here, so find a seat by the stream, soak your feet in the water after your long hike up the wash, and wait for the birds to come to you.

Directions: From St. George, head west toward Santa Clara on Sunset Boulevard (UT 8), and continue to the ghost town of Shivwits. Here the road divides—take the old highway southwest (left) 11.8 miles to the signed turnoff (west) for the L-R Ranch—a private hunting preserve adjacent to the Lytle Ranch. Continue down this gravel road for another 10.8 miles, being careful to follow a procession of small, faded yellow signs to the Lytle Ranch Headquarters.

General information: The Lytle Ranch was established decades ago as a working ranch in the remotest corner of Utah. When the property recently came up for sale, The Nature Conservancy recognized the uniqueness of the setting and arranged for the purchase and perpetual care of the property. The Conservancy then turned management of the ranch over to Brigham Young University, which uses the area for research and teaching.

The ranch does charge a modest entrance fee ($3) for day use of the ranch and an additional fee for camping ($5).

ADDITIONAL INFORMATION

Map grid: 1K
Elevation: 2,780 feet.
Hazards: Remoteness, heat, lack of water, rattlesnakes.
Nearest food, gas, and lodging: Ivins.
Camping: Lytle Ranch.
For more information: The Nature Conservancy, Utah Field Office.

Gunlock Reservoir

Habitats: Lowland riparian, upland desert shrub, pinyon-juniper
Specialty birds: White-throated Swift; Western Wood-Pewee; Willow
Flycatcher; Cassin's Kingbird; Crissal Thrasher; Spotted Towhee;
Lazuli Bunting
Other key birds: Common Loon; Pied-billed and Eared Grebes; Turkey
Vulture; Cooper's Hawk; California Gull; Black-chinned and Broad-
tailed Hummingbirds; Belted Kingfisher; Ladder-backed and Hairy
Woodpeckers; Black and Say's Phoebes; Vermilion and Ash-throated
Flycatchers; Plumbeous and Warbling Vireos; Western Scrub-Jay;
Tree, Violet-green, Northern Rough-winged, and Cliff Swallows;
Verdin; Rock, Canyon, Bewick's, and House Wrens; Northern
Mockingbird; Orange-crowned, Virginia's, Lucy's, Yellow, Yellow-
rumped, Black-throated Gray, and Wilson's (spring) Warblers; Yellow-
breasted Chat; Summer and Western Tanagers; Black-throated and
Song Sparrows; Black-headed and Blue Grosbeaks; Hooded,
Bullock's, and Scott's Orioles; Cassin's Finch; Lesser and American
Goldfinches
Best times to bird: April and September through mid-October for
migrants; May through June for resident breeders.

The birding: There are at least three distinct types of habitat at this site offering
two types of birding experiences. First, the reservoir, while lacking any marshes or
riparian habitat, does attract migrating waterfowl. If you're on your way to or

*The riparian corridor along the Santa Clara River, below Gunlock Reservoir,
promises excellent birding.*

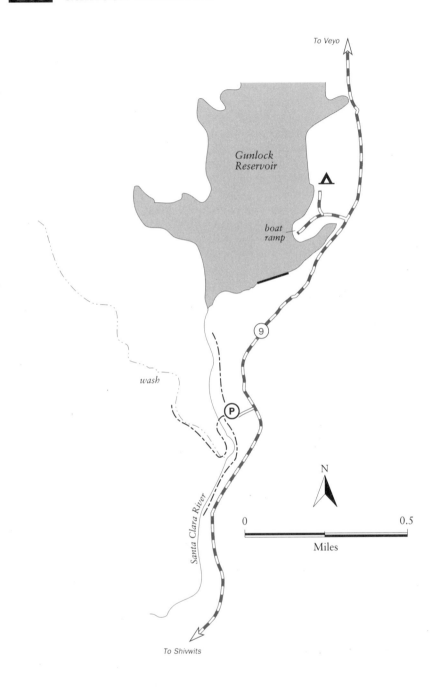

To Veyo

Gunlock
Reservoir

boat
ramp

9

wash

P

Santa Clara River

N

0   0.5

Miles

To Shivwits

through the area, it's worth pulling off by the dam face, in the campground and boat launch area, or along UT 9 as it passes along the east side of the reservoir to scan the lake for Common Loons, grebes, or any ducks heading north or south. With the exception of a few cottonwoods that dot the area, the shoreline is open, so there is little to obstruct your view of the lake. The reservoir is a popular year-round fishing destination, so you and the birds may have to compete with motor-boats for space.

The better birding experience lies along the Santa Clara River's riparian corridor below the dam face; many birders claim that this area rivals or even surpasses the more famous Beaver Dam Wash area farther to the southwest. The riverbanks support a lush overstory of mature cottonwoods with a dense understory of emerging willows and Russian olives. Adjacent to this fairly narrow corridor lies the Mojave Desert, with cacti, manzanitas, pinyons, junipers, and scattered grasses. Consequently, the bird community here, as in the Beaver Dam Wash area, is more characteristic of the bird community along the Lower Colorado River in Arizona and California, with an interesting mix of northern species thrown in for good measure.

There is no trail in the area, so from the parking area (see directions) you will have to make your own way along the river. Choose whichever side of the river will put the sun at your back while you scan the cottonwoods for birds; if you need to cross, the river is shallow and can be waded, or there are logs spanning the banks that can be crossed. I recommend heading downstream from the parking area—if you walk upstream you'll quickly encounter the dam face and run out of birding.

Work your way downstream as far as you feel comfortable hiking, while listening for bird activity in the cottonwoods and in the understory. Because the vegetation is lush here, good aural identification skills are helpful. Failing that, you may spend a fair amount of time wandering in circles trying to find that elusive bird singing in the top of a tree. Another good approach is to simply find a comfortable place to sit and see what comes and goes. Warblers, Summer Tanagers, woodpeckers, vireos, and flycatchers all make use of the river forest. Activity is greatest here in the mornings, but the shaded river corridor seems to sustain at least moderate activity throughout the day.

West of the river, the adjacent desert is also quite interesting. A number of shallow and usually dry washes cut through the red sandstone slickrock to enter on this west side, and sometimes birding along one of these courses can be very rewarding. You're more likely to see Western Scrub-Jays, Bushtits, Juniper Titmice, and the other typical arid lands species, as well as the reclusive thrashers. The wash shown on the accompanying map is only one of many options in this desert.

Directions: Gunlock Reservoir is an impoundment on the Santa Clara River, along UT 9, about 15 miles northwest of St. George. Access to the riparian corridor is 0.5 mile south of the dam face; turn off UT 9 into a graveled parking area by the river.

General information: The riparian corridor both below and above the reservoir is extensive, and the route described here is only one of many possibilities. About 2 miles of the Santa Clara River below the dam (including the section described here) lie on Bureau of Land Management lands; if you choose to explore elsewhere, be certain that the area you're birding is not posted, and note that an extensive stretch of the river corridor south of the BLM lands lies in the Shivwits Indian Reservation, all of which is posted.

ADDITIONAL INFORMATION

Map grid: 1K
Elevation: 3,450 feet.
Hazards: None.
Nearest food, gas, and lodging: Santa Clara.
Camping: Gunlock State Park.
For more information: Utah Division of Parks and Recreation and Bureau of Land Management, Dixie Field Office.

109 West Canyon, Snow Canyon State Park

Habitats: Upland desert shrub, pinyon-juniper
Specialty birds: Peregrine Falcon; Gray Vireo; Crissal Thrasher; Green-tailed and Spotted Towhees; Black-chinned Sparrow
Other key birds: Wild Turkey; Gambel's Quail; Lesser Nighthawk; Black-chinned, Costa's, and Broad-tailed Hummingbirds; Ash-throated Flycatcher; Western Scrub-Jay; Verdin; Rock, Canyon, and Bewick's Wrens; Northern Mockingbird; Le Conte's Thrasher; Yellow, Yellow-rumped, and Black-throated Gray Warblers; Abert's Towhee; Chipping, Brewer's, Lark, Black-throated, and White-crowned Sparrows; Scott's Oriole; Lesser Goldfinch
Best times to bird: Early mornings, May through June

The birding: One of the best days of birding I've ever had in Utah took place in West Canyon, though I'd be hard pressed to explain why this dry desert wash attracts such a remarkable diversity of birds. The Three Ponds Trail is over mostly level ground and about 2.75 miles long (one-way), but the exposure and several stretches of hiking in sand make for a tiring walk.

A short distance beyond the trailhead, the trail climbs gently through a narrow canyon, sheltered on the east and west by sheer sandstone walls. This can be a good birding area, with several species of hummingbirds and sparrows, as well as Spotted Towhees, Lesser Goldfinches, and swallows frequenting the area. A bench set against the east wall is shaded from the morning sun and a good place to sit and observe bird activity in the surrounding shrubs. Beyond this point a long stretch of the trail crosses an open expanse of sparse shrubs and pinyons in a series of open basins separated by sandstone fins. There is generally little bird activity in

The upper end of West Canyon in Snow Canyon State Park.

109 West Canyon, Snow Canyon State Park

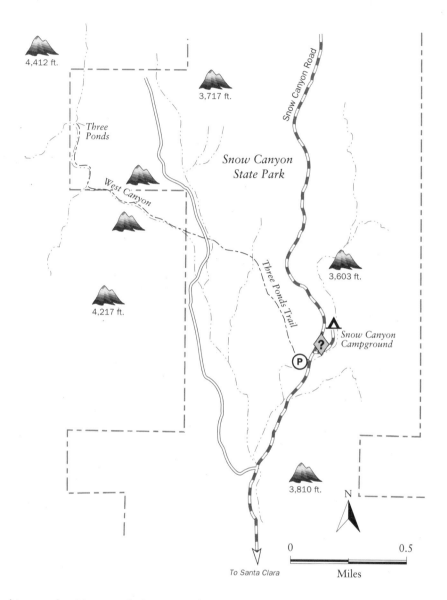

4,412 ft.

3,717 ft.

Snow Canyon Road

Three
Ponds

Snow Canyon
State Park

West Canyon

3,603 ft.

4,217 ft.

Three Ponds Trail

Snow Canyon
Campground

P

3,810 ft.

N

0   0.5

To Santa Clara   Miles

this stretch—it's a good place to pick up your pace to reach the mouth of West
Canyon while the day is still cool.

Shortly after crossing a gravel road, the trail enters the sandy wash that empties West Canyon. West Canyon lies between towering sandstone cliffs, which
appear to guard the entrance like castle buttresses. If you're hiking with nonbirders,
this is probably where you'll get left behind. There are several islands of oak trees

scattered around the wash, and it's worth finding a place in the shade to sit and observe the activity. The oaks attract a variety of warbler species, and sparrows are also abundant.

The trail continues up the wash and through the canyon mouth, at which point the canyon opens up into a sagebrush-covered basin. The edge of this basin supports cottonwood, box elder, and more oaks, and all this structural diversity attracts a commensurate diversity of birds. Continue up the wash, or take the small trail that climbs up on the low bench on the right to follow the edge of the basin. Either way, look for hummingbirds, sparrows, and orioles singing from perches on the tops of shrubs and trees. Wrens call from the cliff walls, woodpeckers forage in the trees, and Peregrine Falcons have been seen here, flying along the cliff face. This is another area where it's worth taking a few minutes to find a spot in the shade and just sit and observe.

Beyond this basin the canyon narrows again and soon reaches Three Ponds. Bird activity is often high right up to the ponds, and a flock of Wild Turkeys sometimes frequents the area around the water hole. This upper region—between the canyon mouth and the ponds—is a good area to look for the thrashers, but these secretive birds often go undetected.

Three Ponds is a series of pools or *tinajas* in the sandstone, only the lower of which is apparent upon approach. The upper two pools lie above the lower pool, and it is possible to edge your way along the sandstone wall—toe holds have been cut into the face—and explore the other pools. It is also possible to continue hiking or scrambling beyond Three Ponds, but the canyon becomes quite narrow and significant bird habitat disappears.

Directions: The trailhead for West Canyon is on the west side of the Snow Canyon State Park road, about 50 yards south of the campground entrance station. Follow the trail signs for Three Ponds, which are at the head of West Canyon.

General information: This hike offers little shade and demands ample water and sunscreen. Don't plan on drinking from Three Ponds; they are usually green and stagnant and best left for the wildlife frequenting the area.

ADDITIONAL INFORMATION

Map grid: 2K
Elevation: 3,600 feet.
Hazards: High temperatures, no water, little shade.
Nearest food, gas, and lodging: Santa Clara.
Camping: Snow Canyon State Park.
For more information: Utah Division of Parks and Recreation.

110 Red Hills Golf Course

Habitats: Lowland riparian, pinyon-juniper, upland desert shrub
Specialty birds: Willow Flycatcher; Green-tailed and Spotted Towhees
Other key birds: Pied-billed Grebe; Turkey Vulture; Osprey (fall to spring);
Wild Turkey; Black-chinned Hummingbird; Black Phoebe; Vermilion and Ash-
throated Flycatchers; Western Kingbird; Bewick's Wren; Northern
Mockingbird; Cedar Waxwing (winter to spring); Orange-crowned, Virginia's,
Lucy's, Yellow, and Yellow-rumped Warblers; Lark and Song Sparrows; Black-
headed Grosbeak; Bullock's and Scott's Orioles; Lesser Goldfinch
Best times to bird: Throughout the day during winter and in spring or fall
migration; early mornings mid-April through June for breeding species

The birding: Red Hills Golf Course offers an oasis in the midst of harsh desert
terrain. While the surrounding red-rock desert is barren and dry, this golf course
offers a perennial stream flowing into a pond, a dense and complex riparian corridor, and plenty of high trees for perches and nests. The downside, if one feels
compelled to look for one, is that maintaining all this greenery requires a lot of
irrigation.

From the parking area, walk away from the clubhouse and toward the first
tee. The riparian corridor is apparent from the edge of the parking lot. Walk over
to the creek and turn left, upstream. The golf course is narrow enough that you'll
be able to see most of the species in the area along this route, whether birds are
nesting in the riparian corridor or using the more open parts of the course for
foraging. A pair of Vermilion Flycatchers have nested here for several years and
can usually be seen perched along the stream course.

Continue to the northeast end of the course—you'll see where the cart path
crosses and a wall of dense vegetation confronts you–and continue back downstream on the opposite side of the creek. You'll have to work your way around an
arm of this narrow grove that protrudes into the course opposite the clubhouse,
and then proceed down toward the pond. A suspension bridge crosses the creek
just above the pond and returns you to the parking area. Birding the pond itself is
likely to be most productive in winter, when overwintering waterfowl and the
occasional Osprey take advantage of the open water.

Directions: The golf course is on the east (right) side of UT 18 as you leave the
outskirts of St. George and head north toward Snow Canyon State Park.

General information: Almost all of the golf courses in the St. George area are
known for their birding opportunities; I chose to include this one for its year-
round accessibility, and because the birding is good spring through fall. There is
not much open water on this nine-hole course, and in winter you may need to go
to other nearby courses to find geese and ducks, but Red Hills is a good place to
start. Red Hills Golf Course is owned and operated by St. George, and management
seems very astute about maintaining and improving their bird habitat. Many courses
in the area are private clubs, so be sure to seek permission if you bird at other
courses.

110 Red Hills Golf Course

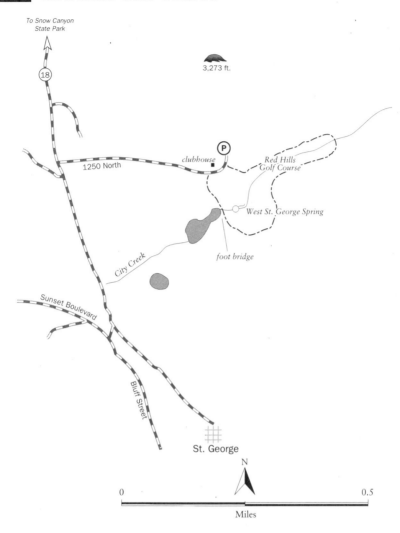

Remember that golfers, not birders, are the primary constituency for Red Hills; respect their game and stay out of the way. If you stick to the riparian corridor, you won't have any problems.

ADDITIONAL INFORMATION

Map grid: 2K
Elevation: 3,000 feet.
Hazards: None.
Nearest food, gas, and lodging: St. George.
Camping: McArthur's Temple View RV Park, St. George.
For more information: Utah Travel Council.

111 Virgin River Parkway and Tonaquint Park

Habitat: Lowland riparian

Specialty birds: Western Screech-Owl, Willow Flycatcher, Crissal Thrasher, Cassin's Kingbird, Lazuli Bunting

Other key birds: Green Heron; Gambel's Quail; Lesser Nighthawk; Belted Kingfisher; Greater Roadrunner; Ladder-backed Woodpecker; Black-chinned Hummingbird; Black Phoebe; Vermilion and Ash-throated Flycatchers; Western Kingbird; Bell's Vireo; Northern Rough-winged and Cliff Swallows; Verdin; Bewick's Wren; Orange-crowned, Lucy's, Yellow, Black-throated Gray (spring and fall), Townsend's (fall), Yellow-rumped, and Yellow-throated Warblers; Abert's Towhee; Song and White-crowned Sparrows; Black-headed and Blue Grosbeaks; Hooded and Bullock's Orioles; Lesser Goldfinch

Best times to bird: Early mornings before 9 a.m., April through June, and during fall migration, September through October. The parkway is also a popular spot for the local Audubon Christmas bird count because it's a good place to search for overwintering birds.

The birding: The Virgin River Parkway is one of the St. George area's highly accessible and bird-friendly municipal parks. The parkway, which is shared by cyclists, joggers, and pedestrians, is paved and runs along a 2-mile stretch of the river below its confluence with the Santa Clara River. The path follows a bench along the west shore of the Virgin River, the floodplain of which is wide here. Vegetation

The Virgin River, shown here near Grafton, flows through classic lowland riparian habitat.

111 Virgin River Parkway and Tonaquint Park

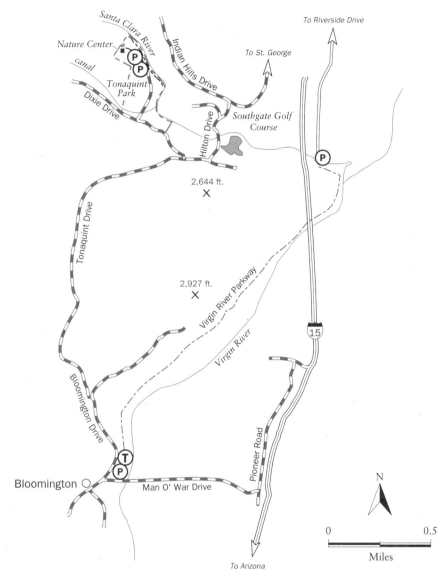

along this corridor is a dense, short mixture of willows, tamarisk, and Russian olive. Floods periodically sweep the corridor clean, providing a view from the parkway of the tops of young trees growing in the Virgin River floodplain.

Birding is usually consistent over the length of the trail, so there is no particular destination. Of course, the farther you walk, the longer you spend on the trail, and the more diversity you're likely to uncover. If you're short on time, walk in from either the north or south entrance and stroll as long as time permits. You could also set up a car shuttle if you only wanted to hike one way, or you could make a morning out of the 4-mile round trip. This is an area where, at least during breeding season, good call identification skills are helpful because birds can be hidden in lower branches. If you know the bird by call, you'll know whether you want to spend time waiting for it to reveal itself.

The primary attraction at Tonaquint Park is a narrow but dense riparian corridor that follows the Santa Clara River as it nears its confluence with the Virgin River. As a municipal park, the site is also readily accessible for a quick but high-quality birding session, maybe even on the way to work. Also, the Santa Clara River is an important migration corridor for many species of songbirds (this site seems particularly good for warblers), and the proximity to populations of Mojave Desert birds means that chances are good you'll see something worthwhile.

Most of the park is open fields and playgrounds, so the riparian forest describing the course of the Santa Clara is readily apparent as you enter the park. The area you'll want to bird runs essentially from the first parking area to the Tonaquint Nature Center, a brick building visible beyond the last parking area. In any case, proceed along the one road in the park and park in any of the parking lots, all of which border the river.

There is a paved bike path that follows the edge of the forest, and one way to bird this area is simply to walk the length of this path, scanning the trees and keeping an eye on birds moving in and out of the forest to forage in the open fields. This is a good way to find the Greater Roadrunner, if any are in the area. These birds probably nest in the forest but wander the fields and parking areas in search of food.

A better option, however, is the informal trail that passes along the edge of the river and underneath the dense tangle of tamarisk. There are a few downed trees along this path and a couple of washouts, but the walking is easy. You can enter or exit this trail at numerous points; just keep an eye on the tamarisk forest until you see an opening where others have wandered. Stop wherever an opening in the canopy allows you to get a view of the river; this is where you'll find birds. The warblers seem to prefer the higher branches of the cottonwoods on the river; Bewick's Wrens forage in the undergrowth and along lower tree limbs and trunks; Lazuli Buntings perch over the river and sing; and Abert's Towhees are a secretive denizen among the fallen leaves on the riverbank. Find an open spot on the riverbank with a view of the avenue of cottonwoods and just sit and wait.

The nature center should not be overlooked. A small artificial pond lies before the center, with a wooden deck built over the water. This is a good area for Black Phoebes, which prefer to forage over still ponds or slow moving streams. Also, a young stand of willows at the far end of the pond provides some habitat and can be another good place to check for warblers.

Directions: To reach Tonaquint Park, head south on Bluff Street (UT 18) in St. George. A few hundred yards before the I-15 interchange, turn right onto Hilton

Drive (a major intersection), and proceed through Southgate Golf Course, which surrounds this road. Immediately after passing through the golf course, bear right onto Dixie Drive (again, a major intersection). The entrance to Tonaquint Park is on the right, about 200 yards along the road.

To reach the north end of the Virgin River Parkway near St. George, take Exit 6 off I-15, or if you're already in St. George, head south on Bluff Street. At the I-15 interchange, Bluff Street becomes Riverside Drive, and a few yards farther south a narrow paved road signed as Main Street departs to the right. Take this turn and proceed to the end of the road and the parkway trailhead.

The parkway's southern access is in the community of Bloomington. South of St. George, take Exit 4 off I-15 and head south on Pioneer Road, then west on Man O' War Drive. This road soon crosses the Virgin River, and immediately on the right is the south access and a parking area.

To get to the parkway from Tonaquint Park, consult the accompanying map.

General information: Because the parkway is shared by a variety of users, it's a good idea to step off the path before raising your binoculars and becoming entranced by a bird. Otherwise, you'll become an obstacle to be dodged by cyclists and others. If you choose to hike the entire trail, be sure to bring along a canteen.

Tonaquint is one of the newer parks in the St. George area, and it remains to be seen how the park will be developed as a recreation destination and, more importantly for birds and birders, how the riparian corridor will be managed. As with so many streams and rivers in the West, the riparian zone here is being overrun by tamarisk, the exotic invader that thrives at the expense of native plants and offers nothing in the way of food for wildlife. Hopefully, the local municipality will find the resources to fight this scourge along this section of river.

ADDITIONAL INFORMATION

Map grid: 2K
Elevation: 2,550 to 2,600 feet.
Hazards: None.
Nearest food, gas, and lodging: St. George.
Camping: McArthur's Temple View RV Park, St. George.
For more information: Utah Travel Council.

112 Washington Fields and Seigmiller Pond

Habitats: Upland desert shrub, lowland riparian
Specialty birds: Ferruginous Hawk; Prairie Falcon; Burrowing Owl; Marbled Godwit (spring and fall); Northern Shrike; Lazuli Bunting
Other key birds: Trumpeter Swan; Greater White-fronted Goose (winter); Snowy and Cattle Egrets; Green Heron; Northern Harrier; Cooper's, Swainson's, and Rough-legged (winter) Hawks; Golden Eagle; Gambel's Quail; Common Moorhen; Greater (spring and fall) and Lesser (spring and fall) Yellowlegs; Sanderling (spring and fall); Western (spring and fall) and Least (spring and fall) Sandpipers; Short-billed (spring and fall) and Long-billed (spring and fall) Dowitchers; Forster's and Black Terns; Yellow-billed Cuckoo; Common Nighthawk; Western Kingbird; Barn Swallow; Nashville Warbler (fall); Abert's Towhee
Best times to bird: September through June

The birding: The St. George area is full of surprises: places that look uninteresting harbor an amazing array of species. Washington Fields is one such place. This is essentially a driving tour through agricultural fields with short diversions to some farm ponds and a bushy area along the Virgin River. Birding here is interesting almost year-round. Summer gets too hot for much activity from either birds or humans. The area appears to be an important overwintering area as well as a stopover for raptors, waterfowl, and passerines.

Take your time driving the rural roads that cross Washington Fields. Keep an eye out for raptors perched on power lines or soaring over the fields and for geese, swans, and shorebirds grazing in the hay fields (particularly in winter). The two farm ponds on the west side of Washington Fields, just off 3000 East, and the cottonwood-riparian corridor along the Virgin River are particularly worth exploring. This latter area can be explored by parking in the trailer court at the northwest corner of Washington Fields and walking over to the river.

Seigmiller Pond, another tiny farm pond on the edge of the Virgin River, attracts an ever-changing pallet of migrating water and shorebirds, as well as hosting some interesting overwintering waterfowl. Because the pond is so small and has no nesting habitat, few of any particular species seems to be present at any given time, but local birders feel the pond is always worth a drive-by.

The pond is clearly visible from the access road. Use your car as a blind and spend half an hour or so scanning the pond, waiting to see what will show up. Binoculars are adequate, but a spotting scope is handy if you plan to differentiate among those species of shorebirds whose distinguishing characteristics are subtle at best.

In addition to the species listed above, it is certainly possible that you will encounter some of the rare transient shorebirds that come through Utah—this is part of the appeal of this site; it's a real potluck!

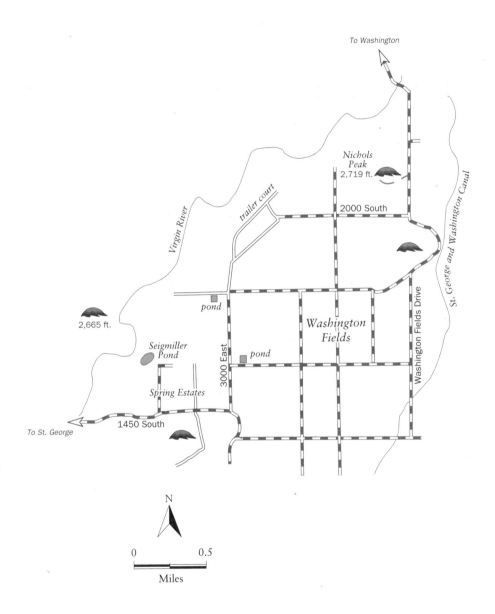

To Washington

Nichols
Peak
2,719 ft.

Virgin River

trailer court

2000 South

St. George and Washington Canal

2,665 ft.

pond

*Washington
Fields*

Washington Fields Drive

*Seigmiller
Pond*

3000 East

pond

Spring Estates

To St. George

1450 South

N

0   0.5

Miles

Directions: From downtown St. George, head east on St. George Boulevard (100 North). Drive under I-15, then turn right onto River Road Follow River Road south until you cross the Virgin River, then turn left immediately—you'll be headed east on 1450 South (a.k.a. Stake Farm Road). After about a mile, you'll see a sign for Spring Estates. Turn left into this development, and follow the main road for about 200 yards as it descends onto the floodplain of the Virgin River. Seigmiller Pond is on your left.

Return to Stake Farm Road and continue east for about another mile, at which point the road will begin to curve sharply to the right, and 3000 East departs to the left. Take this left turn and begin your exploration of Washington Fields (see accompanying map).

General information: Washington Fields has long been a favorite destination for local birders, but like many areas in and around St. George, it is experiencing heavy development pressure. Until recently, Seigmiller Pond was on a private farm where the owner accommodated birders. However, the land was sold and now lies in a new residential development. This has made access easier, but the future of the pond and its value to migrating birds may be at risk. Ideally, this little area will be preserved as a community park and pond.

ADDITIONAL INFORMATION

Map grid: 2K
Elevation: 3,000 feet.
Hazards: None.
Nearest food, gas, and lodging: St. George.
Camping: McArthur's Temple View RV Park, St. George.
For more information: Utah Travel Council.

4. Status and Distribution Chart

CHECKLIST, SEASONAL OCCURRENCE, HABITAT ASSOCIATIONS, AND ABUNDANCE OF UTAH BIRDS

You don't have to be a birder for long before the urge strikes to start keeping track of the species you've seen. Whether birding in Utah is the result of an occasional visit to the state, a daily stroll through your neighborhood park, or a lifelong passion, the following checklist is one way to keep track of your observations.

A debt of gratitude for this list is owed to the Utah Ornithological Society, which maintains a checklist of birds within the state of Utah. The UOS also updates the state checklist periodically and determines which species should receive acknowledgment as having appeared within Utah's borders. This process of updating includes assessing the veracity of rare bird sightings as well as keeping up with changes in taxonomic standing accepted by the American Ornithologists' Union.

Utah's checklist currently includes 408 species. Of those species, 87 are designated as "occasional" visitors, which is to say that they have been sighted rarely, perhaps only once. To see one of these species is a rare stroke of luck and a good day in any birder's logbook. Your chances of spotting the remaining 319 species depends on your location and timing. The information included in this checklist is designed to help get you to the right place at the right time.

The species in the checklist are separated by taxonomic family and follow the order recognized by the American Ornithologists' Union. Each listing includes the species's common name, its habitat association, its ecoregion association, and its seasonal abundance. A key to interpreting the table is provided at the bottom of each page. Both the habitat and ecoregion associations indicate where you are *most likely* to find each bird; you may in fact find a bird outside of its preferred habitat, particularly if it's a migrant. Likewise, the seasonal abundance graphs give you an indication of when you're *most likely* to find a given species. Bird populations are dynamic, fluctuating over both long- and short-term scales, and waxing and waning in response to such vagaries as food abundance, weather events, and habitat availability. Bird populations vary spatially as well, which is to say that territories occupied one year may be abandoned the next, only to be reoccupied in a later year.

Don't let all these exceptions discourage you! Use the checklist and status and distribution guide as a planning tool—and remember, birds do have minds of their own.

One final point—the author welcomes contributions to update the checklist. E-mail: mcivor@digitalpla.net

Utah Birds

Status and distribution

Bird Species	Habitat Association	Region	Season of Occurrence J F M A M J J A S O N D
LOONS			
☐ Red-throated Loon*	LR	G	
☐ Pacific Loon	LR	G	
☐ Common Loon	LR	G, W	
☐ Yellow-billed Loon*	LR	G	
GREBES			
☒ Pied-billed Grebe	LR	G	
☐ Horned Grebe	LR	G	
☐ Red-necked Grebe*	LR	G	
☒ Eared Grebe	LR	G	
☐ Western Grebe	LR	G, W	
☐ Clark's Grebe	LR	G, W	
PELICANS and CORMORANTS			
☒ American White Pelican	LR	G	
☐ Brown Pelican*	LR	G	
☒ Double-crested Cormorant	LR	G	
BITTERNS and HERONS			
☐ American Bittern	LR	all	
☐ Least Bittern*	LR	G	
☒ Great Blue Heron	LR, MR	all	
☐ Great Egret	LR	G, U	
☐ Snowy Egret	LR	all	
☐ Little Blue Heron*	LR	G	
☐ Tricolored Heron*	LR	G	
☐ Cattle Egret	US, LR	all	
☐ Green Heron	LR	G, M	
☐ Black-crowned Night-Heron	LR	G, U	

Habitats

A = Aspen	LS = Lowland desert shrub	PJ = Pinyon-juniper	* = Rare birds,
AL = Alpine	MM = Mountain meadow	SF = Spruce-fir	information wanted;
DS = Desert steppe	MR = Mountain riparian	US = Upland desert shrub	see Appendix A
LR = Lowland riparian			

Bird Species	Habitat Association	Region	Season of Occurrence
			J F M A M J J A S O N D
❑ Yellow-crowned Night-Heron*	LR	G	
IBISES and SPOONBILLS			
❑ White-faced Ibis	US	G, U, W	
❑ Roseate Spoonbill*	LR	G	
STORKS			
❑ Wood Stork*	LR	G	
SWANS, GEESE, and DUCKS			
❑ Fulvous Whistling-Duck*	LR	G	
❑ Tundra Swan	LR	G	
❑ Trumpeter Swan*	LR	G	
❑ Greater White-fronted Goose*	LR	G	
❑ Snow Goose	LR	G	
❑ Ross's Goose	LR	G	
❑ Brant*	LR	G	
☒ Canada Goose	LR	all	
❑ Wood Duck	LR	G, W	
❑ Green-winged Teal	LR	all	
❑ American Black Duck*	LR	G	
☒ Mallard	LR, MR	all	
❑ Northern Pintail	LR, MR	all	
❑ Blue-winged Teal	LR	all	
❑ Cinnamon Teal	LR	all	
❑ Northern Shoveler	LR	all	
❑ Gadwall	LR	all	
❑ Eurasian Wigeon*	LR	G, M	
❑ American Wigeon	LR	G, U	
❑ Canvasback	LR	G	
❑ Redhead	LR	all	
❑ Ring-necked Duck	LR, MR	G, W	
❑ Greater Scaup	LR	G	
❑ Lesser Scaup	LR	G	
❑ Harlequin Duck*	LR	G	

Regions

G = Great Basin   C = Colorado Plateau
W = Wasatch–Uinta   M = Mojave Desert
U = Uinta Basin   all = Statewide

Abundance

■ Common   ▭ Occasional
▬ Uncommon   — Irregular
— Rare

Bird Species	Habitat Association	Region	Season of Occurrence J F M A M J J A S O N D
❏ Oldsquaw	LR	G	
❏ Black Scoter*	LR	G	
❏ Surf Scoter	LR	G	
❏ White-winged Scoter	LR	G	
❏ Common Goldeneye	LR	G, M, C, W	
❏ Barrow's Goldeneye	LR	G, W	
❏ Bufflehead	LR	all	
❏ Hooded Merganser	LR	G	
❏ Common Merganser	LR	all	
❏ Red-breasted Merganser	LR	all	
❏ Ruddy Duck	LR	all	

VULTURES

Bird Species	Habitat Association	Region	Season of Occurrence J F M A M J J A S O N D
❏ Turkey Vulture	all	all	

HAWKS *and* FALCONS

Bird Species	Habitat Association	Region	Season of Occurrence J F M A M J J A S O N D
❏ Osprey	LR, MR	all	
❏ White-tailed Kite*	US	M	
❏ Bald Eagle	LR, US	G, W	
❏ Northern Harrier	LR, MR	all	
❏ Sharp-shinned Hawk	SF, A	W	
❏ Cooper's Hawk	SF, A	W	
❏ Northern Goshawk	A, SF	all	
❏ Common Black-Hawk*	LR	M	
❏ Red-shouldered Hawk*	LR, US	M, C	
❏ Broad-winged Hawk*	PJ, US	M	
❏ Swainson's Hawk	US	all	
❏ Zone-tailed Hawk*	PJ, US, LR	M, C	
❏ Red-tailed Hawk	all	all	
❏ Ferruginous Hawk	LS, US	G, U, C, M	
❏ Rough-legged Hawk	SF	G	
❏ Golden Eagle	LS, US, DS	all	
❏ American Kestrel	LS, US, DS	all	
❏ Merlin	SF	W	

Habitats

A = Aspen
AL = Alpine
DS = Desert steppe
LR = Lowland riparian

LS = Lowland desert shrub
MM = Mountain meadow
MR = Mountain riparian

PJ = Pinyon-juniper
SF = Spruce-fir
US = Upland desert shrub

* = Rare birds, information wanted; see Appendix A

Bird Species	Habitat Association	Region	Season of Occurrence (J F M A M J J A S O N D)
❑ Peregrine Falson	LR	G, C, U	Occasional (year-round)
❑ Gyrfalcon*	PJ, SF	W	Irregular
❑ Prairie Falcon	US, DS	all	Common (year-round)

GROUSE, PHEASANTS, TURKEYS, *and* QUAIL

Bird Species	Habitat Association	Region	Season of Occurrence (J F M A M J J A S O N D)
❑ Gray Partridge	US	G, W	Uncommon (year-round)
❑ Chukar	US	G, U	Common (year-round)
❑ Ring-necked Pheasant	US, DS	G, W, U	Common (year-round)
❑ Ruffed Grouse	PJ, A, SF	W	Uncommon (year-round)
❑ Sage Grouse	US, DS	W, G	Uncommon (year-round)
❑ Bonneville Sage Grouse[1]	US, DS	C	Uncommon (year-round)
❑ Blue Grouse	SF, A	all	Uncommon (year-round)
❑ White-tailed Ptarmigan	AL	W	Rare (year-round)
❑ Sharp-tailed Grouse	US, DS	W, G	Uncommon (year-round)
❑ Wild Turkey	SF, A, MM	G, M, C	Uncommon (year-round)
❑ Gambel's Quail	LR, US, PJ	M	Common (year-round)
❑ California Quail	US	W, G	Common (year-round)

CRANES, RAILS, GALLINULES, *and* COOTS

Bird Species	Habitat Association	Region	Season of Occurrence (J F M A M J J A S O N D)
❑ Virginia Rail	LR	all	Common (spring–fall)
❑ Sora	LR	all	Common (spring–fall)
❑ Purple Gallinule*	LR	G	Occasional
❑ Common Moorhen*	LR	G, M	Uncommon (year-round)
❑ American Coot	LR	all	Common (year-round)
❑ Sandhill Crane	LR, US	G, W, U	Common (spring and fall)

PLOVERS *and* SANDPIPERS

Bird Species	Habitat Association	Region	Season of Occurrence (J F M A M J J A S O N D)
❑ Black-bellied Plover	LR	G	Uncommon (spring and fall)
❑ American Golden-Plover	LR	G, U	Rare (spring and fall)
❑ Snowy Plover	LR	G	Uncommon (summer)
❑ Semipalmated Plover	LR	G	Uncommon (spring and fall)
❑ Killdeer	LR, MR	all	Common (year-round)
❑ Mountain Plover*	LR	W, U	Rare (summer)
❑ Black-necked Stilt	LR	G, W, U	Common (summer)
❑ American Avocet	LR	G, W, U	Common (summer)

Bird Species	Habitat Association	Region	Season of Occurrence (J F M A M J J A S O N D)
Greater Yellowlegs	LR	G, W, U	
Lesser Yellowlegs	LR	G, W, U, M	
Solitary Sandpiper	LR	C, G	
Willet	LR	G, W, U	
Wandering Tattler*	LR	G	
Spotted Sandpiper	LR, MR	all	
Upland Sandpiper*	DS, MM, US	W	
Whimbrel	LR	U, G, W	
Long-billed Curlew	US, DS	G, W	
Hudsonian Godwit*	LR	G	
Bar-tailed Godwit*	LR	G	
Marbled Godwit	LR	G, U	
Ruddy Turnstone*	LR	G	
Red Knot	LR	G	
Sanderling	LR	G	
Semipalmated Sandpiper	LR	G	
Western Sandpiper	LR	G, U	
Least Sandpiper	LR	all	
White-rumped Sandpiper*	LR	G	
Baird's Sandpiper	LR	G, U	
Pectoral Sandpiper	LR	G	
Dunlin	LR	G, U	
Curlew Sandpiper*	LR	G	
Stilt Sandpiper	LR	G	
Buff-breasted Sandpiper*	LR	G	
Short-billed Dowitcher	LR	G	
Long-billed Dowitcher	LR	G	
Common Snipe	LR	all	
Wilson's Phalarope	LR	all	
Red-necked Phalarope	LR	G, M, C, U	
Red Phalarope	LR	G, M, C	

Habitats

A = Aspen	LS = Lowland desert shrub	PJ = Pinyon-juniper	* = Rare birds,
AL = Alpine	MM = Mountain meadow	SF = Spruce-fir	information wanted;
DS = Desert steppe	MR = Mountain riparian	US = Upland desert shrub	see Appendix A
LR = Lowland riparian			

364

Bird Species	Habitat Association	Region	Season of Occurrence (J F M A M J J A S O N D)
GULLS, TERNS, *and* ALCIDS			
❑ Pomarine Jaeger*	LR	G	
❑ Parasitic Jaeger*	LR	G	
❑ Long-tailed Jaeger*	LR	G	
❑ Laughing Gull*	LR	G	
☒ Franklin's Gull	LR	G, U	
❑ Little Gull*	LR	G	
❑ Bonaparte's Gull	LR	G, U	
❑ Heerman's Gull	LR	G	
❑ Mew Gull	LR	G	
❑ Ring-billed Gull	LR	G	
☒ California Gull	LR	G, U	
❑ Herring Gull	LR	G, U	
❑ Thayer's Gull	LR	G	
❑ Lesser Black-backed Gull*	LR	G	
❑ Glaucous-winged Gull*	LR	G	
❑ Glaucous Gull	LR	G	
❑ Black-legged Kittiwake*	LR	G	
❑ Sabine's Gull*	LR	G	
❑ Caspian Tern	LR	G	
❑ Common Tern	LR	G, W	
❑ Forster's Tern	LR	G, W, U	
❑ Least Tern*	LR	G	
❑ Black Tern	LR	G, U	
❑ Ancient Murrelet*	LR	G, U	
PIGEONS *and* DOVES			
☒ Rock Dove	US	all	
❑ Band-tailed Pigeon	PJ, SF	C, U	
❑ White-winged Dove	US, PJ	M	
☒ Mourning Dove	LR	all	
❑ Inca Dove*	LR, US, PJ	M	
❑ Common Ground-Dove*	US, PJ	M	

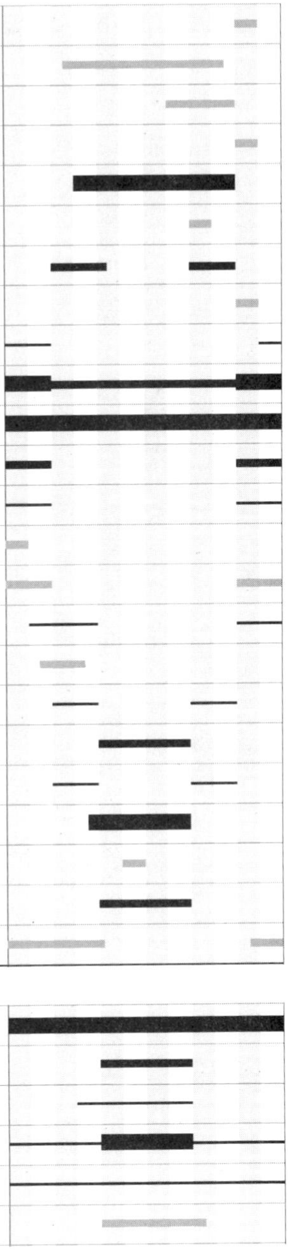

✗ Collared Dove

Regions
G = Great Basin   C = Colorado Plateau
W = Wasatch–Uinta   M = Mojave Desert
U = Uinta Basin   all = Statewide

Abundance
▰▰ Common   ▰▰ Occasional
▬ Uncommon   — Irregular
— Rare

Bird Species	Habitat Association	Region	Season of Occurrence J F M A M J J A S O N D
❏ Ruddy Ground-Dove*	US, PJ	M	▪

CUCKOOS *and* ROADRUNNERS

Bird Species	Habitat Association	Region	Season of Occurrence
❏ Black-billed Cuckoo*	SF, A	W	▬▬
❏ Yellow-billed Cuckoo	LR	all	──
❏ Greater Roadrunner	LS, US	M	▬▬▬▬▬▬▬▬▬▬▬▬

OWLS

Bird Species	Habitat Association	Region	Season of Occurrence
✔ Barn Owl	US	G, U	▬▬▬▬▬▬▬▬▬▬▬▬
❏ Flammulated Owl	SF	W	▬▬▬
Ⓞ Western Screech-Owl	LR, MR	all	▬▬▬▬▬▬▬▬▬▬▬▬
✔ Great Horned Owl	all	all	▬▬▬▬▬▬▬▬▬▬▬▬
❏ Snowy Owl*	US	W	▬ ▬
Ⓞ Northern Pygmy-Owl	SF, LR, PJ	W	▬▬▬▬▬▬▬▬▬▬▬▬
❏ Burrowing Owl	DS, US	G	▬▬▬
❏ Spotted Owl	PJ	C, M	
❏ Great Gray Owl*	US, PJ, SF	W, U	▬▬▬
Ⓞ Long-eared Owl	LR, PJ	all	▬▬▬▬▬▬▬▬▬▬▬▬
❏ Short-eared Owl	LR, US	G, W, U	▬▬▬▬▬▬▬▬▬▬▬▬
❏ Boreal Owl*	SF, A	W	▬▬▬▬▬▬▬▬▬▬▬▬
Ⓞ Northern Saw-whet Owl	MR, A, PJ	all	▬▬▬▬▬▬▬▬▬▬▬▬

GOATSUCKERS

Bird Species	Habitat Association	Region	Season of Occurrence
❏ Lesser Nighthawk	LR	M	▬▬▬
❏ Common Nighthawk	LR, US	all	▬▬▬
Ⓞ Common Poorwill	all	all	▬▬▬▬▬

SWIFTS

Bird Species	Habitat Association	Region	Season of Occurrence
❏ Black Swift	MR	W	──
❏ Chimney Swift*	LR, US	G	▪
❏ Vaux's Swift*	SF, A	M	▬▬▬
❏ White-throated Swift	all	all	▬▬▬

HUMMINGBIRDS

Bird Species	Habitat Association	Region	Season of Occurrence
❏ Broad-billed Hummingbird*	PJ, US, LR	M	▬▬▬
❏ Magnificent Hummingbird*	PJ, SF	M	▬▬▬
❏ Black-chinned Hummingbird	LR, US	all	▬▬▬▬

Habitats

A = Aspen	LS = Lowland desert shrub	PJ = Pinyon-juniper	* = Rare birds,
AL = Alpine	MM = Mountain meadow	SF = Spruce-fir	information wanted;
DS = Desert steppe	MR = Mountain riparian	US = Upland desert shrub	see Appendix A
LR = Lowland riparian			

Bird Species	Habitat Association	Region	Season of Occurrence J F M A M J J A S O N D
❑ Anna's Hummingbird*	US, PJ	M	
❑ Costa's Hummingbird	PJ	M	
❑ Calliope Hummingbird	SF, A, MM	W	
❑ Broad-tailed Hummingbird	SF, A, MM	all	
❑ Rufous Hummingbird	SF, MM, PJ	W	

KINGFISHERS

Bird Species	Habitat Association	Region	Season of Occurrence
❑ Belted Kingfisher	LR, MR	all	

WOODPECKERS

Bird Species	Habitat Association	Region	Season of Occurrence
❑ Lewis's Woodpecker	SF, PJ, MR	U	
❑ Red-headed Woodpecker*	LR	U	
❑ Acorn Woodpecker*	PJ, SF	M	
❑ Yellow-bellied Sapsucker*	LR	M	
❑ Red-naped Sapsucker	A, SF	all	
❑ Red-breasted Sapsucker*	SF, A	G, M	
❑ Williamson's Sapsucker	SF	all	
❑ Ladder-backed Woodpecker	US, PJ	M	
❑ Downy Woodpecker	LR, A	all	
❑ Hairy Woodpecker	LR, A, SF	all	
❑ Three-toed Woodpecker	SF	W	
❑ Northern Flicker	LR, MR, A, SF	all	

FLYCATCHERS

Bird Species	Habitat Association	Region	Season of Occurrence
❑ Olive-sided Flycatcher	SF, A	all	
❑ Western Wood-Pewee	LR, A	all	
❑ Willow Flycatcher	LR	W	
❑ Least Flycatcher*	A, SF	G	
❑ Hammond's Flycatcher	SF	W	
❑ Dusky Flycatcher	A	W	
❑ Gray Flycatcher	US, PJ	all	
❑ Cordilleran Flycatcher	A, SF	W	
❑ Black Phoebe	LR	M	
❑ Eastern Phoebe*	LR, US, PJ	M	
❑ Say's Phoebe	LR, LS, US	all	

Regions
G = Great Basin   C = Colorado Plateau
W = Wasatch–Uinta   M = Mojave Desert
U = Uinta Basin   all = Statewide

Abundance
▬▬▬ Common   ░░░ Occasional
▬▬ Uncommon   — Irregular
— Rare

367

Bird Species	Habitat Association	Region	Season of Occurrence (J F M A M J J A S O N D)
❏ Vermilion Flycatcher	LR	M	▬
❏ Ash-throated Flycatcher	PJ	G, C, M	▬▬
❏ Great Crested Flycatcher*	PJ, A, US	M	▬
❏ Brown-crested Flycatcher	DS, LR, US	M	▬
❏ Cassin's Kingbird	LR, PJ	C	▬▬
❏ Western Kingbird	LR	all	▬▬
❏ Eastern Kingbird	LR	W, U	▬
❏ Scissor-tailed Flycatcher*	US, PJ	G	▬▬

JAYS *and* CROWS

Bird Species	Habitat Association	Region	Season of Occurrence (J F M A M J J A S O N D)
❏ Gray Jay	SF	W, C	▬▬▬▬▬▬▬
❏ Steller's Jay	SF, PJ	all	▬▬▬▬▬▬▬
❏ Blue Jay*	A, SF, PJ	W, G	▬ ▬
❏ Western Scrub-Jay	PJ, US	all	▬▬▬▬▬▬▬
❏ Pinyon Jay	PJ	all	▬▬▬▬▬▬▬
❏ Clark's Nutcracker	SF	all	▬▬▬▬▬▬▬
❏ Black-billed Magpie	US, PJ	all	▬▬▬▬▬▬▬
❏ American Crow	LR, US	W, G	▬▬ ▬▬
❏ Common Raven	all	all	▬▬▬▬▬▬▬

LARKS

Bird Species	Habitat Association	Region	Season of Occurrence (J F M A M J J A S O N D)
❏ Horned Lark	LS, US, DS	all	▬▬▬▬▬▬▬

SWALLOWS

Bird Species	Habitat Association	Region	Season of Occurrence (J F M A M J J A S O N D)
❏ Purple Martin	A, SF	all	▬
❏ Tree Swallow	A, MM	all	▬▬▬
❏ Violet-green Swallow	A, MM	all	▬▬▬
❏ Northern Rough-winged Swallow	LR	all	▬▬▬
❏ Bank Swallow	LR	all	▬▬▬
❏ Cliff Swallow	all	all	▬▬▬
❏ Barn Swallow	all	all	▬▬▬

TITMICE, VERDIN, *and* BUSHTIT

Bird Species	Habitat Association	Region	Season of Occurrence (J F M A M J J A S O N D)
❏ Black-capped Chickadee	LR, PJ, A, SF	all	▬▬▬▬▬▬▬
❏ Mountain Chickadee	SF	W	▬▬▬▬▬▬▬

Habitats

A = Aspen	LS = Lowland desert shrub	PJ = Pinyon-juniper	* = Rare birds,
AL = Alpine	MM = Mountain meadow	SF = Spruce-fir	information wanted;
DS = Desert steppe	MR = Mountain riparian	US = Upland desert shrub	see Appendix A
LR = Lowland riparian			

Bird Species	Habitat Association	Region	Season of Occurrence J F M A M J J A S O N D
❑ Juniper Titmouse	PJ	all	
❑ Verdin	US	M	
❑ Bushtit	PJ, US	all	

NUTHATCHES *and* CREEPERS

❑ Red-breasted Nuthatch	SF	W	
❑ White-breasted Nuthatch	SF	W	
❑ Pygmy Nuthatch	SF	W	
❑ Brown Creeper	SF	W	

WRENS

☑ Cactus Wren	LS, US	M	
☑ Rock Wren	all	all	
❑ Canyon Wren	LR	C, U	
❑ Bewick's Wren	PJ	C, M, U	
☑ House Wren	LR, A, SF	all	
❑ Winter Wren	MR, SF	all	
❑ Marsh Wren	LR	all	

DIPPERS

❑ American Dipper	MR	W	

KINGLETS

❑ Golden-crowned Kinglet	SF	all	
❑ Ruby-crowned Kinglet	SF	all	

GNATCATCHERS

❑ Blue-gray Gnatcatcher	US, PJ	all	
❑ Black-tailed Gnatcatcher	LS, US	M	

THRUSHES

❑ Eastern Bluebird*	LR, PJ	C, U	
❑ Western Bluebird	PJ	G, C, W	
❑ Mountain Bluebird	A, MM	W	
❑ Townsend's Solitaire	SF	all	
❑ Veery*	LR	G, W	
❑ Swainson's Thrush	MR, SF, A	W	
❑ Hermit Thrush	MR, LR	W	

Regions
G = Great Basin   C = Colorado Plateau
W = Wasatch–Uinta   M = Mojave Desert
U = Uinta Basin   all = Statewide

Abundance
▬ Common   ▬ Occasional
▬ Uncommon   — Irregular
— Rare

Bird Species	Habitat Association	Region	Season of Occurrence J F M A M J J A S O N D
❑ Wood Thrush*	A, SF	W	
🗹 American Robin	LR, US, PJ, MM, MR, A	all	
❑ Varied Thrush	PJ, US	W, M, C	

THRASHERS

🗹 Gray Catbird	LR	all	
❑ Northern Mockingbird	US, PJ	M, C	
❑ Sage Thrasher	LS, US	G, M, U, C	
❑ Brown Thrasher	US	G, C, U	
❑ Bendire's Thrasher	LS, US	M, C	
❑ Crissal Thrasher	LS, US, LR	M	
❑ Le Conte's Thrasher*	LS, US	M	

PIPITS

❑ American Pipit	AL, MM	W	

WAXWINGS *and* PHAINOPEPLA

❑ Bohemian Waxwing	US	G, W	
🗹 Cedar Waxwing	US, PJ	all	
❑ Phainopepla	US, PJ	M	

SHRIKES

❑ Northern Shrike	DS, US, LS	all	
❑ Loggerhead Shrike	DS, US, LS, PJ	all	

STARLINGS

🗹 European Starling	LR, US	all	

VIREOS

❑ White-eyed Vireo*	LR, US	C	
❑ Bell's Vireo	LR, US, PJ	M	
❑ Gray Vireo	PJ, US	M, C, W	
❑ Cassin's Vireo	LR, PJ, SF	all	
❑ Plumbeous Vireo	LR, PJ, SF	all	
❑ Warbling Vireo	A	W	
❑ Red-eyed Vireo	LR	U, W, G	

WARBLERS

❑ Tennessee Warbler	MR, SF	G	

Habitats

A = Aspen	LS = Lowland desert shrub	PJ = Pinyon-juniper	* = Rare birds,
AL = Alpine	MM = Mountain meadow	SF = Spruce-fir	information wanted;
DS = Desert steppe	MR = Mountain riparian	US = Upland desert shrub	see Appendix A
LR = Lowland riparian			

370

Bird Species	Habitat Association	Region	Season of Occurrence J F M A M J J A S O N D
❑ Orange-crowned Warbler	US, MR	all	
❑ Nashville Warbler	MR, LR	C, U, M, W	
❑ Virginia's Warbler	LR, MR, US	all	
❑ Lucy's Warbler	LR	M, C	
❑ Northern Parula*	LR	G	
❑ Yellow Warbler	LR, MR	all	
❑ Chestnut-sided Warbler*	US, A	W	
❑ Magnolia Warbler*	LR	G, C	
❑ Black-throated Blue Warbler*	A, SF	G	
❑ Yellow-rumped Warbler	A	all	
❑ Black-throated Gray Warbler	PJ	all	
❑ Townsend's Warbler	A	G,. W	
❑ Hermit Warbler*	SF	M, C	
❑ Yellow-throated Warbler*	PJ	U	
❑ Grace's Warbler	SF	C	
❑ Palm Warbler*	PJ	G, C	
❑ Bay-breasted Warbler*	LR	U	
❑ Blackpoll Warbler*	LR	G	
❑ Black-and-white Warbler*	A, SF	G	
❑ American Redstart	LR	W, U	
❑ Worm-eating Warbler*	LR	W	
❑ Ovenbird*	A	G	
❑ Northern Waterthrush	MR	G	
❑ Kentucky Warbler*	LR	W	
❑ Connecticut Warbler*	LR	G	
❑ MacGillivray's Warbler	A, SF	W	
❑ Common Yellowthroat	LR, MR	W	
❑ Hooded Warbler*	MR	M	
❑ Wilson's Warbler	LR	G, W, U	
❑ Canada Warbler*	A, MR	G	
❑ Painted Redstart*	SF, MR	M	
❑ Yellow-breasted Chat	LR, US	all	

Regions

G = Great Basin   C = Colorado Plateau
W = Wasatch–Uinta   M = Mojave Desert
U = Uinta Basin   all = Statewide

Abundance

▬▬▬ Common   ▨▨▨ Occasional
▬▬ Uncommon   ⋯⋯ Irregular
— Rare

Bird Species	Habitat Association	Region	Season of Occurrence (J F M A M J J A S O N D)
TANAGERS			
❑ Summer Tanager	LR	M	May–Aug
❑ Scarlet Tanager*	LR	M	May (rare)
☑ Western Tanager	SF, A	all	Apr–Sep
GROSBEAKS and BUNTINGS			
❑ Northern Cardinal*	LR	G	Mar–May (faint)
❑ Rose-breasted Grosbeak	US, A	G, C, U	Apr–May; Aug–Oct
❑ Black-headed Grosbeak	LR, A	all	Apr–Sep
❑ Blue Grosbeak	LR, US	C, U, W	Apr–Sep
⊙ Lazuli Bunting	LR, MR, US	W, U	Apr–Aug
❑ Indigo Bunting	LR	M	May–Jul
❑ Dickcissel*	DS, US	W	May; Oct (faint)
SPARROWS			
❑ Green-tailed Towhee	US, MM	W	May–Aug
❑ Spotted Towhee	US, PJ	W	all year
❑ Abert's Towhee	LR, US	M	all year
❑ Rufous-crowned Sparrow*	DS, US	M, C	all year
❑ American Tree Sparrow	US	G	Jan–Feb; Nov–Dec
❑ Chipping Sparrow	A, MM	W	Apr–Oct
❑ Clay-colored Sparrow*	LR, US	G, W	Apr; Sep–Oct (faint)
⊙ Brewer's Sparrow	US, DS, MM	all	Apr–Oct
⊙ Black-chinned Sparrow	US	M	Apr–Sep
❑ Vesper Sparrow	US, MM	all	Apr–Oct
☑ Lark Sparrow	LS, US	all	Apr–Oct
❑ Black-throated Sparrow	LS	M, G	Apr–Oct
⊙ Sage Sparrow	US	G, U, C, M	all year
❑ Lark Bunting	US, DS	W, U	May–Aug
❑ Savannah Sparrow	LR, US	G, W, U	Feb–Nov
❑ Grasshopper Sparrow	DS, US	G, W, U	
❑ Le Conte's Sparrow*	LR	G, C	Jan–Feb; Nov–Dec (faint)
❑ Fox Sparrow	LR, MR, US, MM	W	Apr–Sep
❑ Song Sparrow	LR, US	all	all year

Habitats

A = Aspen	LS = Lowland desert shrub	PJ = Pinyon-juniper	* = Rare birds,
AL = Alpine	MM = Mountain meadow	SF = Spruce-fir	information wanted;
DS = Desert steppe	MR = Mountain riparian	US = Upland desert shrub	see Appendix A
LR = Lowland riparian			

Bird Species	Habitat Association	Region	Season of Occurrence J F M A M J J A S O N D
❑ Lincoln's Sparrow	MR, MM	all	
❑ Swamp Sparrow	LR	M, C, W	
❑ White-throated Sparrow	SF, A, MM	G, M	
❑ Golden-crowned Sparrow*	MM, PJ	M, G, W	
☑ White-crowned Sparrow	MM	all	
❑ Harris's Sparrow	SF, AL	all	
❑ Dark-eyed Junco	SF, A	all	
❑ McCown's Longspur*	DS, US	G, W	
❑ Lapland Longspur	US, LS	C	
❑ Chestnut-collared Longspur*	DS, US	G, W	
❑ Snow Bunting	LR	G, U	

BLACKBIRDS *and* ORIOLES

Bird Species	Habitat Association	Region	Season of Occurrence
❑ Bobolink	US	G	
☑ Red-winged Blackbird	LR	all	
☑ Western Meadowlark	US, DS, LS	all	
☑ Yellow-headed Blackbird	LR	all	
❑ Rusty Blackbird*	LR, MR, SF	M, C, U	
☒ Brewer's Blackbird	LR, US, DS	all	
❑ Great-tailed Grackle	LR	G	
❑ Common Grackle	LR	G	
❑ Bronzed Cowbird*	US, PJ	C, M	
☒ Brown-headed Cowbird	LR, US, DS, MM	all	
❑ Orchard Oriole*	LR	???	
❑ Hooded Oriole	LR, US, PJ	M	
❑ Baltimore Oriole*	LR	???	
☑ Bullock's Oriole	LR	all	
❑ Scott's Oriole	PJ, US	C, M, G	

FINCHES

Bird Species	Habitat Association	Region	Season of Occurrence
❑ Brambling*	US	W	
❑ Gray-crowned Rosy-Finch	US, DS	all	
❑ Black Rosy-Finch	AL	all	
❑ Pine Grosbeak	SF	W	

Regions

G = Great Basin   C = Colorado Plateau
W = Wasatch–Uinta   M = Mojave Desert
U = Uinta Basin   all = Statewide

Abundance

Common   Occasional
Uncommon   Irregular
Rare

Bird Species	Habitat Association	Region	Season of Occurrence (J F M A M J J A S O N D)
❑ Cassin's Finch	SF, A	all	▬▬▬▬▬▬▬▬▬▬▬▬
❑ House Finch	LR, US, PJ	all	▬▬▬▬▬▬▬▬▬▬▬▬
❑ Red Crossbill	SF	all	▬▬▬▬▬▬▬▬▬▬▬▬
❑ White-winged Crossbill	SF	W, G	············
❑ Common Redpoll*	LR, MR	U, W, G	▬ ▬
❑ Pine Siskin	SF	all	▬▬▬▬▬▬▬▬▬▬▬▬
❑ Lesser Goldfinch	LR, US	W, C	▬▬▬▬▬▬▬▬▬▬▬▬
☒ American Goldfinch	LR, US	all	▬▬▬▬▬▬▬▬▬▬▬▬
❑ Evening Grosbeak	LR, US, PJ	all	▬▬▬▬▬▬▬▬▬▬▬▬

OLD WORLD SPARROWS

Bird Species	Habitat Association	Region	Season of Occurrence (J F M A M J J A S O N D)
☒ House Sparrow	LR, LS, US, DS, PJ	all	▬▬▬▬▬▬▬▬▬▬▬▬

Habitats

A = Aspen
AL = Alpine
DS = Desert steppe
LR = Lowland riparian

LS = Lowland desert shrub
MM = Mountain meadow
MR = Mountain riparian

PJ = Pinyon-juniper
SF = Spruce-fir
US = Upland desert shrub

* = Rare birds,
  information wanted;
  see Appendix A

5. Utah Bird Specialties

For many birders who set their sights on this high desert state, particular bird species come to mind. The following section offers 50 maps and accompanying suggestions for finding some of Utah's more "sought-after" species. Each map indicates a habitat-linked distribution for the species. The text that accompanies each map describes the habitat the bird is usually found in, your chances of seeing the bird, and a few key areas in the state where the bird occurs.

What constitutes a sought-after species for you, of course, depends on your personal interests and past experiences. If you are searching for a species that I have not included in this chapter, I would suggest using the index at the back of the book as an aid to finding sites where the species occurs.

Clark's Grebe

COMMENTS: A fairly common breeding bird in northern Utah on most deep lakes and reservoirs, widespread during migration. Found in lower abundance but in the same areas as Western Grebes—distinguishing the two can challenge your identification skills.
CHANCES: Moderate
KEY SITES: Bear River Migratory Bird Refuge, Pelican Lake, Minersville Reservoir

American White Pelican

COMMENTS: Nests only on the Great Salt Lake, but travels widely in daily searches for food. Fairly common throughout the state during migration, even on small lakes and impoundments. Can often be seen circling in moderately sized flocks; its large, black-and-white profile against a cerulean sky is unmistakable.
CHANCES: Excellent
KEY SITES: Cutler Marsh, Wide Hollow Reservoir (migration), Willard Bay

Bald Eagle

COMMENTS: Less than a half-dozen nest in Utah, but in winter this species is fairly abundant. Also seen in riparian areas during migration. Generally associated with riparian areas in winter, where it establishes roosts and often gathers in large numbers.
CHANCES: Excellent
KEY SITES: Brown's Park National Wildlife Refuge, Raptor Loop, Willard Bay

Shaded areas indicate bird species distribution

Northern Goshawk

COMMENTS: This species occurs in low densities in mature montane forests and along lowland riparian areas containing tracts of cottonwoods—it appears to be declining throughout its range. Finding this species can be a matter of luck and alertness.

CHANCES: Poor

KEY SITES: Elk Ridge, Green Canyon, Ferron Mountain Loop

Ferruginous Hawk

COMMENTS: Once probably widespread in Utah, now listed as a state-listed endangered species. Primarily a bird of the open desert; nests at the edge of juniper forests and open, desert steppe habitats. Highly sensitive to human disturbance. More likely to be seen on the wing as you travel the desert, rather than at any particular destination, particularly in west, northeast, and southeast.

CHANCES: Poor

KEY SITES: Devil's Playground, CCC Campground/Tom's Creek, Six Mile Reservoir

Peregrine Falcon

COMMENTS: Usually seen on the wing, high over its territory. Nests on high cliffs, buildings, or platforms, generally near water. A year-round resident of the state. A pair nested in downtown Salt Lake City until 1997. Population in Zion National Park appears to be one of densest in United States.

CHANCES: Moderate

KEY SITES: Ogden Bay Waterfowl Management Area, Pa'rus Trail, West Canyon in Snow Canyon State Park

Prairie Falcon

COMMENTS: Widespread, but in low densities. Found in open desert country with desert steppe and desert shrub habitats and at lower elevations of mountains. Hunts by flying low over the ground to flush small birds. Nests in rocky cliffs or outcrops.

CHANCES: Moderate

KEY SITES: Antelope Island State Park, CCC Campground/Tom's Creek, Randolph Viewing Area

Chukar

COMMENTS: Chukars are native to western Asia but have adapted well to Utah. Prefer rocky slopes or outcrops in upland desert shrub habitat with at least some grass component. The bird's distribution is statewide, where its habitat requirements can be met.

CHANCES: Excellent

KEY SITES: Antelope Island State Park, Fruita, Wide Hollow Reservoir

Shaded areas indicate bird species distribution

Sage Grouse

COMMENTS: Generally goes undetected due to secretive habits. Not particularly abundant, and population is declining due to habitat loss. Most easily found in early spring when both sexes congregate on lekking grounds. Requires extensive tracts of sagebrush; reacts negatively to overgrazing.

CHANCES: Poor

KEY SITES: Brown's Park National Wildlife Refuge, Dinosaur National Monument, Rockport State Park

Blue Grouse

COMMENTS: A fairly common bird in montane forests, occasionally found in lower elevation oak and pinyon-juniper habitats. Migrates altitudinally in winter. Not often seen because it is cryptic and secretive. Approachable and unwary, but females are pugnacious defenders of their broods.

CHANCES: Moderate

KEY SITES: Dahlgreen's Creek, Granite Creek (upper drainage), Stewart Pass Trail

White-tailed Ptarmigan

COMMENTS: Well camouflaged in winter and summer. Prefers alpine or subalpine environment of stunted willow shrubs interspersed with meadow areas.

CHANCES: Poor

KEY SITES: Henry's Fork (upper basin)

Sandhill Crane

COMMENTS: Once extinguished from Utah, this species is making a strong comeback, with about 400 pairs nesting in the state. Prefers open fields and meadows, including agricultural lands; nests in emergent lowland riparian vegetation. Sometimes seen in low numbers in high montane riparian environments. Numbers are greatest during migration, particularly September through October.

CHANCES: Excellent

KEY SITES: Cutler Marsh, Randolph Viewing Area, Six Mile Reservoir

Snowy Plover

COMMENTS: Utah supports the largest assemblage in the world—but they can still be hard to find. Occupies mud and salt flats where they forage for brine flies in shallow water. Much of breeding habitat inaccessible, so easiest to see during migration. Cryptic coloration blends well with salt flat surroundings—watch carefully for movement to reveal the birds.

CHANCES: Moderate

KEY SITES: Antelope Island Causeway, Bear River Migratory Bird Refuge, Salt Hills Flat

Shaded areas indicate bird species distribution

Long-billed Curlew

COMMENTS: Occupies desert steppe, other lower elevation grassy habitats, especially agricultural fields, sometimes in surprisingly arid conditions. Often seen only after flushing from tall grasses.

CHANCES: Moderate

KEY SITES: Antelope Island, Fish Springs National Wildlife Refuge, West Canyon in the Stansbury Range

Marbled Godwit

COMMENTS: Common in migration along shallow lakeshore, including 30,000 which stage annually on the Great Salt Lake.

CHANCES: Excellent

KEY SITES: Antelope Island Causeway, Bear River Migratory Bird Refuge, Layton Marsh Wetlands Preserve

Flammulated Owl

COMMENTS: Fairly common but, like most owls, secretive and hard to locate. Association between this species and ponderosa pines seems to be particularly strong, although it is widespread in the state and adapted to other coniferous and mixed conifer habitats.

CHANCES: Moderate

KEY SITES: Granite Creek (upper drainage), Mill Creek Canyon, Pine Valley Campgrounds

Western Screech-Owl

COMMENTS: Common throughout the state, but also secretive and somewhat difficult to locate. Riparian-dependent and more likely to be found in forests mature enough to have nesting cavities, although this species will also use abandoned magpie nests.

CHANCES: Moderate

KEY SITES: Beaver Dam Wash, City Creek Canyon, Owl Creek

Northern Pygmy-Owl

COMMENTS: Inhabits dense montane forests, conifer, deciduous, or pine-oak. Most active at dawn and dusk. Often found in association with riparian corridor. Like most owl species, probably occurs in greater abundance than they are seen.

CHANCES: Poor

KEY SITES: Mill Creek Canyon, Ophir Canyon, Pine Valley Campgrounds

Shaded areas indicate bird species distribution

Burrowing Owl

COMMENTS: This species has suffered throughout its range from habitat loss—its symbiosis with the prairie dog means it has lost nesting burrows as prairie dogs have been exterminated. Prefers open areas in desert steppe or desert shrub habitats. Often abroad in daylight, hunting or sitting by nest burrow or on nearby shrub or fence post.
CHANCES: Moderate
KEY SITES: Antelope Island, CCC Campground/Tom's Creek, Ouray National Wildlife Refuge

Black Swift

COMMENTS: Distribution highly localized to area around Mount Timpanogos. Highly specialized nesting, usually behind waterfalls, but forages widely and therefore most likely seen on the wing. Very low reproductive rate of one offspring per year. June is the best month to see this species.
CHANCES: Excellent
KEY SITES: Squaw Peak Trail, other areas around Mount Timpanogos

White-throated Swift

COMMENTS: Cliffs and canyons in mountainous country; particularly abundant in southern portion of state. One of the fastest flying birds in North America, usually seen on the wing in search of insects.
CHANCES: Excellent
KEY SITES: Fish Creek, Green River and Split Mountain Campgrounds, Mount Timpanogos Trail

Lewis's Woodpecker

COMMENTS: Inhabits open woodlands, woodland edges, and riparian forests to about 9,000 feet. Prefers ponderosa pine forest or pine-oak mix. Found in lower densities but more widespread in winter.
CHANCES: Excellent
KEY SITES: Ouray National Wildlife Refuge, Swett Ranch

Williamson's Sapsucker

COMMENTS: Year-round resident, nests in high elevation (8,000 feet to timberline) montane forests, including ponderosa pine and mixed aspen-conifer. Appears to exist in low numbers throughout its range.
CHANCES: Poor
KEY SITES: Ferron Mountain Loop, Henry's Fork (upper basin), Pine Valley Campgrounds

Shaded areas indicate bird species distribution

Three-toed Woodpecker

COMMENTS: Distribution closely allied with outbreaks of pine bark beetle infestations. In high, coniferous forests, look for standing dead snags that still retain bark. Male most easily located by its characteristic territorial drumming. Current forestry practices which attempt to control beetle outbreaks have negatively impacted this species.

CHANCES: Moderate

KEY SITES: Silver Lake/Brighton area, Ferron Reservoir, Tony Grove Lake, Trial Lake, Mirror Lake

Olive-sided Flycatcher

COMMENTS: Prefers montane coniferous or mixed conifer-deciduous forests. Also seeks out dead snags; sings from high perch, usually top of snag. Most easily located by its characteristic song, which sounds something like "Quick! Three beers!"

CHANCES: Excellent

KEY SITES: Ferron Reservoir, The Spruces Campground, Tony Grove Lake

Western Wood-Pewee

COMMENTS: Widespread and common resident of riparian, aspen, and mixed conifer-deciduous forests. Highest abundance in the state occurs along the spine of the Wasatch Mountain Range. Fairly abundant along lowland riparian areas during migration.

CHANCES: Excellent

KEY SITES: Dahlgreen's Creek, Duck Creek Reservoir (and stream), Ferron Mountain Loop

Willow Flycatcher

COMMENTS: Locally abundant but declining; southwestern subspecies is a state-listed endangered species due to habitat decline. Nests in mid- to low-elevation (less than 8,500 feet) willow habitats, therefore, most likely seen in lowland riparian areas. Distinguished by lack of eye ring, characteristic two syllable call.

CHANCES: Moderate

KEY SITES: Calf Creek Recreation Area, Lucin, Sand Island

Hammond's Flycatcher

COMMENTS: Found in moist conifer forest (fir, spruce, ponderosa pine) at higher elevations. Distinguished from Dusky Flycatcher by lower mandible coloration and subtle differences in song. Hammond's song described as more emphatic and hoarser than Dusky.

CHANCES: Moderate

KEY SITES: Elk Ridge, Mirror Lake, Spring Hollow, The Spruces Campground

Shaded areas indicate bird species distribution

Dusky Flycatcher

COMMENTS: Utilizes lower elevation habitats than similar Hammond's Flycatcher. Also drier areas, including brush habitats, open coniferous, and mixed conifer-deciduous forests. Fairly common in migration around lowland riparian habitats.

CHANCES: Excellent

KEY SITES: Dahlgreen's Creek, Duck Creek Reservoir (and stream), Warner Lake

Gray Flycatcher

COMMENTS: Fairly common summer resident, well adapted to arid conditions. Its distribution is closely tied to the pinyon-juniper forest type, but it also inhabits dry pine forests and areas with desert shrub cover. Most abundant in the southwest corner of the state.

CHANCES: Excellent

KEY SITES: Beaver Dam Wash, Kolob Reservoir Road, Newcastle Reservoir, Pinto Creek

Cassin's Kingbird

COMMENTS: Similar to Western Kingbird, but distribution more limited to southern portion of state; also fewer in number. Occurs with Western Kingbird in pine-oak-juniper forests, desert steppe, and lowland riparian streamsides.

CHANCES: Moderate

KEY SITES: Enterprise Reservoirs, Hovenweep National Monument, Sand Island

Northern Shrike

COMMENTS: Widespread winter visitor, but low in abundance throughout its range. Prefers lower elevations, primarily desert areas. Look for this bird perched on telephone lines or barbed wire fences near desert shrub, desert steppe, and agricultural fields.

CHANCES: Moderate

KEY SITES: Scott M. Matheson Preserve, Ouray National Wildlife Refuge, Washington Fields

Gray Vireo

COMMENTS: Common summer resident, but restricted in distribution to southern half of the state. Prefers dry, brushy areas, particularly pinyon-juniper forests.

CHANCES: Moderate

KEY SITES: Beaver Dam Wash, Fish Creek, Silver Reef to Oak Grove Campground

Shaded areas indicate bird species distribution

Pinyon Jay

COMMENTS: Common resident throughout the state, but highly mobile and therefore unpredictable in its distribution. Closely allied with pinyon-juniper forests, usually traveling in large flocks that irrupt where pinyon pines produce abundant crops.

CHANCES: Moderate

KEY SITES: Devil's Playground, Kolob Reservoir Road, Strawberry River Valley

Clark's Nutcracker

COMMENTS: A distinctly montane species, generally found in association with whitebark pine, with which it plays a key roll in seed distribution. Also found in other types of coniferous forests. Migrates altitudinally in winter and may be found then in towns or cities on mid-elevation slopes.

CHANCES: Moderate

KEY SITES: Ferron Mountain Loop, Mirror Lake, Tony Grove Lake

Pygmy Nuthatch

COMMENTS: Found in montane, coniferous forests, particularly ponderosa pine, and mixed pine-juniper forests. Travels in loose flocks in the high treetops, calling constantly to one another. Like all nuthatches, forages in improbable poses, often walking down tree trunks or hanging upside-down.

CHANCES: Moderate

KEY SITES: Elk Ridge, Pine Valley Campgrounds, Trial Lake

American Dipper

COMMENTS: Fairly common in permanent streams draining canyons along the Wasatch Mountains. Likes fast moving water, but requires exposed boulders in the stream current from which it makes short forays underwater in search of invertebrates. Present year-round, but makes altitudinal migrations to open water during winter.

CHANCES: Excellent

KEY SITES: Ophir Canyon, Spring Hollow, The Spruces Campground

Townsend's Solitaire

COMMENTS: Prefers open coniferous forests to about 12,000 feet. Probably easiest to locate in winter when these altitudinal migrants concentrate in mid-elevation canyons and mountain slopes, particularly where juniper berries are available.

CHANCES: Excellent

KEY SITES: Bryce Canyon, Mill Creek Canyon, Ophir Canyon

Shaded areas indicate bird species distribution

Swainson's Thrush

COMMENTS: This species seems to have become more rare in recent years. Associated with coniferous and mixed conifer-deciduous forests at mid to high elevations. More often heard than seen with its distinct, upward spiraling and flute-like call.

CHANCES: Moderate

KEY SITES: Silver Lake Boardwalk, Spring Hollow, The Spruces Campground

Sage Thrasher

COMMENTS: Common summer resident of lowland and upland desert shrub habitats. Easily overlooked because of drab coloration, but this medium-size bird can often be seen perched on shrubs or fence posts.

CHANCES: Excellent

KEY SITES: Devil's Playground, Fish Springs National Wildlife Refuge, Ouray National Wildlife Refuge, Stansbury Island

Crissal Thrasher

COMMENTS: A permanent resident in the Mojave ecoregion. A secretive and drab bird, with a habit of running along the ground rather than flying to avoid danger; it frequently goes undetected. Associated with wooded streamsides in desert shrub habitat, including scrub oaks, mesquite, and chaparral.

CHANCES: Poor

KEY SITES: Beaver Dam Wash, Virgin River Parkway, West Canyon in Snow Canyon State Park

American Pipit

COMMENTS: Permanent resident, fairly common in alpine and subalpine settings of meadows mixed with shrubs. Migrates altitudinally in winter, when it can be found in open fields in low-lying areas, particularly near riparian areas.

CHANCES: Excellent

KEY SITES: Bald Mountain, Bear River Migratory Bird Refuge (winter), Brian Head Peak, Henry's Fork (upper basin)

Green-tailed Towhee

COMMENTS: Fairly common in dry brushy habitats, particularly in sagebrush. Occurs at nearly every elevation from low to fairly high in the mountains. Fairly secretive and frequently overlooked.

CHANCES: Excellent.

KEY SITES: Ferron Mountain Loop, Johnson Creek, Strawberry River Valley

Shaded areas indicate bird species distribution

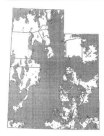

Spotted Towhee

COMMENTS: Distributed throughout the state and fairly common; found in sagebrush, willows, streamsides, brush thickets. Most abundant in southern Utah and Uinta Basin. Male often sings from prominent perch. Common in winter and will forage under bird feeders in urbanized areas.

CHANCES: Excellent

KEY SITES: Starr Springs, Strawberry River Valley, West Canyon in Snow Canyon State Park

Black-chinned Sparrow

COMMENTS: Limited, year-round distribution within the state of Utah. This species is most easily found in the extreme southwestern corner of the state, although a few sightings are reported from north-central Utah in summer. Found on brush covered hillsides, rugged mountain slopes with rocky outcrops, arid foothills, and intermittent desert washes. Sings from top of perch, including shrub or tree.

CHANCES: Poor

KEY SITES: Beaver Dam Wash, West Canyon in Snow Canyon State Park

Sage Sparrow

COMMENTS: Distributed throughout the state, and probably frequently seen—but hard to identify because of its generally drab appearance. Best located in spring and early summer, when breeding males perch on shrubs and sing; otherwise habits are fairly secretive. Prefers lowland and upland desert shrub. Usually runs along ground to escape detection. More common east of the Wasatch Range.

CHANCES: Moderate

KEY SITES: Henry's Fork, Square Tower Loop, Ouray National Wildlife Refuge

Lazuli Bunting

COMMENTS: A common species seen in a wide range of elevations and habitats, including open brush and weedy areas, deciduous woodlands including riparian areas, aspens, willows.

CHANCES: Excellent

KEY SITES: Brown's Park Wildlife Management Area, Green River and Split Mountain Campgrounds, Scott M. Matheson Preserve

Black Rosy-Finch

COMMENTS: A year-round resident that summers in alpine and sub-alpine settings, but migrates altitudinally in winter; often forced to low elevations during harshest winter conditions when it can be seen in large flocks. In summer, nests in rocky scree slopes on the flanks of high mountains.

CHANCES: Moderate

KEY SITES: Albion Basin, Bald Mountain, Henry's Fork (upper basin)

Shaded areas indicate bird species distribution

Pine Grosbeak

COMMENTS: A montane species found in association with coniferous or mixed conifer-deciduous forests. Gregarious and often travels in flocks. Distribution linked to cone production and therefore hard to predict.

CHANCES: Poor

KEY SITES: Ferron Mountain Loop, Silver Lake Boardwalk, Trial Lake

Red Crossbill

COMMENTS: An irruptive species that appears in moderate numbers during years of good pine cone crops, then disappears for years at a stretch. Breeding is linked more to food availability than season and some birds may breed in the same year they hatch. Nests are located high in conifers toward the end of branches.

CHANCES: Poor

KEY SITES: Dahlgreen's Creek, Silver Lake Boardwalk, Tony Grove Lake

Shaded areas indicate bird species distribution

Appendix A

REPORTING RARE AND UNUSUAL BIRDS

Our knowledge about the distribution and occurrence of birds in Utah continues to grow with new sighting records made on a surprisingly frequent basis. In part, this is because bird populations are dynamic over time, with ranges that ebb and advance with long-term environmental trends. Our knowledge is also growing because our hobby is growing—more and more people with good bird identification skills are getting outdoors. And the more eyes we have on the ground, the more we will learn. This is an area in which anyone can contribute. Sighting records are welcomed by the Utah Ornithological Society for birds which may have only been recorded in the state a few times and for those species which have never been recorded within our borders. Species of particular interest to the UOS are indicated in the checklist (Chapter 4) with an asterisk. The outline on the following page indicates the type of detailed information the UOS needs to confirm a rare bird sighting.

Completed accounts of sightings of interesting, rare, unusual, or accidental birds should be sent to:

Utah Rare Bird Committee
Utah Ornithological Society
3868 Marsha Drive
West Valley City, UT 84120

Utah Ornithological Society
Verification of Unusual Sight Record for Utah

Common Name: _____ Scientific Name: _____

Date: _____ Time: _____ Length of Time Observed: _____

Number: _____ Age: _____ Sex: _____

Location: _____

Latilong: _____ Elevation: _____

Distance to Bird: _____

Weather: _____

Light Conditions: _____

Detail Description of Bird: _____

_____

_____

_____

Song or Call and Method of Delivery: _____

_____

_____

_____

Behavior: _____

_____

_____

_____

Habitat: _____

Similar Species and How Were They Eliminated: _____

_____

_____

_____

Previous Experience with this and Similar Species: _____

_____

_____

_____

References Consulted: _____

Description From:

_____ Notes Taken at Time of Sighting _____ Notes Made Later _____ From Memory

Observer: _____ Signature: _____

Address: _____

City: _____ State: _____ Zip: _____

Other Observers who Independently Identified this Bird: _____

_____

_____

Date Prepared: _____

Additional Material: _____ Photo _____ Drawing _____ Tape _____ Other

Return This Form To: Utah Rare Bird Committee, 3868 Marsha Dr., West Valley City, UT 84120

Appendix B

UTAH BIRDING ORGANIZATIONS

Regional Audubon Chapters

Great Salt Lake Audubon Chapter
4726 Wallace Lane
Salt Lake City, UT 84117

Bridgerland Audubon Society
P.O. Box 3501
Logan, UT 843213
Newsletter: The Stilt (Freq : 9)

Salt Lake Birders
420 Parkview Drive
Park City, UT 84060
Newsletter: Bird Tracks (Freq : 12)

Red Cliffs Audubon Society
3287 Swaps Drive
St. George, UT 84790
(435) 673-0996

Wasatch Audubon Society
P.O. Box 3211
Ogden, UT 84409
Newsletter: Mountain Chickadee
  (Freq : 6)

Additional Organizations

HawkWatch International
P.O. Box 660
Salt Lake City, UT 84110-0660
(801) 524-8511
http://www.info-xpress.com/
  hawkwatch/

The Nature Conservancy
Utah Field Office
559 East South Temple
Salt Lake City, UT 84102
(801) 531-0999

Preserve Manager
Scott M. Matheson Preserve
P.O. Box 1329
Moab, UT, 84532
(435) 259-4629
http:/www.netoasis.com/moab/
  matheson

Moab Bird Club
c/o 838 East Oak St.
Moab, UT 84532

Utah County Birders
c/o 2867 North Foothill Drive
Provo, UT 84604

Utah Field Ornithologists
c/o 2226 East 40th South
Salt Lake City, UT 84103

Utah Nature Study Society
c/o Jean White, President
377 East 5300 South
Salt Lake City, UT 84107

Utah Ornithological Society
P.O. Box 1042
Cedar City, UT 84721-1042
Newsletter: Utah Birds (Freq : 4)

Utah Wildlife Federation
P.O. Box 526367
Salt Lake City, UT 84152-6367

Appendix C

CONTACTS

Planning a Utah birding trip

Utah Travel Council, Council Hall, State Street and 300 North, Salt Lake City, UT 84114; (801) 538-1030 or 538-1467; http://www.utah.com

State campground reservations; (801) 322-3770

National park campground reservations; (800) 365-2267

U.S. Geological Survey, 125 South State Street, Salt Lake City, UT; (801) 524-5652

Birding organizations

American Birding Association, P.O. Box 6599, Colorado Springs, CO, 80934-6599; (800) 850-2473; (719) 578-1614; fax (800) 247-3329 or (719) 578-1480; http://compstat.wharton.upenn.edu:8001/siler/patrons/abapage.html

National Audubon Society, Membership Department, P.O. Box 52529, Boulder, CO 80322-2529; (303) 415-0130; http://www.audubon.org

The Nature Conservancy, New Member, 1815 North Lynn Street, Arlington, VA 22209; (703) 841-5300; http://www.tnc.org/index.html

The Nature Conservancy, Utah Field Office, 559 East South Temple, Salt Lake City, UT 84102; (801) 531-0999

HawkWatch International, P.O. Box 660, Salt Lake City, UT, 84110-0660; (801) 524-8511; http: //www.info-xpress.com/hawkwatch

Utah Birdline

(801) 538-4730

Site Information

Use the following phoen numbers and addresses to contact campgrounds and agency offices for informattion on each birding site:

1. JOHNSON CREEK, Sawtooth National Forest, 2647 Kimberly Road East, Twin Falls, ID 83301-7976; (208) 737-3200; **Camping:** Clear Creek Campground, 30 miles west of Snowville

2. DEVIL'S PLAYGROUND, Bureau of Land Management, Salt Lake Field Office, 2370 South 2300 West, Salt Lake City, UT 84119; (801) 977-4300; **Camping:** Clear Creek Campground, 30 miles west of Snowville

3. LUCIN, Utah Travel Council, Council Hall, State Street and 300 North, Salt Lake City, UT 84114; (801) 538-1030 or 538-1467; **Camping:** Clear Creek Campground, 30 miles west of Snowville

4. LOCOMOTIVE SPRINGS WILDLIFE MANAGEMENT AREA, Utah Division of Wildlife Resources, 1596 West North Temple, Salt Lake City, UT 84116; (801) 538-4700; **Camping:** Clear Creek Campground, 30 miles west of Snowville

5. SALT HILLS FLAT, Bureau of Land Management, Salt Lake Field Office, 2370 South 2300 West, Salt Lake City, UT 84119; (801) 977-4300; **Camping:** Clear Creek Campground, 30 miles west of Snowville

6. GOLDEN SPIKE NATIONAL HISTORIC SITE, P.O. Box 897, Brigham City, UT 84302; **Camping:** Golden Spike RV Park, 905 West 1075 South, Brigham City, UT 84302; (435) 723-8858

7. BEAR RIVER MIGRATORY BIRD REFUGE, U.S. Fish and Wildlife Service, 58 South 950 West, Brigham City, UT 84302; (435) 723-5887; **Camping:** Box Elder Campground, Wasatch-Cache National Forest, 3 miles north from Brigham City on US 89

8. WILLARD BAY STATE PARK, 900 West 650 North #A, Willard, UT 84340-9999; (435) 734-9494; **Camping:** Willard Bay (North Marina), 15 miles north of Ogden on I-15 (Exit 360)

9. OGDEN BAY WATERFOWL MANAGEMENT AREA, Utah Division of Wildlife Resources, 1596 West North Temple, Salt Lake City, UT 84116; (801) 538-4700; **Camping:** Century RV Park, 1399 West 2100 South, Westhaven, UT 84401; (801) 731-3800

10. ANTELOPE ISLAND CAUSEWAY and STATE PARK, Antelope Island State Park, 4528 West 1700 South, Syracuse, UT 84075-6868; (801) 773-2941

11. LAYTON MARSH WETLANDS PRESERVE, The Nature Conservancy, Utah Field Office, 559 East South Temple, Salt Lake City, UT 84102; (801) 531-0999; **Camping:** Century RV Park, 1399 West 2100 South, Westhaven, UT 84401; (801) 731-3800

12. FARMINGTON BAY WILDLIFE MANAGEMENT AREA, Utah Division of Wildlife Resources, 1596 West North Temple, Salt Lake City, UT 84116; (801) 538-4700; **Camping:** Lagoon's RV Park and Campground, 175 North Lagoon Lane, Farmington, UT 84025; (801) 451-8000

13. JORDAN RIVER PARKWAY, Jordan River State Park, 1084 North Redwood Rd, Salt Lake City, UT 84116-1555; (801) 533-4496; **Camping:** Camp VIP, 1400 West North Temple, Salt Lake City, UT, 84116; (801) 328-0224

14. STANSBURY ISLAND, Bureau of Land Management, Salt Lake Field Office, 2370 South 2300 West, Salt Lake City, UT 84119; (801) 977-4300; **Camping:** South Willow Canyon campgrounds (Boy Scout, Cottonwood, Intake, Loop, Lower Narrows, Upper Narrows campgrounds), 10 miles southwest of Grantsville

15. STANSBURY LAKE, Utah Travel Council, Council Hall, State Street and 300 North, Salt Lake City, UT 84114; (801) 538-1030 or 538-1467; **Camping:** South Willow Canyon campgrounds, (Boy Scout, Cottonwood, Intake, Loop, Lower Narrows, Upper Narrows campgrounds), 10 miles southwest of Grantsville

16. WEST CANYON IN THE STANSBURY RANGE, Wasatch-Cache National Forest, Salt Lake Ranger District, 6944 South 3000 East, Salt Lake City, UT 84121; (801) 943-1794; **Camping:** South Willow Canyon campgrounds, (Boy Scout, Cottonwood, Intake, Loop, Lower Narrows, Upper Narrows campgrounds), 10 miles southwest of Grantsville

17. SOUTH WILLOW CANYON, Wasatch-Cache National Forest, Salt Lake Ranger District, 6944 South 3000 East, Salt Lake City, UT 84121; (801) 943-1794; **Camping:** South Willow Canyon campgrounds, (Boy Scout, Cottonwood, Intake, Loop, Lower Narrows, Upper Narrows campgrounds), 10 miles southwest of Grantsville

18. RAPTOR LOOP, Utah Travel Council, Council Hall, State Street and 300 North, Salt Lake City, UT 84114; (801) 538-1030 or 538-1467; **Camping:** South Willow Canyon (*see 14 above*) and Clover Spring Campground, 15 miles south of Tooele off UT 36

19. CLOVER CREEK, Bureau of Land Management, Salt Lake Field Office, 2370 South 2300 West, Salt Lake City, UT 84119; (801) 977-4300; **Camping:** Clover Spring Campground, 15 miles south of Tooele off UT 36

20. OPHIR CANYON, Utah Travel Council, Council Hall, State Street and 300 North, Salt Lake City, UT 84114; (801) 538-1030 or 538-1467; **Camping:** Clover Spring Campground, 15 miles south of Tooele off UT 36

21. JAMES WALTER FITZGERALD WILDLIFE MANAGEMENT AREA, Utah Division of Wildlife Resources, 1596 West North Temple, Salt Lake City, UT 84116; (801) 538-4700; **Camping:** Clover Spring Campground, 15 miles south of Tooele off UT 36

22. PROVO BAY; **Camping:** Utah Lake State Park Campground, Utah Lake State Park, 4400 West Center Street, Provo, UT 84601-9715; (801) 375-0731; for group camping only at the birding site; (801) 224-4368

23. PROVO RIVER PARKWAY, Utah Travel Council, Council Hall, State Street and 300 North, Salt Lake City, UT 84114; (801) 538-1030 or 538-1467; **Camping:** Utah Lake State Park, 4400 West Center Street, Provo, UT 84601-9715; (801) 375-0731

24. WARM SPRINGS WILDLIFE MANAGEMENT AREA, Utah Division of Wildlife Resources, 1596 West North Temple, Salt Lake City, UT 84116; (801) 538-4700; **Camping:** Maple Bench Campground, Uinta National Forest, 5 miles south of Payson on Nebo Loop Road

25. BLUE LAKE, Bureau of Land Management, Salt Lake Field Office, 2370 South 2300 West, Salt Lake City, UT 84119; (801) 977-4300; **Camping:** State Line RV Park, Wendover

26. CCC CAMPGROUND, TOM'S CREEK, and GRANITE CREEK, Bureau of Land Management, Fillmore Field Office, 35 East 500 North, Fillmore, UT 84631; (435) 743-6811; **Camping:** Callao CCC Campground, 4 miles southwest of Callao on the Deep Creek Mountains Road

27. FISH SPRINGS NATIONAL WILDLIFE REFUGE, U.S. Fish and Wildlife Service, P.O. Box 568, Dugway, UT 84022; (435) 831-5353; **Camping:** Simpson Springs Campground, 31 miles west of Vernon

28. CLEAR LAKE WILDLIFE MANAGEMENT AREA, Utah Division of Wildlife Resources, 1596 West North Temple, Salt Lake City, UT 84116; (801) 538-4700; **Camping:** Wagons West RV Park, 545 North Main, Fillmore, UT 84631; (435) 743-6188

29. MINERSVILLE RESERVOIR, Minersville Reservoir State Park, P.O. Box 1531, Beaver, UT 84713-1531; (435) 438-5472

30. NEWCASTLE RESERVOIR and PINTO CREEK, Dixie National Forest, Pine Valley Ranger District, 345 East Riverside Dr., St. George, UT 84770; (435) 652-3100; **Camping:** Pine Valley campgrounds (Ponderosa, Upper Pines, Pines, Blue Springs, Juniper Park), 2 miles east of Pine Valley on FR 035

31. ENTERPRISE RESERVOIRS, Dixie National Forest, Pine Valley Ranger District, 345 East Riverside Dr., St. George, UT 84770; (435) 652-3100; **Camping:** Honeycomb Rocks Campground, 11 miles southwest of Enterprise on FR 006

32. DEEP CREEK CANYON and STEWART PASS, Wasatch-Cache National Forest, Logan Ranger District, 1500 East Highway 89, Logan, UT 84321; (435) 755-3620; **Camping:** Logan Canyon campgrounds (Bridger, Guinavah-Malibu, Lewis M. Turner, Lodge, Preston Valley, Red Banks, Spring Hollow, Tony Grove Lake, Wood Camp), starting 5.8 miles east of Logan on US 89

33. HYRUM STATE PARK, 405 West 300 South, Hyrum, UT 84319-1547; (435) 245-6866; **Camping:** Hyrum State Park Campground, same address and phone as above

34. 20-20 PONDS, Utah Travel Council, Council Hall, State Street and 300 North, Salt Lake City, UT 84114; (801) 538-1030 or 538-1467; **Camping:** Logan Canyon campgrounds, (Bridger, Guinavah-Malibu, Lewis M. Turner, Lodge, Preston Valley, Red Banks, Spring Hollow, Tony Grove Lake, Wood Camp), starting 5.8 miles east of Logan on US 89

35. CUTLER MARSH, Utah Division of Wildlife Resources, 1596 West North Temple, Salt Lake City, UT 84116; (801) 538-4700; **Camping:** Western Park Campground, 350 West 800 South, Logan, UT 84321; (435) 752-6424

36. BENSON BRIDGE and OXBOW OVERLOOK, Utah Travel Council, Council Hall, State Street and 300 North, Salt Lake City, UT 84114; (801) 538-1030 or 538-1467; **Camping:** Benson Marina, about 6 miles northwest of Logan on 3000 North (Blacklock Road), or Logan Canyon campgrounds, (Bridger, Guinavah-Malibu, Lewis M. Turner, Lodge, Preston Valley, Red Banks, Spring Hollow, Tony Grove Lake, Wood Camp), starting 5.8 miles east of Logan on US 89

37. GREEN CANYON, Wasatch-Cache National Forest, Logan Ranger District, 1500 East Highway 89, Logan, UT 84321; (435) 755-3620; **Camping:** Green Canyon Campground, about 2 miles east of North Logan on FR 050

38. SPRING HOLLOW, Wasatch-Cache National Forest, Logan Ranger District, 1500 East Highway 89, Logan, UT 84321; (435) 755-3620; **Camping:** Spring Hollow, east of Logan on US 89

39. HIGH CREEK RIDGE, Wasatch-Cache National Forest, Logan Ranger District, 1500 East Highway 89, Logan, UT 84321; (435) 755-3620; **Camping:** High Creek Campground, about 8 miles northeast of Richmond on High Creek Canyon Road

40. TONY GROVE LAKE, Wasatch-Cache National Forest, Logan Ranger District, 1500 East Highway 89, Logan, UT 84321; (435) 755-3620; **Camping:** Tony Grove Lake Campground, Lewis M. Turner Campground, east of Logan on US 89

41. BEAR LAKE NATIONAL WILDLIFE REFUGE, U.S. Fish and Wildlife Service, 370 Webster Street, P.O. Box 9, Montpelier, ID 83254; (208) 847-1757; **Camping:** Paris Spring Campground, about 4.5 miles west of Paris, ID, on 200 South

42. SIX MILE RESERVOIR, Utah Travel Council, Council Hall, State Street and 300 North, Salt Lake City, UT 84114; (801) 538-1030 or 538-1467; **Camping:** Rendezvous Beach, Bear Lake State Park, about 2 miles northwest of Laketown on UT 30

43. RANDOLPH VIEWING AREA, Utah Travel Council, Council Hall, State Street and 300 North, Salt Lake City, UT 84114; (801) 538-1030 or 538-1467; Rendezvous Beach, Bear Lake State Park, about 2 miles northwest of Laketown on UT 30

44. OGDEN NATURE CENTER, 966 West 12th Street, Ogden, UT 84404; (801) 621-7595; **Camping:** Century RV Park, 1399 West 2100 South, Westhaven, UT 84401; (801) 731-3800

45. OGDEN RIVER PARKWAY, Utah Travel Council, Council Hall, State Street and 300 North, Salt Lake City, UT 84114; (801) 538-1030 or 538-1467; **Camping:** Century RV Park, 1399 West 2100 South, Westhaven, UT 84401; (801) 731-3800

46. CITY CREEK CANYON, Utah Travel Council, Council Hall, State Street and 300 North, Salt Lake City, UT 84114; (801) 538-1030 or 538-1467; **Camping:** Camp VIP, Salt Lake City, 1400 West North Temple, Salt Lake City, UT, 84116; (801) 328-0224

47. CITY CEMETERY, Utah Travel Council, Council Hall, State Street and 300 North, Salt Lake City, UT 84114; (801) 538-1030 or 538-1467; **Camping:** Camp VIP, Salt Lake City, 1400 West North Temple, Salt Lake City, UT, 84116; (801) 328-0224

48. PARLEY'S HISTORIC NATURE AREA, Utah Travel Council, Council Hall, State Street and 300 North, Salt Lake City, UT 84114; (801) 538-1030 or 538-1467; **Camping:** Tanner's Flat Campground, 11.7 miles southeast of Salt Lake City in Little Cottonwood Canyon

49. DESOLATION TRAIL, MILL CREEK CANYON, Wasatch-Cache National Forest, Salt Lake Ranger District, 6944 South 3000 East, Salt Lake City, UT 84121; (801) 943-1794; **Camping:** The Spruces Campground, 13.7 miles southeast of Salt Lake City in Big Cottonwood Canyon

50. SPRUCES CAMPGROUND, Wasatch-Cache National Forest, Salt Lake Ranger District, 6944 South 3000 East, Salt Lake City, UT 84121; (801) 943-1794; **Camping:** The Spruces Campground, 13.7 miles southeast of Salt Lake City in Big Cottonwood Canyon

51. SILVER LAKE BOARDWALK, Wasatch-Cache National Forest, Salt Lake Ranger District, 6944 South 3000 East, Salt Lake City, UT 84121; (801) 943-1794; **Camping:** Redman Campground (seasonal), about 1.5 miles west of Brighton on UT 190

52. TANNER'S FLAT CAMPGROUND and ALBION BASIN, Wasatch-Cache National Forest, Salt Lake Ranger District, 6944 South 3000 East, Salt Lake City, UT 84121; (801) 943-1794; **Camping:** Tanner's Flat Campground (*see 48 on previous page*) or Albion Basin Campground, about 3 miles southeast of Alta on UT 210

53. MOUNT TIMPANOGOS TRAIL, Uinta National Forest, Pleasant Grove Ranger District, 390 North 100 East, Pleasant Grove, UT 84062; (801) 785-3563; **Camping:** Mount Timpanogos Campground, 14 miles northeast of Provo on US 80

54. SQUAW PEAK TRAIL, Uinta National Forest, Pleasant Grove Ranger District, 390 North 100 East, Pleasant Grove, UT 84062; (801) 785-3563; **Camping:** Hope Campground, 10 miles northeast of Provo off US 189

55. BOTANY POND—BYU CAMPUS, Utah Travel Council, Council Hall, State Street and 300 North, Salt Lake City, UT 84114; (801) 538-1030 or 538-1467; **Camping:** Utah Lake State Park, 4400 West Center Street, Provo, UT 84601-9715; (801) 375-0731

56. MIDWAY FISH HATCHERY, Utah Division of Wildlife Resources, 1596 West North Temple, Salt Lake City, UT 84116; (801) 538-4700; **Camping:** Wasatch Mountain State Park, 2 miles northwest of Midway, off US 220/224

57. JORDANELLE HAWKWATCH SITE, Bureau of Reclamation, Salt Lake Field Office, 2370 South 2300 West, Salt Lake City, UT 84119; (801) 977-4300; **Camping:** Jordanelle Reservoir State Park, P.O. Box 309, Heber City, UT 84032-0309; (435) 649-9540

58. ROCK CLIFF RECREATION AREA, Utah Division of Parks and Recreation; **Camping:** Rock Cliff Campground, Jordanelle Reservoir State Park, 2 miles west of Francis on UT 32

59. ROCKPORT STATE PARK, 9040 North State Highway 302, Peoa, UT 84061-9702; (435) 336-2241; **Camping:** Rockport State Park campgrounds (Cedar Point, Juniper, Cottonwood campgrounds), 4 miles south of Wanship on US 189

60. TRIAL LAKE, Wasatch-Cache National Forest, Kamas Ranger District, 50 East Center Street, P.O. Box 68, Kamas, UT 84036; (435) 783-4338; **Camping:** Trial Lake Campground, 25.7 miles east of Kamas on US 150

61. BALD MOUNTAIN, Wasatch-Cache National Forest, Kamas Ranger District, 50 East Center Street, P.O. Box 68, Kamas, UT 84036; (435) 783-4338; **Camping:** Moosehorn Campground, 31 miles east of Kamas on US 150

62. MIRROR LAKE, Wasatch-Cache National Forest, Kamas Ranger District, 50 East Center Street, P.O. Box 68, Kamas, UT 84036; (435) 783-4338; **Camping:** Mirror Lake Campground, 31.5 miles east of Kamas on US 150

63. DAHLGREEN'S CREEK, Wasatch-Cache National Forest, Mountain View Ranger District, Lone Tree Road, Highway 44, P.O. Box 129, Mountain View, WY 82939; (307) 782-6555; **Camping:** Henry's Fork Trailhead, 50 miles northeast of Kamas off US 150

64. HENRY'S FORK, UPPER BASIN, Wasatch-Cache National Forest, Mountain View Ranger District, Lone Tree Road, Highway 44, P.O. Box 129, Mountain View, WY 82939; (307) 782-6555

65. SHEEP CREEK LOOP, Ashley National Forest, Flaming Gorge Ranger District, P.O. Box 279, Manila, UT 84046; (435) 784-3445; **Camping:** Carmel Campground, 6 miles south of Manila on UT 44

66. HENRY'S FORK WILDLIFE VIEWING AREA, Ashley National Forest, Flaming Gorge Ranger District, P.O. Box 279, Manila, UT 84046; (435) 784-3445; **Camping:** Lucerne Peninsula, 8.5 miles east of Manila off US 43

67. LUCERNE PENINSULA, Ashley National Forest, Flaming Gorge Ranger District, P.O. Box 279, Manila, UT 84046; (435) 784-3445; **Camping:** Lucerne Peninsula, 8.5 miles east of Manila off US 43

68. SWETT RANCH, Ashley National Forest, Flaming Gorge Ranger District, P.O. Box 279, Manila, UT 84046; (435) 784-3445; **Camping:** Greendale East Campground, 1 mile north of the intersection of US 191 and UT 44 off US 191

69. BROWN'S PARK WILDLIFE MANAGEMENT AREA and NATIONAL WILDLIFE REFUGE, Bureau of Land Management,Vernal Field Office, 170 South 500 East, Vernal, UT 84078; (435) 781-4400; Utah Division of Wildlife Resources, 1596 West North Temple, Salt Lake City, UT 84116; (801) 538-4700; Brown's Park National Wildlife Refuge, 1318 Highway 318, Maybell, CO 81640; (970) 365-3613; **Camping:** Indian Crossing Campground, 7 miles north of Dutch John on US 191, then east 22 miles to Brown's Park Swinging Bridge and Crook campgrounds, Brown's Park NWR

70. STRAWBERRY RIVER VALLEY, Utah Division of Wildlife Resources, 1596 West North Temple, Salt Lake City, UT 84116; (801) 538-4700; **Camping:** Starvation Campground, Starvation State Park, P.O. Box 584, Duchesne, UT 84021-0584; (435) 738-2326

71. DESERT LAKE WATERFOWL MANAGEMENT AREA, Utah Division of Wildlife Resources, 1596 West North Temple, Salt Lake City, UT 84116; (801) 538-4700; **Camping:** Huntington State Park, P.O. Box 1343, Huntington, UT 84528-1343; (435) 687-2491

72. SAN RAFAEL RIVER RECREATION SITE, Bureau of Land Management, Price Field Office, 125 South 600 West, P.O. Box 7004, Price, UT 84501; (435) 636-3600; **Camping:** San Rafael Recreation Site Campground, 25 miles southeast of Cleveland

73. FERRON RESERVOIR and FERRON MOUNTAIN LOOP, U.S. Forest Service, Ferron Ranger District, 115 West Canyon Road, P.O. Box 310, Ferron, UT 84523; (435) 384-2372; **Camping:** Ferron Reservoir, 28 miles west of Ferron on Ferron-to-Mayfield Road; Twelvemile Flat, 19 miles east of Mayfield on Ferron-to-Mayfield Road

74. FRUITA, Capitol Reef National Park, HC-70 Box 15, Torrey, UT 84775; (435) 425-3791; **Camping:** Fruita Campground, 11 miles east of Torrey on UT 24

75. BRIAN HEAD PEAK, Dixie National Forest, Cedar City Ranger District, 82 North 100 East, P.O. Box 580, Cedar City, UT 84721-0580; (435) 865-3700; **Camping:** Cedar Breaks National Monument (seasonal), 82 North 100 East, Cedar City, UT 84720; (435) 586-9451

76. PANGUITCH LAKE, Dixie National Forest, Cedar City Ranger District, 82 North 100 East, P.O. Box 580, Cedar City, UT 84721-0580; (435) 865-3700; **Camping:** Panguitch Lake North, about 26 miles south of Parowan on UT 143

77. DUCK CREEK RESERVOIR and STREAM, Dixie National Forest, Cedar City Ranger District, 82 North 100 East, P.O. Box 580, Cedar City, UT 84721-0580; (435) 865-3700; **Camping:** Duck Creek Campground, 30 miles east of Cedar City off US 14

78. TROPIC RESERVOIR, Dixie National Forest, Cedar City Ranger District, 82 North 100 East, P.O. Box 580, Cedar City, UT 84721-0580; (435) 865-3700; **Camping:** Duck Creek Campground (seasonal), 30 miles east of Cedar City off US 14

79. BRYCE CANYON NATIONAL PARK, Bryce Canyon, UT 84717; (435) 834-5322; **Camping:** North Campground, east of Park Headquarters

80. PINE VALLEY CAMPGROUNDS, Dixie National Forest, Pine Valley District, 345 East Riverside Dr., St. George, UT 84770; (435) 652-3100; **Camping:** Pine Valley campgrounds, (Ponderosa, Upper Pines, Pines, Blue Springs, Juniper Park), 2 miles east of Pine Valley on FR 035

81. SILVER REEF TO OAK GROVE CAMPGROUND, Dixie National Forest, Pine Valley District, 345 East Riverside Dr., St. George, UT 84770; (435) 652-3100; **Camping:** Oak Grove Campground, 21 miles northeast of St. George off I-15

82. KOLOB RESERVOIR ROAD, Zion National Park, P.O. Box 1099, Springdale, UT 84767; (435) 772-3256; Dixie National Forest, Cedar City Ranger District, 82 North 100 East, P.O. Box 580, Cedar City, UT 84721-0580; (435) 865-3700; **Camping:** Lava Point Campground (Zion NP), 26 miles north of Virgin off UT 9

83. POTATO HOLLOW, Zion National Park, P.O. Box 1099, Springdale, UT 84767; (435) 772-3256; **Camping:** Lava Point Campground (Zion NP), 26 miles north of Virgin off UT 9

84. PA'RUS and EMERALD POOLS TRAILS, Zion National Park, P.O. Box 1099, Springdale, UT 84767; (435) 772-3256; **Camping:** South or Watchman campgrounds, south entrance to Zion National Park

85. REMEMBER THE MAINE PARK, Utah Travel Council; **Camping:** Steinaker State Park, 4335 North Highway 191, Vernal, UT 84078-7800; (435) 789-4432

86. GREEN RIVER and SPLIT MOUNTAIN CAMPGROUNDS, Dinosaur National Monument, 4545 Highway 40, Dinosaur, CO 81610; (970) 789-2115; **Camping:** Green River Campground, 5 miles east of Dinosaur Quarry, Dinosaur National Monument

87. PELICAN LAKE, Bureau of Land Management, Vernal Field Office, 170 South 500 East, Vernal, UT 84078; (435) 781-4400; **Camping:** Vernal KOA, West on US 40, Vernal, UT 84078; (435) 789-8935

88. OURAY NATIONAL WILDLIFE REFUGE, 266 West 100 North, Suite 2, Vernal, UT 84078; (435) 789-0351; **Camping:** Vernal KOA, West on US 40, Vernal, UT 84078; (435) 789-8935

89. SCOTT M. MATHESON PRESERVE and COURTHOUSE WASH, The Nature Conservancy, Scott M. Matheson Preserve, P.O. Box 1329, Moab, UT 84532; (435) 259-4629; Arches National Park, P.O. Box 907, Moab, UT 84532; (435) 259-8161; **Camping:** Various commercial campgrounds in Moab or camp on BLM lands; Devil's Garden Campground, 20 miles north of Visitor Center, Arches National Park off US 191

90. DEAD HORSE POINT STATE PARK, P.O. Box 609, Moab, UT 84532-0609; (435) 259-2614

91. WARNER LAKE, Manti-La Sal National Forest, Moab Ranger District, 2290 South West Resource Boulevard, P.O. Box 386, Moab, UT 84532; (435) 259-7155; **Camping:** Warner Lake Campground, 25.7 miles east of Moab off US 191

92. ELK RIDGE, Bureau of Land Management, San Juan Field Office, 435 North Main, P.O. Box 7, Monticello, UT 84535; (435) 587-2141; Natural Bridges National Monument, P.O. Box 1, Lake Powell, UT 84533; (435) 692-1234

93. FISH CREEK and OWL CREEK CANYONS, Natural Bridges National Monument, P.O. Box 1, Lake Powell, UT 84533; (435) 692-1234; Bureau of Land Management, San Juan Field Office, 435 North Main, P.O. Box 7, Monticello, UT 84535; (435) 587-2141

94. SAND WASH, Bureau of Land Management, San Juan Field Office, 435 North Main, P.O. Box 7, Monticello, UT 84535; (435) 587-2141; **Camping:** Sand Wash Campground, 2 miles west of Bluff

95. SQUARE TOWER LOOP, Hovenweep National Monument, McElmo Route, Cortez, CO 81330; (303) 529-4461; **Camping:** Hovenweep National Monument Campground, 20 miles north of Aneth off UT 262

96. HACKBERRY RUINS, Hovenweep National Monument, McElmo Route, Cortez, CO 81330; (303) 529-4461; **Camping:** Hovenweep National Monument Campground, 20 miles north of Aneth off UT 262

97. STARR SPRINGS, Bureau of Land Management, Henry Mountains Field Office, P.O. Box 99, Hanksville, UT 84734; (435) 542-3461; **Camping:** Starr Springs Campground, 50 miles southwest of Hanksville off UT 276

98. HARRIS WASH, Bureau of Land Management, Escalante Field Office, P.O. Box 225, Escalante, UT 84726; (435) 826-4291; **Camping:** Escalante State Park Campground, 710 North Reservoir Rd, Escalante, UT 84726-0350; (435) 826-4466

99. WIDE HOLLOW RESERVOIR, Utah State Parks and Recreation, 1594 West North Temple, Suite 116, P.O. Box 146001, Salt Lake City, UT 84114-6001; (801) 538-7220, (801) 538-7239 (hearing impaired), (800) 522-3770 for reservations; **Camping:** Escalante State Park Campground, 710 North Reservoir Rd, Escalante, UT 84726-0350; (435) 826-4466

100. CALF CREEK RECREATION AREA, Bureau of Land Management, Escalante Field Office, P.O. Box 225, Escalante, UT 84726; (435) 826-4291; **Camping:** Calf Creek Campground, 15 miles east of Escalante on UT 12

101. COTTONWOOD CANYON, Bureau of Land Management, Grand Staircase-Escalante National Monument, 337 South Main, Suite 010, Cedar City, UT 84720; (435) 586-2401; **Camping:** Kodachrome Basin State Park, P.O. Box 238, Cannonville, UT 84718-0238; (435) 679-8562

102. THREE LAKES CANYON, Utah Travel Council, Council Hall, State Street and 300 North, Salt Lake City, UT 84114; (801) 538-1030 or 538-1467; **Camping:** Ponderosa Grove, 14 miles NW off US 89 on Hancock Road

103. KANAB CREEK, Utah Travel Council, Council Hall, State Street and 300 North, Salt Lake City, UT 84114; (801) 538-1030 or 538-1467; **Camping:** Ponderosa Grove, 14 miles NW off US 89, on Hancock Road

104. SPRINGDALE POND, Utah Travel Council, Council Hall, State Street and 300 North, Salt Lake City, UT 84114; (801) 538-1030 or 538-1467; **Camping:** Zion Canyon Campground, 479 Zion Park Boulevard, Springdale UT 84767; (435) 772-3237

105. COALPITS WASH, Zion National Park, P.O. Box 1099, Springdale, UT 84767; (435) 772-3256; **Camping:** Zion Canyon Campground, 479 Zion Park Boulevard, Springdale UT 84767; (435) 772-3237

106. GRAFTON, Utah Travel Council, Council Hall, State Street and 300 North, Salt Lake City, UT 84114; (801) 538-1030 or 538-1467; **Camping:** Zion Canyon Campground, 479 Zion Park Boulevard, Springdale UT 84767; (435) 772-3237

107. LYTLE RANCH PRESERVE, The Nature Conservancy, Utah Field Office, 559 East South Temple, Salt Lake City, UT 84102; (801) 531-0999; **Camping:** Lytle Ranch, about 32 miles west of St. George

108. GUNLOCK RESERVOIR, Bureau of Land Management, Dixie Field Office, 345 East Riverside Dr., St. George, UT 84720; (435) 628-4491; **Camping:** Gunlock State Park, P.O. Box 140, Santa Clara, UT 84765-0140; (435) 628-2255

109. WEST CANYON, Snow Canyon State Park, P.O. Box 140, Santa Clara, UT 84765-0140; (435) 628-2255

110. RED HILLS GOLF COURSE, Utah Travel Council, Council Hall, State Street and 300 North, Salt Lake City, UT 84114; (801) 538-1030 or 538-1467; **Camping:** McArthur's Temple View RV Park, 975 South Main, St. George, UT 84770 (435) 673-6400

111. VIRGIN RIVER PARKWAY and TONAQUINT PARK, Utah Travel Council, Council Hall, State Street and 300 North, Salt Lake City, UT 84114; (801) 538-1030 or 538-1467; **Camping:** McArthur's Temple View RV Park, 975 South Main, St. George, UT 84770 (435) 673-6400

112. WASHINGTON FIELDS and SEIGMILLER POND , Utah Travel Council, Council Hall, State Street and 300 North, Salt Lake City, UT 84114; (801) 538-1030 or 538-1467; **Camping:** McArthur's Temple View RV Park, 975 South Main, St. George, UT 84770 (435) 673-6400

Glossary of Terms

altitudinal migration: the movement of species along an elevational gradient to avoid inclement weather or to take advantage of elevationally discrete resources. Although this type of migration is associated with seasonal changes in weather, for some species altitudinal migration occurs on a shorter time scale and may be induced by the passage of particularly severe weather.

crepuscular: active during twilight hours.

diurnal: an adjective that describes a behavior or phenomena that occurs during daylight hours.

ecotone: the gradient between two ecosystems. Often this zone is marked by a greater diversity of species than either of the adjacent ecosystems, as species from the adjacent ecosystems gather to exploit the resources in the transitional zone.

hack: a term associated with falconry; the falcon is dependent on, and returns to, its handler for food but is free to come and go at will.

latitudinal migration: the seasonal movement of a species; the pattern of species movement that most people refer to when they speak generally of fall or spring migration. In North America this phenomena occurs on a north-south axis.

lek: a place where male grouse gather to perform a mating display and to attract mates. Only those species which evolved to utilize open habitats (desert steppe, desert shrub) gather on leks. Forest species such as Blue Grouse and Ruffed Grouse do not congregate on leks but display individually instead.

nocturnal: active at night.

phenology: study of the temporal or time-linked aspects of recurrent natural phenomena, and their relation to weather and climate.

Selected References

Offered below is a partial list of references consulted in the writing of this book. If you are interested in studying Utah's bird life in more depth, the citations below are a good place to start.

Aikens, C. M. 1970. *Hogup Cave*. University of Utah Anthropological Papers # 93. Salt Lake City: University of Utah Press. 286 pages.

Behle, W. H. 1981. *The Birds of Northeastern Utah*. Occasional Publication # 2. Salt Lake City: Museum of Natural History, University of Utah. 136 pages.

———— 1990. *Utah Birds: Historical Perspectives and Bibliography*. Occasional Publication # 9. Salt Lake City: Museum of Natural History, University of Utah. 355 pages.

Behle, W. H., and M. L. Perry. 1975. *Utah Birds: Checklist, Seasonal and Ecological Occurrence Charts and Guides to Bird Finding*. Salt Lake City: Museum of Natural History, University of Utah. 144 pages.

Behle, W. H., E. D. Sorensen, and C. M. White. 1985. *Utah Birds: A Revised Checklist*. Occasional Publication # 4. Salt Lake City: Museum of Natural History, University of Utah. 108 pages.

Cole, J. 1990. *Utah Wildlife Viewing Guide*. Helena, Montana: Falcon Press. 88 pages.

Edwards, T. C., Jr., C. G. Homer, S. D. Bassett, A. Falconer, R. D. Ramsey, D. W. Wight. 1995. *Utah Gap Analysis: An Environmental Information System*. Logan: Utah Cooperative Fish and Wildlife Research Unit, Utah State University.

Flack, J. A. D. 1976. *Bird Populations of Aspen Forests in Western North America*. American Ornithologists' Union Ornithological Monographs # 19. 97 pages.

Hayward, C. L., C. Cottam, A. M. Woodbury, and H. H. Frost. 1976. "Birds of Utah." *Great Basin Naturalist Memoirs* 1:1-229.

Jennings, J. D. 1970. *Danger Cave*. University of Utah Anthropological Papers # 27. Salt Lake City: University of Utah Press. 328 pages.

Perry, J., and J. G. Perry. 1985. *The Sierra Club Guide to the Natural Areas of Colorado and Utah*. San Francisco California: Sierra Club Books. 316 pages.

Roylance, W. J. 1982. *Utah—A Guide to the State*. Salt Lake City: Utah—A Guide to the State Foundation. 779 pages.

Ryser, F. A. 1985. *Birds of the Great Basin: A Natural History*. Las Vegas: University of Nevada Press. 604 pages.

Sorenson, E. 1996. "Birding Utah, Part I." *Winging It* 8(3):1, 4-7.

———— 1996. "Birding Utah, Part II." *Winging It* 8(4):1, 4-8.

———— 1996. "Birding Utah, Part III." *Winging It* 8(5):1, 4-7.

Wauer, R. H. 1993. *The Visitor's Guide to the Birds of the Rocky Mountain National Parks: United States and Canada*. Santa Fe, N. Mex.: John Muir Publications. 420 pages.

———— 1997. *Birds of Zion National Park and Vicinity*. Logan: Utah State University Press. 183 pages.

Wauer, R. H., and D. L. Carter. 1965. *Birds of Zion National Park and Vicinity*. Springdale, Utah: Zion Natural History Association. 92 pages.

Species Index

Numbers in *italic* type refer to photos.

About the Author

Don McIvor holds degrees in Environmental Sciences from the University of Virginia, and in Wildlife Ecology from Utah State University. His field research has led him through Virginia, North Carolina, Florida, Arizona, Wyoming, and most extensively, Utah. His bird-related work in Utah includes research on Sandhill Cranes (for which he earned a Master's degree), two seasons of intensive Neotropical breeding bird census-taking, and a habitat restoration project on Utah's Bear River. He has published extensively in both popular and scientific outlets. As an avid outdoorsman, Don has explored Utah by foot, canoe, raft, and bicycle.